We'll Buy Another on Monday

JEAN BROWN

$\langle P \rangle$

Books of related interest:

Jean Brown, *We'll See the Cuckoo*
(Palatine Books, ISBN 1-874181-22-5, 520pp, published 2004), £17.00

Geoffrey Mather, *Tacklers' Tales: a humorous look at Lancashire*
(Palatine Books, ISBN 1-874181-19-5, 160pp, published 2003), £7.95

George Ingle, *Marriner's Yarns: the story of the Keighley wool spinners*
(Carnegie Publishing, ISBN 1-85936-103-X, 192pp, published 2004), £10.00

David Hey, *'County of the Broad Acres': A History of Yorkshire*
(Carnegie Publishing, ISBN 1-85936-122-6, to be published 2005), £20.00

We'll Buy Another on Monday

Copyright © Jean Brown, 2004

First published in 2004 by
Palatine Books,
an imprint of Carnegie Publishing Ltd
Carnegie House
Chatsworth Road
Lancaster LA1 4SL
www.carnegiepublishing.com

British Library Cataloguing-in-Publication data
A catalogue record for this book is available from the British Library

ISBN 1-874181-25-X

Typeset by Carnegie Publishing
Printed by Alden Press, Oxford

Currer Walls

Dedicated to Harry, our inspiration.

They are black, this morning, against the snow,
Dry-stone, frost-crusted, gaunt and still;
Conquerors of a thousand Pennine winters
Custodians of the good soil of this Yorkshire hill.
Unearthed and gathered, laid by roughened hand
Of patient monk and peasant craftsman, early old,
They stand serenely, blessing each new generation,
Guarding boundaries, fencing field and lane and fold.
Beloved stone! Be harvest slow
And the price of fattened cattle low,
There are riches on this walled and rocky hill
For those with muscle, strength and skill.
January 1958

Introduction

It was a day like so many others at The Currer, albeit considerably warmer than the New Year's Eve I remember forty-two years ago. Drier, too, for on that memorable occasion it rained heavily and towards evening that turned to sleet and then to snow and by morning there was a carpet, a foot deep, whiter than white, softer than down.

At some time in anyone's life there is the experience of a perfect day, a day to remember more than any other. For me 1 January 1958 remains foremost in a multitude of good days, wonderful days, extraordinary days in our calendar memorabilia. No other day, in what has already been a fairly long lifetime, holds a candle to that New Year's Day.

On that never to be forgotten day, my sister Margaret and I walked the untrodden path across the five fields separating the village from the derelict farmhouse which was to be our home. It had no panes in the windows and the ancient doors failed to swing on broken hinges. Snow had drifted through the gaping, eastern mullions, lying thickly on the stone flags of the parlour and hanging precariously through the rotted floorboards of the bedrooms above.

But the giant walls and stone slates of the roof were intact, impervious to the elements, breathing a saga dating back to the sixteenth century; and the surrounding land, one dating back to the beginning of time. We were unaware that we were about to prolong the story, rescue the house from ruin, use it, share it, record and covenant it to ensure, as far as is humanly possible, its preservation in perpetuity.

On that memorable morning, in brilliant sunshine, we strode through the snow towards it with all the energy of our youth and all the joy and determination of our resolution. The fire we lit in the rusted hearth, with the rotted window frames, leapt up the chimney, a beacon, a flame of friendship which, though we did not know that either, was to welcome strangers from all corners of the world which seemed so big and now seems quite small.

We stood at the gate of the year, on the threshold of opportunity, visualizing a life which promised to last for ever and is now dwindling frightfully fast. Suddenly it was another New Year's Eve, but this time we were waiting for the door to open onto a new millennium and I was resolving to pick up the idle pen and record the last years of the twentieth century and step, with my remaining family, into a new era. Time, I decided, must be found to write another chapter for posterity, if not for the publisher, in the long history of this Yorkshire hillside.

If I were a man I would liken life to an innings, each one batting until bowled out. I am a woman and my life has been spent teaching children, so I will liken it to a skipping game. The rope is turning perpetually, as is the earth, and when it is your moment you run in and jump for as long as you can before the turning rope catches you out. We have been jumping together, Margaret and I, for a good long while but we are not exhausted yet.

The final years and months and days of the last millennium had been but a moment in time in the history of a world so magical, so beautiful, so amazing as to be unimaginable without a creator. They had been but a moment but they had not been uneventful in the pastoral, domestic, unworldly atmosphere which is the only environment we have ever known. The new era approaching might herald a new beginning for some, but we did not expect or wish ours to change.

Though friends and neighbours were having to sell their farms and embark upon new careers, we were taking into the twenty-first century a dedicated determination not to quit.

I am sure I was not alone in pondering on the inexplicable on that unique day in the Christian calendar. The world is a mathematical wonder and its creator must be a master of art and science, both. There was no better time, surely, than the end of one hundred decades to ponder on the simple facts that put the complicated ones in perspective. If there is no creator the unanswerable question is 'How?' and if there is I, too, am anxious to know, 'Why?'

Time fascinates me. Two days before Christmas I went into the low pasture where, in the furthest, lowest corner of our land stands the holly that has provided our modest seasonal decoration for as long as I can remember. Reclimbing the hillside gave me a favourite view of the farmhouse we have lived in for one fiftieth of the recorded years since The Nativity. Of course we have owned the property longer than that, for Grandfather bought it in 1929 and seventy years is only one thirtieth of the two thousand. Multiplying the years since Mother was born by nineteen takes us back to the crucifixion. Twenty times the age of Hilda, spending Christmas with us, and we are back in Roman rule. A year is but a moment, a drop in the ocean of time.

We were sitting in front of the television, waiting for the last hour to pass before Big Ben announced the arrival of the third millennium since the birth of Christ divided time into before and after. The programmes, meant to interest the watching public, failed to entertain us. Seated round the log fire were the two nonagenarians. I did not know what they were thinking. Hilda seemed to be preparing for bed and Aunty Mary was nodding in her chair. Our seventy-two-year-old disabled brother was not interested in domes and pop stars, only in dates and calendar complexities. Margaret, I suspected, was full of wonder. The occasion was, after all, unique.

Together she and I had completed the evening chores and witnessed an uncommonly bright moon. They, whoever they might be, said that it had been nearer to the earth than usual. It had certainly been possible for us to see cattle in the straw without torchlight or electricity.

Feeding animals every evening is a winter chore dating back to early childhood. Margaret had preceded me by enough time to fill the ninety-foot calf manger with corn. Until this was done it was impossible for me to push past the sturdy babies in order to spread the straw which gives them a comfortable bed for the night.

As I left the lighted doorway of the house my shadow went before me and, as always, rose vertically against the solid wall of the calf-shed door. It takes only a little imagination to interpret it as the silhouette of Father, our friend and mentor and workmate, who died during the deep snow of 1979. It always seems to be his work-bent shadow, his slightly bowed, trousered legs and wellingtons, his jacket and the back view of his flat cap. My legs now walk his elderly gait and speed and he accompanies me through the door before disappearing as I enter.

The interesting thing is that, though she is the younger and slimmer daughter, the shadow which resembles Father accompanies Margaret, too, and when we go towards the shed together there are two of him and I am reminded that, just before he died, he said, 'Don't worry, there are two of me now.'

The night was cloudless and who wants an artificial dome when the natural one is bespangled with a myriad of stars? Occasionally a moving light indicated a plane heading for, or leaving, Yeadon Airport. The evening star is best seen from the hollow where the road crosses the cattle grid and the stream flows out of the duck pond. There we had seen it, twelve months earlier, converge with Jupiter teasing us that there was but one planet of exceptional brilliance. They, those cleverer ones than I, said the two planets had not done that for two thousand years and might well have accounted for the mysterious brightness of the star that announced The Nativity. Who knows!

The night was calm. There is seldom wind in the hollow and the gale which almost perpetually sweeps down the Pennine valley was no more than a whisper. Chores done, it was a night to sit on the wall beneath the silver birch, or, had I been Emilie from Lyon, on the Altar Rock, used by Druids for sacrifice more than two thousand years ago. But one must not leave the family on the eve of a millennium.

Instead, I was in an armchair in the sitting room still decorated with Christmas cards and lighted tree. I was grateful for the background pollution of the television, pondering as I was on the mysteries of time and space and wondering if there really was an eternity. One tired old lady went to bed. Aunty Mary was dropping asleep in her chair. Harry was obviously disappointed. He was never a telly-addict but he remembered, several years ago, when we all enjoyed *The White Heather Club*, singing and piping and dancing us into a new year.

Margaret was getting increasingly nervous. Outside the sheds were full of contented, ruminating animals and the noise of distant traffic was scarcely a whisper. Should the New Year be celebrated noisily in the town, two miles away, and there be a loud volley of fireworks, she feared commotion in our animal kingdom. Danny was safely beside her chair and Jess was on the hearth rug. She had been brought in under pressure for her preferred evening activity was to bark at her echo down in the Five-Acre.

I was expecting the long-awaited moment of midnight to be a nothing. We are not an emotional family. There would be no cheering, no hugging, no lifting of the glass to toast the occasion and no singing of *Auld Lang Syne*. Though I am no stranger to celebration and have done more than my share of creating magic, when alone we are not demonstrative. There was a long period of time when, among children and Guides, I was the ignition. To unite, to laugh and sing and to paint occasion after occasion with indelible joy was my responsibility. Twenty years ago this special moment, in the history of mankind, would have been just what we needed as an excuse to light a fire on a hilltop and sing until dawn.

But on the eve of the year 2000, while the rest of the world was in festive mood, we were just sitting idle, disappointing Harry whose mathematical interest had been embracing the unique date on the calendar for simply ages. The celebrations of those in the self-catering cottages would go unheard. Bertie and Janet Bullock, in The Mistal, had gone to church. The lady in The Loft was a local woman escaping, with her dog, the rampaging she believed would accompany a street party outside her home. Though local, she was a stranger and would not intrude. No one would phone. The cattle dealer who used to do so had been dead many years. There would be no one for us to ring. All the many hundreds of people we know would be too busy, for New Year's Eve is a personal affair.

Norman and Heather Wallis were celebrating with friends in the bed and breakfast area we let for self-catering groups at Christmas and whenever.

They had come as a close-knit group of friends to celebrate the milestone together.

So we in the un-curtained parlour, whose eastern mullions encompass the wide sweep of the Aire Valley and a hillside which climbs to the ridge of Ilkley Moor, were alone, apart, isolated as we would be in a few days' time when the seasonal holiday-makers went home and only animals would be our neighbours and only feeding them our pursuit.

When the midnight hour came and the chimes of Big Ben echoed in every house in the land, Margaret called from her window seat vigil. Because the curtains are seldom drawn in this house, she saw the first firework shoot into the sky.

'Come quickly!' she called. Together we hauled Harry to his feet and staggered with him to the window. Aunty Mary continued to watch the screen. For her, at ninety-three, the millennium may not hold the exciting future it might for us.

For a moment the three of us stood locked together and gazed towards Heaven in wonder. The entire dome was artificially spangled with cascading stars; brilliant red and blue, green and gold, purple and white. We turned to the five mullions on the south wall and there, too, the display was stupendous.

We dragged Harry through the living kitchen and out through the entrance porch into the clean, night air. We leaned against the cold perimeter wall in awed silence. There were no bangs, or shouts, or exclamations, just one extraordinary display, a celestial performance unprecedented. Margaret ran for the wheelchair and our coats for the temperature was chill and in the morning the grass would be silvered.

The moment was perfect. We were joined by the Wallis group. The lady from The Loft came down and the returning churchgoers clambered out of their car. No one was vocal. Here, almost on the summit of our Pennine hillside, only the silhouette of the house interferes with the dome of Heaven. Here, there and everywhere, orchestrated and in unison, coloured lights shot into the air and cascaded earthwards. It was as if those lighting the fireworks had planned prematurely so that there was order in their continuity, as if they had purposefully rejected noise for the preferred magic of silence. It was perfect. There were not more reds than blues, no more greens than gold. Purple and orange and white were scattered evenly across the already star-filled sky. It was magic, silent, awesome, so breathtaking that applause would have been inappropriate. The cattle did not even stand and the dogs were unafraid. We were all sufficiently united in wonder, warm and spellbound with amazement. We were immensely grateful to all those Yorkshire people who, from their distant homes, their gardens, streets and villages had participated in the unrehearsed, spectacular performance. Each would be, unknowingly, enjoying his private display. Maybe only we, from our unique vantage point, saw the finale to the twentieth century complete.

For almost half an hour the display kept up its momentum. Then as suddenly as it had begun, it was over. Only then did we link arms and go inside, me with my new year's resolution firmly in place. I must, I surely must pick up my pen.

Margaret, Mother, Harry and me, with Lucky and Jess, 1988.

Chapter One
(October 1996)

God comes in little things
With brown, bright eyes and gentleness.

'Hey, don't you wish your name wasn't Miss Brown?' Joan once said with that wicked smile in my direction.

'Frequently,' I answered from the circle of my eager school children. 'Very frequently!'

It's funny what out-of-context memories come from nowhere when you are travelling. Sitting uncomfortably on the back seat of the Range Rover I ought to have been looking ahead to the next routine job on our autumn calendar, buying calves on Monday, but instead, sitting cramped between two dogs and Harry, I was watching the A534 and remembering my long-term colleague. Joan had taught beside me all the twenty-one years of my village school headship and had died in the spring. She had been such a positive person and memories were happy ones, often funny for she had a delightful sense of humour.

Aunty Mary was nodding on the front seat. Margaret was driving. Jess, our bitch, dozy with her tranquillizer for she travelled badly, was occupying what little space there was between Harry and me, and Danny lay on my feet. The whole of the back space belonged to Lusky, always.

We were returning from Aberporth, a minute village on Cardigan Bay, and we were going straight home without stopping to buy calves at Beeston Castle Cattle Mart as we had done for so many years. We were going home to buy at the local markets on Monday. Some in our profession were seriously wondering whether they would continue, for farming was definitely in crisis with BSE and all that fiasco. Father's motto had always been to replace his sold or fallen stock. 'Come on,' he would comfort himself and us, 'we'll buy another on Monday!' Keeping going had been his lifelong achievement and we must follow suit. Somehow or other we must ride the current storms, as they came. We must replace the twenty-three-month-old bullocks we had sold in September and buy at least seventy week-old calves on our return.

Why, for goodness sake, was I not thinking about that instead of about Joan asking me if I wished my name wasn't Miss Brown?

I seldom hear that title nowadays, but a primary school teacher hears it constantly. It was relatively easy to insist that 'Miss' wasn't enough and had to be followed with a surname. It was much more difficult to limit its use. 'Please can we have rounders, Miss Brown?' and not, 'Miss Brown, please can we have rounders, Miss Brown? Please, Miss Brown? Miss Brown, can we? This afternoon, Miss Brown?' 'Oh, thanks, Miss Brown,' and turning to friends, 'Miss Brown says we can have rounders!'

They prefixed every sentence with my name and used it to end every query. No wonder I wearied of it, yet to turn the clock back and hear them again would give me the greatest pleasure. I have to admit that it was a warm and comfortable name to have to hear often. Imagine being Miss Fortune, Miss Happs or Miss Mellor, or horrendously long like Popplethwaite or full of 's's like Spittlehouse!

To be called Skipper was acceptable, too, and I heard that often enough. To have been called Captain by Guides and their parents might have rankled but because I was skipper of the Sea Ranger Crew also, it was universally adopted and definitely preferable. Once, during the long summer camps we enjoyed on the shores of Hebridean islands, Hazel Belsey asked, 'How many times have you heard your name today?' As often as I'd heard the gulls and kittiwakes calling and the oystercatchers strutting on the beach. I did not mind for it's a friendly name and that is important if it must be heard often. I still hear it but those who use it are ageing too.

I was born to be called Jean, which can become a bit of a wail if repeated several times. It was mostly unused in my middle years but now I have hardly any other. I am destined to hear that constantly also, which puts me not just in the working class but most definitely in the servant class. Only our multitude of animals cannot use it, but they would if they could for I am their servant also. All our holidaymaking guests, even those who are children, address me so and if anyone used my name more than school children did it was Harry. Whenever within hearing distance he shouted 'Jean!' repeatedly and forgot what he wanted in the first place. His speech problem made Jean easier to say than Margaret. Thankfully she responds to my name as often as she does hers and because, though physically handicapped, he was otherwise a perfectly normal brother he often got sisterly short shrift.

No one was using my name as we drove gently towards home after yet another lovely holiday in Aberporth, our Autumn Retreat. It's the nearest we get to peace. Because we have recently sold more than seventy quite enormous bullocks we leave only the responsibility of yearlings to Dorothy and George who have been standing in for us since the 1980s. These are all out at grass and, hopefully, need little care. Our barn, by that time, is filled to capacity with hay and straw, and work, even if it were we who were at home, would be at its lowest. Annually, though how long this will last, we have a spate of mishaps before we leave, relative peace while we are away and normal for The Currer when we get back. Real trouble seems to take a holiday when we do. He does not go with us, thank goodness. We are far from confident that this will be always so and we tremble every time we squeeze into a telephone kiosk to ring home.

Our residence at The Cedars that year held but one trauma. It came before we drove the last few yards up the steep approach to the chalet. We decided to pull into the car park, overlooking the bay, and phone home.

Dorothy greeted us with, 'Oh, I'm not a happy woman today!' We had been away from home only one day and Dorothy was reporting Trouble. Why hadn't he packed his bags simultaneously with us?

'What's up?' I heard Margaret say, and we both held our breath. To leave The Currer in the hands of friends, however capable, is a risk we are only prepared to take in the interest of survival. Perpetual work, sixteen hours a day, seven days a week, past retirement age is a recipe for disaster.

'Oh, everything,' Dorothy groaned. 'The goat's knocked the side mirror off Mr Fane's car and it's cost £50.'

'Aw, never mind that. Tell him to put his car in our garage. Tell him we'll pay.'

Any price must be paid for peace when we are away.

'The money wouldn't go into the meter in The Loft cottage.'

'Did you poke it with a knife? That works!'

'We sent for Mike. He changed the meter. The washer went on the hot tap in the kitchen and soaked everything.'

'What did you do?'

'George mended it. Our dog Skye has gone missing. We've searched everywhere.'

We were really sympathetic. We know how awful it is when an animal goes missing. It is very stressful. Fortunately they usually turn up. We comforted Dorothy, but we relaxed. There was nothing, yet, to warrant our return. We replaced the phone and together said, 'Phew!' It's a word we constantly use. We say it nearly as often as we say, 'Mind!' using that as a verb and not as a noun. All my life, it seems, there have been things to fall over. As a child my wobbly brother was always underfoot. Then it was animals, then pupils and Guides, tent pegs and kitbags. Once again it became Harry, Aunty Mary's legs on the hearthrug, cases belonging to guests and their heads when I am serving an evening meal. In winter bales of hay are always in the way and bullocks' heads impede my way along the manger at feeding time. 'Mind!' I have said many times all my life. I say it with resigned tolerance, sometimes prefixed with 'never' and seldom ending it with 'out'.

'Phew!' we said with real relief, then, 'Mind,' as we stumbled over Danny who always squeezes into the kiosk when we do. We got into the car and drove the remaining short distance up the steep approach to The Cedars. We let ourselves in and unpacked.

Hours later I said, 'Where's my purse?' We searched everywhere. I'd had it in the phone booth, so we went down to the car park and searched there.

'I'm sure you brought it out,' Margaret said. I had no recollection of anything except that we'd been stressed, fearing a re-call home. We searched the garden with a torch. It was the beginning of the holiday and because we'd been travelling there was far too much money in that purse when Charlie, our goat, had just cost us £50 and a new meter would be to pay for. It was no way to start a holiday but, as Mike the electrician once said, it would pass. We never found the purse, but Dorothy's dog came home next day and the most amazing thing happened when we went to the Cardigan swimming baths. I found some money in the pocket of the bag we always use for our towels and swimsuits, be it the Keighley pool or the Cardigan one. It is a Reader's Digest give-away bag with a pocket in which I keep the pensioners concession cards and when I thought the zipped compartment felt to have more than a couple of plastic cards, I opened it and found five £20 notes. They must have been pensions put there one day and forgotten. We hadn't been to the baths for ages. We had hysterics and I was accused of being no longer fit to manage the family purse. We never found the lost one but we didn't have to go to the bank and thereafter we had a trouble-free holiday. It is worth mentioning, however, that we had not learned our lesson, for the very next year, coming home to our chalet after a day at Aberaeron, we stopped alongside a kiosk just outside Plump, eight miles north of Aberporth, to phone home. Next day we were preparing to go south, to Haverfordwest, to visit friends who spend holidays in The Mistal. My purse was missing. After looking everywhere we began to fear it must have been left in the Plump phone box. I was very embarrassed because I always hold the purse. We decided to go the eight miles back. It was eighteen hours since we'd phoned but someone might have taken it into the pub or the village shop. We need ask at neither, for the purse was still sitting on the ledge in the kiosk. Either everyone passing had a mobile or, which we prefer to believe, all Welsh people are honest. Now we leave the purse in the car and take only a handful of coins into the phone box.

It was funny that, with plenty to think about, a pleasant holiday behind and a calf-rearing future ahead, all I could think about, travelling homewards, was Joan saying, 'Hey, don't you wish your name wasn't Miss Brown?' Joan who had bravely fought but lost her encounter with cancer in the spring, Hazel who had appreciated how many times 'Skipper' was called and Harry whose continual call for attention sometimes drove me around the bend. It must have been the silence in the moving vehicle. Being increasingly immobile Harry seemed incapable of getting anything for himself. Handkerchief, more tea, spoon, sugar, pills, Gaviscon, jigsaw, glasses, towel, salt, pepper, telephone directory, *Radio Times* and more wood for the fire. And, after the wonderful dentist lady successfully made him a set of false teeth, he wanted his Teeth Mug. She bravely made him a bottom set which none of us thought he would ever wear. Having done so, she persisted in trying to put them in while he snorted and spluttered, forgetting to take a breath. Defeated, she handed me the lower jaw with a look on her face which indicated she, too, had her misgivings. I put the dentures in my pocket and took them and Harry back to the Range Rover.

At home I gave them to Margaret who is the most capable and the most vocally positive. She grabbed him like a calf and held his mouth open and fumbled without success. 'You're not trying!' she yelled at him. 'Make an effort. Breathe properly. Don't be stupid!' Then in despair, 'Oh, I give up.'

Exhausted, our brother sat there still without his bottom teeth. His mouth was different from the norm and saliva had always been a problem. Without any bottom teeth his tongue would not stay in, but we couldn't prolong this stressful activity. Even if we succeeded there was no guarantee they would stay in or that he wouldn't choke and then we would be guilty of manslaughter. (I remember a child who queried why someone should have to go to prison for man's laughter!)

And then I said such a simple thing. I said, and indeed it was a school marm command, 'Oh, Harry, put them in yourself!' and he did, which is why he was sitting beside me in the back of the Range Rover, handsome and displaying lovely white teeth whenever he smiled.

We turned off the eastbound road to go north and as we passed Beeston Castle Cattle Mart we began to talk. It was Saturday and empty but I was back in the present. The big job of calf buying loomed ahead. Normally we had left Wales on Friday and bought our calves at Beeston Castle on our way home. This market was always heaving with them. At 8.30 a.m. Margaret would have been at the ringside ready to bid. I would be in the collecting shed, stationed outside a pen on which our name was chalked, listening for the auctioneer to announce Margaret's successful bids. 'Mrs Brown!' he would shout.

Why, in an era when so many couples do not marry, do we who never have always get addressed as Mrs? The auctioneer would call 'Mrs Brown!' close on seventy times and first one collecting pen would be filled, then others. But the Saturday market sheds were empty and we were going straight home to buy locally. Due to the BSE tragedy thousands of calves were going straight to the abattoir to be shot. It was Government policy so a premium of over £100 was paid to farmers for their bull calves. Those of us who wished to rear had to outbid the Government which meant buying would be very expensive. It was a shambles, but farmers are renowned for doing as they are told. We do not make any of the rules. We might grumble but we follow them all right.

For the first time ever, I was scheduled to go alone to Otley Mart at the same time as Margaret would be at Skipton. The thought sobered me. Crikey! I thought. I was six years past retirement age and would have to learn to bid. I'd be a novice in a new profession but Margaret was Bossman. It would have to be. I regretted having to pass the market at Beeston. I was happier remembering teaching days.

For the first time our journey home from Wales had offered the freedom to leave Wrexham Travel Inn at a reasonable hour and dawdle over coffee by the riverside at Winslow watching amateur canoeists compete with professional swans. We'd had an opportunity to appreciate the autumn glory of the Peak District and to push Harry's wheelchair leisurely along the woodland trail, after lunch, in the Hayfield Nature Reserve. Moreover the return home promised to be quite carefree, too. We'd phoned Dorothy and all seemed fine. She was just putting a casserole in the oven for our evening meal. Because we were not buying in Cheshire we would not find that the newly bought calves had arrived home before us and needed attention. Our herd, we thought, could not possibly have increased. There would only be the seventy-five bovine yearlings, two donkeys, four goats, seven geese, one stray cat semi-resident in the bullock sheds and a flock of pigeons far too numerous to count. In the house would be the two ancient moggies, Chintzy getting thinner and thinner and Tommy still living though Dorothy had pronounced him dying on our return from the Isle of Man in the spring. Margaret had coaxed him into revival and he continued to wend a zigzag path to the door whenever it was necessary.

Heavens, we thought, the house and its converted barn will be empty as it used to be in the days we sometimes yearn for. The thirty Dutch students, who would occupy every bed space, would not arrive until Sunday. We could enjoy twenty-four hours of bliss. When the long bus from The Netherlands emptied itself of tall boys and girls the silence which accompanies isolation would be lost, but they would be self-catering and pose little problem. We would be free to go to neighbouring markets on Monday to buy, not one but

many. Goodness me, we might even unpack our cases. On previous years we had not even lifted them from the roof rack for nearly a week.

To be coming home without calves may even have fooled neighbours in the village along the top road. The Browns have come home from Wales without calves! They are going the way of many and giving up. People thought that in 1951 when Grandfather died leaving us with what seemed an impossible overdraft. They believed that again in 1979 when Father died, but each time they had been wrong and if they thought we were quitting in the autumn of 1996 they were once again deceived. I am sure that relatives thought, when we came to the ruin in 1958, that we must be opting for The Good Life. Without buildings surely we could not farm. But Father never went to the market to buy a few. He never built a small shed. He was not a smallholder. He was a farmer and to him big numbers of cattle and long hours of work were a way of life.

When he died during the big snow of 1979 it came as a shock to many that, with an old mother, a disabled brother and a sister who was a head-mistress, Margaret was prepared to soldier on. They smiled when we began to convert the barn into holiday accommodation and remarked, 'Oh, that is what they are doing. They are giving up farming. We knew they would!' They were wrong again. If they thought that by coming home from Wales without calves we were at last ready to quit they would have to change their minds when we went to market on Monday.

But first, before routine imprisoned us, we were to enjoy this gentle homecoming of peace and solitude. There would be so little to do. The house would be cleaned for our return. The sheds would be empty, the cattle grazing, the casserole made. It would last two meals at least. What could one ask for more?

As we drove down Currer Lane all was quiet. The flock of far too many pigeons soared into the silence. Aunty Mary broke it by singing softly, 'Now thank we all our God.' As we pulled into the yard no baby voices called. No noise came from the calf shed fans which had been still all summer and would not be needed until Monday. Only Dorothy's car was parked in the yard. Only she and George welcomed us and even they left shortly. We could not thank them enough.

We gathered round the log fire to eat casserole from steaming bowls and to wonder what to do. We are not acquainted with inactivity. I opened my pile of post. A man booking a November holiday wrote, 'Welcome home!' Margaret went out to feed the stray cat and look at some new water bowls John had put in the calf-shed in our absence and check that Mike had put a lamp in the enclosure we always call the Poorly Pen and hope we do not have to use it. Cattle had been visible on the skyline but too far away to count before dark. Everything was ready. We were on the starting line waiting for the whistle.

After years of farming one grows sensitive to the presence of animals. Both Margaret and I know, without looking, whether a shed is occupied or empty. No noise is needed, no ruminating murmurs or heavy breathing. The knowledge is intuitive. Passing the top bullock shed Margaret knew it wasn't empty. She looked within and flashed her torch. There in the darkness she saw the four startled eyes of two red Limousin heifers, maybe five months old, with market stickers on their rumps and definitely not belonging to our almost totally masculine herd. Suddenly frightened, they bolted and threw themselves against the back wall of the shed. Margaret hastily shut the door and turned off her torch and came indoors.

'Well,' she reported, 'we seem to have two more than when we left!' and next morning I amended that to three. Arising first as I always do, I found another similar heifer outside the shed door, trying to communicate with her mates. I was just shutting the yard gate when Margaret came intending to let the animal into the shed but it turned and easily jumped my five-barred gate. I had to dodge its spread-eagled legs.

'Whatever you do,' Margaret said, 'do not buy a Limousin heifer!'

We have three neighbouring farmers all called David. One who lives nearly a mile away bought a Limousin heifer at Bingley market some years ago and brought it home in his Ifor Williams trailer. He reversed to his shed door believing all he had to do was open it and let down the trailer ramp. But that animal could fly. It soared over the trailer gates and bolted for the main road. David gave chase, saw it turn left and gallop towards the village. Guided by brief glimpses and startled bystanders he followed the heifer along the top road leading to our entrance. The airborne animal easily leapt the cattle grid, galloped down our lane, over the grid at the foot of the hill, through our farmyard and over the gate under the sycamore tree. We had not been witnesses and were surprised to see this very red-faced farmer burst into our yard in hot pursuit. Middle-aged or no, that man could run!

We women are far more laid back about chasing animals than men. We watched this man run down into the Five-Acre remembering Jack, a haulier, chasing cattle of ours he wished to load. They had escaped and he gave chase. We knew, if left, they would encircle the field and return exhausted and more controllable. David chased his animal all round the field and up through the Dyke field, the Footpath field and into the intakes where our herd took an interest and galloped towards home. The runaway joined them, Margaret opened a shed door and the sillies all ran in. David, with his face redder than beetroot, followed not too far behind. We did not think he would have any strength left to walk home for his trailer but he had. Seeing him a year later we'd asked after his heifer. 'I never let it out again,' he said.

There was no way, we decided, we were going to buy a Limousin heifer or chase ones which appeared from nowhere and leapt five-barred gates, so we came indoors and had some breakfast. The third red animal returned to the shed door and called for its mates within and Margaret, who can do these things, just opened the door and let it in. Then she set about phoning neighbours to see who had recently been to market. It is confusing to have three all called David. She rang the nearest. He'd recently spent some time sitting at our kitchen table trying to persuade Margaret that half-grown heifers were a good buy. Granted there was no subsidy on heifers but they were very cheap. Half-grown they could be bought for the same price as a good bull calf and there would be no early rearing problems, no milk feeding, weaning and all the work entailed with the very young. Margaret told him she was sticking to her preferred method. She rescued baby bulls which would otherwise go to be killed. They were a bi-product of milk production and she liked her herd to be reared by her and no other. She knew it was harder work initially, but when grown her animals were manageable. They did not take fright and gallop through the village. They knew the land and they knew her and me and the subsidy made the price difference. This David had gone away defeated. She had not changed her mind. She thought perhaps he had taken his own advice and bought three wild heifers at a recent sale. She phoned him. The heifers were not his. Neither did they belong to the David capable of running a marathon. The owner was the third David. He'd actually bought six and three had played truant. We were home! No doubt about that. I leaned out of the kitchen window to say, 'Hello,' and felt water pouring down the inside stone mullion. Trouble had come home also. He'd left after us and returned earlier. We didn't trust him one bit.

David's trailer had barely left the yard when the abnormally long Euro-bus from Holland squeezed itself into the yard and emptied its contingent of thirty students into the dining room. They were annual visitors who knew the ropes and we were freed to investigate the water coming through a broken overflow from the central heating tank. We jostled the ballcock about and the deluge stopped. We knew it was only a temporary repair but our cases were to lift from the roof rack ready for the calf-buy. The lovely silence had been disturbed for the Dutch giants have loud voices, but we do not complain for they feed themselves and bring their own sleeping bags. I love those kind of people.

Margaret counted the cattle and checked the boundary and when the television was switched on after dark, we curled up beside the burning logs and slept. I had had two restless nights. Almost always I can sleep as soon as my head touches the pillow. I could wake, attend to Harry and fall asleep immediately. In camp I could wake, walk round the tents of sleeping children and return to my sleeping bag and be unconscious at once. Not many things keep me awake, but buying calves at Otley market was doing just that. I am only the farmer's man not the business manager.

There is no local market the size of Beeston Castle and we'd never, previously, thought we could buy seventy in one day. We'd be lucky to get forty at Skipton and fewer than twenty at Otley. Things were different with no export trade. If we bought simultaneously at both places we might come close to the number we wanted.

I think I am a very good farmer's man. Margaret seldom complains but she buys and I scivvy. I'd protested when she'd suggested this plan but hadn't a hope of winning.

We both went to Skipton where the buying starts first. Black and white Friesians were not even being put through the ring. They were being penned in twenties and taken straight to the abattoir. Because export of calves was prohibited, there was this fantastic surplus. Those who thought farmers were over-producing but continued to want milk and dairy products should have been told that, to have these, a calf must be born every year. To witness birth and nurture a baby only to have it shot was heartbreaking for the dairy farmers and when they saw Margaret they crowded round her, before the sale, begging her to take their babies and rear them at The Currer. The pen marked 'Mrs Brown' had several in it before the auctioneer lifted his hammer.

I returned to the Range Rover with its usual contingent of dogs, very old Aunty and Harry, none of whom would ever be left at home. I drove silently to Otley. For a lady who'd dared to do many things in her life, I was extremely nervous. I had a private word with Ernest, the auctioneer, and told him to look in my direction for, on that occasion, it was my responsibility to nod. He found it quite amusing for I was quite well known as a village school head-mistress who had recorded for posterity but who was probably too old to learn new tricks.

There was a lethargy in the profession. It wasn't fun any more but when the farmers saw me, and not Margaret, at the ringside there was a glimmer of amusement. When I bought my first calf Ernest played on the lighter atmosphere by knocking the calf down to, 'The author!' instead of to Mrs Brown. Everyone laughed.

I'd come a long way from Jean, Jean; Miss Brown, Miss Brown; Skipper, Skipper; to the elevated title of Author. Joan would never have let me live it down. Had we been still teaching together she'd have had tremendous fun out of that.

We bought a lot of continental breeds that year. The calf processing scheme did not include them until November so many were not as expensive as the black and whites the Government were willing to pay so much for, just to get rid of them. We bought quite a number of Limousin bulls which seem to be much more docile than their sisters. One, I remember, was big and rather frisky and when the Barbaults came from Lyon we complained that it was French. Bernard christened it Jacques Chirac and it remained so named. Normally only he and his small daughter came for her November holiday week but that year his wife Yveline came and we had a great time. Her English was quite good. Emilie's was almost non-existent. Just a few calf rearing nouns and verbs. 'It's the blue,' she would say, 'Milk,' and, 'Squirt.' Amid all the fun, BSE (blast it) could be forgotten.

But the paperwork now necessary could not. Farmers were drowning under wave after wave of it!

Holiday-makers are uninterested in calves. I cannot understand why! They will spend a whole week here, like the Dutch students do, and never go down to the shed to see them. Our babies have a spacious shed to leap and dance about in, warm and airy and carpeted with straw. I suppose we should be grateful for the first few weeks are critical and Margaret wants few distrac-tions from her constant vigilance. Caring for babies, animal or human, is a scary business. We are, however, so appreciative of the beauty of the newly born, the miracle of it and the mystery of it that we cannot understand those who walk past and never see.

The shorter journey home from local markets had benefited the calves and they settled in well. Only one was ill. It was a bonny Limousin which came with an abscess under its belly. This had not been noticed in the ring. Had it been Margaret would probably have bought it anyway for she is good at curing infected navels. She's a very good vet. I told a qualified one once that he and his colleagues could safely bet their last shirt on the fact that if Margaret said there was a problem, there was. She never mistakes illness for health. What others cannot see, she detects and ninety-nine times out of a hundred she can diagnose and cure it.

But this abscess was not on the navel. 'We ought to be able to take this calf down to the surgery,' Margaret said. Vet fees are high and the calf was only small so we backed the Range Rover to the shed door, walked the calf out and lifted it into the space usually occupied by Lusky. Margaret crouched in that space, too, to hold the calf steady. With Harry on the front passenger seat I drove very carefully down the steep, cobbled snake of a road to the by-pass roundabout on which stands the efficient new, veterinary surgery. It was a perilous journey, steep, winding and very bumpy.

'This is stupid!' Margaret said, in and among the exasperated commands of steady, not so fast, what are you doing, do be careful, watch it, too fast! I was dizzy with the effort to drive smoothly but every time we went slowly round a bend Margaret and the calf were in collision with the back seat.

The vet dressed the wound and bound it tightly with a bandage. He gave it an antibiotic and instructed that we take it back in a week. Margaret was critical. She thought the tight bandage would do more harm than good and she worried in case another hazardous journey, in such a limited space would be dangerous to a healing wound.

'What we need,' Margaret said, next morning, 'is a small Ifor Williams trailer. Small enough for us to handle. Just big enough for us to walk a calf in, if we want to go to the vet.' Vet bills are expensive.

As always we immediately latched on to the idea. What we want, we want immediately. We phoned Lindley Pate, agricultural merchants at Gisburn. They had just one, second-hand, sheep trailer in almost mint condition. Just what we wanted.

'A trip out for you, Harry,' after morning chores were done and Aunty Mary had been roused. She can always get up if we are going somewhere. Everything about the little trailer was right, except the price which was much more expensive than we had expected. We'll have to farm a long time and take a lot of calves to the vet to save enough on farm visits to pay for that, I thought, writing out the cheque.

The bandage was a disaster, uncomfortable and keeping the abscess in rather than letting out the pus. That same evening we took the little fellow back to the surgery. It was a different partner and he took off the dressing revealing a messy, inflamed wound. For a few days his new treatment, without the bandage, seemed to be working and the brave little chap was bright and perky. Then, suddenly the wound opened and emptied pus and gut and dear knows what and the next use we had for the smart little trailer was to take the dead calf to the knacker's yard. We had hoped to save life by having an ambulance. What we had prevented, perhaps, was injury to ourselves. Struggling to heave a dead calf into the back of the Range Rover had never been too easy, not even with a bale as halfway landing before the final heave into the vehicle. To drag it into the trailer was easy, though infinitely sad.

That autumn both our old cats died. First Tommy, then Chintzy. Tommy had threatened departure for a long time. Chintzy got thinner and thinner. She could well have been nearing twenty. Tommy was an antique who had been accident-prone all his life. Their departure left us with only our stray cat, a tiger tom who came and went for months before finally deciding to stay. We decided not to encourage him to come into the house. Enough animals littered the hearth for Harry and Aunty Mary to fall over. The old cats had long been useless as vermin hunters. Tommy, in his youth, had patrolled the barn. Chintzy had caught her prey along the field walls, down towards 'Jack Field', the farm below us where she had been born. When they had retired from the hunt the tiger tom had made a sustained effort to take Tommy's place in the barn, but when the local Cat Protection Society was asked by the council to remove all cats from Bradford Market, we were asked if we could take two. They were not house cats and they would be neutered and would make good farm cats. We agreed and in due course a lady from the society brought two big animals, one mostly black and one all grey. The barn was full of hay at the time with doors locked and bolted against village children who do so like to make a mess of bales. It was safe to release the two cats without much danger of them being able to escape. Margaret put food out for them each day. It always went, but it was months before we saw the cats again. What we did notice was a growing pile of pigeon feathers behind the corn bin. After a while we realised that the flock of far too many was a great deal smaller. We had released not one cat among the pigeons, but two, and there is no greater truth than what happens if you do that. There is no more stupid bird than a pigeon. It is a sitting target, allowing predators to creep up close enough to grab. What had been an embarrassing problem we hadn't known how to solve had suddenly become no problem at all. Indeed the priority became how to keep some alive. Seeing one or the other cat creeping along the ridge of a shed, towards a docile pigeon, sent us scurrying into the yard yelling, 'Shoo! Shoo!' to both hunter and hunted. All-out annihilation was unthinkable but quite possible.

For the first time since our arrival here in 1958 we had no cats in the house. It was safest. We were always afraid of the elderly and infirm falling over one animal or the other. Danny, the beautiful collie we had brought back from

Luskentyre in 1995, never goes into the sitting room unless Margaret is there. A guest named him Super Glue because he almost adheres to her, and to me sometimes. We fall over him constantly. Lusky was always safely under the kitchen table. He, too, had been brought from Luskentyre, in 1983. Harry had christened him the Lord of the Isles. Unfortunately, right from the start he had had problems with his back legs, his hip joints having shallow, almost non-existent sockets. The vet advised making the pup walk and discouraging it from running until movement had had a chance to wear deeper hollows in the baby bone. This treatment worked for Lusky and he could eventually run as fast as most dogs. He couldn't leap up perpendicular heights such as walls and he always needed help to get into the Range Rover. At the ripe old age of thirteen, arthritis had set in with a vengeance so that he began to drag his hindquarters somewhat. The same vet told Margaret to lift his tail and walk beside him and that solved the problem for a long time. Lusky learned to grow old and accept disablement with absolute dignity. With mostly any other owner he would have been put to sleep. This alternative was never discussed. Our beautiful Lord of the Isles learned a contentment many humans would be wise to copy. It did not distress him to sit long hours in front of the house, Monarch of the Glen, relatively immobile. On holiday he would sit happily with the rear door of the Range Rover open. We, together, lifted him in and out and were prepared to do so for as long as it took. He was never incontinent, as such. With the help of a hand holding his tail he could make it to the nearest grassy patch. If we were not at hand when nature called and he was obliged to wet the towel we always placed beneath him, he was patient until we came and he told us in a language we soon learned. His indoor domain was under the kitchen table, unseen from transient guests. His coat never lost its thickness nor its shine. He allowed Margaret to do everything for him. I was only allowed to turn him over. Promptly at six o'clock every morning, he barked so I needed no other alarm. I got up, dressed and came downstairs and turned him over. He sighed with happiness and slept again having done his daily task. He had roused the workforce.

Margaret was his personal slave. The hours she spent looking after that dog could not be counted. We had thought that, when we went to The Isle of Man, in the spring, it would be Lusky's last holiday, but no. He went to Wales in the autumn, to the October cattle markets to buy calves, to Gisburn to buy a trailer. He'd accepted disablement and Margaret was dedicated to caring for him.

Mother had once said, when Bess our twenty-year-old dog recovered from another heart attack, 'You won't get rid of your old folks easily, either!' How accurate she had been. Lusky was far from ready to go to whatever Heaven is reserved for dogs as faithful and as beautiful as he.

We'd brought Jess, our bitch, from the Lake District in 1988. She expected pedestrians in the house to step over her. She liked the Aga mat. Cooking breakfast for all our numerous guests was a problem for she would not leave the warmth, so I fried eggs with a foot on either side of her. She was outside during the day but in the evening she insisted on sitting on the front room rug and, unfortunately, she liked to lean on Aunty Mary's feet. This angered the old lady who didn't like our lovely dog at all. As only a spark from the fire would send Jess scurrying from the rug, I resorted to making a cardboard cage for protruding feet, so that they could not be sat upon!

We called Jess Harry's dog because when we scolded him, mostly in jest, she ran to his defence. If we said, 'Where's Harry?' she would climb on his knee and lick his face. Though approaching seventy, Harry had never had a problem with animals. In his youth he had mingled with them unafraid. Recently he had watched them from a distance, without resentment. I suppose this had been encouraged because he became more vulnerable to being knocked over and it was safer for him to be on the other side of the fence. Sitting in an armchair, on the outside bench, or on the back seat of the car, he did not need protection so she could climb on his knee and sit close when driving. She loved Harry and was serenely confident that we loved her. Aunty Mary did not, hence the cardboard cage, but the little collie never stopped trying to win her affection, waste of time though that was!

In the heat of August we had received news of cancer operations for two of our dearest friends. As October went into November, news of apparent success was very encouraging. Tommy, a frequent, disabled guest was making a good recovery and Janet, the first Guide we had taken to the Hebrides, was beginning to put the experience behind her. Just before Remembrance Day, I found the husband of another Guide selling poppies on the library steps.

I stopped to buy and he said, 'Did you know my wife is in hospital having a mastectomy?' Whenever we are up, we come down again. Margaret and I went to see her next day. I find that all my Guides, whatever age they are, sit with knees up or cross-legged as if round a camp-fire. Janet was always found with her knees up even at sixty, and Valerie, also over fifty, was sitting cross-legged on the bed smiling with pleasure that we had come.

'I'll tell you what,' she said, 'when I came out of the operation I was muttering, "A Guide smiles and sings under all difficulties".'

'When I learned the Guide Law,' said Barbara, one of my other early members, 'I was only ten but I was deadly serious. Every law meant my obedience. It was what my Guider believed was right, what my parents believed, and my teachers and the minister at the chapel and God himself. And now,' she continued, remembering the struggle of parenting teenage children, 'all these role models seem to believe different things. There's no longer one standard, one set of rules.'

The Guide Movement had terrific power and appeal in the early days. It, more than the Church, moulded and shaped our lives. Wouldn't I just love to be Guiding and camping and giving today's children the discipline and character training they deserve and many do not get. The Guide Movement taught all these things while having tremendous fun. Suddenly confronted with the fragility of life, Janet and Valerie wanted to go back to the islands and a seed was being planted out of which would grow an idea and eventually a reunion.

For some life ends far too soon. For Aunty Mary it was treating her well. On 3 December she became ninety and the occasion was marked by the arrival of friends and family. A cousin's daughter made a beautiful cake and iced it professionally. The news that it was her birthday travelled round the town and even people with whom she had worked, thirty years ago, came to see her. To end work at sixty and live beyond ninety is to be retired for a very long time. Personally I think it is too long, but few would agree with me.

Aunty Mary certainly enjoyed her special day. She had sold her house and come to live with us in 1989 saying she thought it wise to make this move while she was still able to help us. Indeed she had adjusted herself to our very active environment and had given valuable help. She was a good biscuit maker and she did our ironing and she was able to call us from the yard and buildings if Harry needed assistance. She was popular with guests and was called Aunty by hundreds of people.

After her ninetieth birthday she decided to retire. She had a wonderful excuse for doing nothing and one cannot criticise one so old even if one is sure it is important to keep agile. For Aunty Mary, becoming ninety was a milestone where she was happy to sit. I do not think Margaret will let me do so when I reach that age. We realised how much help Mother had given when she died. We also felt it when Aunty Mary stopped working and we had no help at all with the Chapel Ladies' Christmas Dinner we had been providing, mid-December, for several years. It came at a time of the year when feeding cattle was a full-time occupation. I could expect no help from Margaret to assemble the extra chairs and tables needed to seat so many well-proportioned ladies. It came at a time when there was always the possibility of snow and ice closing our road and we began to think it was a very risky business to prepare for a gathering that might well have to be cancelled at the last minute.

There is always a feeling of guilt at Christmas time if one neglects to continue a seasonal ritual so we were hesitant to back out. This was the only opportunity we had to do something for the village, half a mile away. This chance to prepare a lovely Christmas dinner for thirty old ladies should have brought more joy than it did. It would have done, I'm sure, if it had not been so impossibly hard. We were physical wrecks by the end of it, but the ladies loved it and left saying, 'See you next year!' Pulling on dirty trousers, we did not share their confidence. We left the piles of dirty dishes to be washed after we had fed the one hundred and sixty herd but the extra chairs and tables stayed in the dining room for several days. 'Oh, heck!' we groaned, season of goodwill, who would believe it?

In December 1996 we housed more than seventy little bull calves and a similar number of yearling bullocks and one heifer. We do not buy heifers for the simple reason that we can choose the gender of our animals by only bidding for bulls. There is a premium on them but not on their female relations. If Government has introduced a system, and you are to survive and are able to work it, then you are wise to do so. So why had we bought a heifer in 1995 and why can I see her and her brood, in the shed across the yard, several years later, writing for posterity?

I am not sure if we bought the heifer or if it was given to us. The calf sale was over. We had bought most of the calves at Beeston Castle and were just topping up our number at Skipton. We were leaning over the side of the pen, looking at the half dozen we had bought, when a farmer came and asked Margaret to buy two calves. We do not know whether he had arrived too late to place them in the sale or whether he had bought two he didn't want. Either way, Margaret being always a soft touch where babies are concerned, feared they might otherwise go to be killed and said she would. He asked for £40, which was really only the value of the strong bull calf. The other was a heifer which was a pure bred Friesian. As it was practically a give-away we presumed it would be a twin, a freemartin. Friesian heifers rarely leave the farm on which they are born for dairy farmers keep them to join the milking herd later. Twins are ninety-nine per cent infertile and are sold for a song.

The latest additions to the herd were taken home and with them this pretty, rather fragile baby who was never named. When we referred to it we said, 'the heifer'. It was not destined for fame, only to accompany its male contemporaries to the store market two years later. The modest sum it would fetch would not be assisted with a Government premium, so if it made a small profit it would only be because it had cost nothing to buy.

Between the Chapel Dinner and Christmas we usually brought in the vet to dehorn the calves before the horn buds grew too big. I had long since left behind the age at which most ladies retire. It was sixteen years since my somewhat early retirement from teaching. These had been rewarding, demanding and exhausting and I should, by rights, have been wearing a bit thin. There seemed little evidence of that, though the unpleasant activity of de-horning is strenuous and lasts all day. Hour after hour we hauled twelve-foot gates around the pens to make temporary crushes and, one by one, we pushed healthy calves in a direction they did not want to go. Each had to be handled twice, once for the anaesthetic and ten minutes later for the burning off of the horn bud. I was quite pleased with my performance but increasingly we began to think there might be a better way. A local farmer told us to try applying a paste immediately we brought them home from market and thereafter we did and found it about sixty per cent successful, which was a blessing. In 1996, however, we man-handled the lot and lying in bed, too battered and bruised to sleep immediately, I pondered on the extraordinary, demanding years, sixty-six to be exact, of my too busy life. Always, from early childhood, jobs have had to be completed. There has never been an opportunity to dodge them. The last bale must come off the lorry, the last animal fed, the last load of muck taken out, the last guest accommodated and fed, the last bed made.

When was it any different? The ability to keep right on to the end of the road was not learned tardily. The necessity to mark the last exercise book, hear the last child read, walk the last mile, pitch the last tent was taught by Father in the cattle sheds, singing as we milked the last cow, 'Keep right on to the end of the road'. He would be proud to see that we were still keeping on, finishing, as far as possible in our lifetime, the job of making The Currer productive and beautiful.

If his legacy had been our ability to keep going then Mother's had been the knowledge of how to shap! This dialect word describes activity with purpose, to do a job properly, quickly; to make dust fly. We are continually asked how we can find time to do so much. We answer with confidence, 'Because we were taught how to shap!' We do not dawdle or take the long way. We do not walk empty-handed. We do one job going and another on the way back. Guests who had just asked the way to the village pub didn't believe me.

'There must be more to it than that,' they argued.

'All right then,' I said, 'Perhaps it's because we don't go to the pub!'

Mother was a master of the art of shapping. She never made one cake. In a day she would make enough for a confectioner's shop. She multiplied every recipe and she made sure her daughters could do the same, and her son. What jobs he could do he did methodically and he finished, though he could hardly be dragged to his chair when he had done so.

I think we have always known what needs to be done and what can safely be neglected. Some things we need and some we can well do without. The former are few and the latter are many, yet most people would put many in the 'can't do without' category. As children we did not have money. While those in my class had Saturday pennies when they were five and spending money when they were teenagers, I had none. My family had none to spare, only to share. The same applies now. We are living proof that hairdos, cosmetics, toiletries and jewellery can equally well be done without. Only a limited wardrobe is necessary and 'best clothes' can last almost for ever. I have but one dress that suits all occasions. I remember going to a funeral in it twenty years ago. I mostly wear a jacket and my one coat I made from beautiful, Luskentyre woven Harris Tweed to go to a Guide's wedding in 1978. An annual visit to a Damart sale seems to meet most other needs.

Shoes are seldom necessary. It is possible to work twice as hard without them and we discard them indoors. Dirty soles are no detriment, bare feet never smell or feel cold and skin is the most hardwearing material of all. Wellingtons, in our profession, are necessary. Gloves are not.

We spent thirty-five years of my life without a car, declaring to all and sundry that one was not needed when we could all, including Harry, walk the half mile to the bus with ease. We did not, then, have to shop for a multitude of guests. A vehicle is now necessary and it must be an over-lander with four-wheel drive to climb the hill in snow, but it can be an old one. Ours have always been bought when they were pretty ancient.

Relatively recently cleanliness in society has become an obsession. A daily bath or shower in our climate is a luxury, not a necessity. A daily hair wash is a waste of time and water. Hand washing precedes everything we do appertaining to guests but we have ample proof that to drink coffee and eat biscuits while mucking out in the cowshed does not end in salmonella or e.coli. Buying meat from a butcher who does not separate raw from cooked might. Not storing it properly or cooking it thoroughly might cause you to be sick, but with animals we have eaten more muck than most and it has never done us any harm.

For obvious reasons clean sheets and towels are necessary for paying guests but, with often twenty to wash each day, to change one's own is often forgotten. Apparently it does not matter. Compared with my contemporaries who have not lived on the land, where mud and muck are neighbours others would prefer not to live beside, I am the most fit and agile. While they have arthritis and digestive problems I can only confess to broken fingernails and a painful little toe I stubbed on the table leg.

Knowing what is important and what is, for me, totally unnecessary is a time-saver of real significance and a money-saver no one can dispute. Alcohol and cigarettes, meals out, computers and videos *et cetera* would give us no more pleasure than we get already: certainly no more fun, just considerably more stress.

A dog, two dogs are necessary, and a friend, a workmate, for most jobs need two and laughter really needs to be shared. For us a social life is not important; an armchair is and a fire, a log one. I know it is easier and cleaner to press a switch but electric is not for me. The brasses on our family mantel-piece do not have to be cleaned every week as Mother did when we were children. The world would not come to an end if they were never cleaned at all but I like the occasional chore and the shine that follows.

We are not one bit critical of how other people spend their time and money. We just have to explain continually how we find time to do the things we have to do.

'How do you find time to write a book?' is the most frequent question. That's an easy one to answer. Some dawn-riser wants an early breakfast. Having provided it I then have an hour to scribble before the more considerate guests get up.

Christmas used to be the busiest time of all when we catered for many during the festive season. Since making a separate B&B kitchen it is possible to let all our accommodation to self-catering groups. We take advantage of this especially at Christmas and New Year.

A dozen years ago, before Mother died, we exchanged a traditional Christmas dinner for a quiet run out in the Dales. Chores had to be done before and after it and in 1996 we noticed that we had to assume the job of preparing the picnic. This had previously been Aunty Mary's job but she had retired. She took advantage of being ninety, laughingly told people, 'It's nowt being old' and got up late, much later than her friend, five years older, who always spent Christmas with us.

Not a year passes but we spend time and money organising so that life is easier. Working our twin businesses must become increasingly simplified if we are to cope with the rapidly growing task of caring for dependent relatives. We think we are experts at innovation but we can scarcely keep up with the speed at with other things become more difficult.

For the second year running Hilda rang in the middle of the afternoon on Christmas Eve to ask if we had forgotten to collect her! We'll swing for our oldies one day! There was a white, hard frost and next day there was snow. A white Christmas! The self-catering guests were ecstatic! We hurried feeding the herd. One phone call only comes on Christmas Day. Joan Entwistle, a much loved guest whose legs were amputated fifty years ago, comes every August with her husband, and never forgets to ring.

A white Christmas! There are few these days. The highways were busy taking families to get-togethers but the road we took from Blubberhouses, over to Greenhow Hill on the B6265, was covered with undisturbed snow. No other vehicle but ours had travelled it or the road we took to Grimwith Reservoir. My, how cold it was. Grim, but wonderfully white. The windows of the Range Rover became frozen with patterns seldom seen on glass in these days of central heating. When does one ever wake to find Jack Frost's artistic drawings of leaves and ferns on the bedroom window? Everything was silver: even the sky, for the sun shone weakly through cloud. Everything glistened. Every breath we gave the outside air was visible.

We were alone, just our car on the icy tarmac. We ate our picnic in comparative silence, clutching our hot mugs of tea for warmth. The icy beauty left us spellbound. How stupid can you get, we wondered? Should we really have come to this isolated wonderland, on Christmas Day, with two very old ladies and a brother who needed a wheelchair? Were we just two selfish females who wanted to eat ham sandwiches beside a frozen lake rather than cook turkey and plum pudding? We were miles from anywhere and pretty vulnerable. If we needed help it was not to hand and a mobile phone was not within our experience.

We struggled across the iced tarmac to the frozen toilets, one on each side, one dependant at a time. We're crazy! When each was safely back, Margaret and I walked the dogs along the lakeside, happy and healthy. Every blade of grass was a crystal miracle though every intake of breath was sharp. It was a Christmas Day to remember, clean and white and utterly beautiful.

It would have been lovely to return to the cosiness and comfort of The Currer, with its blazing log fire and twinkling tree lights, with freedom to be lazy. But no, we had to don working clothes and feed the herd. The only real hardship is the transition from comfort to work, the getting up and changing gear. Once in the sanctuary of the sheds, among the cattle, we are fine. We do really, truly, honestly like feeding cattle.

Margaret.

Chapter Two

*Give me, amidst the confusion of my day,
the calmness of the everlasting hills.*

Without a doubt, the most tranquil place on our little bit of the planet is the hollow where the road home crosses the trickle of a stream flowing gently under the cattle grid, from the pool we still called the Duck Pond. It had become somewhat overgrown since Reynard and old age had deprived us of ducks some time ago. In the spring a couple of mallard annually spent some time there and something must live in it for a single heron often stands there in waiting.

The wall which plummets down the steep hillside, from the quite ancient hawthorn to the miniature wetlands, marks the boundary between the land we own and the fields we rent from George. We know exactly how long the road is, which follows it from the farmhouse to the summit grid and the gate which enters the tarmacked road into the village. We know because, in 1959, we sledgehammered its foundation, yard by back-breaking yard, uphill all the way. When we were relatively young we smashed the top stones of the eighteen inches of jumble, thrown from the eastern wall, into the ruts of the cart tracks, by an ancestor of the modern JCB owned by the Yorkshire Electricity Board.

We know, too, how long it is because, twenty-five years later, we paid an astronomical sum to have it surfaced with, the men said, 'Motorway tarmac'. A representative from a firm, backed by a headed invoice and a written estimate per yard, unexpectedly arrived when we were contemplating employing someone to tarmac some of the road. Not for us, for guests! They did not complain but some commented that the road was bumpy. We, in the Land Rover, never noticed but, one day, someone gave me a lift in a car and drove more quickly than we do and I had to agree. The journey was a bit rough.

So we'd seriously discussed improvements. The foundations hadn't moved but twenty years of rain water hurtling down it had disturbed the quarry bottoms with which we had surfaced it. Some had been swept downhill to lie deeper than necessary on the floor of the little valley.

29

We had just arrived home from holiday when this road maintenance vehicle pulled into the yard and this yellow coated, helmet-wearing workman said he had a load of hot tarmac in excess of what was needed on the bypass and could we use it? The man was unsure whether the load would cover the whole quarter of a mile but we assured him we couldn't afford more than just wheel tracks and we signed a written agreement thinking how lucky we were. Someone had turned up at the right time, to do a job we knew was essential.

The lorry arrived and behind it was a piece of professional apparatus into which the tarmac was gently tipped and which smoothly and expertly clothed the road from side to side. We were too busy to monitor the activity and when we eventually went to look we were horrified. It looked beautiful, an edge-to-edge carpet, new and black and perfect but not the wheel tracks we had agreed. We protested. The man had not told us that his efficient contraption could not do tracks, only the ten-foot width. Too little of the road had been done but the man was reassuring. Not to worry. He'd already sent for another load to complete the admittedly perfect job. The cost was astronomically high. We realised we'd been taken for a ride. In spite of the headed invoice, the firm wanted cash and I had to make a frightening phone call to the bank manager. We learned an important lesson and were reminded of it every time the cheerful workmen, in their maintenance van, passed us on the road. Working in the area we saw them several times and they waved in a friendly way. We had to acknowledge they were excellent road surfacers. Fifteen years later we still have a good road. Its quarter of a mile length is a symbol of our ability to keep going right to the end. Had we stopped short of the summit we would not have reached the top road and a track which doesn't get there is no good at all. It is also a symbol of our being able to pay for what we get, albeit with considerable help from the bank!

The lesson learned was not wasted. Many years later a second generation of workmen was driving up our road, one day, as we returned from town. They said they were gritting the road in the village. The last workmen for the council had not come the final hundred yards to our entrance gate. When we'd asked the authority why, we had been told the final stretch wasn't theirs. It made no difference that we told them we had owned the property for seventy years and that the road had been tarmacked by the council all those years. Because they had suddenly denied responsibility potholes had appeared on the road. Periodically I'd filled them in but always, after several months, the filling had disappeared.

'If you are doing the top road are you coming right to our gate?' we asked these current workmen.

'Oh, yes,' they said. 'We just wanted to know if anyone would be driving out in the morning while we're doing it?'

We were full of holiday-makers who would be driving out in their cars at around 10 a.m. 'Just give us ten minutes warning,' they said. 'We'll make way!'

Next morning, around about 5 a.m., Margaret heard a disturbance among cattle and got up to see all was well. She noticed huge vehicles at the top of the road and presumed the roadworks had started early and the top of our road was being used as a turning circle. We cannot see the road from the kitchen window. I rise at six and it was at least an hour before a holidaying dog-walker told me that workmen were resurfacing our road.

'That's not our road,' I said. 'That belongs to the council. Our road is this side of the grid.'

'That's what they're doing,' he said. I ran out to the yard entrance and sure enough he was right. I forced Margaret out of bed and together we ran up the road.

A hundred yards had been tarred and scattered with chippings.

'What are you doing?' we shouted.

'We've just sent for another load,' the man said. We were emphatic. We had never agreed that he should do ours. They'd said they were doing the top road. We didn't want ours doing. No way. We'd never, ever have chippings. In a downpour they'd all end up at the bottom of the road in the grid well.

They tried persuasive tactics but, once bitten, we were forever shy. 'We'll only charge £3 a yard,' the man said.

'A square one or a linear one?' I asked.

'Oh, a square one,' he answered as if that were the lesser cost.

I was quick. I'd been there before. 'That's about £4,000,' I said. 'Don't be daft. You come here at five o'clock in the morning thinking you can get away with it. No way!'

'Well, you can't have us working, using materials for nothing,' he complained.

'Oh yes we can,' we said. 'We don't want them. Take them away. We didn't order them!'

'£400,' he begged. 'Well, we'll settle for £200.'

'Right,' I warned. 'If you don't go I'll ring my solicitor.' With that the men scarpered, never to reappear. Saying they were doing the top road was a hoax. The potholes remain and Margaret was right. Most of the loose chippings, thrown with a shovel across the wet tar, ended up in the grid well. Sooner or later we will have to scoop them out, lying on our bellies, with a garden trowel.

We and our road have a shared history. Climbing it to the more civilised heights of the road into the village does not interest me and this is not because, growing older, I tackle the steep hillside slightly less easily. Returning to The Currer has always been preferable to leaving. Only occasionally does it excite me to go away from here and coming home always thrills. The opportunity to do so was mine every day when I was teaching. For the most part it was in daylight when the view, whatever the weather, is spectacular. From November into March it was in darkness and the lighted hamlets on the opposite hillside and the floodlit A650 in the valley dazzled my descent. It is downhill all the way, to the footbridge where the hollow is, where the pond fills the glacial depression, where the tiny stream flows out of it, beneath the cattle grid and disappears down a drain under the yard and the cattle sheds. These John Sugden built for us in the hollow, so that they are below the house and take away none of its majesty

All the way from the entrance gate, on which there is the modest name-plate of our domain, only the roofs of the sheds can be seen and the sixteenth-century house stands proudly against a pastoral background. A valley separates us from the opposite Pennine slope, patterned with green fields and walls of millstone grit until the winter snow line is reached and the moorland where you will catch your death of cold if you recklessly go without a hat.

Descending our road the farmhouse appears to be low and sheltered but, having reached the hollow and crossed the bridge, the road rises and those approaching see that the house is on a hillock. Instead of its roof intermingling with the pattern of the Airedale hillside it is suddenly silhouetted against the sky, that ever-changing canopy in daylight, that mysterious umbrella of the night.

This small depression, made for us in the Ice Age, thirty yards from the farmhouse, is my quiet place. It endeared itself to me, long ago, when coming home from my pleasant headship of Kildwick Church of England School, five miles up the dale. There is always a wind on the hill. The west wall separating our land from the fields we rent from George is meant to protect foot travellers from the ravages of the prevailing wind but it fails totally. When we built the road we were vandals. We took away the opposite wall for its foundations so that an east wind is a killer. The west wall is pretty useless, too. The canny wind takes an easier route as it hurries up the valley and tries to blow away all those descending, whose feet are not firmly on the ground.

The sudden, round the bend dip into tranquillity cannot be missed. No matter where else one's thoughts lie, the sudden peace obliterates them all. An invisible door has been shut on the wind and the silence amazes. A safe harbour has been reached. Warm air caresses cheeks reddened and chilled by the journey down. Lungs, fighting to maintain regularity, suddenly breathe easily.

I have remarked once before that perhaps one's life mirrors the terrain on which one lives. If so, that is the reason why moments of calm are short-lived at The Currer. There is only a moment of quietness in the hollow before striding uphill to the yard entrance and being swept ferociously from behind by a wind threatening to impale human beings on the silver birches as easily as it does an airborne plastic bag.

Now, when it is twenty short years since my retirement, the balm of the hollow could be a forgotten experience. I must not let it be. Before we had water piped to the cattle sheds, we had to fetch it from the pond, or the ever-gushing spring, but now that chore is no more, opportunities to experience the healing qualities of the glacial hollow are limited to the winter opening of the field gate into the stock-yard, for the evening return of cattle and whatever artificial excuse can be made. Wellingtons don't have to be washed in the pond, nor the evening star viewed only from that vantage point but, if there is a moment to spare, that is how we choose to fill it.

The reasons we built the sheds in the hollow were several. The principal one was for them to be viewed from the kitchen window. We are farmers and when we are not outside we are constantly keeping a vigilant eye from within. As I write this I can see the only cow we have, the heifer that was, and her brood who have spent the night indoors, in the first shed we built way back in 1960. We built the walls from stone we took from the intake walls. We were vandals then, too poor to buy materials and we hadn't been infected with the preservation bug. If the calf-shed door is open we can see, from the kitchen window, whether peace is reigning there. Because the sheds are built on lower ground than the house we can see above them to the fields where cattle pasture. We can see the water trough at the foot of the First Intake, where town water has been brought so that there is always enough, even in drought.

Daily the herd congregates there. With binoculars Margaret can monitor their arrival and, when they have satisfied their thirst and settled for their midday sit-down, she can go and count them and satisfy herself that none is ill.

In one way we were unwise to cluster the bovine city in the valley of tranquillity, for the wind which hurtles though the farmyard so violently that, sometimes, it is dangerous to cross, has to be taken artificially into the sheds with fans and plastic tubing.

Our first guest of the year 1997 arrived even before it did. The New Year guests had not left which meant that she had to be housed in the spare room. She was bringing two poodles and, because that room is quite small, we manhandled the double bed out and put in a single one and a table where she could eat until the seasonal party left and she could be re-housed properly. She was here for several weeks on a dog-grooming course in the town and had asked for permission to bring two poodles, standard ones she said. In my ignorance I thought standard meant normal and that normal meant small. I nearly died when she arrived with two enormous, fancy-clipped creatures, one black and the other white, both bedecked with ribbons and bows. They practically filled the spare bedroom.

It was a trying but funny few days with frost and snow outside, bullocks galore in the shed, Mr and Mrs Bullock in the Mistal Cottage, every bed-space full and two whopping great fancy-pants parading as if they were at Crufts. Each morning they took their mistress walkies, dragging her unceremoniously by the lead, their bows and ribbons blowing in the wind. Fortunately they preceded her into the car and went to the salon with her.

When the New Year guests went we transferred her into a legitimate bedroom but as she was mostly our only guest, her dogs paraded in the dining room while she ate, which was against all hygiene rules, and they had a field day in the snug. Outside she dare not let them off the lead and, of course, the inevitable happened. The black one got loose and disappeared completely into the dark night. Her owner was distraught and paced the vicinity of the farm calling its name repeatably between her sobs. Getting no response she came to us, told us and said she was going to look lower down our hillside. That is not a sensible thing to do if you are a stranger. She was firmly attached to the white festooned monster. Had it been that dog she had lost it would have been seen more easily. Fearing for the woman's safety down our rough and wooded hillside, Margaret elected to go with her. We tried to muster up some tolerance. On a dark January night, with all our evening feeding to do, it wasn't easy. I remember preparing the woman's evening meal with something very near to exasperation.

They went down to the coppice we call Jimmy's Wood and along the foot-path beside our relatively unseen boundary-neighbour's house, 'Jack Field', then past Rawson Chad's 'Royd Field' and along the track to the village. They did not think such a large be-ribboned animal could go unnoticed on lighted streets but it was nowhere to be seen. They followed the bus route back to the track which leads to the cricket field and the remaining four fields to The Currer. They could do nothing more so they came home, Margaret to feed cattle and the good lady owner to eat very little of what I had prepared. I do not think she slept but sometime just after 6 a.m. the errant animal returned to scratch and whimper at the back door.

We deal with much bigger animals than standard poodles but, from the realms of dog, they were far too big for me. Give me a little collie any day. Arrogance is not something I can cope with and, as you must be aware, I am uninterested in being 'dolled up'!

The weather was mild and dry and frequently the herd of semi-wild fallow deer roamed the fields, below the house, those we call the Five-Acre and the Low Pasture. There was some disapproval from a non-farming landowner in the valley who believed the herd should not have been introduced to the hillside. Deer can jump even high fences and there would never be any way he, or we, or any of us on this hillside, could keep them out. Most of us who rear and nurture domestic animals have a great love and respect for the wildlife sharing our kingdoms. We certainly love the deer and when they come we run with binoculars, to count them and make sure no poacher is being successful. They are not the only trespassers. Harry Raw's sheep should stay on his side of the boundary wall but all too often take a free holiday-weekend in the Low Pasture. We are not going to quarrel with a good neighbour about that. The sheep are farmed and if they come, they go. The shepherd sees to that. The deer do exactly as they please but, as they are a holiday-maker attraction, they are welcome. Guests are far more interested in deer than in cattle. Isn't that sad? The native roe deer are seldom seen. They are far too shy to leave the cover of the woodland but the fallow deer, briefly, venture close and we love them.

The man who had introduced the herd of fallow deer to the area came to tell us to be on the lookout for poachers with dogs. I think he even meant we had to intercept them! I would have to be firmly behind a locked door before I would accost a trio of men with dogs. Seldom does any such unpleasantness intrude upon us. Of course we fear for the beautiful animals and have far more respect for them than for many of the so-called superior race but in all fairness, we have never encountered poachers. They do not work in daylight. We give no man permission to shoot and if poachers there are, they are not very successful ones for the herd grows rather than diminishes. Of this I am not surprised because, quite frankly, I would not choose to scramble among the rocks and bracken, the tangle of bramble and gorse and the natural tree growth. More humans would be injured than deer. I am confident of that.

The local landowner objected to the deer, but they were supported by neighbours who wrote to the paper and they still roam freely, so all is well.

On the day of the Annual Guide Reunion, Margaret found a huge, five-inch nail in a bullock's hoof. It had entered from below and protruded above. Such a discovery is made with foreboding. A big animal must be manhandled into the crush, a foot rendered painful must be grabbed and uplifted forcibly and whatever foreign body removed, with varying degrees of difficulty and quite a lot of danger. For a problem like this to present itself on Guide Reunion day was not unknown but doubly unacceptable. I was blamed for the wood-bearing nail which was trespassing in the gateway. I am invariably scapegoat. When presented with a difficult and dangerous job, such as removing a five inch nail, almost totally lost in a bullock's hoof, in at the bottom, out at the top, it is fortunate if there is a sister to blame and to shout at. That sister is used to verbal abuse from the lady who actually will be the one who has to struggle with the resistant animal in the crush, lift up the heavy foot and claw out the nasty nail. Of course, the one being blamed will have to help for it will be a two-woman job, but mine is mostly a minor role so, if it relieves the one doing the worst job of a weight of built up tension to shout loud and long and accusingly at her sister, so be it.

Actually, on this occasion, the nail was removed without too much difficulty and, having pierced a hole right through the hoof there was hope that it would drain of infection naturally. Nevertheless Margaret washed it thoroughly and injected an antibiotic for safety. I searched the area for any more dangerous pieces of wood which might have gone walkabout in gateways from the pile destined for the sitting room fire and, tardily, returned to my job of getting ready for the Seventeenth Reunion of Guides who had camped with us in the Hebrides.

Sitting with Barbara Sherriff (née Binns) and her husband, Arnold, drinking our last cups of coffee before midnight and their imminent departure, I tried to analyse why we are so afraid of Reunion Day. Barbara argued that it was nonsense to say that we could do most things without stress and then to say that to anticipate an annual reunion was to trigger a nervous breakdown. Nonsense or no, it is true. We go about our professional jobs, we farm, we cater, we are handymen, we are carers. I was a teacher and a leader. It is our nature to be calm and confident and yet we are all in a panic when our grown children come to see us. Barbara insisted that it was stupid. We had just had three hours of joy. What could be easier than welcoming friends who want to come together in remembrance of childhood fun, who vote annually with their feet simply to recall memories of adventure, laughter and song?

'It's because we are tired,' said Margaret. The long winter is not over on the first Saturday in March. The barn is still a quarter full of hay and straw and more loads will have to be bought before winter is really over. The dykes are full of black or white (February Fill Dyke is a local description of the wet month when dykes (ditches) are full of either water (black) or snow (white)), the cattle are housed, the dogs are dirty and we haven't even begun the massive spring clean. Remnants of Christmas and autumn calf-rearing time must be whisked away from an untidy porch. Cagoules are splattered with cow muck and wellingtons are dirty and wet. Walked-in mud adds an extra layer to the parquet tiles in the entrance and must be scraped off.

'That's silly, too,' said Barbara. 'You don't have to do that for us!'

We have our pride! Paying guests we can keep in the part of the house reserved for them which is always respectable. Past Guides use our entry, invade our kitchen and sit on our carpet.

'It doesn't matter a bit,' Barbara reassured us. 'They all love you both!'

That may be the reason we get in such a tizz. Maybe that is the answer. When they were children they needed us to take them to magical islands, to feed them, to keep them warm and dry and safe. Their acceptance of us was casual. We were taken for granted. There was never any demonstration of affection. We were neither mum nor favourite aunty. We were Skipper and Flim and they were Guides, going away to camp far, far away from home. Together they all had fun because we were their security, in the background, working like galley slaves. Every year camp began with an excited gathering on the station platform, they greeting each other and ignoring us. It ended on the same platform nearly three weeks later without any show of gratitude. Tired and sad that the magic was over for another year, the relationship had not changed. It was still them and us. The way it should be. They disappeared with their parents without so much as a backward glance. No hugs nor kisses, not even thanks. Margaret and I would shoulder our rucksacks and go home satisfied. This was the role we knew so well.

It was many years later that the realisation dawned on each of them, just how wonderful their experiences had been, just how tough they had had to be, how independent and, amidst such beauty, how spiritually aware they had become. With maturity had come more sensitivity to life in general and they had begun to evaluate their childhood experiences and become more aware of the part Margaret and Hazel and I had played. They had even exaggerated our importance and glorified us as extraordinary people. They had encircled us with haloes we did not wholly merit and our new status was never as comfortable as the old.

It was 1997, just forty years since we had taken the first children to camp on the Island of Tiree, in the Inner Hebrides, and seventeen years since the last camp on Harris, in the Outer Hebrides. All our Peter Pans had grown up but for them their experiences had not dimmed. On the contrary they were indelibly bright and each had begun to think she had been singularly blessed having shared something others had missed.

I have always segregated people into those who have camped and those who have not. Those who can sleep on the ground, carry their drinking water a quarter of a mile, build themselves a shelter and cook on an open fire fed with driftwood and peat, are different from those whose bed is permanently soft, whose water comes from a tap, whose home is centrally heated and whose food can be heated in a microwave. With an arrogance I hope I do not really possess, I have always sub-divided those who have camped into those in general and those who have camped with us. They, I know, are more positive than I am about this. 'Our experience was unique!' they assert with confidence, and the older they become, the more adamant they are that their holidays were incomparable. They descend on us every first Saturday in March full of that confidence. It has nurtured real affection. They feel their own children have been deprived of an opportunity now not on the market. They bounce into our home like friendly dogs, embracing us with laughter, a song on their lips and a love in their hearts with which we do not know how to cope.

And when they go, three hours later, we will not see them again for a year unless we are lucky and one brings her children to see us or sadly one is in hospital and we are informed. I once said that I would most like to be remembered for having taken so many children to the Hebrides. I can see no reason to change my mind. Indeed the first Saturday in March might well be the most important day of the year and why I am all of a do-dah anticipating it and completely exhausted when it is over.

Most of our children now live too far away to attend Reunion but some do come long distances. In 1997 came the first awareness that some really did want to return to the islands. It wasn't just a fantasy. Some of those who were the pioneers were discussing among themselves and sending waves of determination in my direction.

If I have had one dream more than any other, since retirement from teaching and Guiding, it has been that I take another island camp, never very successfully. In-sleep fantasies never are. In private, Margaret and I had dismissed any possibility of a reunion on an island. We had Harry and Aunty Mary. We were not free. Neither was there suitable accommodation on Tiree. Even without Harry and Aunty tents were out of the question. A few of us, including Margaret and me, would still be happy under canvas. Those of us who had been mature when the opportunity to continue a nomadic life had been snatched away from us, would find a return to a tent no problem. Most had not slept on machair for decades. A reunion was quite impossible but we were not believed by the conspirators. Because it was a long way off I said flippantly, 'Oh, you never know. Perhaps in the millennium!'

'I'm coming,' said the Valerie I'd last seen in hospital, undergoing surgery for cancer. They lifted coffee mugs and toasted the millennium. So help me, I thought, this isn't just a gentle lapping on the shore. At the least it is a spring tide, at the most it is a veritable tidal wave.

It was 4 March and, according to Harry, the day, had he lived, when Father would have been a hundred. Mother, had she done likewise would have reached that milestone a few months previously. We had expected her to reach her century for she had been as lively as a cricket until she was nearly ninety-four. Then, quite suddenly she was diagnosed with cancer of the pancreas and died four months later. We had lost an active member of the workforce and a companion with whom to leave Harry. We had also lost a large portion of the fun of living at The Currer.

The Range Rover had been losing oil excessively. The trouble had begun back in October. It embarrassed us that we had left a mark on the clean concrete outside our chalet in Wales. We'd reported the leak when the vehicle had been in the garage for a minor repair. 'Bring it in, sometime,' the mechanic had said. 'We'll repair it.' Sometime had been neglected and it was already

March. To take the Range Rover in to the specialist garage in Thornton is a bother to be avoided unless really necessary, but we have used the Simmonite garage since we first got a four-wheel drive vehicle rather later in life than most people do. I was already thirty-five and our parents were in their seventies before we admitted one was necessary. Thereafter we have left the maintenance of successive vehicles to David Simmonite. We may well be his longest customers. When we first met him he was just a lad in a barn up Squirrel Lane and he's occupied his spacious premises in Thornton Road for many years.

Our problem is that when we leave the vehicle for repair we are eight miles from home by road and six miles on foot. The latter used to be no problem when time was not at a premium. There is a bus terminal nearby but the route is into the city extending the return journey to twenty miles. To walk to the village of Denholme to pick up a bus travelling the shorter route is a good two miles. In the early days we always opted for the six miles direct rather than the two into Denholme. They are along country lanes and through villages with very un-British names. There is Moscow and Egypt and Jerusalem Farm and, should you deviate, there is a hilltop terrace of houses called The Bay of Biscay. Until recently demolished, the tall wall below the hamlet of Egypt was always known as The Walls of Jericho. More and more often we have accepted the offer of a lift into Denholme. Why not? There is always work needing to be done urgently at home but to walk to the bus is warmer than to be taken to it by one of the mechanics and left shivering on the pavement until one or other of two possible buses passes through the village.

On the morning of the day Father would have been a hundred, I was left standing at the bus stop in front of the massive, many-storeyed mill by David Simmonite's daughter. She and her sister are famous in rally driving circles. I told her that, in a filling station on the Isle of Man, the man at the pump noticed the garage sticker in our rear window and had eagerly asked if we were the Simmonite Girls. They are young and we are greying. In view of the gentle forty miles an hour we do the suggestion was hilarious. Once we had been stopped at dusk, by a young policeman in Wensleydale, for travelling too slowly and guests had once joined a queue of traffic, travelling at thirty miles an hour locally and had jokingly remarked, 'I bet that's The Browns in front!' Eventually passing the slow-going Range Rover they had found their prediction true!

The famous car driver set me down in Denholme. It was bitterly cold even for March. I marked time at the bus stop trying to keep warm. When driving one never puts on enough clothes to stand waiting for public transport. The thing to do in such freezing temperatures is to let the mind wander, not a difficult thing to do just one hundred years since father's birth, waiting for a bus in the village where my maternal grandmother had been born.

It is always cold in the expanding village of Denholme. The snow lies deeper there than anywhere else locally and still occupies the field corners long after it has left The Currer. Because it featured frequently in my mother's childhood it has remained a part of our background history.

What a leap man has taken in just one hundred of the millions of years his brain has been developing. In the fifteen minutes I waited for that afternoon bus, juggernaut lorries from all over Europe noisily passed, nose to tail, belching out their exhaust fumes! An articulated monster, of incredible length, was expertly reversed into the mill yard. As recently as my generation, mill workers wended their way to the same mill yard in clogs and shawls, in collarless shirts and flat caps and buried their children, because of tuberculosis, in the full churchyard. Sadly that church, where once the same vicar christened my grandmother, married her to my grandfather and christened all their children, is now closed. Something infinitely precious has been lost and been replaced with instability.

Amid the noise and fumes, I tried to remember that this was the sleepy, quiet village where my most recent ancestors had plied their diverse skills. There at the Royal Hotel Great Grandfather William Booth had been both tailor and publican. He had died prematurely of a broken heart after his wife's death from Bright's Disease. His demise had orphaned six children, five girls and one boy. Julia, the eldest, had assumed responsibility. Annie was in service at the local doctor's and Jane, my grandmother, joined her when she was eleven. Annie married and her husband, landlord of the Black Bull, was also the village dentist. His primitive tools had been passed to our cousin Michael who was a present day dental surgeon with more efficient equipment.

Jane had married Grandfather Tom Smith, middle son of the eleven children of Joseph Smith, cab proprietor in Keighley. His livery stables housed twenty-two horses and almost as many carriages in days, not long ago, when the only way to get to this now-polluted village was by horse or by a now extinct steam train to a station almost a mile away. Great Aunt Julia, wishing to visit her younger sister in town, used to beg a lift on the flat cart of The Carrier.

The twentieth century was fast coming to a close in a different world from the one Father had been born into at the close of the last one. Cars and aeroplanes, space rockets and computers, telephones and televisions had all emerged in a matter of one person's lifetime. Such rapid change may never happen again. Father and I had delivered milk by horse and cart and measured it out from a metal can long before bottles and refrigerators and, not all that much later, had watched men walk on the moon.

The bus came and I took a window seat. There was The Royal where Aunty Mary had been born. She boasts blue blood in her veins! Public transport goes slowly through straggling villages with several stops en route. There was the cottage where Great, Great Aunt Elizabeth had lived. There was the Black Bull and there, on the left, Lower White Shaw Farm where another great aunt had farmed with her husband. Only one of the five sisters had lived away. Her marriage and departure to Scotland had formed the Glasgow connection which had been important in our introduction to the Hebrides. Aunt Minnie's children were all Yorkshire born for she had journeyed south for each confinement.

Only Annie had lost children to tuberculosis, which was amazing as all the cousins had lived near or visited regularly without the precautions of modern medicine. There are only two daughters left of Aunt Minnie's family and only Aunty Mary here to remember the lifestyle of the last generation. When we go, only these ramblings will remain.

The moment comes when we let the six-month-old calves out of their shed during the day prior to complete freedom. Preparation for this means we have to re-fence the widening gaps in the walls of the Five-Acre. We took the wherewithal to do this temporary fencing down the field on the trailer we use with the quad bike. Halfway down the field it disintegrated. I've never seen anything collapse more efficiently. It had transported too many heavy bales in the winter (Margaret beware!) and had not had covered accommodation. It was a potential loss. Admittedly it had not been a hundred per cent useful for loading bales, for the floor space had been fractionally too small and the eighteen-inch sides had been a nuisance, but we could not possibly do without it.

Our job completed we brought the ruined trailer home. All that was left were the excellent wheels and axle and the sturdy tow-bar. We hadn't a clue how to repair it!

Sometime in the future, through Countryside Stewardship, will come the turn of this Five-Acre wall to be repaired and two of the gaps will be properly gated and the others walled. This will mean the end of the spring chore necessary for little more than one week every year. During that short period of being contained in one field, the calves learn how to come home at night and the dogs re-learn their job of encouraging them to do so. Thereafter the gap fences can be taken away and the calves given greater freedom in the sure knowledge that they will come home.

One night, that March, there was a incident I will not forget. Margaret had gone to the twelve-foot iron gate of the calf-shed door to open it for the returning sturdy animals. Like many of our gates it was only fastened with binder twine. I was putting hay into mangers in the bullock sheds and Danny was, as usual, getting under my feet. He was suddenly alerted to the premature, hurried arrival of all seventy-plus calves at once and he shot out of the manger intent on helping Margaret. Instead he frightened the baby herd which sought immediate shelter in their shed. I heard the crash of the iron gate as the binder twine securing it snapped. Where was Margaret? In a panic I followed Danny. Only one calf was visible. Only the south wall at the other end of the shed had halted them. The gate was flat. It had fallen inwards onto the bedding muck. One calf only had not leapt over it. He was on his back, feet in the air; on the gate and underneath the gate, on her back, pressed into the softer muck of the gateway, was Margaret. With my heart in my mouth I rolled the heavy calf over, and it scrambled to its feet. Then I lifted the heavy gate from imprisoning my prostrate sister. Was her back broken? Would she crawl out? How damaged was she? Was this to be the moment when the life we had created suddenly came to an end? There was an imprint of the gate on the well-trampled manure and a ditch where the front feet of the jumpers had landed. Those less athletic had left deep footmarks between the bars of the flattened gate. Margaret stirred and tentatively rolled over, testing herself as one does who is dazed and bruised and humiliated. She got on to her knees and found she could stand. Bedding manure is dry but not at doorways where hundreds of hooves knead it into putty. From head to toe the back of her was coated in manure.

'Phew!' she gasped as we both realised that life, as we have created it, could still continue. Then, of course, came the outburst, the pointed finger of blame.

'What did you do? You did something to frighten them!'

'Me? It wasn't me!'

'Well, it was something!'

'It might have been Danny. It wasn't me!'

'Well it was something,' the poor woman said, helping me to re-tie the gate with binder twine before going into the house to peel off her dirty clothes.

This was just another example of how dangerous daily life is on a farm, how easily a herd can be startled, how near safety is to tragedy. A fast car entry into the yard, headlights switched on, a horn blown, a new noise, the sudden appearance of a guest at the shed doorway can cause chaos. Cattle are unpredictable and will even refuse to pass a tipped load of logs but lick all over someone's car. To be in the midst of them is to dice with disaster for, since farmers gave cattle freedom, life has become much more dangerous. When we were children the herd was tethered in the cowshed and human progress within was relatively safe. Now, with increased freedom and bigger numbers, to walk among them is only safe if no one startles them.

We seemed particularly accident prone that spring. Always by March/April the depth of manure needs to be taken out but we try to hang on until turn out. The animals get bigger and those in the top bullock shed find they can not only overlook the dividing wall, they can hang heads right over to communicate with their colleagues in the lower shed. They cannot touch noses because a manger runs along the wall in which we strew hay and scatter corn.

Whenever our activity includes carrying bales of hay or straw we wear hooded, plastic jackets. When not carrying, the hood hangs loosely behind but without it, when we do, little bits of straw stray into our feminine underwear. There is nothing more uncomfortable than a hayseed impaled in next-to-skin clothing.

Margaret was loosening bales when this next, more amusing but potentially more dangerous accident occurred. She had cut the binder twine on the bale and was stooping over the hay when she felt herself being lifted completely off her feet. A bullock on the other side of the wall was eating her hood. She felt a tightening round her neck as the bullock easily took her weight and she realised she could quite possibly be hanged. That moment when you realise you are in real danger is a frightening one. She had only one hope. The plastic was that of a cheap market jacket, useless against rain but all right against hayseeds. It couldn't stand her weight and when it tore she was unceremoniously dropped back into the manger. The half-eaten, torn hood was no longer usable and another jacket had to be bought!

It is quite frightening being attached to whatever is disappearing down a bullock's throat. I had taken the binder twine from a bale behind the iron bars of the walk-along manger and had wrapped it a few times round my hand while distributing the hay to the ever-hungry animals. One found the dangling bit and began to eat it. If there is a piece of twine anywhere in the manger a bullock will find it within seconds and everything that goes in disappears immediately. Ruminating animals swallow at once and chew later! I felt the twine tighten round my hand which was being rapidly drawn through the vertically parallel bars of the manger. I was not going to be eaten. Bullocks are not capable of that, but I was going to lose an arm or at least have it riven from the socket and I was going to have a mauled hand which was dangerously near to the monstrous mouth. When in danger I call and Danny responds in an instant. He daily thinks I need protection and when I spread straw he comes with me and holds back the herd with a fixed glare. When he comes quickly into the feeding trough heads back out quickly one after the other. With my other hand I grabbed the fast disappearing red ribbon and when my bullock backed out of the manger an amazing length of it was drawn out of his stomach. All my fingers were swollen, bloodless and deathly white. Eventually they became a purple deep enough to exhibit. They were painful for some time and now I do not wind baler twine round my fingers. A determined bullock is stronger than I am and nothing, I repeat nothing disappears down an animal's throat more quickly than twine.

For some time a couple called Hepplestone occupied the Loft Cottage for the first two months of each year. They lived in a caravan on Baildon Moor but some Green Belt regulation prevented them from being resident all twelve months. They came for several years on 1 January, until they eventually bought a house.

Because of fire regulations all our doors have to open outwards and this makes the Loft Cottage very vulnerable in wind. The prevailing one always helps to open it and a gale snatches it out of your hand and bashes it against the retaining wall at the top of the loft steps. Over many years this wind power must have put considerable strain on the hinges and persistent rain that winter must have swollen the wood. Whatever the reason the door wasn't locking properly and one blustery morning, nearly at the end of their stay, the door blew open. A freak wind came down the chimney, before the couple was awake. It roused them rapidly enough! We did what we could with binder twine tied to a handle in the living room and urgently phoned a local joiner. He repaired it and told us our window frames were rotting, too and that we'd be losing panes before long. We decided they'd have to wait. Jobs like that cannot be done in wintertime if they can be put off.

Even when Easter comes, winter has not left our hillside. Daffodils may be out in the south but here they are barely in bud. Cattle still need feeding and walls tumbled by the frost have to be repaired. Fences rotted by constant moisture tend to collapse and allow cattle to trespass where they are not supposed to go. If this happens to be Jimmy's Wood it is a nightmare getting them out which is why we had it professionally fenced to permanently prevent cattle access but that word is a challenge to bovine animals. Any land ring-fenced must have a gate in and a gate out not just for people walking the somewhat overgrown footpath, which passes through, but also to drive out cattle for whom the fence is a challenge they can overcome. Of course gates are left open by inconsiderate walkers, everyone knows that! We put springs on the gates into the woodland so that walkers were assisted in closing them. This fascinated Jess. We could barely get through before she and the spring had closed the gate. It was a lovely game to play for the closure came with a bang followed with a growl. We could not halt her little party-piece, so we stopped trying, and were very quick to get through the opening before she performed her trick. We never taught her to shut the sitting room door when she came in. She knew exactly how to open it but it was left to one of us to get up and shut it.

What with one thing and another we were short of spring-cleaning time and when Margaret saw an advertisement for a rapid emulsion paint spreader she ordered one. It was described as easy to use and was a modern replacement of the Black and Decker Paintmate Margaret had been using but for which we could no longer get replacement pads. This newer equipment was a great improvement, the advertisement said, which was stuff and nonsense. She used it with difficulty for one season and then gave it away. Bags of special paint had to be bought and carried in a knapsack. It was heavy. When doing ceilings there was grave danger of overbalancing and falling off the ladder. Of all the stressful jobs Margaret has performed this, she declared, was the one she feared would trigger off that nervous breakdown we promise ourselves when we have time!

But there wasn't time. Tom and Judy Pearson came and a lady with three small children from France. Tom and Judy were both in wheelchairs and it was a funny combination round the dining table. The French lady had no car and it terrified me to know what to do with her and three small children, every day for a week. Three quarters of a mile to the bus is a long way with a small family. It amazes me that the Ministry of Agriculture can be so ignorant of what a B&B diversification can mean. I racked my brain to think of some activity for them. The thought of blending Tom and Judy with small French-speaking children made me wish diversification to that place my mother always called Umanick!

Unbelievably the disabled couple and the family from Europe got on like a house on fire. Tom and Judy were regular visitors always on the receiving end of everyone's kindness. Tom had a huge van suitably adapted for him to drive from his wheelchair. There was plenty of room in it to take the French family to Bolton Abbey one day and somewhere else the next and each day was an adventure. Tom was the giver and Judy no longer a receiver. It was wonderful. They had never enjoyed themselves so much before. They had never felt so important.

One day we hosted the annual visit of the residents from White Windows Cheshire Home. Our paying guests stayed behind and joined in the fun. The French lady proved herself both a carer and a worker as she flitted from sitting room to kitchen as if it were her profession.

Shortly after this our own French boy, Denis, came for two weeks and he tied an iron sheep-hurdle onto the axis and tow bar of the bike trailer, with the ever-useful binder twine and, hey presto, we had a far more useful piece of equipment. It had no restrictive sides and could easily be loaded with bales. Good old Denis! What would we do without him? There are few better mechanics. None cheaper for we only have to feed him!

I filled in the annual IACS form which is no longer a difficult task for we have no change. Until the Government alters the form I can cope. We were about to involve ourselves with much more paperwork, however, for we had at last been accepted on the Countryside Stewardship Scheme.

Long before this debatably environmentally friendly scheme came into existence, we had been quietly employing a drystone waller to repair our miles of field boundaries. We had received a percentage grant from the Ministry and we repaired at a speed we could afford. We were prepared to do this, when and if our purse would allow, until the enormous task was completed.

Quite unexpectedly this wall grant was discontinued and replaced by a stewardship scheme. The only way of continuing was to apply for membership. The aim of the scheme was to encourage farmers towards a less intensive way of farming and to recreate landscapes without the use of fertilisers. So doing would mean the return of England's wild flowers and fauna. Traditional methods were encouraged and stone walls would receive grants. It all sounded fine but when we'd first applied we'd been turned down. Seeing our unfertilised fields and our carpet of meadow flowers, the inspector had said ours was already an example of what they meant to achieve and money must go to those who must be encouraged to change, not to those who never had. And the walls, we asked? Hard luck! No scheme, no walls!

Someone in 1995 advised us to send in another application. We could lose nothing by doing so but again our application was rejected. However, the new CSS advisor suggested he came and discussed our application to see if adjustments could be made to ensure an application in future was accepted. We must never again spread calcified seaweed as this contained a little fertiliser. We must not spread farmyard manure nor keep horses or donkeys. We began to think such a scheme a nonsense but, since our covenancy with the National Trust, the building of the dry stone walls had became a top priority.

We were prepared to argue. All right, we would stop the use of calcified seaweed but the farmyard manure was essential. To continue a traditional manner of farming and maintain our flower cover, surely we had to scatter the bedding manure as we, and our predecessors, had done since the beginning of farming time. To cease this spring activity would be to allow the wild flower meadows Grandfather had bought seventy years ago to return to the pre-monk days when all this hillside was moorland, tufted with heather and bilberry, rushes and cotton grass and acres of bracken. No way! Even if there was any possibility of magicking away the winter accumulation of bedding manure we could not agree. We were on the point of backing out but we managed to come to an agreement when the man learned that we only spread it after composting it for a year and that we only had enough to cover a third of the land each spring, in rotation. The donkeys were allowed to stay. Had they had to go we would definitely have backed out of the scheme. We do not suffer fools gladly!

We had to do something to satisfy the Government that we deserved a grant for re-building our walls. The Dewpond, which had been constructed a few centuries ago, had dried up even before Father had died over twenty years ago. We had mourned this loss but had found there was little we could do about it financially at the time and the deep, cobbled cone had become overgrown with grass and weeds. If we were prepared to restore this relic of bygone times and rebuild a Civil War lookout, locally called Fairfax Coppy, we may be accepted.

The outcome of all this was that we were. And Tim Walker and Graham Foster began the mammoth task of re-building most of our walls, the cost of which would be shared sixty/forty by the Government and us over a ten-year period. Never since the National Trust covenancy had we been more pleased. Nothing is more beautiful than a drystone wall. The cost to us would be phenomenal and we would have to continue the bed and breakfast lark for another ten years at least and defer growing old. It amazes me that a government was prepared to make a contract with two women farmers, one who was sixty-seven and the other fifty-eight, which was to last ten years. It shocked us as much as the bank manager, seventeen years ago, who was prepared to lend us money to convert a barn into holiday accommodation when there was no guarantee that any tourists would come!

Diversification is recommended to farmers who find profits from the land are not viable. Government seems to think that those who are finding it impossible to make ends meet can find the money to convert property to satisfy tourists who must now have en suite accommodation, or enter into environmental projects for which they must find forty per cent of the cost.

Our own holiday was approaching and after that would come the summer of Harry's seventieth birthday. He who had not been given seventy minutes to live had survived seventy busy years! We decided to buy him a lightweight wheelchair. It is not impossible, yet, for me to throw the wheelchairs high enough to be caught by Margaret standing on the roof rack but, I must admit, it is not as easy. We have never bought presents within the family for we only have one purse. We knew, however, that all our guests would ask Harry what had been bought for him by his sisters. We could say, 'The wheelchair' and not feel guilty. We went to Brighouse to buy this lighter model four months before his birthday so that we could take it on holiday.

Nationwide, election fever raged but it did not affect us at The Currer. No canvassing would-be politician comes out here. I am sure they were giving farmers a wide berth, anyway, so great was the crisis in our industry. We were spared the excited activity everywhere and could get on with preparations for the holiday undisturbed.

Chapter Three

I heard again the Gaelic speech, the scrunch of keel on shingly beach;
I saw the little lochs where lie the lilies white as ivory.
With buoyant step I went along, whistling a Hebridean song
That Iain Og of Taransay sang one enchanted day.

Anon

W e are disaster prone just before we go on holiday but everything, during the first few days of May, went incredibly smoothly. So quietly and easily we were scared. On Wednesday evening, the day before we were to leave, we drove the Range Rover out of the garage, carried down our packed cases and prepared to load the roof rack.

'This can't be true!' we said. The house was tidy. All we had to do was put up the luggage and, believe it or not, we could have a bath. It was not a normal activity to have a bath before we left for holiday. Ever since 1979 there had never been time! That was the year we had decided to convert the barn into holiday accommodation. Following Father's death in February, life had become increasingly hectic. We had been tired out by October half term so we had decided to snatch a few days' holiday in Grange-over-Sands, Cumbria. We had not been able to leave until after a brucellosis test on all our heifers. Mother, Harry and Aunty Mary, dressed for holiday, had watched through the window while we'd got increasingly hot and dirty. The Land Rover was packed. We'd told the vet that when he'd finished we were off on holiday. 'When do you get your bath?' he'd asked. 'When you get there?'

Indeed, things had not changed over the years. The rest of the family always bathed before holiday. Margaret and I always had ours at the first Travel Inn en route. May 1997 looked like being an exception. There was going to be time!

'Come on,' I urged Margaret, 'Let's get the cases on!' But the phone was ringing. Mr Davison, at Upper Transfield, was calling to say our cattle were wandering all over his paddock. This was appalling news. To get into his property our cattle must have the breached the boundary and romped all over the council-owned moorland which surrounds the Druids' Altar. To get them back onto our land they would, once more, have to cross the heather and bracken, this time uphill. Not an easy activity. It is strewn with rocks and is unfenced. They would most likely refuse to go back through the breach in the wall, wherever that was, and may even head for Bingley. The job was virtually impossible.

We jumped into the Range Rover and drove overland to the furthest corner of our land, looking for a gap in the boundary wall. We noticed quite a number of our one hundred and seventy cattle still at home and we could not find an exit hole so we climbed out of the vehicle and scrambled over a wall onto the track that leads to Upper Transfield. We catapulted down the hillside to the Davison's pleasant property and there were cattle in his paddock but they didn't belong to us.

'I know. I'm so sorry,' the embarrassed man said. 'I phoned to tell you but you had left.' The relief was enormous. We had no criticism for the man whose error had tortured us. There was only this wonderful, relaxed enjoyment of good news.

The straying animals had come from below, not above. There was a temporary hole in the hedge where they had pushed through. We tried to coax the animals back the way they had come but, as always, they wouldn't oblige so Mr Davison went in to phone and, laughing and waving, we climbed back up the hillside and over our un-breached boundary wall.

'That was a shock!' Margaret admitted. 'Let's drive all round the boundary and make doubly safe.' So we did and darkness was falling as we returned home.

The calves had returned to the shed without any encouragement from us. All seemed well. Cattle or children have to be counted. Large numbers have always been our responsibility and counting a necessary chore. Margaret went to take her evening roll-call and found six calves were missing. She was not unduly concerned. If one animal is missing it means we have a problem. Several means they are usually safe, unless they have jumped a boundary. It was surely the most beautiful night, yet, that year. There is always the first night when calves decide it's time to sleep out of doors. These six would be warm and dry. Their bellies would be full and the call of the wild would be tempting them to sleep under the stars for the rest of the summer.

The risk, however, could not be taken so, happily thinking about the coming holiday, Margaret searched the fields we rent from George and she found the six campers, placidly ruminating, as content as could be. She let them be. On returning she made one of her rare mistakes. She left the calf-shed door open in case the wanderers returned.

Harry and Aunty Mary bathed but we did not, nor did we load the roof rack, nor did I get to bed before well after midnight. At close on 2 a.m.

Margaret prepared for bed and as she did so, a fox jumped onto the wall close to the shed which houses the geese overnight. It began to scream and there is no noise more terrifying to prey. Presumably our feathered friends would create a dramatic, chaotic diversion. Who wouldn't, hearing that awful scream? Margaret dashed out to chase away the noisy fox but she was too late to prevent near disaster. The flapping, squawking geese had spooked the seven-month old calves who stampeded to the open door of their shed and hurtled through it in one maniacal torrent. They continued alarmingly quickly through the low paddock into the Five-Acre. Their momentum increased when they reached unobstructed space and they began to gallop round and round the field perimeter. Turning left at the gateway their journey took them careering down the steepest slope of the field to the ring fence round the woodland which blind Samson, three years ago, had jumped easily.

The thudding of three hundred hooves awakened me. A stampede is very frightening. Cattle running are not stampeding. That is a different thing altogether. It has perpetuity. It is blind. It is unstoppable until exhaustion controls it. To step in its path would be fatal. We stood at the sitting room window watching, with horror, the repeated 'takes' of a Western movie. Each time the herd careered past the window we prayed it would be their last time. A ten-metre strip of the field was bare and black with the ploughing of their hooves.

'Well, that's the end of going on holiday!' Margaret said. 'All of them will have pneumonia!'

An hour, it took, for them to slow down and stop. We dare not disturb them for fear they would start again. Some may have crashed through the fence into the woodland but we dare not investigate although the darkness was turning into day. We went to bed and lay, sleeplessly, determined not to go on holiday.

Rising early we found all the calves had re-entered the shed but were standing paralysed with heads facing the wall, like devout Jews at the Wailing Wall. Their coats were still wet with the sweat of their unreasonable activity but a count found them all at home. There was not a blade of grass on the ten-metre racecourse.

By mid-morning normality was being reached. Given hay the calves were eating. No one was panting. By midday we were seriously thinking we might leave, after all. We still wonder how we dared to do so. The calves ventured out quite happily to graze and we thought, perhaps, no harm would come of our putting the cases onto the roof rack. Margaret never stopped checking her calves. It would be awful to go and have to come back and silly to stay if there was no reason. At 1 p.m. we decided the risk was greatly reduced but we were shell-shocked, unbelieving that the experience seemed to have left no damage. We were still amazed that none had hurtled over the fence. The edge of the quarry, from which the building stones for the farmhouse had been cut over four hundred years ago, is only feet from it and to jump the one, at speed, is maybe to fall over the other.

We rang Dorothy who replaces us twice a year so that we can re-charge our batteries. We told her what had happened but that normality seemed to have returned. 'We're going,' we said. 'We'll phone from Ayr and if there is anything wrong you must tell us and we'll come home!' At 2 p.m. we were voting in the General Election at Parkwood First School, already on our way to the Hebrides.

The atmosphere in the Range Rover was somewhat strained and silent. On most previous occasions we had begun to relax almost as soon as we'd pulled out of the farmyard. That year it took us a great deal longer. Aunty Mary has never grown any farm awareness. What goes on outside is a total mystery to her, though she has been with us for many years. All that time she has believed, quite seriously, that everything we do is automatically wrong. When things go awry she knows it isn't her fault so it must be ours. When they go well she is not convinced that it is we who have manoeuvred it. We were already late which to us is, regrettably, quite normal but worrying for we do not like driving in the dark. Neither do we like going north on fast highroads so we always go what Aunty Mary calls, 'The fields way,' which takes longer but is less stressful. Nearing the point where we turn west towards Dumfries we approached a road diversion and were directed to take a roundabout, longer way. That, too, she thought was our fault and we began to worry what would happen if we had to say, after phoning home, that we must re-trace our steps next day and go home.

Darkness fell long before we reached Ayr Travel Inn so we were tense and did not relax until we had made the crucial phone call home. Dorothy reported that all calves were counted and all were happily in bed. Aunty Mary and I soon followed but Margaret and Harry, in the adjacent room, were relaxed enough to stay awake watching election results until Keighley was announced shortly after midnight.

We were heading for Oban via the Isle of Arran, boarding the steamer for Broddick at Ardrossan and we'd decided to breakfast on board. Harry ordered porridge, which Caledonian MacBrayne cooks make rather well. Harry was always a sweet tooth and sugared everything more than anyone else, so Margaret helped herself to lots of sachets. Two she scattered on Harry's breakfast and two she put in his tea. She tested the porridge and said, 'It's salty this morning! Do you think they've used sea water?' and sprinkled on two more of the sachets for good measure and to disguise the salt. Even so he could not eat it. Aunty Mary scooped up the unused sachets and, when the waiter came, while we had taken Harry to the toilet for disabled, she remarked that the porridge had been far too salty. The waiter had not replied. He had just gathered up the empty sachets and taken away the rejected porridge. For Harry not to enjoy a breakfast on holiday is stressful and we fought to regain a relaxed atmosphere. We always enjoy holidays but we have to work hard for the tranquillity we yearn for. We worked very hard that holiday!

We drove from Broddick to Lochranza and crossed by ferry to Claoniag on the lovely Mull of Kintyre. It was the most beautiful of days and gradually the sail and the motion of the car along the narrow lanes fringed with a profusion of gorse, calmed our shattered nerves. We took a diversion down memory lane to drink our mid-morning flask of coffee on the shore at Skipness, a village in which we had spent happy holidays with Father before his prostate cancer operation. Then we took the lovely west coast road north to Oban. On a grassy plateau, elevated above the road overlooking the bay, we made our evening meal. We lit our camping gas stove and boiled some bagged 'fish in parsley sauce'. With a kettle of boiling water almost every menu is possible. There is instant everything these days, instant soup, potatoes, gravy, custard and coffee. There are several things that can be boiled in bags. It's a doddle. We do not need a restaurant at a Travel Inn, just a kettle of boiling water and a tin opener to have canned fruit as dessert. A local lady thought we were about to pitch camp and came to direct us to Ganavan. When she realised we were only having a picnic, she joined us for a while. We like meeting the real people of the Highlands.

We thought everything was going just fine but Harry was not enjoying his food. We were working so hard to neutralize the atmosphere and we weren't succeeding very well. In fact we were struggling. We were well on our way to Fort William before we solved the problem. We were aware of the effect but couldn't identify the cause. Harry had indigestion and needed Gaviscon. I was driving and I suddenly said, 'Did you put those MacBrayne extra sugars in your bag, Aunty Mary?' She said she had and I asked her to get one out and we saw at once that it was not filled with sugar. They all contained salt. No wonder Harry felt so awful. Were we so stunned by the stampede that we couldn't read sugar from salt? Phoning home we'd found the calves were fine but we, tragically, couldn't tell sugar from salt! Now we can laugh. Then it didn't seem at all amusing.

Neither was the fact that, when we got to the Travel Inn, the two rooms we'd been allocated each had only one bed, a double one! I had been very definite, when booking three months earlier, that we needed adjacent ground floor rooms. I stressed we had a brother in a wheelchair and a very old Aunty. I am good at this reservation job. We'd booked well in advance because we needed rooms to be next to each other and our dependents could not climb stairs easily. The lady at the other end of the phone had been helpful. She'd asked if I would like the room for the disabled. We don't really need it but we had decided to sample it. It is often funny to see what facilities otherwise intelligent people think suitable for the handicapped.

On arrival we found that there had been a total mix-up, even of our names. The room for the disabled had been allocated all right but the other room was upstairs, miles away. And both rooms had only double beds! We had never come across this before. Previously all rooms had had a double and a single bed. I explained that I had booked a disabled room for my seventy-year-old brother and myself. The receptionist said there was only ever one bed, a double one, in the room for the handicapped.

'But that's not sensible,' I protested. Not all handicapped people are married. Those who are often cannot sleep with anyone, however close the relationship. Most are brought with relatives or carers. I was emphatic. 'It's our profession,' I explained. 'We cater for disabled holiday-makers. Only a few want a double bed.'

'There isn't enough room for two beds,' she said. Indeed she was right. Far more space than was necessary had been allocated to the en suite facilities.

'Have you got a put-up bed?' I asked.

'We have but it's already in use,' she answered. 'I could try and get you hotel accommodation in the town.'

Twin bedded rooms, ground floor, adjacent and en suite, late at night? She could try but the success factor would be low! And, anyway, we couldn't cope with breakfast. These were all positive reasons why we appreciated Travel Inns and Lodges. I felt sorry for the receptionist. It wasn't her fault so I said that we would cope. It is really no big deal to cope with sleeping on the floor. We do it regularly at home.

We took Harry, in his wheelchair, to see Fort William at night. It was not a pretty sight. Since we had last stayed there overnight, the main street had been closed and converted into a shopping precinct but there seemed to be many more pubs than shops. Living out in the country we never see anyone the worse for drink. The open doors of the dimly lit saloons spilled out noisy, singing customers. Two elderly ladies pushing a seventy-year old man in a wheelchair were strangers. In Scotland but out of place! We could not believe that this Highland community could be so noisy. We had always thought that Fort William, which is only a main street and a cluster of hotels, was for the élite not the boozer! At night-time we felt extremely uncomfortable in it so we returned to the Travel Inn. I took rugs from the Range Rover and two bits of foam we have on the back seat and, that night, I slept on the carpeted floor of the room for the disabled! I slept well, reassured by the knowledge that the morning would bring a fresh start, a lovely journey via Spean Bridge and Loch Garry and, ever northwest, along Loch Cluanie and under the shadow of the Five Sisters of Kintail to Shiel Bridge and Loch Duich, passing the Eilean Donan castle and through the flowering gorse towards the lovely Isle of Skye, isle of mountains high! Who wouldn't sleep?

We were doing this somewhat longer journey, ignoring our favourite Road to the Isles via Mallaig and Armadale, because Harry wanted to see the new bridge which now spans the Kyles at Lochalsh. To do so must be a great inconvenience for those on foot who used to take the little ferry from Kyleakin to do their shopping. The bridge is quite a way from either village and, without a car, is a long walk! So much for modern technology! We crossed it with interest and nostalgia. The ferry had been part of the joy of our holiday.

The road crossing Skye, to Uig and the Outer Isles ferry, is now a wide highway and, were we speedoholics, we could do the journey in record time. But we are not, and Skye, though we think it does not compare with the Outer Islands, is still too beautiful to hurry through, no matter how urgent is the desire to get aboard the RMS *Hebridean Isles* for the last leg of our two-yearly visit. That year it was an evening sail across the Minch to Harris, and the scent of peat and tweed and all the magic of our much-loved island.

Our first full day was Sunday and it was far too wild to venture out with a wheelchair. We'd planned to leave the cover on the roof rack all holiday so that some things, including Aunty Mary's wheelchair, could be housed there. Having our mid-morning coffee in front of the large sitting room window of our cottage, we noticed that a starling was eyeing it over as a possible nesting place. When he started bringing back the wherewithal to build we tried to shoo him off. He was very persistent and we had to take off the cover or take him, his wife and his imminent family home with us. It was a breezy, precarious job to remove it and empty the objects we'd hoped to leave there. We spent much of the afternoon watching a turbulent sea crashing on the beach below us at Scarista and then, because Harry was itching to venture out, we drove round towards Leverburgh. Even in a heavy Range Rover, we could feel the gale trying to overturn us. Just beyond Northton we met a walker striding out in her Sunday hat, presumably going to church. Such a hat should not be worn in a gale and long before we met and passed her, the hat had begun its flight to the island of Berneray. She did not even give momentary chase. It was gone in an instant. We drove on and paused on the water's edge in the shelter of Leverburgh but even there the wind threatened to take the Range Rover, even as it had the hat. We decided Harry must wait for outdoor entertainment until morning and we retraced our road home to the cottage. Passing the Northton turnoff we saw the hat-less lady striding out ahead of us and, drawing level, we stopped to offer her a lift knowing that she must be heading for Scarista Church, some three miles away.

'Were you intending to walk all the way?' we asked.

'Well, no,' she replied. 'Someone would have come along.' True. On Harris whoever came would have stopped.

Sunday, we know, is a sacred day on the islands and so it should be. The Sabbath peace is a medicine which would benefit us all and of which most of us are deprived. We do not visit our friends, however welcoming they might be, on a Sunday unless we have no alternative, so it was Monday morning before we headed for Luskentyre, the haven we used for so many summer camps with so many healthy, happy children. We had wakened to snow. A couple of inches of it whitened the machair bordering the white beaches. It had gone from sea level before we drove to Luskentyre but it illuminated the hills for several days.

The minute township of just ten crofts houses our closest friends, those incredibly tolerant and wonderful people whose support gave us security when weather was bad and we were under canvas. These were the people who had made the Harris Tweed from which some of our clothes have been made, who knitted the socks in our wellingtons and the pom-pom caps on our heads, who had made us crowdie and cloutie dumplings, scones and pancakes galore.

On the water's edge live Katie and Angus, who had given us Lusky many years ago and from whom we had taken Danny on our last visit. Lusky was only a pup and, though we are sure he remembered Angus, he was an all-Currer dog. Yorkshire had been his home and Harris his holiday venue for as long as he could recall. He had no memories of it as a place from which he had been uprooted, and Angus was not a master who had rejected him. Lusky was not a rescue dog.

Danny was! He had had three homes on Harris. He had been born some-where up at Maaruig, where the north track left for Rhenigidale, before the building of the road. He had been born in the home of the policeman and I am sure Danny had never, ever been ill-treated. He is such an affectionate dog he could never have suffered physical abuse. He had just been passed on which was sad for Danny's heart is big and it had been broken three times. His second home had been with an elderly couple at Bunavoneadar. They loved him dearly (who wouldn't) but a young dog needs to be active. Angus's daughter, Kathleen, is district nurse and she brought him home for Angus to train for the sheep. Danny is a cow dog. He was not interested in sheep which is why, at three years old, Danny was given to Margaret.

All dogs love Margaret but none adored her as Danny does. Some dogs are excited by their love and are all over their idol. Not Danny. He makes no fuss. He just adheres to Margaret like sticking plaster. Other people leave their dogs alone, at home all day. Some, though we disapprove, leave their dogs in our cottages when they come on holiday. Danny we never leave. His heart would break again. I'm sure he loved his other owners. He knows how to do so more than most but he remembers rejection and fears it may happen again. He need not worry!

Danny looks out of the window when travelling, and when we turned on the Luskentyre road, on that Monday morning two years after we'd taken him away in a British Airways box, he recognised the geography of the place and attempted to crawl under the seat.

'Danny! What are you doing?' We were disappointed. We had looked forward to returning with him to the beaches of his boyhood. 'We're going to see Kathleen,' we said but his head was hidden under the seat and no way was he going to respond positively. His back end, the only visible bit of him, was trembling. It was such an anti-climax. We had told him daily, for at least a month, that we were going to Luskentyre. It hadn't occurred to us that he might be petrified of our leaving him there.

When we rounded the bend and gasped, as always, at the sheer beauty of sand and sea, mountain and sky, our canine friend's head lay well and truly under the seat. Lusky could smell the ozone and he whimpered pleasure from his back space, Jess was alert with anticipation but Danny remained imitating an ostrich. When we reached the cottage, which stands so close to the sea one could imagine it might fall in, Danny almost refused to extricate himself from below. He is normally the most obedient of dogs. He had not resisted when we'd taken him away, two years earlier. He had worn a resigned, refugee look, a sad, bewildered acceptance of the fact that any withdrawal would be futile. The look returned as he reluctantly allowed himself to be coaxed out of the Range Rover.

How dearly I would like to know what thoughts occupy a dog's mind. Danny makes few decisions of his own which is why we allow him to climb the road to the gate and do not call him back or worry if he decides to gently move the calves through a gateway without permission. We all have to do something off our own bat, sometimes. He allowed Angus and Kathleen to fuss around him but his eyes did not light up and when Margaret told him he could get back into the car he did so with obvious relief. Over the fortnight the idea that Margaret might leave him behind gradually disappeared. His memory was acute. Twice, at home, he had crawled under the seat. On both occasions we were being followed by a police car. His first master had had one but we had not understood why Danny had behaved so. Now we knew. We became aware of what might happen if we took him to see the old couple at Bunavoneadar but we were told they would love us to do so. We found the cottage but the door was locked. A neighbour said they would be in Tarbert, having lunch at an old folk's centre and we must just go and introduce ourselves. We did and Danny reluctantly behaved himself and allowed the old lady to fondle him. She amused us by lifting one ear and chuckling, 'One ear up and one ear down,' as if it were some remembered puppy joke. Danny behaved like a gentleman and left wagging his tail. The penny was beginning to drop that we were not going to abandon him.

It was not Harry's best holiday but it was lovely nonetheless. The island doctor sorted him out. He had always been a worrier and the stress before we left and the journey up and one thing after another necessitated that we push him miles and miles of magnificent Harris road and track and beach until he was healed.

Mary Ann and Donald MacSween take B&B guests in their own house as well as owning the cottage we call The Cloisters. Temporary residents met Margaret on the shore. They had just bought, 'A Song to Sing and a Tale to Tell' in the craft shop in Leverburgh. They were a Yorkshire couple living in Cleckheaton, called Bagot, who had spent holidays on Tiree and in the Connemara, a one-time favourite place of ours. We had many shared experiences to talk about.

Visiting friends occupies much of the time we spend on islands. We love to hear the Gaelic being spoken in the kitchens of our friends. Mamie's grandson, four-year-old Alan, spoke both languages fluently though Gaelic was the one he used to family. He owned two of the pet lambs and, wishing to hear the native words, we asked him what he called the lambs. He looked at me incredulously. How could I not know such a simple thing as that? With a sigh, which bordered on disgust, he said, 'Sheeps.' Now if people ask a silly question we answer, 'Sheeps!'

I must confess we really do not know anything about sheep except that Harry Raw's can always find a way onto our land. We do not know the routine of a shepherd, the when and how of dealing with dipping and shearing and of when to run the ram with the ewes.

We only know about cattle and, to our surprise, it was three-weekly obvious that our heifer wasn't infertile. She was regularly a-bulling but among a fully castrated herd she would never be in-calf. The dilemma was what to do about this unexpected situation. Of course we could just sell her with the bullocks in September, as we had planned. Or, because she was a pure bred Friesian, we could get her in-calf and sell her to a dairy farmer, giving her a longer life. As that is always our endeavour, this option was the most favoured. We had no intention of calving her ourselves. We were too long out of practice. We did not debate the problem long. We had rescued the little heifer nearly two years ago when she had cost so little. Perhaps we should do so again. Our reward would be the knowledge that her life expectancy would be much longer and we might get more money for her in-calf than just as a store. We have to be businesswomen or we will become bankrupt! So we sent her to Tim Walker's red Limousin bull and she came home due to calve at the beginning of March the following year.

Reunions are all the vogue at the moment perhaps because contemporaries have been scattered across the globe. A friend of Margaret's, Mavis Readman, was home from Illinois, USA, so she let the word pass round and invited any school friends, still in the area, to a reunion at The Currer. It is an undisputed fact that if you have shared the experience of school days, Guiding, a neighbourhood or a holiday encounter it is very easy to talk. The intervening years just slip away and it is as if you have never been parted. May is a busy month but we made time for that wonderful day Margaret shared with her friends.

The busiest days in May 1997 were those when we accommodated and fed students from the Raffles College in Singapore. There were over thirty of them so both cottages were used as well and, even then, some had to be found sleeping space in Haworth. All wanted the evening meal and there was no way we could have coped with this had the Asian students not been so nice. They all looked exactly alike and they all thought The Currer was 'Cool!', that the meals were equally cool and that to help serve the meals was really cool! We loved having them and could find no fault with their manners, their helpfulness or their loud appreciation of everything, but we were shocked by their untidiness, the state of their rooms and the impossible jumble of clothes all over the floor. We mentioned this to their teacher, an English man, who told us the students came from very rich families and had servants to do everything. We made their beds but refused to pick up their belongings.

Towards the end of the month Harry, Margaret and I were invited to a dinner at East Riddlesden Hall. Now and again our association with the National Trust is an item. Normally we would accept no invitation to eat out. Harry was never happy to go into a café or a restaurant. He ate better in public than in private but it was a tremendous effort to do so and he avoided it like the plague! For weddings and anniversaries we were glad if we had a suitable excuse for the struggle to eat, when excited, left Harry a wreck.

However, he really did want to go to this National Trust dinner in the newly roofed barn of the seventeenth-century property. We know that the building of our house preceded that of the Hall because the Paslews who lived in the old hall, now largely a ruin, sold our house to Arthur Currer in 1571. It was in the fourteenth year of the reign of Queen Elizabeth 1, when one Paslew was imprisoned in the Tower of London. Our home is very modest compared to the elegance of the Hall. Until Grandfather bought it in 1929, it rarely housed owners and tenants do little to improve, or beautify rented property.

There was one reason why Harry thought he would like to accept this invitation. Strange as it may seem he coped better outside the extended family than within it. With strangers he could be calm and composed. With family he was a nervous wreck. We always believed Harry would go to Buckingham Palace or the Antarctic or wherever opportunity took him. He was an extrovert in almost every situation, interested and confident unless it involved relatives and then he found nervous excitement too difficult to control. We knew that, providing he could cope with the meal, he would really enjoy this invited experience.

So Margaret and I hunted out the dresses we own, suitable for every occasion, and we drove to the Hall in our fast-deteriorating Range Rover. Our vehicles are old when we purchase them and our lifestyle, as hill-top farmers, ensures they encounter plenty of muck and persecution. We washed the dust off and cleaned the windows for we have our pride. We are proud, too, of our association with East Riddlesden Hall. The National Trust has reclaimed it sensitively. It is old and built with local stone. Its roof and floor are flagged traditionally. It is mullioned and beamed and for all these we have a reverence. It is beautifully kept by a workforce we recognise as friends and it stands in lovely grounds from which The Currer is seen to great advantage.

The dinner was held in the newly roofed barn to celebrate its completion and Harry really enjoyed himself. He was very proud of our connection with the Trust and, if Harry was enjoying himself, so were we! He was even eating well and joining in the conversation. There was just one moment of panic. We had left Jess with Aunty Mary, for company. Neither had we taken Lusky. Just Danny, who is afraid to be left. Because we had had to get Harry's wheelchair out of the car we had left it parked beside the lake instead of in the car park. In the middle of the speech given by Dennis Healey, Lord Riddlesden, Danny began to howl. Once he begins to do this he does not stop of his own accord and Margaret had to excuse herself and go to quieten him. The mallard on the lake were ignoring him completely. All told it was a very pleasant evening. One we will not forget.

There are guests we will not forget, some because of their cordiality, others because of their unpleasantness. Of these no season is completely free but fortunately they are few. If I record them in the same paragraph it does not mean that they came in the same month or even in the same year. Two winter guests, coming to visit family, cancelled immediately. We suspected that their family had insisted they stay with them, which is usually what happens, but their excuse was that we hadn't swept under the bed. Bed bases are only two inches from the floor these days and to vacuum under them means moving the bed completely and is not necessary every day. The alternative is to take off the castors and make the bed sit on the floor but then the bed cannot be moved at all. The lady said she had dropped an earring that had bounced under the bed. Retrieving it she had found an unopened, very small stick of rock. Children had used the room before them and one must have lost his sweetie and it had rolled too far under to poke out. People's excuses are varied and undermine our confidence far more than they should since they are generally feeble.

Some excuses hurt us but amuse the other guests so that, in the end, we laugh also. One couple left because I hadn't told them that, in our farmhouse, guests sit at the table together. Had I told them they would not have come! They said that the 'unintelligent conversation at table was unbearable'. They were so unpleasant that their departure was not only welcomed by the other guests but their excuse was deemed very amusing. Our customers return, year after year, for the pleasure of table talk. I told them that their evening meal would be served, in future, on separate tables and they said they would all leave and not return. The Vinces, who have been coming since we opened in 1981, now, when booking, ask if we have individual tables and all those resident at the time comment and laugh every time they return. But, as I've remarked, experiences like these are less pleasant for us.

A family came to celebrate an anniversary of some sort. They reserved the B&B half of our conversion to self-cater for their large group. They booked three days but, having stayed two and celebrated whatever it was they came here for, they decided to go home early. We should, of course, ask for pre-payment of bookings. Other people do but we have only ever asked for a deposit and produced the final bill at the end of their stay. I said that this family would be required to pay for the full three days they had booked. I could have taken bookings for this lost day had they only booked two in the first place. It was far too late now!

The senior member refused to pay for the unused day and said they hadn't been satisfied. They had appeared to have had a wonderful time! Why, I wanted to know? 'Well, 'the man said, 'actually my wife is allergic to the smell of furniture polish!' He was adamant that he would not pay in full but made an amazing proposition. 'I am a gardener,' he said. 'Next time we come, I'll bring some tools and do your garden for you!'

'But there will not be a next time,' I said.

'Oh, we'll come again,' he promised.

'But there isn't a next time for people who don't pay the full amount they've reserved,' I explained.

'Oh come,' he protested. 'You're a Christian. You wouldn't turn me away!'

Try me!

Dealing with human beings is more unpredictable than coping with animals. We have absolutely no idea what the outcome will be when we agree to provide accommodation for strangers. A group of five men, touring with some unidentified exhibition, booked B&B for one night. They occupied three rooms so one bed space would not be used. They arrived late but went out immediately and did not return until the early hours of the morning. Before breakfast I was crossing the yard when I saw one man sneaking out, in his car, with a young lady. I barred his way and asked who the young lady was and where they were going. He had obviously picked her up somewhere, the night before and hoped it wouldn't be noticed. It is not for me to criticise or pass judgement but it is my responsibility to see that people pay for their accommodation so I told him he must do so. He said he couldn't because he had no money and the leader of the group was paying for him.

'Well! Go and get some money from your boss. If this lady stayed the night you must pay,' I told him. Very angrily the young lady pulled out her purse and paid the very small sum we charge for bed and breakfast and the young man put his foot on the accelerator and sped up the hill. Margaret says I get more like a seaside landlady every day!

Aunty Mary's working days appeared to have come to an end but she was determined to make the biscuits for the chapel fête that had been held here annually for some time. It was increasingly obvious that our workload was heavier each day. June becomes invaded with special needs children and finding a suitable Tuesday, a day fixed by the chapel ladies, was becoming almost impossible. The coffee morning began before Margaret and Harry even started washing the breakfast dishes and those coming for afternoon tea arrived before 2 p.m. and chatted with their friends, supping cups of tea and eating all afternoon. Very reluctantly we told the secretary that, thereafter, we'd have to cut out the coffee morning as Aunty Mary had found the biscuit-making too great a task at ninety. Little by little the extra straws must not be allowed to break the camel's back. It is particularly important, to us, that the pressure of work does not eliminate that element of fun so necessary in our diet. Laughter is a hallmark of our life at The Currer. All work and no play is no good at all especially when play, at our house, is increasingly hard work!

One play day is when we go strawberry picking. Not long ago, when Mother was still alive to help top and tail the fruit on the evening of the gathering, we allowed ourselves two days at the pick-your-own fields. Once for strawberries and once for raspberries. Without Mother we had cut the excursion down to the single day and picked intensively first in the strawberry beds and then along the raspberry canes at Birstwith. In 1997 we inadvertently chose to go on the busiest day of the Great Yorkshire Show at Harrogate and the A59 was jammed with traffic.

Margaret and me with special needs children on holiday at Currer Laithe.
Also Danny and Jess.

As always we had collected Hilda, Aunty Mary's friend five years her senior. We left the two of them sitting in the sun, by the farm shop, while we pushed Harry down the bumpy field to watch us while we frantically picked fruit to last all year. We gathered so much the bill was enormous and warranted all five of us being given a free ice cream. The manager had recognised us from our previous one-day marathon picks. It is impossible to go anywhere incognito with our peculiar assortment of dogs and oldies especially when our custom is so profitable. Every year we earned the bonus of free ice cream.

The trouble was that by the time we had gathered and paid and stowed our harvest on the roof rack and taken our dependents individually to the toilets, we were pretty near exhaustion point. We were hungry and dirty and unreasonably intolerant! So much for a play-day! Guests would be waiting for their evening meal and the promised strawberries and cream. The twenty baskets over-brimming with blackcurrants, raspberries and strawberries would be lifted down with their clean, helping hands and, after the meal, all fruit must be prepared for the freezer lest our harvest be spoiled.

We were weary. Margaret climbed slowly into the driving seat and we waved to the manager, promising to call again next year.

Margaret said, 'I don't fancy trying to cross the Harrogate/Skipton road. It will be full of people just leaving the Show. I think if I turn right, instead of left, we will come to the roundabout and get onto the Otley road easily.'

We had not brought a map and we found that turning right was taking us due north and nowhere near the roundabout. Margaret was unconvinced even though the hot sun was streaming through the back window. She insisted we'd soon see the golf balls at Menwith Hill Early Warning Station. Until we saw a signpost saying we were going to Knaresborough she still insisted she was right.

We are a very vocal family and all of us talk at once. Any guest will confirm that. 'You are wrong,' we all complained. 'I'm looking for the golf balls.' 'They are behind.' 'You'll have to turn round!' 'I can't. There's no turning place.' 'You'll have to!' 'Don't be silly. Where is there any place on this narrow road where we can turn?'

Harry said, 'Where are we?' He always wanted to know. 'Oh shut up,' Margaret said. 'All of you shut up!'

'No idea,' I said but ahead a village was appearing and its name was emblazoned on a post on the roadside. We all read the unbelievable: BEDLAM.

The atmosphere in the Range Rover became hysterical. It was one of those unrepeatable experiences which trigger off so much laughter. Unable to control it Margaret pulled into the kerb and we let all our tension come away in laughter. Good, noisy, tear-dropping laughter. We held our sides and wiped our eyes and then Margaret found a place to turn and we retraced our journey back to the Skipton–Harrogate road and crossed it without any problem at all. By the time we went to bed it was morning!

That summer we had the Bracs family. Mother, father and adult son came for two weeks and, almost at the end of their stay, the old man was taken into hospital so they stayed for three. Arnold was good at throwing bales of hay onto the mow and as it was the season when loads were being delivered daily, he frequently stayed behind to help.

He also got rid of suspect youths who, in a large van with tinted windows, often parked at the top of our road on our side of the cattle grid. This van would then be joined by one or two more cars and local people began to suspect there was some drug dealing going on. Whenever Margaret and I climbed the quarter of a mile to ask them plitely to go, they did so courteously but they always came back. We couldn't always be climbing the hill. The police offered no help. 'If they are on your land, doing no harm, just tell them to go,' they said, which was no help at all.

Arnold was! I was busy making the evening meal when the collection of cars assembled as usual. Margaret asked Arnold to accompany her and when they reached the top of the road no one was visible. Arnold went close to the darkened windows and knocked. 'Look here,' he said. 'I'm on holiday but I've a good idea what's going on here because my job is with the CID. If I see you here again I'll soon find out all about you!' It was all a pack of lies but he must have sounded convincing for we never saw those cars again. Youths must now be quite wary of who might be here on holiday for they seem to no longer take risks.

Our experience of the drug trade is nil but we are not unaware of the misdemeanours of the outside world so when Margaret found a suspiciously hard brown packet by our roadside she sent me to the police station. The sergeant on duty eyed it with suspicion and took it into a back room while I sat on the bench provided and speculated on why the others waiting at the desk might be there. The sergeant returned with the opened parcel which was nothing more than nylon stockings compressed to make a firm packet.

'I think it might be a dog throw,' the smiling policeman said. 'One the owner throws and the dog brings back. Like a homemade ball!'

No reward for finding drugs! We both laughed! I felt a bit of a Charlie. 'It did look as if it might be,' the policeman admitted. Someone really did find drugs under a stone on the Altar Lane, worth a fantastic amount of money. Soon after, lifting a fallen stone back onto the wall, Margaret found a note secreted beneath it saying, 'If you want your dosh back ring this number.'

We took the letter home and rang the police and told them what we had found. 'Oh, we left that there,' said he. 'It's our number. Put it back!' Do they really think a drug dealer would put himself to so much risk as to ring an unknown number?

Both Denis and his sister Emilie came for the first fortnight in August before being joined by their parents, after which they all drove up to Harris to spend some time with our Luskentyre friends, while staying with Katie and Angus on the shore. The Barbaults are very widely travelled city dwellers. They've been to India and Burma, Italy, Russia, Germany and more but they had not had many, if any, encounters with remoteness so empty as the Highlands and Islands of Scotland. Most people, even the British themselves, think of this island as being over-crowded. Maybe it is, south of The Currer, but from here to the north of Scotland, with the exception of the Glasgow/Edinburgh belt, there is only farmed pasture and moorland, hill and dale to the Borders, mountain and glen beyond. We avoid Carlisle on the west and Newcastle on the east and miss Glasgow by crossing the Clyde so from here to there we see only the occasional hamlet and pass only the occasional car.

Travelling further north there is only the in/out experience of Fort William before the greater emptiness of 'The Road to the Isles'. Skye is just a fantasy of mountain and sea loch, craggy landscapes and peat bogs, and Uig, from which the Outer Island steamer sails, is just nothing at all. A few houses, an inn and the Caledonian Macbraynes' warehouse. Even this remoteness does not prepare you for the moonscape of Harris. The Western Isles are out of this world and the Barbaults found them so and returned to The Currer wide-eyed, unable to put into English their Luskentyre experience. It was not necessary. We've been there more times than I can remember. Had they enjoyed themselves? That was the only important question. Of course they had!

They came back to The Currer on the eve of Harry's seventieth birthday. Three score years and ten, in anybody's life, is an important milestone. In Harry's it was a miracle.

Because we have always been isolated by our profession and, for the past forty years by our out-of-village location, Harry was not known to many. I may even say to no one outside the nuclear family. Neighbours and extended family knew he existed and he was recognised locally by hundreds just because he was always with us, but few knew him as a person. Society neglected all those of his generation who were disabled. There was no education, medical care, no financial help when he was born nor throughout most of his life. That it had been a struggle to walk and talk and eat all these cumulative years had gone unnoticed because people had been taught not to stare. This was interpreted as not to look so they did not see. When walking and talking and eating became increasingly difficult society looked the other way even more. Disabled people are very sensitive to being by-passed. Harry didn't like being ignored. For seventy years most people thought it safest to pretend he didn't have a problem. It is easy to say that this scarcely mattered within a close and happy family, such as ours, as busy as we are, as active and adventurous as we are, with a constant stream of people coming to The Currer. We holiday twice a year in delightful places and always have some on-going project. There are daily trips out necessary to the running of our twin businesses and phone calls coming regularly from all corners of the world. What a good life he has, so able-bodied people thought. He had no responsibility for financial problems and no relationship worries. They forgot his struggle and the long-time caring responsibility of his parents and his siblings. Because he was always in the car when it went out and always with us when they came to see us it went unnoticed that no one came to see him. He hardly ever needed a doctor. The physiotherapist whose advice had been recently sought came once to bring a useless piece of equipment and once to take it back again. People come to see me, or Margaret. They came to see our parents and now they come to see Aunty Mary. No one came just to see Harry. No schooling meant no school friends. Our playmates never became his. When neighbouring children, or cousins, came to play on the farm they did not form any relationship with Harry. Only his siblings, his parents, grandparents and Mother's sisters did that. Life for the disabled nowadays is much more extrovert and they can form friendships and have experiences outside the family, which is a good thing. However, because of our lifestyle Harry gained more than he lost and had a great deal of real fun which is lacking in many able people's lives.

As children we had a two-week holiday in Blackpool, before the war put a stop to that for several years. To celebrate Harry's seventieth birthday we decided to drive over to this once-familiar resort and take a walk down memory lane. We all loved our annual holidays of the thirties and the few years immediately after the war. Then Margaret and I got the island bug and began to devote our holidays to taking children camping in the Hebrides. Though we had happy memories, neither Margaret nor I had the detailed ones Harry had retained. So much had happened since then but Harry recalled everything. We had negotiated with our paying guests not to have an evening meal that night so we had time galore to push wheelchairs almost the length of the promenade and back. We walked slowly to allow Harry, who did not read, to name all the hotels on the Esplanade. It was magic!

Some things were different. The beach was not crowded as it used to be. The sun was maybe not hot enough for today's softer generation who use it for sunbathing and not the energetic games we always pursued. In our childhood the beach was for cricket and rounders, for racing and splashing about in the water however cold the day. Also the promenade was for parading along, in droves, arm in arm, so closely behind those in front that the view ahead was people, people, people and, should you hesitate, you would be trampled on.

On that return to Blackpool for a day in the summer of 1997, while the Barbaults were on Harris, there was hardly anyone on the beach and few on the promenade so that it was safe to push two wheelchairs, to stop when the fancy took us with no danger to the public. We routed our journey down the narrow street, St Chad's Road, where we had lodged. Harry, not we, knew the number of the house. He knew the layout of the stairs and bedrooms. He knew exactly where we bought the best ice cream, the morning newspaper and where we collected fish and chips for supper. The day was one enormous success.

On 29 August he had an extraordinary seventieth birthday and, for the first time, everybody came just to see Harry. They came to see him! Not Margaret nor Aunty Mary nor me. They came to see Harry! Our Bank Holiday holiday-makers got up early and decorated the house and yard with balloons and banners. Visitors began to arrive almost as soon as Harry got up. He never got washed or shaved and he never had breakfast. His pile of presents grew and when all friends had gone and the opened pile of them was investigated we could not establish who had been the giver, such was the wonderful chaos of the day. We knew exactly who had brought just one gift, however. Tony and Pauline Ainley had had a specially printed tee shirt made with a picture of the farm, a 70 m.p.h. road sign and the words, 'Harry at 70. Been there, done that, got the tee shirt.' He wore it proudly all the rest of his seventy-first year.

Too true, Harry's was a success story. He had won and deserved commendation. He had not grown old as other men do. In a few ways he was still a child. Because society had virtually ignored him the world had not left its scars. He was unspoiled. He had not made mistakes. He had not had to sort out relationships or be the breadwinner. He was not an old man content to sit in a chair and sleep. Every day he wanted to do something and go somewhere. He did not want to miss a word of conversation. Young at heart he was a very nice man and totally unselfish.

The Barbault family gave him the ultimate gift, though he did not receive it until Christmas. A jigsaw arrived in a paper bag with no picture of what it would be when completed. Harry began assembling it immediately and, little

Harry's Seventieth, with the Barbault family (from left to right: Emilie, Yveline, Harry, Denis and Bernard).

by little a lovely, laughing photograph began to appear, of himself, behind his birthday cake and surrounded by Denis and Emilie, Bernard and Yveline. The finished masterpiece was framed and hangs on the sitting room wall and Harry showed everyone, smiling with the same delight as he does on the birthday photograph.

Chapter Four

*So narrow is the dividing line between right and wrong, joy and sorrow,
between calm and unrest, harmony and discord.*

We'll See the Cuckoo.

Harry's birthday banners were left flying and the following day was one of sunshine and smiles. The atmosphere was idyllic. Everyone seemed safe and well. Janet, the close friend who was fighting cancer, had looked her normal self when she came to the celebration. Because it was the Bank Holiday week, Tommy, also apparently back to normal fourteen months after his encounter with the same monster, was unbelievably well. Twelve months ago we'd almost cried when he'd joined the annual Bank Holiday crowd who meet up together every year. Tommy was disabled physically only. Since birth his legs had been a problem but, like Harry, he walked. Unlike Harry his arms and shoulders were abnormally strong. Tommy could do anything. He never came to the farm without repairing broken objects and whatever we wanted he knew where to buy it. He and Veronica always joined others who had met here years and years ago and, enjoying each other's company, rebooked to be together again every August Bank Holiday. They had a wonderful relationship with the Entwistles, that amazing couple who have overcome disablement more than anyone we know. Patrick, born with cerebral palsy and brought up in a children's home, is the author of the book, *What's in a life*, and proud recipient of an MBE. He is married to Joan who has reached pensionable age walking on two artificial legs for fifty years or so. Tommy and Patrick shared the same wonderful sense of humour.

My, were we all feeling good after Harry's birthday! God was in His Heaven. All was right with the world. At dinner table I paused to extend my pleasure at Tommy's grand recovery. 'You look just great!' I said.

He pulled out his wallet and opened it and took out the lucky half of a chicken bone. 'I got this here last year,' he said.

Remembering his condition when he'd been here then, I said, 'It worked!'

'Yes, it worked!' Tommy said.

'I got the other half,' said Patrick, fumbling in his pocket for the unlucky half he had kept. Looking mischievously at his laughing wife, he said, 'Mine worked, too. I've still got her!'

We were all so happy. Life was all joy. Disability did not affect the soul. The flags of birthday celebration and the balloons danced on the washing line. Whoopee!

The next day was Sunday. The atmosphere of a Sunday is always a little different even in these days of public ignoring of its balm. Never before did the atmosphere at The Currer change so dramatically as it did on the Sunday morning of 31 August 1997. Before we had begun to prepare breakfast for the full house, news came over the radio and television of the accident which caused the death of Diana, Princess of Wales. Many of the guests of Harry's birthday were still here but joy had fled. The shocking news turned celebration into mourning. No one could have anticipated how much pleasure Harry's birthday would have generated and no one could ever have believed that the death, even of a princess, could provoke such emotion. Breakfast was a solemn, almost silent routine, eaten quickly but without enjoyment. It was important to everyone, from this country or from overseas, to get into the sitting room quickly to watch the television, in silence and mourn, not just with the nation but with the world.

Dishes had to be washed, but apart from that we did nothing all day either, but sit in front of the screen. Those leaving for home did so reluctantly and late, and in tears. Those staying did not want to enjoy the summer glory of the Dales. All they wanted to do was to sit in our sixteenth century room and mourn the death of our twentieth century People's Princess. They sat with eyes glued to the screen, watching the emotional portrait of she who had wanted to be, and had become, a modern day Queen of Hearts. We did not want to join our guests. The shock-fall from joy to sorrow was too painful. We needed the privacy of our own front room. With the August sun streaming through the mullioned windows we, like the millions everywhere, neglected everything. We were hypnotised by shock, disbelief that it was an accident, horror and sadness. We were gripped, as was everyone, by the lethargy of the post-accident hours and days.

Nobody grumbled about putting their holiday on hold. Nobody wanted to escape sharing by viewing. The pen which writes this cannot explain the atmosphere of the week that followed any more than journalists and commentators could account for the unique togetherness of the nation and the world during the pre-funeral days.

Floral tributes carpeted the landscape. Acres of flowers everywhere. Everything was on hold. We are not telly addicts. We have too much work but we watched daily, as did the nation and everyone was behind closed doors for the funeral. And when it was over all one wanted to do was to watch it again, to witness the silent crowds along the streets lining the route to the Minster, to listen again to the tribute of Diana's brother and hear the applause in Hyde Park, which began as a murmur and became a crescendo. We, members of the Guide Movement, wanted to hear the choirboys sing again, 'My Creed'.

> I would be true for there are those who trust me,
> I would be pure for there are those who care,
> I would be strong for there is much to suffer,
> I would be brave for there is much to dare.
> I would be friend of all the foe the friendless.
> I would be giving and forget the gift.
> I would be humble for I know my weakness.
> I would look up and love and laugh and lift.

I did not know then that my Guides were taking printed cards of 'My Creed' out of their Bibles and showing them to their children.

And as the cortege approached Diana's final resting place bystanders threw flowers galore on to the passing hearse and cars came to a standstill on the motorway to watch with awe and respect.

All mourning, all tragedy and all beauty has to become just a memory.

Neglected work has to be resumed and life must go on. But few would argue that this shared experience had not left its indelible mark on all of us.

We picked ourselves up, prepared for the annual sale of our cattle and the holiday which was to follow. Incredibly, Lusky was going with us once more. It had not seemed possible that he would ever see the sea again when we left the Isle of Man eighteen months ago. But he had been to Wales and then to Harris in the spring and, lo and behold, our physically disabled dog was going to Wales with us in October. On the Isle of Man we had learned how to cope. It had been possible, there, to daily wash the towels he sat upon like an emperor. He was not ill. He just could not walk any more but he had adjusted to his immobility as all wheelchair users eventually do. It no longer worried him. He was happy in the car so he did not mind that he had to be lifted in. He ate well and was in his element by the sea. We knew that ninety-nine per cent of the population would not have enslaved themselves to a disabled dog as Margaret did. They would have had the vet put him to sleep. That we could not possibly do while he had no pain.

One day he was sleeping peacefully under the table, when Tim, the waller, became concerned. Lusky's lungs were so good his breathing was inaudible. 'Is 'e alreight?' said the big man putting out his hand to touch the dog under the table. Lusky was not only alive. His reflexes were excellent and had not Tim withdrawn his hand quickly he might well have lost a finger.

It was relatively easy to handle a dog which was down. It is another story with a billy goat of quite enormous proportions. We received the news that Charlie was down while we were in Aberporth. Dorothy reported that he had squeezed himself between the hay-mow and the corrugated tin wall of the top bullock shed. To move him, she said, seemed impossible. They had tried. They had struggled a long time but he would not get up. As we were due home in a matter of three days, we told her to leave him there and we'd do something when we returned. Three days later, on our return, poor Charlie was in some distress. We couldn't move him either so we got out the ATV and a rope and with determination to overcome the difficulty, we attached Charlie and slowly pulled him out of his ill-chosen hollow. He was wet with the sweat of struggle and the heat of the hay-box that had been his bed and he smelt strongly of four days' urine.

At the doorway we tried to urge him onto his feet but without success so we brought a loose corrugated tin sheet and rolled him onto it. He sat up alert and watched us make holes in the tin to attach the rope from the ATV. On Charlie's face was the amusement of a goat at the incredible antics of members of the human race. We took him on a lap of honour round the farmyard and drew up at the door of his own shed. Inside, with the hard floor under his feet and a sack under his belly, we managed to lift the goat onto his feet but when we let go he sat down again. We repeated this activity three or four times a day for weeks on end, so strengthening his legs until he walked again and grazed happily in the paddock. He always needed the initial heave onto his feet but he lived the good life for six months more and then died with dignity.

Hours of non-profit making time can be spent on the Luskys and Charlies of this world. To lift and care for them needs two of us. So many jobs require both Margaret and me to be together. This was fine while we could safely leave our human dependants long hours alone. This was particularly necessary at calf-rearing time when each feed would require both of us for two hours. There seemed to be no other way but, increasingly, one of us should be in the house if the other was out. The problem was that Harry was still mobile. As long as he could walk alone, he was in danger of falling. We installed a buzzer in the calf shed to recall us if there was an emergency and went to the cattle markets and bought sixty calves. We planned a second visit the following week to top up the number.

'Next year let's look into a self-feeder,' Margaret said. 'Both of us out of the house for hours is dangerous. Before we have a real accident, let's buy a self-feeding machine.'

'Next year's a long way off,' I said. 'It's too risky trying something new on seventy calves. What happens if it doesn't work? Buy one now. Try it out. We need ten more calves. Try it out on them this year. What d'ye say? Run two systems at once and only have ten on trial.'

Don't we just like to make instant decisions? Margaret reached for the phone and rang Bill, our corn merchant's traveller, and he gave her the number of a Mr Lawson who was representative of a firm that made automatic feeders and she ordered one. Just like that! We who spend no money on ourselves can just, in a matter of seconds, order a milk machine costing over a thousand pounds. We like things to be delivered at once and this could not come tomorrow, but we could have it in just under a fortnight so we did not go to Otley to buy the extra ten on Monday. We delayed a week longer and concentrated on the sixty we were feeding by hand. Then we went to the market and bought fifteen which is NFU, normal for us, and Mr Lawson brought the machine and fitted it up for our trial run.

'It will feed half the seventy-five calves,' he said. 'It would be wasted on just fifteen!' So he fitted teats in half the shed and we jumped into the experiment with both feet, which was more than we'd bargained for. The newly bought fifteen adapted quickly to having 'Mum' available all the time. When the twenty we had trained to two feeds a day switched to *ad lib*, they drank so much we feared their bellies would burst. One we named Tabletop because he drank so much his back became square and the white pattern looked like a tablecloth hanging over it. His greed frightened us so much we put him back into the twice a day pen. We were understandably a bit nervous.

The two systems running side by side meant much more work but the ones on *ad lib* feed progressed quicker, were ready to be weaned in half the time and we were positive we'd made the right decision. We agreed to buy a second machine the following year and feed all the calves in this way. It did not make life all that much easier for Margaret, for vigilance was more important than ever, but it did mean that it was not necessary for me always to be there when it was getting more and more unsafe to leave Harry for two hours at a time. Occasionally we took him into the shed to watch but the fans drawing in the clean air made the atmosphere cold and he could not stay long without freezing.

Learning the new skill was not easy. When all calves were fed at the same time, we knew when one was reluctant and could investigate the cause. When all were drinking at any old time, picking out the sickly one was none too easy. It was more than ever necessary to be frequently in the shed, always checking, always looking for the one with an empty belly, the one not chewing its cud, not licking itself. More than ever, it was necessary to check a temperature and, if needed, inject the antibiotic. We laughingly offered Margaret a bed in the calf shed. It seemed she was always there.

But, hard though the twin systems were during the trial year, we were confident the advantages out-weighed the disadvantages and we were enjoying the novelty of a new project. It was exciting and invigorating. I hope we never reach stagnation point. In every profession the way must be forward. There must be a challenge round every corner, however old you are.

If we can do it ourselves we do. For forty years at The Currer, and many more before at the Home Farm, we had been making homemade, wooden hayracks almost annually. Cattle systematically eat away anything which is wood. Tongues and teeth wear away stalls and barriers and demolish mangers and hayracks just as a pup in the house will make short work of chair and table legs! As this had become almost a yearly renewal, little by little we had introduced more permanent eating bays of concrete and we had acquired several iron crates for hay during the first month of rearing calves. But when the weaning was over and the *ad lib* teats removed, the wooden, slated hay mangers were re-hung. That in itself was a big job so we visited agricultural merchants looking for uneatable mangers. We could not find what we wanted so ordered made-to-measure ones locally. These cost us an arm and a leg but I think they will still be there when we are gone. Like the laid-on water, the troughs and bowls which mean no more carrying of buckets from the spring, like the florescent lighting, the well-placed corn bins, the ATV and the thistle mower, all these innovations are supposed to make life easier for the ageing workforce. How come we are as busy as ever? The ninety feet of iron hayracks were expensive but certainly they represent money well spent. A tremendous amount of money, earned by accommodating holiday-makers, has gone into making the bovine city a place to be proud of, with its purpose-built sheds, their air-system fans and tubes, their concrete floors, the stockyards and hay barn. We appreciate the fact that we can go from shed to shed under cover, that doors and gates are positioned sensibly for management, for we have come all the way from no sheds at all, no road and deep mud everywhere, from feeding bales to out-wintering cattle in rain and snow, carrying water, and working without electricity, to the comparative luxury of the present day. Yet the truth is that things have not got easier. Animals are bigger and, to make a living, farmers have had to keep more, many more. Bales of fodder and straw are heavier than ever before. And the paperwork! That is a job in itself. Margaret says it isn't, because it can be done in the warmth of the kitchen, but in the old days we never had to de-horn and ear-tag. It all adds up to the fact that, though expensive, so-called labour-saving equipment is a pleasure, work doesn't get much easier and leisure is still at a premium. Though to be honest, I suppose, without them we might already be pushing up the daisies!

Why do we continue? Well, some do and some don't. In December frightened farmers were already beginning to protest loudly. Unfortunately farmers cannot strike. They have to run home at milking time.

It wasn't the farming which nearly finished us, that December, it was the Chapel Christmas Dinner. Margaret was far too busy to help with the preparations. I remember manhandling the table and extra chairs from the Loft Cottage, sliding them down the bedroom steps in an un-feminine and dangerous manner. Thirty old ladies wanted the Christmas dinner too early in December. This meant a premature trip to the nearest holly tree and a far too early decoration of the spruce which must not drop its needles until after the New Year. The new milk machine alongside the older-fashioned way, the de-horning and the bad weather meant we were struggling more than we dared admit.

At the back of our minds was the fear that, after all my preparations, at the last minute the weather would cancel all. Our road becomes impassable very quickly. It weeps water in winter and the first frosts make a glacier. We do not have to wait for snow to close the road. Ice does so extremely efficiently. What's more, the yearling bullocks come home every night to be fed and bedded down and routine work is an all-day affair.

We coped, 'in a fashion', as Mother would have said. Everyone was splendidly fed and all enjoyed the annual get-together. Each returned to her more gentle environment unaware of the enormity of the clear-up which had to wait till morning. We didn't even remove the dirty dishes from the table. We shut the dining room door and donned dirty clothes to go out to feed the cattle and when we had finished that, there was little enough of the day left to get Harry and Aunty Mary to bed.

Next day, after the morning feed, the great clean-up began. Is there anything worse than unwashed Christmas dinner dishes left until the morning after? There is only the undisputed blessing of piping hot water to save the day. For the not-quite-emptied tureens we have hungry, feathered friends waiting outside. Struggling alone to return the borrowed chairs and table from The Loft cottage, I acknowledged we were beaten. We had continued longer than we should have done already. It was the wrong time of the year to cope. The weather could be enemy number one, a farmyard emergency could suddenly cancel all opportunity to mass cater. I was adamant that we should not push our luck any further. Before it ran out we should tell the secretary to find another venue. We were sorry. We do not like to disappoint but, if I remember rightly, the weather the following year would have put a stop to the booking anyway.

For nearly a decade we had closed our B&B business for Christmas and New Year and for seven of those years we had opened it for self-catering groups. When everyone was in festive mood and cooking masses of food, we had escaped to some Dales beauty spot to eat ham sandwiches in wonderful isolation. In 1997 that was impossible for gales swept the area, blowing down trees and causing havoc everywhere. They blew our telephone wire down and strewed it across the entrance at the Moor Gate cattle grid. There was no way we could abandon The Currer while tempests roared, so we resigned ourselves to the first stay-at-home Christmas since 1986. The wind abated for Boxing Day so we pretended that was Christmas Day and drove to Bolton Abbey. All the way fallen trees had been dragged from the roadways and debris was scattered in the fields and caught in the hedgerows.

We had barely left the village when all pretence that it was Christmas Day had to be abandoned. While everyone is at home on Christmas Day, celebrating with family or friends, everyone was heading for Bolton Abbey on Boxing Day. It could have been Whitsuntide Sunday. All the world and his neighbour paraded the banks of the River Wharfe. We couldn't believe it. The sun shone quite strongly. The river was high and tree debris floated swiftly on the torrent and, yes, we enjoyed rubbing shoulders with the crowd nearly as much as we enjoy isolation. Harry certainly did for he liked to watch people from his wheelchair.

And so the year ended and gave way to a new one. I am not sure I like stepping into the unknown and I treat most New Years with caution. It is not wise to anticipate what the future holds in store. Perhaps it is that I prefer to look back, gratefully, on what has been. In January I tend to pick up my pen and record for whoever might be interested, but mostly for my family, the way it has been. The way it will be I leave to the Inventor of Life. He'll make it interesting, I am sure.

We'll See The Cuckoo had been well received and was in its second edition. The clamouring for more of The Currer story became louder. To write is not really a problem for me, because I invariably get up early and there is plenty to tell if it happens to be what enough people want to read. If not it is still self-satisfying to record thoughts and ideas and remember minor miracles and laugh again at what has been so funny. I am still surprised that some people enjoy reading about this demanding corner of Yorkshire and our pastoral and traditional way of life, enough to natter continually for more. I cannot say, 'of the same stuff' for every day is different here, more so, maybe, than in a town.

Writing is a pleasure. Typing is time-consuming when two fingers seem to be all that I have. Trying to interest publishers takes far too long when people don't like waiting. Perhaps, after all, I am extremely big-headed if I dare to think that the thousands who've read my books are anything but a drop in the readership ocean. Perhaps publishers are busy enough trying to supply millions and think, with me, why does anyone want to read about ordinary, simple things? Demand, if the media is anything to go by, is for tragedy, crime, heartbreak and disloyalty, for selfishness and abuse.

Nevertheless, you bet I was writing, even if our lifestyle was none of these things. Those asking for another book wanted it immediately. Mother and her daughters, too, liked things instantly. Life, I am increasingly aware, is extremely short and years begin and end faster as one ages. *A Song to Sing and a Tale to Tell* had to be produced quickly for the parents of my children who could not wait until their children were grown before they learned of the fun of camping in the Hebrides. Thule Press, in the Shetland Isles, had taught me how to publish quickly. I had paid for the first edition and thereafter they had assumed responsibility. I had not lost money. Similarly I had subsidised costs of the first imprint by Pentland and again, further editions of *We'll see the Cuckoo* had been met by the publisher. To do this is always a risk I am half afraid to take.

When *We'll Trace The Rainbow* was written I sent it to a book agent. Three months later it was returned with comments and rejection. It was charming, he said! Nonsense! We may live a charmed life, but we certainly do not live a charming one. I hoped my writing did not disprove that! The agent said our holiday guests could be exploited much more. There was real subject matter in them. There was too much buying of calves which would not be of universal interest and I should leave out references to cancer. It was inappropriate.

I asked Tony Ainley, who had prepared *A Song to Sing and a Tale to Tell* for its publisher in 1979, and he and his wife Pauline prepared the new manuscript and inserted the drawings of Pauline and Joe Walters, and we sent it straight to a printer and bookbinder in Halifax. The speed at which all this happened was wonderful. I took the decision in memory of Mother and Father's brave and dignified encounters with cancer, of the similar experience of Joan Armstrong, my competent infant teacher, and of several of our guests whose fortitude and cheerfulness I could not ignore. I have no regrets. The agent was wrong. We buy calves. We are farmers. We respect ninety-nine per cent of our guests and cancer, sadly, is part of life, for far too many people.

We are do-it-yourself people. We always have been. To 'do-it-yourself' publish was a huge risk. The agent was wrong about recording the vagaries of our customers. Recording some encounters with the human species can occasionally be far from pleasant and happy memories are more satisfying to write about. However, not all our guests fall into the category of having acceptable behaviour.

Two workmen, who'd been having B&B in December, decided to rent The Loft for all January. Comings and goings of Loft cottage people are not seen from the house. We cannot see their car but we can see the light in their sitting room which tells us they are home. Workmen are out all day and often work overtime. Most get a pub meal. These two men had paid promptly when having B&B. I did not think they would not do so when they used the cottage. For three weeks we only saw a light in the evening and I began to think it was time they paid. I made a special effort to catch them but no light came on. We could not remember when we had last seen it. We began to wonder if there had been a light yesterday, or even the day before. Even as we know if there is no animal in the sheds we instinctively know when cottage occupants have gone. But in this case I was reassured that the two men had not left without paying for their packed bags were in the passageway. As they went home at weekends we presumed they would be collecting them later that day to do so, or even to leave prematurely, before the absolute month was up. Workmen sometimes finish a job early just as often as they stay a week longer because they have miscalculated. In actual fact they never returned. They did not pay their rent and they did not collect their bags. When we re-let the cottage we removed them and eventually we opened them. They contained clothes which we washed and took to a charity shop, and a brand new pair of trainers we gave to another workman. Bits and pieces went in the bin but the almost new holdalls we kept for holidays. I sent letters to the address they had given me but heard nothing.

We have been providing accommodation long enough to observe change. People have grown more inconsiderate in our twenty years' experience. It is maybe only a small proportion but it is significant. A generation ago, those who booked came. A growing few now book but do not come or cancel at the last moment and think they owe nothing. To some, it means nothing at all that we have kept our part of the bargain and reserved their cottage, or their room. A woman rang asking if I had a cottage free. Both had occupants but the season was early and there was no one in the B&B accommodation, nor likely to be in the next few days. As we let this larger space to groups, and as the woman seemed genuine, I said she could rent this for the same price as a cottage. She said her husband was coming over from France arriving at Leeds railway station at about 8 p.m., that she would pick him up and come straight here.

The heating was still on for four Americans who had just left. We left it on all day but the expected couple never came. The lady never rang. At midnight we turned off the electric and stamped off to bed. Everyone has access to a phone. If they can ring to book, they can ring to cancel!

There are moments when we are totally fed up of people! We seldom feel that way about animals. Constant feeding of cattle in the wintertime is exhausting but anger against human beings, however short, is soul destroying.

A friend said one day, when we were discussing our own behaviour faults, 'It's not what I do which worries me. It's what I think!' Angry thoughts are destructive and on these occasions it is best to escape from The Currer and think about something else.

It was a fine Sunday so we put three wheelchairs in the Range Rover, collected Aunty Mary's friend, ninety-five year old Hilda, and drove to Yeadon Tarn. Around it there is a concrete path, slightly tilting towards the water. Two wheelchair users, who propel themselves, told us so. On the tarn, on a Sunday, the waterfowl have competition in the shape of multicoloured yachts and Jeremy Fishers, with opened umbrellas, line the water's edge. It is a nice place to spend the afternoon pushing wheelchairs and walking dogs and quite hilarious if there are three chairs and only two pushers. The unhampered walkers smiled and laughed openly as we passed and they chatted with whichever passenger we had left behind waiting for a member of the relay team to return and collect. The bleaching sun, the exertion and the hilarity cleansed us of anger. As our French girl Emilie says, you've got to laugh! It is the only way!

March came in neither one thing nor the other. The nine months' gestation period of the first calf to be born at The Currer since 1982 was nearly up and we began to talk of what we would do about that. We had originally thought to sell the still-nameless heifer before she calved. We were out of practice and we thought it best to sell her and let some expert dairy farmer cope.

However the calf situation was very bad indeed. The Calf Processing Scheme was ensuring that most calves born in the milking herds were taken straight to the abattoir. If the calf was a bull, being a Limousin cross it might have a chance. If it were a heifer it would be useless to the milking herd and bring no Beef Special Premium as a beef animal. Heifers were almost throw-aways. It was wrong. The whole subsidy system was wrong. It always is, for the public believes it is a give-away to the farmer, when its purpose is solely to make food cheap to the consumer. Subsidising at source sends the wrong message. I have always thought government help should go to the buyer and the producer be paid an appropriate price. The farmer would not then be subjected to so much criticism.

We decided to let the calf be born at The Currer after all. If it were then it would live, for no way would we deprive it of at least two years on this lovely hillside. Gradually we realised we had no intention whatsoever of selling the heifer before she calved. We'd just go to the market and rescue another destined for the abattoir and rear both of them together. Keeping the heifer was a different thing. She was a dairy cow, destined to give gallons and gallons of milk. We could drink some ourselves but with hygiene rules what they are, we could serve none to our guests. We would have to sell her and, we believed, that would be a fairly profitable thing to do because, every day, she became more and more beautiful.

We went on a fact-finding visit to Skipton Cattle Mart, on the day newly calved heifers were sold, and we came away very nervous. All the animals to be sold were standing quietly tethered in the market stalls awaiting their call to be shown in the ring. Our heifer had never been tied. She'd never had a rope round her neck. Her two and a half years of total freedom had made her somewhat arrogant. You bet, she'd behave badly if we tried to tether her. Heifers in our dairy herd, nearly forty years ago, had learned, almost from birth, not to object to a rope. She probably would. She'd had no training for such. So help me, we anticipated troubled times ahead. Tim said we ought to introduce her to her future role in life before she calved for we'd have to milk her during the few days between her calving and the market sale. We did not relish this idea.

For the first twenty-five years of my life and the first sixteen of Margaret's we had been dairy farmers. We had been accustomed to tying up cattle and breaking in frisky heifers. I'd spent many years milking by hand. We had always taken away the calf unaware how stressful that was to baby and Mum. Then had come the twenty years of a suckled herd when there had been no reason to separate them. The years with a suckled herd had been happy. They had been years of struggling with overdraft and cattle accommodation problems but they had given great joy at calving time. Babies should be brought up with mother in an ideal world.

We had become aware, however, that far too many calves were being born nationwide. Father, sensitive to his earthly responsibility, realised that it was maybe better to rear those already born than to increase the country's calf population. Ever since then this has been our philosophy. As long as people require milk calves must be born. These we will rear. Thousands sent to abattoirs each week is not only wastage, it is a sin.

Forty years of rearing animals in freedom had not prepared us, forty years older, to suddenly tie up a heifer. We wished, wholeheartedly, that we had never brought her from Skipton Cattle Mart. In so doing we had created a situation for which we were ill-prepared. The farmer, who had persuaded Margaret to take the unwanted baby, knew she was an easy touch, a softie who would never send a baby to be killed if she could offer it life. Two and a half years later we had misgivings!

Recently, however, this almost unknown animal had begun to show signs of elegance. She had begun to stand out as a lady among the all-male herd. And what a lady! Every day Margaret said, 'The heifer's beautiful!' Indeed she was. She was evenly marked. A black and white British Friesian with none of the Holstein blood recently introduced into dairy herds. She was fit, her back was absolutely straight and her filling udder was perfect. There wasn't a wart or a blemish on our beautiful, in-calf heifer, who hadn't even a name. We became increasingly big-headed about her.

'I'm sure she'll win First Prize at the sale,' we said often enough. None could be superior unless, of course, she behaved badly when restrained, presuming, of course, that it was possible. Taking her calf away from her was not discussed between us for it was too painful to anticipate. We filled our minds solely with the swollen ego of having reared such a lovely animal. I regret to say we made no attempt to teach her restraint, cowards that we were.

The other really beautiful animal was Lusky, our Lord of the Isles according to Harry. His long hair still shone, the black as ebony, the white as snow. From his bed beneath our huge pine table in the kitchen, he called to me in the bedroom immediately overhead, exactly at six o'clock every morning. Thus bidden, I rose, rolled him over onto a clean towel and put on the kettle. I spent the next hour writing at the table above him, while he went happily back to sleep. There was no change in the pattern of his behaviour. There was no occasion whatsoever to wish his end to come. Just now and then we wondered if he would survive another holiday in the Hebrides. We hoped he would. We had managed perfectly for several excursions to Wales and Scotland and we were confident we could cope again. He was eating well, sleeping a lot and he had a language we could interpret to supply all his canine needs. He was happy.

Increasingly we knew that our heifer's end-of-March calving would take us joyfully and sadly down memory lane. We awaited the birth with a certain awe. We had not had a calf born in sixteen years when Joanna, our Jersey cow, had had her last calf in the early days of our B&B experience. We remembered the gynaecologist, staying with us at the time, whose clinical language had been so different from ours. Slacks and cleansings and calf bed had him baffled. 'A cow and a Countess,' my father used to say. 'Nowt to choose between em. Nine months waiting, born t'same way. Both'll suckle t'young an' both'll dee!'

The mystery of birth and death is being tarnished by this sophisticated and promiscuous society and its pre-occupation with genetic manoeuvring and abortion of unwanted babies and massacre of surplus calves. There is beauty in each when responsibility is left to The Maker, yet there is little on the silver screen other than the reporting of interference with both.

If we had searched our souls, Margaret and I, we would have realised that something was missing. Our lives were not without babies. They had not been without children. We annually bought between seventy and eighty-week-old calves but we had not witnessed or assisted their birth. Our last kittens came from a neighbour. Someone had abandoned them in his dairy and pups have recently come to us at eight weeks old. It was eleven years since we had had a flotilla of ducklings hatched on the farm and our last chicken had been born just before Christmas five or six years ago. Sadly the geese had become too old to reproduce. What a pathetic state of affairs this was, now we had time to think about it. Farm babies there had been in plenty when we were children. Now even the birds were not nesting on our doorstep anymore and Harry Raw's sheep went home at lambing time.

There is a distinct difference between adoption and giving birth but we strongly believe, in this age of surplus calves, that the former is our role rather than adding to the surplus in general, but we still think that we have lost something of infinite value. We were rather excited that, for once, just once, we were going to let this happen. The heifer's baby was going to be born at The Currer. Like all our other calves, sadly it would lose its mother, but it would have Margaret and she would care for it longer than its mother would have done.

We watched our in-calf heifer religiously, I in the early hours of the morning and Margaret in the quiet hours of the night. The nameless bovine lady grew more beautiful every hour, her coat shinier and silkier, her eyes more liquid. We marvelled at the perfection of our young expectant mother. Personally I prefer 'expectant' or 'in-calf' to the hard sound of the modern 'pregnant'.

My children would have been taught to say, 'Is she going to have a baby?' and not, 'Is she pregnant?'

We began to be nervous lest our beauty queen put a foot on a rusty nail or scratched her coat on the barbed wire of the fence. She was big and wide, as fit as a fiddle and far too impulsive. Though they still slept overnight in their shed, she and her two bullock companions were let out daily to graze in the pastures we rent from George. The door was rather small for the enormous belly of the heifer and she would recklessly barge her way through with no thought for her safety. Then she would carelessly gallivant down the hillside. 'I'm going to be a nervous wreck!' Margaret said.

The heifer had spent the winter with two bullocks we had thought too thin to be sold at the September sales. They were now fat and heavy and almost thirty months old. This is the age cattle must be sold if their meat is allowed into the human food chain since the advent of BSE. We hoped the birth of the calf would coincide with their forced departure so that the heifer would not suddenly be bereft of friends. On the Sunday before the bullocks left on the Monday, Margaret put all three animals into the barn. There were about eight or nine six-month-old calves penned in a corner and, when the bullocks left, next day, the heifer had company. Aloneness is what cattle fear most. To be separated from the herd frightens them more than anything. The barn was very nearly empty of hay and straw and, as it was only the end of March and we were still supplementing their diet of new grass, Margaret had ordered another load to be brought.

Late on Monday night our heifer became uneasy and we reckoned she would calve within the next twenty-four hours. Tuesday morning was damp so we did not let any of the calves out though they were used to daytime freedom. The bigger bullocks were being released as the phone began to ring. The load of ordered fodder was on its way. So was the baby. Everything was about to happen at once!

Tim had called at the farmhouse on his way down to the Dyke Field boundary wall where he was currently building. We said we'd call for help if we needed it. We dragged a twelve-foot iron gate into the barn to restrict the area allowed to the heifer and separate it from the laden lorry due to deliver its goods. The two front feet of the calf were protruding as the huge lorry backed into the barn, emitting its nasty exhaust fumes.

Margaret yelled at me to fetch Tim and I ran (I still can) down the Five-Acre and into the Dyke field. Tim and I jumped into his Land Rover and we drove back to the barn. All four of us including Mark, the driver, began throwing off bales with unusual speed, leaving the heifer to get on with the relatively normal job of giving birth. The two things should not have been happening at the same time. Indeed there was progress in only one department. The bales were coming off the lorry apace but the calving was at a standstill. The mother-to-be was getting nowhere, she was down, she had tried. Having failed she had given up in disgust. Her human friends had deserted her. In her time of need they had abandoned her and played with four hundred bales instead! Two little hooves and three inches of leg was the best she could do. The two men put a rope round the protruding feet and pulled until they were beetroot faced. We decided to get the vet and his tackle and I ran to the phone. Had things been normal in the farming world, this heifer would have been a valuable animal. As things were in our tortured profession, even with a First Prize, the price would not be high. She would be sold, next Monday, to some struggling dairy farmer maybe for only a song, but these worldly thoughts were not those invading our minds. The only thing that mattered was that the heifer lived and that the calf was born alive.

Having phoned the vet, I ran back to the barn. Tim was alone for Mark and the empty lorry had gone and Margaret was putting the dogs out of the way, into the Range Rover. As I ran to help him the heifer began trying again, somewhat half-heartedly, but each time she heaved, we pulled and the head of the still living calf appeared. It was big, far too big for a comfortable birth. We pulled even harder and the hefty shoulders came and the hips jammed. Margaret returned. For some days she had been reading R.W. Blowey's *A Veterinary Book for Dairy Farmers*. It had warned that there might be a necessity to rotate the calf, slightly, if this happened. We followed this advice and the first calf to be born at The Currer for many years slid onto the clean straw. Tim grabbed its back legs and, jumping on a nearby bale, shook it till it breathed. Then he laid it in front of the heifer and she licked it vigorously.

Exhaustion evaporates quickly with success. I dashed to the phone and cancelled the vet's visit. Returning to the barn I saw his car already coming down the hill. He had received the call en route but continued just to see all was well. He joined the admiring group, smiling broadly, as were we all.

In a world where time has now been counted in millions, where space and its infinity is being explored, belief in Heaven and a resident God comes in fits and starts. The enormity of everything suggests there must be a regulator. The whole of life cannot be based upon chance. We feel it an immense privilege to be present at birth, and death, mysteries even the scientists cannot solve. We certainly liked being there when that baby calf was born, yet in our happiness there was sadness that this was to be a one-off experience and that the next few days were not ones we would choose. We were in the business of rescuing surplus calves, not starting a suckled herd. We've been there and done that and our priority now is to give what happy life we can to those calves coming off the conveyor belt of milk production and destined for no life at all. When a friend's fourth baby was born she was overcome with sadness, knowing that this was surely her last child. That is how we felt also.

We had waited a long time for this. Our last calf had been Joanna's. Our Jersey house cow had had a name. She had provided all our milk and cream and our parents had churned some of this into butter in the days we remember with such gratitude. We sat quietly, each on a bale of straw, for some time after Tim left, watching our un-named heifer lick her newly born baby with all the expertise of one knowing exactly what to do. We had taken her from a harassed farmer at Skipton Cattle Market believing her to be a freemartin. We had been wrong. We had never expected this, two and a half years later. She had been happy with us but she would have to go. She was a dairy cow and we were not dairy farmers. She must go into a milking herd to produce milk for an uneducated society who were supposed to know all about the birds and the bees and didn't ever know that a cow had to have a calf every year to produce milk. This animal would have a calf annually, but not with us. She would be loved, for dairymen love their animals, but she was ours and we knew of no way that we could keep her. We watched her adoring the new born knowing she must spend the rest of her life having babies taken away from her so that the milk God meant should be theirs, could be sold in the supermarkets of the town. We were going to feel extremely guilty when we took her to market in six days' time. The new baby was a wye calf, a heifer, black as ebony, half Limousin. Future calves would probably be purebred

Friesians. The females would be kept and reared by hand to join the milking herd. The males would join the surplus queue. Our moment of joy was nearly over. We mourned, as Barbara had, that this would be our last baby.

We had problems to solve, but the next sale was not until Monday so we had several days to sort things out. Until the successful birth was over it had been premature even to anticipate what must be done. With six days' grace we shelved our problems again. Why distress ourselves further? First there was the trip to Gisburn Calf Market, on Thursday, to buy one more similar wye calf as soulmate for ours when Mum disappeared.

The black, wet beauty deserved more than that. The mother was obviously devoted. Before she stood Margaret milked out enough of the precious liquid to give to the baby should she refuse to drink or her mother not know how to stand still. It was wasted effort for the newly bonded mother and daughter knew exactly what to do. In less than half an hour both were standing and the baby was suckling and the newly drawn milk was being put into the freezer to be thrown away several months later. In the wild, animals know exactly what to do. Not all domesticated animals have instinctive knowledge of how to behave and some have post-natal depression and reject their babies. We had clear memories of a cow called Meg, in our suckled herd, who annually was aggressive towards her young, battering it with her head. Her new offspring had to be taken quickly away, unlicked and unloved until the disturbed, bovine brain righted itself and madness turned to motherliness. Then, carefully at first, the two could be re-united and all would be well.

Our new mother had never witnessed birth. She had never seen another in the herd give birth and suckle but she knew exactly what to do. She had never been handled since being a baby herself. Her swollen udder was probably overful and tender but she did not mind the eager mouth seeking its first experience of food. We could leave them both, confident that we were no longer needed, angry at fate which dictated that we had to eventually separate them.

We shut the door firmly on the dogs and goats. We did not know how the heifer would react to strangers, human or otherwise. She might become very protective. A wise farmer leaves a newly calved cow alone for a while but the heifer we had labelled impulsive, headstrong, mad even as she fought for more than her share of corn in the manger, seemed suddenly benign, gentle and quietly serene.

We knew this could be an illusion. We would find out in the next few days when we had to introduce her to extraordinary things like being tethered and hand-milked. Just now, however, all these things could wait until after our visit to Gisburn for the one playmate for the home-farm baby. We are good at putting off awful things.

When we had converted the barn into holiday accommodation we had preserved one of the ancient cow stalls for posterity. It had been removed to the Dutch barn and when that had been demolished in 1991 we had taken the stall down to the new barn. We thought this would be the place to tie the heifer but it needed some sorting out for there were bales in it and we delayed doing that also. We've plenty of time, was our excuse. Struggling with newly calved cows had been routine in the dairy herd forty years ago. We were forty years older and out of practice, so every thing could wait until the weekend. There was time. Tim said he'd take her to market for us but that we must take the calf away soon enough for the udder to fill evenly. I must admit we didn't really listen to anything he said. When it was necessary, only then, we would think about it.

On Thursday we let the herd out early and drove over to Gisburn in plenty of time, we thought, for the calf sales. We even sauntered into a petrol station to fill up with fuel. We felt professional with the trailer jogging along behind and we wanted one calf, not seventy. We wanted a Limousin cross heifer to match the one we already had and both could be introduced to the milk machine. They would be a time-consuming job during the busy tourist season but there was nothing we could do about that!

The sale began at 10.30 a.m. and when we arrived at 11 a.m. it was nearly over. We couldn't believe it for usually there were plenty of calves. We hurried to the ringside. A Hereford heifer was just being sold. In a panic lest there be none other, Margaret's hand shot up. Heifers were mostly unwanted and Margaret's bid had no competition. 'Mrs Brown!' said the auctioneer.

A second Hereford heifer from the same farm entered the ring, 'Come on, Mrs Brown,' the auctioneer urged. 'Take the two!' The hammer came down. We had bought two calves, two Herefords when we had wanted a Limousin.

'Come on,' said Margaret. 'Let's go.'

The last calf was being pushed unwillingly into the ring. It was very small, a Limousin heifer, just what we'd wanted had we dared to wait. Margaret hesitated and bid. 'Last calf to Mrs Brown. Thank you everybody!' The sale was over.

Let me tell you this about Margaret. In some things she looks ahead. In two years' time she would sell those heifers, probably to suckling herds and she would want them to go into the ring and be sold as a pair so that they entered their new herd with a friend. The two Herefords would go together and the two Limousins. Perfect!

The sale was over and strangely we felt more shattered hastily buying three than casually buying seventy. It was the wrong time of the year. Margaret turned to me as we wandered back to the car. 'What have I bought three calves for?'

'We've got the milk machine,' I said. 'Huh!' said my sister. We did not know how true a statement that was, about the milk machine, I mean. I thought I was talking about the *ad lib* feeder. I was but it wasn't the artificial one which gave us so much joy. We had no idea what pleasure there was in store for us so we went back to the Range Rover, weighted down with care, and opened the coffee flask preparing to wait for the bills of sale to be made out in the office.

'Have you got one?' Harry asked.

'I've got three!'

'What for?' asked a laughing brother.

'Dear knows,' Margaret answered, 'God only knows why I've got three more!' He knew all right. I'm sure of that.

We drank our thermos coffee discussing how best to get the trailer to the loading bay. We've never really solved the problem of reversing a small, two-wheeled trailer. We would make a mess of it, if watched by more competent farmers. We decided to do what we always resort to doing, which is to unhitch it and manually push it accurately into place.

First we had to go to the office and pay and collect all the masses of paper-work. The old man who had sold us the last calf was at the desk getting reprimanded because his wife had written the wrong date on his form and altered it. This is not allowed so the office lady was kindly making him out a new form. This is red tape gone crazy! The old softie's wife had made a mistake but the old softie was overjoyed that he had sold his little baby to Margaret. No farmer wants his calves to go to be killed. All farmers, whether their interest is in sheep, or pigs, or cattle, are awed by birth and want all their animals to complete whatever is their life expectancy.

We returned to the Range Rover and drove to the loading bay. In full view of amused farmers, we unhitched the trailer and pushed it in. Who cares? Arriving home we'd have the same problem but this time the trailer would be heavier. There would be three calves inside it. The new arrivals looked like Christmas trees with ear-tags in each ear and market stickers on their backs.

There are two entrances to the barn. The pen we had prepared was at the east end, more difficult to negotiate. With one calf only, manually reversing the trailer would have been easy. As we had three calves we decided to draw up at the west door. We could do this without the necessity to reverse. There was, however, the bigger problem of a newly calved heifer to pass. We had no guarantee that she would not charge intruders with calves which did not belong to her. We decided to take the risk, to open the door a fraction and dash in with two of the calves before she could comprehend what was happening. This would have been fine had there been only two calves or three people to cope. We slammed one gate of the trailer shut and squeezed into the barn with the little Limmy and the smallest of the two Herefords As we did so we heard the left-behind Hereford escape from the inadequately gated trailer and scamper up the slope to the ungated 170 acres of pasture.

There was nothing we could do but abandon the two within the barn and chase after the one that had escaped. Fortunately the gateway mud was deep and the calf floundered enough to be caught. There was rising panic as we wondered what was happening to the two left to the mercy of the newly calved heifer. They might have both been tossed quite brutally. Struggling with the muddy calf was not easy. A two-week old calf is a slippery customer even without a coat of mud. We hardly dare open the barn door and push in the truant for fear of what chaos was within, but we were to stand spellbound for several minutes, backs against the closed door behind us. The heifer, looking wide-eyed and maternal, was eyeing the newcomers with wonder not distaste. She was thinking, no doubt, 'Whatever is the world coming to. First there was all that pain followed by a baby. Then the door opens and I get three more!'

Memories of previous struggles to foster calves, when we had a stillborn, had not prepared us for the way this unique member of our herd was welcoming strangers. Her tail swished from side to side. From head to toe she was kindly. The new Limousin could not believe her good fortune. A new mum! Cor! How wonderful!

We stood transfixed, aware of some sort of a miracle about to solve all the problems we had pushed aside. The milk bar was open. The little Limousin, whom village children soon called Lucy, began suckling immediately. We sat on bales watching the extended family bonding, listening to the heifer lowing, talking baby language to the two Herefords, inviting them to share her reservoir of body building milk.

It was then that the heifer was christened. 'We must call her Diana. She loves children!' I said.

'And we don't need to sell her!' Margaret added with sheer relief.

We could not keep a heavily milking Friesian to feed just one calf. If we had had the opportunity and the time to take the excess milk every morning and night, there would have been too much for us to drink for Diana would give many gallons a day. Milk and cream and butter for the family would have returned us to the sixties and seventies when we had a house cow. We'd never had a Friesian, specially bred to produce milk in abundance. Stringent Health and Safety rules prevented us serving unpasteurised milk to paying guests but there were no rules at all about adoption in the herd. Diana was telling us clearly that she was prepared to rear and nurture all these orphaned children of her kind, if we would only keep her at The Currer. You bet we

Diana and family.

would! We could forget tethering, market hazards and the self-service feeding machine could stay dust-sheeted. We weren't interested in First Prizes. When had we ever wanted to show off our animals? We never ever wanted to sell. We only ever did so when it was impossible to keep them any longer. Diana could stay. We could relinquish all responsibility. She would pay for her keep in no time.

We had been relieved of a big decision. We make our modest living by being farmers not sentimental smallholders and, in this case, we did not even feel guilty. There were plenty of dairy cows out there, producing milk for the city folk. Our decision was a sensible business arrangement arrived at by two level-headed ladies.

There was another, wonderful advantage of deciding to keep Diana. She would have a calf annually. She might lead our herd for a dozen years or more. And every spring she would calve. A baby would be born at The Currer. Unlike Barbara we had many more to look forward to.

Diana's baby was always Baby Di. The twin Herefords Harry named Jacqui and Josie, the only twins who have yet come here on holiday.

Chapter Five

So I laugh when I hear them make it plain
That dogs and men never meet again.
For all their talk who'd listen to thim,
With the soul in the shining eyes of him?
Would God be wasting a dog like Tim?

W. M. Letts, from Elizabeth Goodge's *Book of Comfort*

As it turned out it was much more necessary that we should be at home on the following Monday, than at the Skipton dairy cow sales. On the Sunday evening Lusky had not eaten his supper. This was most unusual and very worrying. Our happiness in the decision to keep Diana and the extraordinary way in which she had adapted to her large family had filled our weekend agenda. We had talked of nothing else. Mother and quads in the paddock, she grazing contentedly and they frisking joyfully, meant that we frequently neglected work just to watch and to wonder. Fate has so many surprises.

It was with a sudden jerk from serenity to concern, that we realised our old dog wasn't very well. It is a fact of life that just a moment in time can bring everything tumbling. Just as the Pennine ridges make you first climb up and then come down, so does life treat us. Sometimes we are allowed to walk across the ridge, in the clouds, but sooner or later down we come again.

The fact that our laughing, cheerful dog, our friend for sixteen years, did not rouse for his evening meal brought us down to earth on that Sunday night following Diana's confinement. Margaret, anxiously, got out of bed several times during the night. His breathing was shallow and laboured.

He did not bark to rouse me, as usual, at six o'clock and when I turned him on to a clean towel I found he was quite dry and it was unnecessary. He wagged his tail feebly but he didn't want his milk. He just lay there, regal and beautiful. For such an old and handicapped dog, he was very handsome. His coat, thick and long always, looked shampooed for he no longer dirtied it in the cattle sheds. His working days had ended long ago. Danny and Jess came home filthy. Lusky was immaculate, even though he would never allow grooming or scissors to come near him. He always had such a happy face. Jess could look daggers drawn if so inclined. She, our loving and affectionate bitch, who instinctively came to comfort us when we were sad, could frighten away trespassing village children just with a look. Danny can look forlorn for he has had three rejection experiences and, no matter what, only death will part us and him. Lusky was different. Lusky was always happy. Lord of the Isles that he was, he could not look unhappy if he tried.

Usually, by the time that Margaret dragged herself out of bed, Lusky and I had had two hours of undisturbed companionship. With Lusky it was a reserved relationship. He never showed affection, like Jess did, or looked soppy like Danny. He would sleep with his head resting on my feet, not because he wanted to be close but just because it was comfortable. He never wanted to join the family in the sitting room, occupy the hearthrug as Jess did or press against Margaret's armchair like Danny. He never snuggled up to us in the Range Rover. It was beneath his dignity but he was the only dog, maybe with the exception of Shep, many years ago, we knew would protect us. Danny protects me from cattle. Lusky we knew, for sure, would protect us from people. He was known to bite any amorous guest, getting out of a car and heading towards us with arms outstretched.

Usually he had had two bowls of milk before Margaret appeared but on that sad Monday he never barked. My sister was up earlier than usual, for when uneasy she is wakeful.

'He's not well,' I said when she came down.

'I know. Has he had a drink?' she wanted to know. We had been so pre-occupied with Diana we hadn't been fully aware of his increasing doziness. 'I don't think he's been sitting up for days,' she commented.

We knew he had been eating, that does not go unobserved, but he hadn't been sitting up as much and had been sleeping more. He'd enjoyed being fondled by Margaret. She never neglected that. He wouldn't let me for he was a one-man dog. Though his back legs were useless there had never been any paralysis of his tail. We had a large rubber groundsheet beneath him and when he wagged it, the thumping could be heard in the next room. The groundsheet was a relic from our left-behind camping days and it had made life easy for a long time.

Margaret tried him with a little milk and was distressed when he was sick. It was obvious that he was very ill and uncomfortable. Only very rarely does Margaret send for a vet to help an animal die. The thought of having to do so for Lusky had never entered our heads throughout his courageous disable-ment. That morning Margaret admitted that she could not bear to see him suffer. Many would have thought that a dog that couldn't walk was suffering but we knew, in Lusky's case, that was not so.

Sometimes, we are told by those who profess to know, it is necessary to tell a terminally ill person who is hanging on to life that it is all right to say 'Goodbye' and die. Margaret told Lusky so, and together we went out to feed the herd and release them to pasture. As spring asserts itself there is less and less work for me in the bovine city. I came in earlier than Margaret. We had no B&B guests, Aunty Mary and Harry were still sleeping so I mashed another cup of tea. We mash tea in Yorkshire. Else where, I believe, they brew it.

It was year end and I was working on the balance sheet. All was silent. No noise from breakfasting people or animals. No conversation from the dining room. No wind. No murmur from the Air Stream, silenced when the cattle were let out. The Currer was flooded with sunshine and a blackbird gave a brief call from the sycamore. I watched a starling making a nest. I wasn't at all interested in the balance sheet. It is never a satisfactory occupation. We spend too much on better facilities for animals, on walls and necessary fencing.

Alone in the silence, Lusky's breathing seemed to be all expired; like some inner tube, little by little going down. Then I heard him make the same noise as Father did when he died during that dreadful snowfall of 1979, that unmistakable noise lungs make as they try to inhale their last breath and cannot. I knew that Lusky's doggy soul had gone elsewhere and I went slowly outside to tell Margaret.

His earthly remains lay in state under the table nearly all day for callers came and put paid to all but routine. Some we did not tell that the dog under the table was dead. He did not look so. Bill, the corn traveller came. He had called Lusky 'Fangs' ever since his teeth had been clipped by the vet, to prevent him bursting any more tyres. Most collies chase cars. Only Lusky could puncture tyres! Bill could not believe the dog was dead. Tim, the waller whose hand had been nearly severed when he'd thought Lusky was not breathing once before, did not risk it again. Brian the builder, who'd known Lusky since we brought him home as a six-month-old pup, was quiet. It was a quiet day during which all of us could believe the dog was just sleeping. We did not know what our table would look like without a dog under it.

We waited for some privacy. Village children came to tell us that Lucy had climbed the stile into the field adjacent to the paddock. They did not tell us they had encouraged it. I'm sure they had been letting it suck their fingers. Of course it would follow them. We sorted that out and sent the children home and then we went into the fenced land beside the stream on the other side of the calf shed and we dug a deep grave between the daffodils and under the silver birches. We had not long ago had the calf shed lengthened and the soil disturbed by the building was easy to dig.

'There is no more beautiful place than this,' Margaret said.

'Have you seen the loading pen?' I asked. In autumn when cattle are being sold their excited hooves churn up every blade of grass and the ground is brown. That March the whole of it was a cobalt blue carpet of Germander Speedwell.

We realised that Lusky had lain in state for over nine hours. We laid him gently in the wheelbarrow and pushed him through the stockyard and into the enclosure. There we buried him as we have so many other dogs and, having completed our task, we walked sadly back to the house. Usually, when one dog dies, we must think of replacing it. On this occasion, Danny, Lusky's successor, was already a member of the family. We had never intended to have three dogs but on Harris in 1995, Angus had persuaded us that Danny was the dog for us. Danny had done his share of pleading and we'd given in. We had never regretted our decision and on Lusky's death there was no need to look for a replacement, no need to buy another on Monday.

We have never found it difficult to accept a new dog, or calf, or whatever, to fill the space left by one that has died. People who say, 'I could not have another dog,' are depriving themselves of pleasure. Because we are now quite old ourselves we have had many dogs, most of which have lived more than what is considered a doggy three score years and ten. All have been different. Now and again one briefly behaves as another did and we say, 'Just like ...!' but actually no dog is a clone of another.

March had come in nondescript but it was most certainly going out like a lamb and the hawthorn was green. When it became white we would be heading for our first holiday on Tiree in four years. The daffodils in the orchard were more numerous than ever. They were not only reproducing but we had added to their number by planting the hundred bulbs left by the Dutch students in October. Every morning the silver birch buds had grown and soon they would burst. Easter was just around the corner. For sixteen years and possibly thirty holidays, Lusky had been our annual island fun-dog. The beach was his natural environment. If his doggy soul was still around the farm, and Margaret discounted any suggestion otherwise, surely it would accompany us on the RMS *Lord of the Isles*, to Tiree in May. It would accompany us free of earthly disablement, able to flit along the beach unhampered by arthritis, ahead of the sea birds, not behind. We could not fret. We could mourn, but memories were pleasure and though death is a frequent visitor where many living things lodge together, birth is also a spring phenomenon. Diana's calves softened the blow of Lusky's departing and photographs went home on the cameras of all our April guests.

The way was smoothing out for Dorothy and George to take over while we rejuvenated on Tiree. The four years of our absence seemed like a lifetime.

Everything we had to do was squeezed into the thirty days of April. There was the annual day-visit of the residents of the Leonard Cheshire Home at Sowerby Bridge. There was the redecorating of many rooms. Almost all had to be re-whitened. Having given away the clumsy Black & Decker contraption, Margaret resorted to the simplicity of a paint pad. The Young Farmers' motto, KISS, Keep It Simple, Stupid, takes some beating. Brian was restoring mullions and replacing the rotting window frames with hard wood. The house was looking good.

Charlie, the billy goat, died with dignity having lived six months after his gruelling experience while we were on autumn holiday. Jo Tewson, an acclaimed actress, was busy reading *We'll see the Cuckoo* for Talking Books for the Blind. She occasionally rang for information on pronunciation. 'This is your other self,' she would begin.

We wormed the cattle and we replaced the lost ear tags lest an inspector descend on us. The fire service sent out their inspectors. New rules on fire alarms had to be obeyed. The noise had to reach a certain number of decibels in each bedroom. Ours failed and £1300 was spent on new equipment. A bullock was found to have Foul. And another. What was new? The day before we left, enough copies of my new book *We'll Trace the Rainbow* were delivered to enable me to take gifts for our Tiree friends.

In spite of everything there comes the day one goes on holiday and what is not done is left until your return. Whatever obstacles present themselves beforehand, there is the moment you must go if you are to get to your destination, the moment when you pull out of the yard and head north towards those beckoning islands which lie dreaming in the west.

We have long since given up any idea of travelling along motorways. We even avoid A roads whenever possible. Our preferred route is via Wharfedale and our first stop was for refreshment at the home of Julia and John Horner, who farm Redmire, in Buckden. Julia was one of my pupils, a Guide, a Sea Ranger, an island camper and is now a friend. Redmire is owned by the National Trust and generations of Horners have been tenants. It is a very beautiful house and its situation, in a Dales landscape, is incomparable.

We shouldn't have stopped but we had promised and our route passed the Redmire entrance. We were late and Julia had had to collect a son's friend and we had to await her return. John told us to make ourselves a cup of tea so we put the kettle on the shining new Aga and waited for it to boil. Margaret took one mug from the dresser top and three from hooks. We mashed the tea and Margaret poured it, talking ten to the dozen to John. Once farmers start it is impossible to stop them! I tasted my tea and it was vile.

'Did you put sugar in Harry's?' I asked. She nodded. 'Well, you put salt in and have given it to me!'

'No I haven't. This is the sugared one,' she insisted, tasting it to make sure.

We poured the tea out of my mug and found that over half the contents were salt. Julia, returning at that moment, laughed, 'I've been salting some beef!' There was semi-hysteria and we told the story of the Caledonian MacBrayne porridge and then Julia wanted to show us round her house and we talked B&B language for she takes tourists, too, and time was running out. We looked at the clock and it was 4 p.m. Sensible people, wanting to arrive in Ayr before dark, should be approaching Dumfries by now! We were only at Buckden, on narrow roads, climbing moorland tracks leading to Hawes, still in Yorkshire. Once again we would approach the Travel Inn in darkness, for us the greatest of all punishments. When we visit Julia again we will be en route to nowhere. We'll have a full day, one without an evening meal to make.

Making virtually the same journey north each year, we have tried to vary our route. We do not try to get from A to B at speed. We are on holiday as soon as we pull out of the yard and our long journey is all such, gentle and enjoyable. We had booked a two-day stop at a place near Ford, just off the Loch Gilphead to Oban road. The lady advertised short stays in her self-catering cottage but it had already been booked so she gave us the option of a six-berth caravan. Aunty Mary was adamant that, having never slept in one before, she was far too old to start. Having taken her on holiday twice a year since 1970 we reserve the right to do it our way. By this method we have now survived twenty-five years of always having an eighty-year old and over, with us. Aunty Mary's comment is, 'Well you'll be used to it!' So we are.

Take it or leave it, she came or she didn't. We booked the caravan and she really enjoyed it. We approached this first bivouac by crossing the Clyde from Wemyss Bay to Rothesay, on the Isle of Bute. We skirted the resort and took a narrow road round the island. We had not expected to be so immediately in love with it. In the morning sun it was a beautifully farmed island which appealed to the crofter in us. We crossed the Kyles from Rhubodach to Colintraive on the Cowal peninsula and thereafter sailed to Tarbert from Portavadie. Driving through Tighnabruaich, we noticed that the pier had become a ruin. Harry remembered getting off the Kyles of Bute steamer, with Father, just for the fun of it and having to pay 2d to get off and 2d to get back aboard. This levy had apparently been insufficient to maintain the pier after all! The last time Margaret and I had been on the Kyles of Bute ferry had been with a party of seven, forty years ago, trekking with trike carts and camping on one island after the other.

Arriving at Tarbert we had travelled south to Ardrishaig, to spend a couple of hours with friends we'd first met on Mull. Then we continued to the caravan at Stroneskar, near Ford, where Aunty Mary behaved herself perfectly. We were as comfortable as could be inside the caravan and we would have been happy there longer if Tiree had not beckoned so determinedly. Our hostess, Sheena McNair, was extremely welcoming. It was a large caravan and Aunty Mary had her own bedroom and once inside there was a cottage atmosphere of which she approved.

We have an affinity with all farmers. These had a suckling herd of Galloways. They were never idle but, because we were on holiday, we had moments to spare to watch their activity and, once or twice, we chatted with them. They were taking suckled calves, beautiful ones, to the Oban Sales on the day we were to leave and they spent a long time grooming them. Selling all ours on one day, or at the most two days, we do not have time to groom even if we had docile animals which would allow such beauty treatment. We watched the hair dressing with great interest. Oban is renowned for its good quality cattle. These Galloways were pure bred. Ours are always dairy cross. We think ours are good but acknowledged that these were the real McCoy. The farmer's wife wanted us to call at the market on our way in to Oban. We would not have suggested it. We find guests watching us sell cattle at market rather stressful. She not only invited us but chose to sit beside us. To our dismay, all the cattle we saw sold, including the McNair's, fetched shockingly low prices. Surely the farming industry could not survive this recession much longer. We boarded the RMS *Lord of the Isles* tingling with anger at a public consumer who expects us all to work so hard for so little return.

We had never, in forty-five years, stayed anywhere on Tiree other than at Salum. In our twenty-five years of camping with children, it had always been on the machair bordering the bay. Salum boasts only three houses. Right at the water's edge still stands Salum House, home, in those wonderful camping days, of Calum MacLean, known to even a wider world than Tiree, as Calum Salum. He had been our friend and mentor, our security, the father figure of all the children, the piper at our dances and the shopkeeper who had provided our food.

Then there is the croft where live our longest Tiree friends, the MacInnes family, on whose land we camped and whose newly adapted steading cottage was to be our new holiday home at Caolis. Lastly there is the cottage we used to rent, belonging to the MacLean family which, since the death of our dear friend Charlie, has been extended and modernised only for family use.

This had left us without Tiree accommodation but, fortunately, Hughie MacInnes was talking about converting a steading on land he had at Caolis. Things move slowly on islands and the permission to do so, and the work on the conversion, had taken four years. It was only ready for occupation within minutes of our arrival. Work had been persistently delayed by bad weather. The hole dug to receive the septic tank had filled with water so that the modern, plastic sphere had floated. News from Ellen, Hughie's Glasgow-based sister, had been continually negative. At one point she had said we'd have to stay with her mother at Salum. We are used to the last-minute finishing of projects, overnight struggles to complete before a deadline and we did not get too worried. 'Don't worry about the septic tank,' we hastened to comfort her. 'We can always bring a chemical loo!'

Hughie, who never ever opts for second best or compromise, completed only minutes before the arrival of the steamer. The key to the one-bedroomed cottage was waiting for us as we drove up to the Salum croft to collect it. Hughie had already had one experience of building a house. Several years ago, to our horror, he had taken down the thatched one which he'd inherited from generations of his ancestors and in which he and his four sisters had been born. It was in this tiny Tiree cottage that we had first met our friends in 1951, in which we had ourselves stayed when we came to the island with Mother and Father in the mid-sixties. We, who didn't have to live with its inconveniences, were very sad when Hughie pulled it down and built a house with plumbing and electricity. Tiree people were moving on and once they began to enjoy the twentieth century and technology, they began to leave us, at The Currer, far behind. They who had been behind took a sudden leap forward, and we who had been slightly ahead were left a long way in their wake. Hughie had built a lovely modern cottage for his parents and himself. His herd increased, he bought tractor and equipment, he was moving forward at a pace. Converting a steading into two holiday cottages was child's play. Only the prolonged winter had been the obstacle.

Even so we had had a few misgivings. The one bedroom, of course, must be for Aunty Mary. The other three of us must use the sitting room. Hughie had promised to put a bed in the corner for Harry. This arrangement mirrored the sitting room accommodation at home. Harry frequently used the bed behind the curtain and Margaret and I sleep equally well on the floor, as easily as we always have done, since our respective teenage years. That is no problem, only it is just a little more difficult than it used to be to get up from ground level! The wardrobe for the one bedroom had not arrived from the mainland. I'd visited the Argos Shop in Keighley and ordered a portable one for I knew that Aunty Mary's case would hold almost all her many dresses. Things run more smoothly if we are prepared and ready to forestall any complaint. The frame and plastic one advertised was not kept in stock and we had collected it from the store on our way north. We are last-minute people, too!

We were delayed going straight to Caolis. We knew we would be for Effie always has the kettle on. In her younger days she had made lunch for a third of the campers at the beginning of our summer camp. Fifteen had sat round her table. The others had been entertained by Charlie's mother, and at Salum House by the housekeeper, another Margaret Brown.

For the purpose of these records we should, by rights and out of respect for our readers, become more widened travellers. If they are bored with our obsession for the Hebrides they must skip a few pages for there are not all that many years left for us to risk missing one. I have friends whose retirement has provided them with opportunity to explore the world, who could write a book about distant and exotic places and we, who can see no future retirement ahead, count the remaining annual holidays on the islands as far too few.

The newly made cottage at one end of the steading had used less than a third of the whole. Approaching it from the Caolis road we – that is Margaret and I – nearly had hysterics. It had taken years to get the planning permission and then bad weather had hampered progress. Whatever had been done within was not visible. Apart from a new door, the outside looked as it always had. We had not expected roses round the door but it amused us that it didn't look like a cottage. Harry and Aunty Mary didn't see it at all and were looking elsewhere. There had not been time or dry weather to whiten the outside walls. They were weathered with the winds and storms that, though they never seem do so in May, can sweep angrily in from the Gunna Sound and the Atlantic. Just two small windows and a door made the diddy cottage look like something from Goldilocks and the three bears.

Our hysteria became tempered with foreboding. Not on our behalf. We could have slept in a cleaned-out pigsty but Aunty Mary had to be appeased and Harry used to go to pieces if she criticised. Our friends Hughie and his sister Ellen, over from Glasgow especially to see the new cottage christened by the Browns, led the way driving to the rear of the steading in their Land Rover Discovery. We followed and the two of us alighted to inspect the cottage before introducing our dependants to whatever living accommodation it provided. It is totally disgusting that our faith in Hughie, for a few brief moments, had disappeared. We followed our friends into the cottage and it was BEAUTIFUL. The workmanship was superb, the decor just lovely. It was spacious and light and excellently planned. The walls were rough but Persil white. There was a window on both east and west walls so that whichever way you looked you saw the sea. At one end was a modern kitchen area with more facilities than provided in our sixteenth-century cottages. On the east side of the breakfast bench, the sitting room area was deeply carpeted and comfortably furnished and Harry's bed was lost in a corner, no problem. Aunty Mary's bedroom was just right, next to the bathroom. Oh boy! It was lovely. We couldn't wait to bring in the others. Anyone wanting a holiday on Tiree, this is the place to be. For one thing the Caolis beaches are so beautiful. Certainly there is no better place to convert a steading and to do it so excellently will draw people to the island like a magnet. We think so, anyway!

When our friends had gone back to Salum we unpacked and erected the fold-up wardrobe for all Aunty Mary's dresses. We had the happiest of holidays. As always we talked a lot of farming. Hughie had built himself a feeding bay for wintering cattle. Margaret said it was what we needed on the other side of our barn so that hay could be thrown out directly into a manger. If we had one, fewer bales would have to be carried and any innovation which would do that would be more than welcome. Margaret carries almost all of the bales and I spread them. Her back is bent and has been for thirty years. As it doesn't seem to get any worse I try not to worry but I definitely supported any idea which meant fewer bales to be carried. For food and bedding we use at least forty a day.

That year we had the added pleasure of having one of my school children, a Guide and a Sea Ranger, living on the island. She had fallen in love with Tiree when camping with us throughout her teenage years. Now she lives there and loves it. Driving to visit her one day, we encountered a badly injured seagull on the road in front of us. Margaret investigated and found it so badly hurt it could not walk or fly. She was lifting it into the back of the Range Rover when it suddenly attacked her quite viciously with its very able beak and she arrived at Sylvia's somewhat bloodied.

Later, more educated as to its potential beak warfare, she put it into the unconverted part of our steading. It was frantically hungry and for several days she fed it masses of food. It was flapping all over the concrete and it became pretty obvious that hospital treatment was useless. Feeding it was doing more harm than good. It was getting very dirty and its feathers needed water so she decided to take it down to the shore and put it on the sea. She did and the joy it suddenly felt could be witnessed by all. On the water, floating on the rise and fall of the waves, it looked a healthy gull. Its legs were probably useless as propellers and its wings would never again lift it into the sky, but for a day or two or three it would be very happy. Each day, taking the dogs on their morning scamper along the bay, I scanned the area for a dead seagull. Each evening Margaret did the same, expecting that the tide would have abandoned its lifeless body on the high water line but, while we remained on holiday, it never did.

There are no beaches quite like the Tiree ones. They are whiter, even, than the shores of western Harris, and that is almost an impossibility. On Tiree most of them are accessible by Range Rover. There are the bigger bays of Gott and Baugh along which you can drive more than a mile, the lesser ones of Salum and Balevullin and the cosy, sheltered beaches at Caolis on which you can drive only a few yards but which are so beautiful they must be part of paradise. If they are, there is no one there, only the sea birds and the seals, for Caolis is the best place to watch their swimming antics and to tempt their curiosity. There the sun is invariably behind so that the sea is always turquoise. Mary's house stands sentry, silhouetted on the almost flat skyline. She was the first of the Salum children to come to The Currer, just two weeks after our removal from the village, in 1958. She and her husband and family are back on the island after a working career in Hong Kong. They are both island born and their roots lie deep in the rocky headland of Rosigal.

We had one moment of concern which sent us driving late to the doctor at Baugh. Harry avoided every episode of the soap opera Emmerdale he possibly could. So do we but Aunty Mary joins most of the watching public, at 7 p.m. every weeknight. Harry used to watch, twenty years ago, when the village life portrayed and the moral standards of the farming community matched our own. Now we prefer to watch Dales Diary, for Emmerdale and its villagers must come from some other planet!

On this particular Tiree evening it was too cool and breezy to tempt Aunty Mary out of our cosy cottage, but Harry was determined to escape the torture of watching our own locality being maligned. Having eaten our meal, Harry begged to go out before it was properly digested. So we drove over to the Scarinish end of Gott Bay and, with the wind behind us, we walked along the hard sand, Margaret throwing a ball for the dogs and I was pushing the wheelchair. It was absolutely the wrong thing to do for the biting wind we had put behind us kept dodging round to catch our breath. Almost immediately Harry's hiatus hernia began to give pain. Margaret hurried back to collect our vehicle and drive it the short distance we had gone and we couldn't get Harry back into the warmth quickly enough. We expected things to improve rapidly when we got back to the cottage but the pain persisted and we decided to phone the doctor and ask for advice. We were told to drive Harry over to the surgery, if possible, so, at approaching 10 p.m., we went the eight miles or so and all the way the pain got better and better and we began to be glad we had not asked the doctor to come to us. Indeed we felt embarrassed to trouble him at all. He was very tolerant and, just to be sure the pain had not been anything to do with his heart, he gave Harry an ECG, the result of which showed that his heart was perfectly normal. That news was worth coming for, if nothing else. A clean bill of health is a valuable thing to have! Especially if you are hundreds of miles from home, on an island and have just had a nasty pain!

Cautiously we explored the possibility of a millennium Celebration, on Tiree, should we allow ourselves to be persuaded by the 1957 Guides. Would it really be possible to return with the Song to Sing children and venture down

Memory Lane? Hughie planned to make at least one more cottage out of the steading and there were other holiday cottages close by at Caolis, which is a straggling township of ten houses, perhaps more. At Salum there had only been the one. At our new location perhaps a reunion could be arranged.

On the night before we left, we joined the MacInnes family for an eightieth birthday celebration. Effie's birthday was the day after mine which always came while we were on holiday. It would do so in two years' time. In the millennium I would reach seventy. What better thing than to re-unite for that occasion. We all knew this wasn't idle thinking. In two years we were coming back with some of our enormous family. Nothing was going to stop us!

Dorothy said, when we arrived home, 'This is the list of phone calls asking for accommodation and they all want en suite!' This had been happening for some time. 'Tough!' my reply had always been, but put a little more politely. This is a sixteenth-century building. Twenty years ago, when we converted it, no one knew about en suite and the Tourist Board never encouraged us to see into the future. No guests ever minded, but nowadays even regular guests were wishing they had their own facilities. A new Joe Public was emerging expecting even farmhouses to be The Ritz.

Tim rang to say one of our bigger animals had put its foot through a roll of sellotape and that there was considerable swelling. We did not immediately think a roll of sellotape could possibly be a problem but Margaret hunted up the animal and brought it into the shed. Tim was right. Somehow or other it had managed to put its foot centrally into a roll of parcelling tape. The card round which the tape is wound is rock solid and dear knows how the hoof had managed to go through. The animal's front leg had an armlet, a very tight one and there was considerable swelling above and below it. We were amazed that grass had not soaked the cardboard allowing it to disintegrate. We didn't know how to tackle it best. We managed to get the bullock into the crush. This is not always the easiest thing to do. We invariably manage it but often have to persuade the animal with a tempting amount of corn. With its head securely held Margaret examined the foot. Its tight bracelet would move neither up nor down and a knife made only a scratch on the hard surface of the cardboard. Swelling either side made a hacksaw impossible. In the end she had to get sharp hoof clippers and slowly and painstakingly cut through it. Fortunately she managed to do so without amputating the foot. How the bullock managed to get the ring on in the first place is a mystery we will never solve.

Busily washing dishes, one day, Margaret had a sudden idea. If one is to survive one must move with the times as far as possible. We had not totally dismissed the provision of en suite accommodation as impossible. We realised that to have one or two rooms converted would make problems. In our profession, especially when nowadays people book well in advance for even overnight stays only, it is not possible to allocate a specific room. We have to be able to rearrange where necessary. En suite had to be all or nothing. Margaret's idea meant the sacrifice of the single room. She suggested we divide it into two. One half could be entered from inside one double bedroom and give space for a toilet, washbasin and shower. The other half already had a door from the passage. This could become the private facilities of the other double and the existing bathroom, opposite the twin be for the use of those occupying that only.

We had been busy all spring replacing the soft wood window frames and, with this opportunity, ordered our builder to put a stone mullion in each window. Twenty years ago, when every penny had to be borrowed, we had stopped short of doing this. It is silly to say we regretted not doing something we couldn't afford. In those circumstances there is no choice but now, having to put in new window frames, we took the opportunity. Our purse was still lean but, with business a continual operation, repairing windows had to be where and when a room was empty. The last mullion was installed in 2001, so frequently were rooms in use. The opportunity to make two toilet-shower rooms was easier. Work could be confined to the one room being divided, until the very last minute when the door had to be made into the double room. We had to wait until that room was vacant and then make a dash for it. Increasingly we used the end bedroom on our family passage and had a door opening into the garden. People in this bedroom had private use of the family bathroom and lately we have enclosed the two rooms by putting a door in the passage making them quite separate

So now four of our six rooms did not share a bathroom. We sent for the National Trust land agent, Andrew McVety, and acquired permission to build a small, lean-to addition to the twin entered from the dining room and almost always used by disabled guests. It is suitable for wheelchair users and over the years has been in great demand. This would give a fifth bedroom en suite facilities, though not immediately for planning permission had to be applied for and building was not started for many months. Eventually Brian built the extension and no one could tell that it had not been built in the sixteenth century, like the rest of the house. This left one room not converted and we searched for a way. The solution followed work on the dining room twin. The existing walls are so thick Brian increased the space by pulling down the outside wall, which was to become an inside one, when the lean-to was built. He re-built this with bricks and inserted an iron girder. In so doing we gained the two feet of floor space we desperately needed.

Brian said we could use this method within the remaining downstairs bedroom, which is adjacent to the staircase. Brian said we could use the space under the stairs, which had been a cupboard for seventeen years. Then, if we reduced the thickness of the outside wall, we could make enough room to install toilet, wash basin and shower. Hey presto! We could do it, if we worked during the winter months and booked accordingly.

Denis, when he saw the finished improvements commented wisely. 'Now, Jean, they'll want a menu!' Over my dead body! The way we go is for more self-catering groups. No way do we, with me at the helm, become a restaurant! We must steer a course towards an easier life, not a harder one.

To do this was to discuss, with John our shed builder, the possibility of a feeding bay. Space for improvements outside is becoming limited, too. We wanted it between the lower wall of the hay barn and the stream. Would there be enough room? There was, just. Hughie's had not been roofed. John insisted ours must have one. Here we go again, we feared. If John is employed the job must be a perfect one. Ours must have a roof! When we suggest a minor improvement John perfects it to become an expensive project.

It looked as though we would never get the bank overdraft dismissed and we were getting a long way beyond our youth. On returning from our Tiree holiday I had paid the printer/bookbinder a frighteningly large amount for a colossal number of books so we decided to launch *We'll Trace the Rainbow* from The Currer. Many people came. Orders came from all over the place and, very quickly, a third of the books were sold.

News, which had been so good, of Janet in Leeds and Tommy in County Durham, began to worry us. People do conquer cancer and many tumours remain in remission indefinitely. Neither was true for our two friends. It seemed so unfair that the illness in both should bounce back. It claimed Tommy first. We had thought his body was indestructible. It was not but his soul will be. Heaven would welcome Tommy and will be a better place because of him. Inevitably, with so many guests returning every year, so many school children continuing to visit me and Guides every which way, it is only natural that we are going to be involved, more than most, with the lives of others. We are looked upon by them as almost family. They can cope with us as a minor extension of theirs. For us it is much more difficult. They add us to their Christmas card list unaware that ours has already over three hundred names. We welcome their good news and congratulate them on their achievements. We love to greet them and our door is always ajar in the hope that they will visit. We are pleased when they phone. If their news is sad we commiserate and if it is of bereavement we grieve with them. We do all these things sensitive to the knowledge that our family of outsiders is so big we could not inform them as they do us. We could not even attempt to.

Our friendship with Janet had lasted close on fifty years. She had been my most enthusiastic Guide when I came out of college and began my thirty years of Guiding joy. Janet had been the first teenager Margaret and I had taken to the Hebrides and she had been one of the small group we had taken trekking from island to island in 1958. Since then she had been a not-too-distant friend, eventually marrying and living in Leeds. She had always radiated joy. She was a friend one could talk to all day. She thought all she had learned had been taught by me, which wasn't true, and she thought she knew me, what I would think and how I would react and that wasn't altogether true either for no one completely knows another. That is a proven fact. One thing we did know about Janet was how she would react to a terminal illness and we were proved right. She, I'm sure, would have said she knew exactly how I would but I don't even know that myself. I would certainly not handle it as well as she did for, at the moment anyway, I seem to have too much responsibility to leave behind with Margaret to be prepared to go with acceptance, as Janet did. 'I have no problem with dying,' she said and she never lied. Initially she, and we, thought that she had won the battle. Hers was the only home we felt comfortable taking Harry to a meal. She was an excellent cook and hostess and Harry was always so at ease with her, the stress he normally felt when eating was not present at all.

Janet's cancer had been operated on and was believed to have been controlled. It lay dormant for a little while and then bounced back again. She expected to have another operation but her consultant told her it could not be. She was always impeccable, most often in white, far cleaner and more elegant than I have ever been.

She had asked the simple question, 'Is there anything I can do?' Surely there is an answer to this. The specialist should have known several. His clumsy, 'Just keep yourself clean, Mrs Beard,' would have offended most of his patients. Janet found this little story well worth telling. That she had been taken by surprise was part of the story. That she had been wearing white trousers and Aran sweater to match and was always a good story teller and actress, caused her listeners first to gasp and then to laugh with her.

It was not necessary for the specialist to answer, 'What ever you want to do, go and do it.' Each day is a day to live. This was Janet's philosophy and it would always be. A good friend of mine had said she would want to be told if she had terminal cancer. I had, at that time, thought differently. Father's prostate cancer was spreading but we had decided not to tell him believing ignorance was medicine in itself.

'Why, for goodness sake?' I had wanted to know.

'So that I could get my soul in order,' she had answered.

'If it isn't in order start now,' I had laughed. 'You might have a heart attack tomorrow.'

Janet didn't need to get her soul in order. Her faith was stronger than mine. She was absolutely sure. There were, however, many things she wanted to do. Most important was to finish some project she was developing for the young people of her church. This was of primary importance to her and quite beyond my understanding and involved others and not ourselves. There were two things she wanted to do which did involve us. She wanted a reunion with the seven who, forty years ago, had pushed trike carts from island to island in the Hebrides. The unique experience of sailing from Tiree to Barra, from there to the Uists, to Eigg and Rhum and Skye, in the days when most children just went to Blackpool, was one of her most precious memories. I was a young teacher. They were all teenagers. 'Remember when we'd just begun, remember when we rode the sun?'

All five were married. Janet was in her early sixties, Ann lived in Aviemore, Toots in Delph, Foxy and another Margaret a few miles up Airedale. All four were in their mid-fifties and hadn't seen each other for several decades. We did not agree to meet just because Janet was ill, though each understood that the seed had been sown and nurtured by her. We met because it was forty years ago exactly, and each wanted to meet the other. It was never apparent that Janet was ill. The joy and laughter seemed always to be rooted in health. She was always fun to be with. So were they all. They even looked the same. Age had crept up without altering attitude and distance had not separated us from the teenage relationship which had been such an adventure. I re-packed the trike cart and the local newspaper photographer made sure the occasion had a place in the *Keighley News*. A real reunion was talked about, a Tiree Experience for them and for many more, as if Janet's illness was a fantasy that could be dispelled by, 'Keeping Clean'! Margaret and I knew it wasn't and so did Janet and when she expressed a wish to re-visit Tiree immediately, before it was too late, we phoned Hughie and booked the lovely new Caolis cottage for her and her husband. The visit was such a success, and the future was unpredictable, so they re-booked for the following year. It was so like Janet to live and think positively.

The summer was surprisingly wet. It rained continually for the Chapel Fête, imprisoning everyone indoors. We'd had great difficulty fitting this annual occasion into our over-full timetable. June was heavily booked with schools. Aunty Mary, who had been a source of help each year, baking and entertaining, was suddenly no help at all. Indeed she appeared to have forgotten what day it was. She habitually rises late and for this reason we had abandoned the coffee morning part of the day. I hastened to rouse her and she couldn't understand why. 'It's your Fête Day!' I shouted, for she is very deaf.

'It isn't today,' she insisted and wouldn't believe me.

We struggled through an event which should be pleasure, anxiously wondering if we'd complete the festivities before the return of our paying guests and if we could possibly get through the washing up before beginning the evening meal for many. We realised that things had changed in our household, that we had lost Aunty Mary's valuable help and that holiday-makers were more numerous and demanding. We reluctantly decided we must suggest the Fête venue be elsewhere next year. It was a decision we hated taking but, at that time, other members of the congregation were organising events in their own homes and gardens satisfactorily and I think they understood that the pressure on us was increasing.

We decided to accept an invitation from FWAG, the Farming and Wild-life Advisory Group, to inspect a meadow where fertilizers had not been recently used and wild flowers had been allowed to run riot. We followed the Leeds ring road to the award-winning meadow and parked in pouring rain outside the gate. Margaret and I donned wellingtons and raincoats and followed other flora enthusiasts along the indicated paths. Rain had lain much of the tangle of flowers and standing water lay everywhere but we found the experience interesting and were confident that, were our pastures not eaten, there would be the same variety. Indeed, even with cattle grazing we had flowers in abundance.

We were very wet and intent on escaping the barn where members of the committee were serving strawberry teas. We deemed it too wet to unload Harry and Aunty Mary and stagger up outside barn steps to the improvised tearoom. We failed. Our car was stopped and we were encouraged to drive in and partake. We suffered wet trousers and rivers of water trickling down our necks, just watching Harry's enjoyment of the novelty. Then we man-handled our brother down the difficult staircase in torrential rain. Margaret returned for Aunty Mary and found her, protected by a lady's umbrella, pausing on the steps, reciting poetry. What's new? She recites poetry to everyone!

It rained and rained so much the earth steamed when the sun came out and with it an unprecedented number of midges. These Highland pests are seldom seen at The Currer. They frequent the valley and the riverside foliage but rarely trouble us. Two single mothers were occupying The Mistal cottage. After the wet spell they were taking advantage of the climate change and were sitting out of doors, late on the Thursday evening. On the Friday morning they displayed badly bitten ankles and told us we had bugs in the beds. We had never been told anything like that before! We tried to think who had been previous occupants. It is amazing how quickly you forget even yesterday. Who rented the cottages last week is a mystery which often takes some time to solve. We searched the beds for signs and one woman brought me evidence. A minute insect rested a moment on her finger and then flew away. This was Friday and the next day there would be a change over. The two young women were ready to be downright awkward so we went into town and ordered two single beds to be sent to The Currer! Then we went to the vet and asked what a bed bug looked like.

'That's nothing like the insect which flew off her finger,' I said.

'Did you say flew?' said the vet. 'Bugs don't fly. The midges were atrocious last night!'

How could we be so slow? Why, with all our experience of Mull and midges at Tobermory, of Rhum when an opened tin of mandarin oranges immediately attracted a dense black skin of literally hundreds, why didn't we who had travelled on the train to Spean Bridge with a lady who had declared you could win a war with midgies, why didn't we know what had bitten? When we told the ladies they did not believe us and argued otherwise.

We were expecting the arrival of Bernard and Emilie, from Lyon, for she was going to spend five weeks of the summer here, to improve her English, just as Denis had. Bernard has a delightful sense of humour and found the bed bug incident very amusing. He had accompanied Emilie, as it was her first experience alone, but he returned to France the next day. As he left he advised Margaret, 'You must go to the flea market tomorrow. Get some more!'

We embarked upon the most wonderful summer with Emilie. We found she could be trusted with every chore be it animal husbandry, housekeeping, cooking or entertaining. She could make cakes and pies that I could not better. It is unusual to be able to allow a fourteen-year-old to make puddings for holiday-makers. We laughingly taught her to sing, 'Anything you can do, I can do better!' and had to admit, that with youth on her side, she probably could.

We were experiencing an unusual teenager. Had she been a member of the Guide Company, thirty years ago, she might not have been so unique. In those days there were many with few possessions and very little money but craved for neither. Her father left her with an emergency purse but she spent none of it. Guests loved her but found it strange that she appeared to have nothing and want nothing. Her wardrobe was small. She washed her clothes frequently overnight and wore them again next morning. She had few toiletries, no jewellery or make-up. Going into town, one day, I reminded her of the money her father had left in my safekeeping.

'Take some if there is anything you would like to buy.'

She replied, 'Jean, I am fourteen years old and money is not my problem.'

Imagine, if you can, a beautiful Gallic girl, stepping into womanhood with no problems about money, fashion, cosmetics or jewellery yet looking as if she would make all heads turn in her direction. When her stay was up she was to go camping in Greece with unknown children of her father's work mates. 'I hope there is just one more girl who doesn't like stick-lip!' she confided.

We had promised her a trip to the seaside. 'I would like to go to Blackpool,' she said. This Lancashire resort had been mentioned in her English lesson at school.

'OK. We will go there,' we answered the city girl who spent every weekend with her brother and parents in the country, winter holidays in the French mountains and summer holidays with us in the Yorkshire Dales. She had travelled to the North West of Scotland last year, and sailed to the remoteness of Harris and The Uists and she wanted to see what Blackpool was really like!

The week before our excursion to the glamour of the triple piers, the tower (which is more universally known than the Eiffel Tower in Paris), the Golden Mile and the Pleasure Beach, it was the World Cup. When England won in 1966, we and our army of children were on Harris. When the French won, Emilie was with us, sitting on our hearthrug cheering. There was such excitement I think even the guests were pleased that the French team were winners. They thought that Emilie should celebrate and gave her five pounds to do so. She did not display it triumphantly, as she had the two-penny piece she'd found on the carpet while making beds. Then she had declared, 'Look! I am rich.' She said, 'Thank you,' and spent it on ice-cream for all of us when we went to Blackpool.

We'd asked what she would like to do there. 'When I go to the seaside,' she said, 'I make sand castles!' So I found an empty plant pot and we took the small metal shovel we use for the Aga and put them in the back of the Range Rover with three wheelchairs, two dogs and the picnic things and we collected Hilda and went to Blackpool. We drove slowly along the promenade, from north to south, looking for a parking area. Emilie's eyes were popping. When we were children it was so much more gentle on the eye than it is today. Brilliant colour offends me. I think it was much more gaudy than the French girl had expected. Certainly there is no place quite like Blackpool. There is no compulsion to see the sea for the round-the-year, ready-to-light illuminations and the cartoons on the trams are a distraction! I must be one of the few people who have never seen the autumn lights. Then they must be quite spectacular but before switch-on they are unnecessary clutter on the sea front.

We could not find anywhere to park and unload our vehicle until we reached St. Anne's-on-Sea where the tide was almost out of sight. The wide, twice daily washed sands were nearly empty. We pushed the three wheelchairs onto the beach and had our picnic. We watched Emilie, our happy teenager, make her sand castle and then she and Margaret took the dogs to meet the incoming tide. Compared with most days, that very wet summer, a weak sun shone all day but failed to dry the sand. I seem to remember that drifts were blown, daily, onto the promenade when we were children and that, if there was a breeze, its stinging particles could be felt on our bare legs. That day, as on the birthday visit of the previous summer, there was no dry sand but the day was a success. There was no doubt about that. If we had had a teenager attracted to slot machines and theme parks, we would have been sorry company for her.

So, too, the day we took Emilie to Malham was also a success, though that was one of very heavy showers, typical of the wet summer. Harry had never seen Malham Cove. In the days when he could have walked the quite considerable distance, along the bank of the baby river to the famous rock face, we had not had a car to get us to Malham in the first place. Recently the National Trust has made a path wide enough and smooth enough on which to push a wheelchair. We decided to disregard the possibility of a heavy shower and risk taking Harry for his first close-up view of the giant face. The track begins elevated above the stream, which flows from beneath the Cove a considerable distance away. Then it appears to drop quite steeply towards the floor of the valley and I caffled, as we say in Yorkshire.

'You go without us,' I said to Margaret. 'It's too far and too steep. I'll push Harry back to the village. You and Emilie go alone.'

So the two of them strode off alone, downhill, and when they had gone a few yards, Emilie turned. I was still standing watching their progress and I waved. Emilie turned to Margaret and halted her. 'I can't leave them,' she said. 'It's too sad. Harry has never seen the Cove!' So she came and took the handles and pushed the wheelchair all the way there and all the way back. Emilie is a rare breed. There should be a preservation order on such!

Chapter Six

Autumn tints and shadows, winter storms and snow,
Daffodils in springtime and the hills aglow

Campfire round

A unty Mary had not had what she calls her MOT, her annual check-up. Our doctor had left the premises he had used for many years and joined a larger practice on the opposite side of town. Because of his removal this annual test for someone as old as Aunty Mary had been forgotten. I reminded the receptionist and asked that Harry have this annual opportunity because of his disability and the fact that he never had cause to go to the doctor. Every six weeks or so his prescription had been renewed for the last thirty-five years but Harry had very infrequently had to see a doctor. I thought he should now he was in his seventies. The appointment was just to see the nurse for blood and urine tests and a check on blood pressure.

We found the new premises very difficult to cope with. The car park was spacious but full and our very old Range Rover was too big to leave conveniently. I had come without Margaret. I parked far away and struggled with the wheelchair alone. Previously we had, on those very rare occasions, parked just behind the surgery and Harry had walked in. At this considerable distance a wheelchair was essential. The swing doors into the clinic wouldn't stay open and I had to call for help. Then I had to return to the car to collect Aunty Mary. She came away with a clean bill of health and Harry, it was found, was extremely low on white blood cells. He was given an urgent appointment with the haematologist at the hospital. His immunity would be very low, we were told. One of the doctors in the practice told us it would mean he could not take antibiotics by mouth but, if he had an infection, we must insist this was given by an injection.

The pre-autumn holiday was preceded by a rush of guests. For many years, indeed right from our 1981 beginning, Mr Van Caeneghem had been coming from Belgium. We loved him. He was now in his eighties and his family had insisted that he did not come. Two years earlier he had been taken ill here and been treated in our local hospital for pneumonia. He phoned first to say he was coming, then to say his daughter would not allow him to make the journey. A few days later he phoned to say he was coming and would we see that he was met at the airport. Friends he knew well who were staying at The Currer, collected him from Yeadon and 'a red carpet' was laid in welcome. He asked permission, as usual, to phone home and announce his safe arrival.

'They do not know I have come!' he said. 'I did not tell them because they would have prevented me!' We spent an anxious week hoping he did not need any hospital treatment. He is a very nice man, a retired actor, a wise, kind gentleman whose annual visit we, and our guests, have always enjoyed immensely.

The disturbing news we had been given about Harry worried us but did not seem to affect his general health. No medication was available to right this disorder. It was just necessary that we knew his immunity was impaired. The summer deluge continued and fields were saturated and rivers swollen. One of Harry's ambitions had been to go to Kilnsey Show which is held at the beginning of September. The opportunity had never presented itself for us to satisfy this craving so we decided to make one and go regardless of the wet weather. We drove up soggy Wharfedale with our two old ladies in the back complaining that we shouldn't be going any where near a cattle showground in these conditions. They were right but it didn't deter us. We pulled onto the mud of the rutted field and parked. We left them still grumbling on the back seat and attempted to push Harry wherever was possible and laughed as if it were a huge joke, which indeed it was.

The mud was inches deep everywhere and the wheels of the chair sank into the mire. The mood of the crowd was commendable. Everyone was trying to make believe they were having a great time but the fell runners were falling all over the place and tractors were continually employed pulling out cars. It was a fiasco and Harry was acutely disappointed. One sister had to push while the other pulled. We had hysterics but his enjoyment had already taken a blow by the criticism of the two old ladies and this was the last straw. When we eventually returned to the Range Rover, muddied and red in the face, the OAP reception helped not at all. Harry and Margaret and I could cope with weather. We have been doing so for long enough. And we can laugh. We have to, for our life is a situation comedy, but Harry could not cope with the disapproval of the old ladies. So much for a visit to Kilnsey Show! We will not go again while Aunty Mary lives!

As often happens in very wet summers, there comes a day which is blisteringly hot. One Sunday, when the Pennine hillside steamed and sweat poured down our faces, Mr Davison from Upper Transfield rang to say our boundary wall was down and cattle could get out. We had plenty of grass and we could see the satisfied herd chewing their cud on pasture from which moisture was rising in a thin mist. There was no immediate need to make a dash for the gap reported, so we filled a flask with coffee and took Harry up in the Range Rover to investigate.

First we drove round the boundary along the south of our land and, where the view was stupendous, we paused to have our picnic. Breaches in the wall seldom take too long to repair. The heat was intense and the distance shrouded in the haze peculiar to very hot weather. We leisurely enjoyed being away from the farmhouse for a while. We had no premonition of the scale of the damage to the wall reported down. Gaps, capable of letting a whole herd escape, usually only take half an hour to repair. On this memorable occasion a hundred metres of wall had literally been pushed over to a level all one hundred and seventy cattle could have stridden at once. Along the low side of the wall the pushed-over stone lay in a ribbon. This, we were sure, could only have been done with a gang of youths all pushing at once.

We did not speak. Margaret went to the west and I to the east and, in all our years of hard work, we have never performed as we had to do on that very hot Sunday afternoon, throwing stones back onto that wall to raise it sufficiently to deter the herd. We did not stop to choose our material carefully. Every stone we lifted we threw back onto the hundred-metre stretch. We sweated until we were as wet as we would be in a downpour and our faces became beetroot red. We manhandled boulders until our muscles were in cramp. We'd come without gloves and our hands became torn and bleeding but we raised that wall until it was four foot high. It would not have won any competition but it was secure.

'Are you all right?' Margaret eyed me anxiously when we met. 'You are red. Do you think you've got blood pressure?'

'Can't have. I'd be dead by now!'

Indeed we must be fit to pull out of the bag of energy what we did on that very hot afternoon. It was good fortune that Sunday evening meals are salads and the trifles, to follow, had already been made. We reported the damage to the police who asked what would be the cost of repair. Fortunately that stretch was the next on Tim's agenda. Within weeks he would pull it down and rebuild it to Countryside Stewardship specifications. It would cost £18 a square meter and that would total £2000.

Late in September the second *ad lib* self-feeder milk machine was delivered and the two inventions were wheeled to the manger and the tubes and teats arranged for the calf buying, which would follow close on the heels of our return from holiday. The first had been so successful we had no qualms about buying a second, in spite of the expense. Little by little we were equipping ourselves for whatever the future might hold in store. Aunty Mary had stopped working and Harry, who had always been a minor care, was becoming more and more immobile, more and more dependent. Come what may, we had to endeavour to be prepared. We were leaving solvency very late in life. We were fully aware of that!

We were certainly not prepared for the dramatic events in the sitting room on the Saturday night, six days before we left. We prepare to leave The Currer by selling the twenty-three month old cattle. Routine procedures go well for they are planned and organised and well rehearsed over many years. The rounding up of the cattle, the assembling of the Cattle Passports, the loading of bullocks for transport to Otley and the waiting in the auction ring for our turn in the draw, to show and sell. We do not enjoy any part of this annual performance but we are professional about it and know the way to conduct it successfully with little stress to animals and, though we are pretty wound up, the most awful day of the year passes. Time is a kind friend. We had put the moderate cheque into the bank to pay for the winter feed and turned our attention to the immediate task of preparing for holiday in Aberporth.

It is useless to try to be prepared for pre-holiday events other than to say expect 'something' to happen, for it will. There is no doubt about that! What it will be is the mystery. I suppose, if I am being cynical, this adds to the excitement and provides suitable subject matter for my autobiography. The events of that September Saturday could never have been predicted in our house where animals, domesticated and wild, live outside. Only the dogs walk in. As Margaret is mostly out, even they are seldom in the house. Everything else has comfortable accommodation outside. The wildlife of our sheds and pastures only infrequently trespass. An occasional bird has flown down the chimney. Now and then a goat kid has been known to take a look inside. A large sow once entered and up-turned the bread-bin. Frogs have been seen in the front porch and silver trails on the parquet floor tell us slugs have been in and gone out again. Donkeys step their front feet onto The Mistal cottage kitchen floor but never come near ours. Hitch-hiking mice, brought here by a lorry load of straw and not born in the barn, have occasionally had to be taught proper manners, but in general the wildlife know their place. Apart from these minor diversions our animals could be classed as 'hefted'. They know their space. They are never hungry so they respect unfenced boundaries. Only when new to The Currer do they make the mistake of trespass. Our cats are excellent hunters. Only rarely do we see a mouse when we lift a bale, so either they are few in number or know how to conduct their lives in secret. Rats are not common, seldom resident. Like tourists they are on the move. They come and go, thank goodness, and keep their distance. Father used to say that if there were weasels there wouldn't be rats and we see those sometimes.

The weekend of our departure, in the autumn, coincides with a Belfast Dog Show which Dorothy always attends. Because of this Sandra and her family hold a get-together weekend prior to Dorothy's return. When we first opened for holiday-makers, Sandra was able to look after our business for the whole fortnight but since marriage and children she has been too busy. The September weekend is enough.

There are not many scraps of food left in our hungry household. Guests leave nothing on plates and we eat whatever returns from the table in tureens. The geese thoroughly enjoy bread leftovers and goats eat the external leaves of cabbages and cauliflowers. There are some leavings which, every few days, Margaret offers to the birds. Her practice was, and I emphasise the past tense of that verb, to put these scraps behind the house where crows and magpies removed them immediately, we thought.

On the Saturday before leaving for Wales we were all sitting round the fire in the front room, having just watched the news. I only saw a movement, it was so quick! Something went from the hearth, across the rug and disappeared under Harry's chair. Aunty Mary saw nothing and is very deaf so did not hear Harry splutter and Margaret say, 'Did you see that?'

'What was is?'

'A rat!' she whispered. 'It's under Harry's chair!'

We didn't know what to do. It was important that we got Aunty Mary to bed as quickly as possible. This is not easy because she is so slow but it was unthinkable that she should know. She is petrified of a mouse. We remembered she and her sister had gone to sleep at her brother's house, the time they had seen a mouse when living in the street. If she saw a rat she would have a stroke.

'Are you ready for bed?' I asked. 'I'm tired and I can't go until you do.'

There was no indication that she would go quickly or even go at all and I began to panic. If the intruder moved again and she saw it she would not sleep all night. She's not a countrywoman. She is not animal-friendly at the best of times. She is scared even of a beetle and has hysteria over a moth flitting round the light.

I said, 'Aunty, we want you to go to bed. Now. Margaret has just seen a little hamster run under Harry's chair. We want to catch it. Someone will be worried about it.' Any sensible person would have replied, 'Don't be silly!' Margaret nearly exploded with laughter. Harry chuckled openly. Maybe the news just did not register but she did gather up her belongings and she did go to bed. We were flabbergasted.

Without her Harry couldn't keep quiet. He'd seen a rat! It was under his chair! Did Aunty Mary believe such a silly story? It was all right for him to laugh. We had to do something. Quickly! We opened the little door leading from the sitting room into the cubicle containing the wash-basin and the open door to the toilet. In the four hundred years before we came, the outside door to this was its only entry. When we had built on the wash kitchen we had opened an entry into it from within and much later had asked our builder-cum-everything to put in a downstairs toilet. The window was wide open.

'I opened that. It's my fault,' Margaret said.

We opened the door onto the outside and left an inviting exit for a rat which was probably very frightened indeed. The room is big with an added alcove Mother always called 'The New Do' and we could not police the escape route and disturb furniture at the same time. We never actually saw the intruder go but we eventually agreed he must have done so for no amount of under-furniture poking and chair shifting caused a sighting.

We sat shivering within the cold draught of the open door for a long time, until we could feel quite sure the animal must have escaped. A rat is a big animal, unlike a mouse which can, so a pest controller told TV viewers, get through any hole through which a biro can be passed. A rat, we thought, was too big to hide.

'Well,' Margaret said at last, 'That's a first. That's never happened before. It's the food I've been putting out at the back. I won't do it again!'

We were quite shaken. Rats are something we can well do without. We hadn't seen one in the barn since it was built and the disturbance, caused by pulling down the old and building the new, dispersed any vermin we had. We went to bed fairly sure that we had no unwanted lodger, but next morning, when Margaret opened the sitting room door, the first thing she saw was the rat. We couldn't believe it, but we were alone. Aunty Mary and Harry were safely in bed. We had no guests likely to interrupt so we closed the door firmly behind us and we moved furniture to clear a road to the outside door. We blockaded any escape route and we guided the intruder out. I saw him go through the back door. We heaved a sigh of relief and re-instated all the furniture. Margaret hadn't seen the animal go out but I had so we had some breakfast, looking at each other occasionally and opening our eyes wide. What next, we wondered? Having eaten Margaret went back into the sitting room and the first thing she saw was a rat.

'I don't know what you saw,' she said accusingly. 'Whatever it was it wasn't the rat.'

'It was! I know it was. I saw that rat go out of the door!' A mouse is quick and small and one can be forgiven if one imagines a scutter, but a rat is big and slow and I'd seen it plainly.

Once again we went through the ritual of barricading doors and corners. We used the mattress and base of the bed-behind-the-curtain, we overturned the chairs and we disturbed the rat. Margaret saw it go out herself and was satisfied. She thinks I am incompetent where animals are concerned. When the room was once again back to normal Harry and Aunty Mary had breakfast and were put into the Range Rover and Aunty Mary was taken to and left at Chapel. When Harry and I returned Margaret greeted us with, 'There is still a rat in the front room!' She was nearly in tears.

Until then we had believed there was but one rat. Then we remembered that rats and mice are never loners. One mouse may seem happy enough hunting alone but both are family orientated. Rats follow their leader. How else could the Pied Piper have been so successful? We hadn't been dealing with one, there had been three! The last was the most difficult to remove. Alone he was frantic. Only Margaret with the fireguard as shield diverted him successfully in the direction of the door.

We did not put back the furniture immediately. Behind that closed door we searched every possible retreat. We lifted up the carpet edges to make sure there were no holes. Margaret is addicted to looking for mouse holes in holiday cottages and B&B places but we found no internal entry. To make doubly sure Margaret put bait in the drystone wall below the sitting room window and we left our sixteenth-century chest proud of the inside wall and put a pile of bait behind that.

I am sure those rats were of the travelling variety, just passing through. We never saw them again, alive or dead, and no bait was taken but it was not quite the end of the story because, having just had a picnic by the riverside at Winslow, we were heading for the Travel Inn at Wrexham, when Margaret suddenly whispered, 'I never removed that bait in the sitting room!' Sandra has three small children and a puppy and we had left her with a pile of bait behind a chest proud of the wall. We stopped at the first telephone booth and alerted her. 'We had a little mouse last week,' we lied. 'We left some bait and forgot!' I wonder if Sandra looked at the large pile and wondered why on earth so much was left for one small mouse.

This was an incident we kept secret from everyone, until now, so we were unable to share our laughter when, some months later, watching a television programme called Holidays from Hell, we heard distraught tourists abroad being reassured that the infestation was not rats but hamsters. We couldn't even tell Aunty Mary what we were laughing at!

Then the alarming incident had to take second place and be quickly designated to the history book because on the Thursday, the day before we left for Aberporth, the receptionist rang from the doctor's surgery to tell us Harry's thirty-year long prescription of Phenytoin must be changed to Epilim. He must come off the original drug immediately. A prescription would be waiting for him on Friday morning and must be collected before midday. We were taken by surprise. A supreme effort had to be made to leave early and pick up the prescription, en route, before the surgery closed. We were not able to see the doctor and we were going on a two-day journey to a fairly remote coastal village in Wales. We went to the nearest chemist and the pharmacist made us a print-out of the instructions appertaining to the new drug. These instructed him not to take Gaviscon or Cemetidine within one-to-two hours of the drug and told us the side effects may be nausea and an initial loss of hair. We were decidedly nervous and agreed not to start the new medication until we reached Aberporth, where we had a fairly dodgy fortnight, seeking help from the local hospital and the pharmacist at Boots Chemist in Cardigan. We stopped the Cemetidine altogether but during the three-month run-up to Christmas problems with the Epilim increased substantially.

We bought seventy-eight calves and put them on the two milk machines and all went well. Minor farming problems were over-shadowed by Harry's reaction to the new drug. It made him aggressive, mostly towards himself, so that he tore his fingernails to bits and with the jagged edges scratched his arms and bald pate until they bled. We were convinced this was due to the change of drugs and a discussion with a neighbour, whose adopted child had had to be taken off them due to aggression, increased our suspicion.

Christmas came and went with a pleasant Holy Day picnic at Bolton Abbey. For the first time in many years, Janet did not visit us on Boxing Day. Our concern for her was growing but her spirits continued to be high. She was going to go on a journey to some place she believed would be good. As soon as we had a minute we went over to Leeds to see her. Her body looked ill but not her laughter. It bubbled up from within as it always had. She was fond of cats and a stray was giving her great pleasure. 'It's been sent to make me happy,' she said.

Shortly into the New Year Harry had a blood test and this time he was short of red cells and was given a transfusion. This helped him physically but the aggression remained and stressed not only him but us also. There was also a different kind of stress which will be appreciated only by those coping with another's handicap and that was our almost impossible task of getting Harry to the doctor's surgery. Both Margaret and I had to go. Parking was so difficult. Getting the wheelchair out of the back of the car was a two-man job. Visiting the doctor was a new experience. All his life Harry had been healthy. A phone call only had been necessary to renew his prescription. Now a visit had to be made or a letter sent to do what the telephone had done. It is half a mile to our post box. We had all the winter chores, the bales to carry, the animals to feed so we decided to do what we should have done years ago, or at least when the doctor's premises moved. We changed to the village doctor's practice and almost all our problems were solved. The best thing was that the haematologist said Harry's blood disorder was old age, not

Phenytoin. She said there was no reason for change and, slowly, very gradually, the old medication was resumed. That Harry recovered well from the
shattering experience we attribute to a Skipton homeopath. We were advised
to try this lady by Joan MacInnes, a pupil of mine who had been a Guide,
camping many years with us in the Hebrides. She had become a nurse and
later in her career she had counselled those with cancer and ministered to
those in a hospice for the terminally ill. Long before Father died, in 1979,
she and her husband Steve were helping her parents house-sit at The Currer.
She had reared a daughter and twin boys but had returned to nursing in time
to be staff nurse in the surgical ward when Margaret had an operation. She
was working among cancer sufferers when Mother was diagnosed in 1990 and
her knowledge was invaluable.

Almost immediately she had been taken ill herself and eventually ME had
been diagnosed. Her help had come from complementary medicine. She told
us to take Harry to Sue Asquith in Skipton. No harm can come of homeopathy and, as Margaret has proved with animals, a great deal of good can
sometimes result. Accepted medical advice told us Harry's blood would not
return to normal. It was continually monitored and very occasionally it was
boosted by a transfusion, but mostly tests said one wasn't necessary. No one
knows how indebted we are to Joan and to Sue Asquith, in Skipton.

We did not want to have to cope with anyone being ill. No one does. Aunty
Mary continued in sound health and so did her very old friend, and Harry's
was on track again. As Colin from Australia said, so say we. He comes with
his disabled wife to revisit family in Bradford and they stay for six weeks every
two or three years. The year he brought his elderly parents as well was quite
traumatic. One day we said with authority, for we have problems and we knew
how things were for him, 'Are you all right, Colin?'

'I'm fine,' he replied. It was one of the decrepit family's good mornings.
'If they're all right, I'm all right.' That's how it is with us. It doesn't matter
how annoying guests are, and those at the beginning of the season can be
impossible! But, if family and animals are fine, so are we.

A party of seven photographers wanted self-catering accommodation for
four days. I suggested both cottages for the price of one for the whole week,
just £60. The leader phoned several times. The two cottages were one above
the other, I said. Yes, they could all eat together but two cottages would give
them double the number of bedrooms, a bedroom each nearly. If they used
the alcove bed they need not share at all. Just what they wanted, he said. No
deposit was sent. There was barely time for that.

It was very cold. I turned on the heat and made up the beds and saw that
everything was cosy for their expected late arrival of 9 p.m. They did not
come and at 11.30pm they phoned to say they were lost at Micklethwaite on

the other side of the valley. I gave instructions and eventually, long after midnight, their mini-bus drove into the yard and parked close behind our Range Rover. I showed them into the lighted warmth of the cottages and said, 'Goodnight', and that I'd see them in the morning.

I went to bed. Margaret never follows immediately. About 1 a.m. she conducted her last check of the calves and put out the lights. The cottage lights were all on and there was some activity between house and mini-bus. 'Is everything all right?' she called. 'Goodnight!'

Coming to bed she heard the minibus being moved. Good, she thought. We don't like being imprisoned from behind. Rising early next morning I noticed that the photographers had got up and away before me on whatever work project they were here for. We expected them back in the evening but they did not come and next morning I unlocked the doors and went in only to find they had never stayed at all. Not a bed had been slept in. None of the electric had been switched off. Only when the money in the meter was used had lights and heating ceased. Margaret had not heard the mini-bus being re-parked. She had heard it driving away. The only evidence that they had even been within the cottages was a full bin of empty beer cans. Though I wrote twice we received no money and no explanation! Things like this do not matter if our nuclear family and our animals are well but we are allowed to spit a bit and we do. It always seems to happen when we are at our most accommodating, when we are trying our hardest to please, when it is winter-time and we are fully occupied feeding cattle.

For some time we had been discussing a new floor covering in our three kitchens. The farmhouse kitchen was currently carpeted. When we first came to The Currer we had paid for it to be tiled. It was a luxury, one of the very few we allowed ourselves at the beginning. Mother had made rag rugs. She was incredible. She had not only semi-covered the kitchen floor but she had fully carpeted the first floor corridor, all eighteen yards of it, and the stone staircase. The variety of tiles available in the fifties had not withstood the years. When they began to crumble we laid a carpet over them. This Margaret and Father bought from a man at the door. It was enormous but it cost £60 and I remember being critical when, on returning from school, I found they had spent so much! The salesman had said it was a ship's carpet and I had to admit, years later, that it had been money well spent. It endured all the traffic of three decades. In particular it withstood the dirt of the barn conversion. We washed it repeatedly and it came up like new. Strips of it remain to this day, years later.

But there comes a time when things have to be renewed. I had laid the lino in both our other, uncarpeted kitchens. Sooner or later I knew the hygiene inspector would insist we had this done professionally. One freezer was leaking. She would notice that. Where there is water, joinings and wall edges must be perfect or it will run beneath and I was ready to hand over, to a skilled craftsman, the jigsaw of laying it down the steps which separate the two kitchens and extending it through the door and into the downstairs loo.

Since we had become caterers, a carpet in our farmhouse kitchen was not ideal so we drove over to a firm on the outskirts of Leeds and ordered inch-thick parquet tiles for it and non-slip, industrial lino for the rest. It would take about a week, the firm manager said. He told us to remove all furniture from each room so that his craftsman could work. We are getting old for this lifting of heavy furniture lark. The B&B kitchen equipment went into the shower room. The old freezer we took to the tip. Tables and kitchen cabinets went into the sitting room where Margaret and Harry and I slept for three weeks, he on the bed behind the curtain and we on the floor. Aunty Mary was confined to her bedroom, access to which, most of the time, was barred. It may seem to others that it is a nonsense to have empty bedrooms in the B&B area and to opt to sleep on the floor but the thought never enters our head. If it did we would dismiss it as wholly impossible with brother and Aunty and dogs. The farmhouse is home and the B&B for guests ...

Those three weeks we remember as some of the most difficult we have ever spent. The inconvenience was offset with the ease with which we can now clean floors. We have a particular liking for parquet tiled ones and these Canadian maple ones we left unstained. Harry was not there when a visiting cousin's husband said to his wife, 'Look! They've got an artificial wood floor!'

On being told Harry said, 'What did you say?'

'That it isn't artificial,' I smiled.

Harry had a lovely sense of humour. With a wicked gleam in his eye he pointed at me and said, 'Rockefeller!'

We have an affinity with parquet tiles. We once laid nearly ten thousand of them all over the floor of our conversion. They were not new. We had found them in a huge pile in a hayfield at Wyke and bought them, uncleaned, for just £100. Their history and ours coincided for many weeks in the summer of 1980.

There was a buzz at the March Guide Reunion. A year ago I had said, 'Two thousand. Maybe!' Nothing was going to deter these young middle-aged ladies, who had sailed to Tiree in 1957. They were unstoppable. Their shouts to return were not to be silenced. Whatever the obstacles they were determined we would overcome them and we would celebrate the year of the millennium by returning together to see if the magic they had experienced when they were young was still to be found.

'Remember when we rode the sun?'

Would it be the same? Would they remember the island or each other?

All were married with grown children and even grandchildren. Would they still be able to dance to pipe and accordion? Would the campfire kindle the same spirit, would it create the same magic?

'Remember when we'd just begun?'

Only Margaret and I rested comfortably in the knowledge that it would.

So the seeds were sown. The idea was conceived and the gestation period would be fourteen months and then, God willing, we'd ride the sun again.

April and Easter came and with it guests galore, and Denis from Lyon and one day the phone rang. It was Barbara Sykes from Golcar Farm, at Eldwick. She is a capable shepherdess who has a successful business giving sheepdog experiences and excellent advice to interested people from all over the country and beyond. She even offers collie owners the opportunity to try working their own pet collies and she will train sheep owners how to use their dogs. We rank her among the professionals and support her by offering accommodation to her clients, who come from a distance and need somewhere to stay while they attend her interesting sessions.

Olga Beardswood happened to be visiting us and was being entertained in the sitting room when I got up to answer the phone. Barbara said she hoped she had not put me in a spot but she'd just given my name to a caller wishing to book a sheepdog experience in July. It was for a blind date, she said.

'What's the problem?' I couldn't see one for we frequently house people who have kept the Sheepdog Experience a secret from a husband or a child for whom they've booked it as a birthday present.

'I said Blind Date,' she emphasised her statement. 'Blind Date. You know. Cilla Black!'

I was stunned. 'You've what?'

'I've had to give your name to the producer of Blind Date. He's just phoned and booked a young couple who will choose to have a sheepdog experience in the Yorkshire Dales and he wanted suitable accommodation.'

'Well, ours isn't.' I was firm about that.

'Well,' she said. 'I offered him a five star hotel in Ilkley. He didn't want that. I suggested a family-run hotel locally and he told me to keep going so I said that there was a farmhouse across the valley. He said that was what he wanted. He's going to ring you. I'm awfully sorry!'

'Well, we're not suitable,' I insisted. 'We're not posh enough. We haven't got a licence. The man must be crazy!'

'He'll ring you. I thought I'd better tell.' We laughed together. We actually thought it was very funny.

I went into the sitting room and Olga and Denis and all the family thought it was funny too, then the phone rang again and this producer asked, as Barbara said he would, and I told him we were not suitable, as I had said I would. But he would not listen. He said we were just what he wanted for a 'different' July Blind Date and though I protested and even belittled our accommodation, he would not take no for an answer. I went back into the sitting room and this time only Olga laughed. She said she'd tape it and send it to Lyon. We couldn't because we haven't got a video.

Twice in the three months to July, I phoned to repeat that we were really not suitable for an occasion such as this. We had not seen many Blind Date programmes for they are shown at evening mealtime. What we remembered of the few that we had seen was that unsuspecting young couples were flown to exotic places and returned to tell Cilla Black that they hated each other. Finding that they were scheduled to go to an unlicensed farmhouse, in this country, would not be a good start. I said I thought that, not being given the excitement of a trip abroad, they should at least have splendid accommodation and that ours was sixteenth century on a working farm! Nothing I said would put the man off so we prepared to wait until whoever it was came to see for himself and nobody did. No one came to check what facilities we had for such a programme. Everything was taken on trust. Amazing!

Janet lived just long enough to laugh at the Laurel and Hardy situation we had got ourselves into. Her cancer was terminal but her humour, her faith and her determination to live life to the full, right to the end, filled us with love and admiration. Visiting her renewed our somewhat damaged faith in human beings. It is impossible to live in the modern world, with human frailties constantly being shown on television, not to sometimes wonder if evil outweighs good. A visit to Janet was to leave feeling otherwise. She displayed no weakening of character and her ability to laugh at her illness at the same time as respect it, was quite unique. She couldn't blind us to how ill she was but I am quite sure she deceived many. When she died it was inconceivable that her soul would not be elsewhere.

She had planned every bit of her funeral, including the fact that I must give the Eulogy. She wanted to be in control to the very end, and perhaps she was. The service was to be a celebration of the joy her life had been. The hymns and prayers and readings were of hope and gratitude and the church was full and the singing jubilant. Did she think that I could cope with that joy or did she know that I was incapable of that? I could only remember the other side of Janet, the one which could be deeply moved, the one which could shed many tears. I trembled a lot when delivering my prepared tribute. There was a sudden contrasting silence in the crowded church. I sincerely hope that she, in Heaven, did not mind that for a few moments I deflected the mood of jubilance to one of great sadness. There was a silence. Everyone was listening. Tears were falling. I believe they were hearing what they wanted to. To celebrate Janet's life was insufficient without the opportunity, for a moment, to mourn. Bereavements can only be healed that way. Margaret, and those that came to thank me after the service, said Janet had chosen me to do just that. Perhaps she had.

Chapter Seven

Come share my place,
a green jewel of an island in a peacock sea.

Anon

In life, especially in a farmer's life, birth and death are almost routine. Janet believed in re-birth and this is not easy to disbelieve in springtime. To hope that there is a new life ahead for animals is comforting but to think there will be another for me, in which this one I have recorded is completely forgotten, fills me with horror. Joan Entwistle reminded me, recently, that 'This is not a rehearsal!' and I think it best that both life and death should be allowed to remain a mystery. It is foolhardy to tamper with either.

Diana's second calf had a difficult entry into the world of The Currer. This time we had no Tim and so we sent for the vet and his equipment. He brought along a student and between us we didn't need any tools. Diana is an excellent mother. She only requires humans once a year. At all other times she keeps her distance and makes her own decisions. She is not a pet and never has been but she is a giver-upper when it comes to calving. Normally I couldn't touch her with a barge pole but, in labour, she will rest her head in my lap and her eyes will be lifted to Heaven, a clear indication that she thinks her end has come.

Guests named the new black baby Dodi, but to us this annual edition to our herd is always just Diana's. We hurried to the market to buy three more, slightly anxious in case the miracle did not happen twice. We bought three little Aberdeen Angus babies and she took to them immediately and they thought they were in Heaven with a real mum to suckle them.

There were two, not very minor, incidents to worry us when a holiday was less than three weeks away. Diana didn't cleanse properly and we had to recall the vet to take away the rotting afterbirth. Then a bug one of the little Angus calves had picked up at the market nearly cost him his life. Calves do come from auction with loads of germs and sick ones are put into the Poorly Pen and nurtured back to health. Having put this baby immediately into 'Care' we were loathe to take it away from Diana. The little family had the spacious luxury of the whole barn with its deep-straw carpet so Margaret decided to take a chance and leave the baby to maternal nursing. She helped by giving the necessary antibiotics daily but the rest she scarily left to nature. Mark, delivering a necessary load of straw, said the calf would die but Little Toughie was so named because he lived and because Janet, who loved little boys, so named a farmer's four year old, when we were in Denmark nearly forty years ago.

We rarely stopped thinking about Janet in those after-the-funeral days. Although we did not know it then, we had a year ahead which would cause us another worry over a friend with what we believe is a far worse disease than cancer. Janet had remained vocal until she died. She was a born dreamer and philosopher, talking in depth and provoking conversation. She had talked frankly about dying and had no problem with the inevitable. She was just very short of time. Returning from a visit to Janet the mind was refreshed. Her deepest thoughts and ideas had been on the tip of her tongue ready to be expressed and shared.

With Betty it was different. We had first met in teacher training college fifty-one years earlier and had become life long friends. Though she only lived ten miles away we rarely met except at College Reunion in Ripon and at our every-other-year get-together here at The Currer. Occasionally she brought her toddler grandchild over to see the animals. The child was called Emily and Betty annually brought her to see our Emilie, from France. She had done so in August '98 and we didn't see her again until the April '99 Reunion. In the August she had confessed to a vague awareness that her hand was not moving quite as it should. The problem had increased and begun to affect all her movements and in March she was diagnosed as having motor neurone disease. Another close college friend brought her to the April gathering and we were all alarmed at the rapid progress of the illness. Her mobility was decreasing fast and her speech was going but her fun-loving personality was unchanged. At nearly seventy, her youthful ability to poke fun at herself was still there. It seems to me, as I write this, that I have collected somewhat extraordinary friends. Betty was no exception.

After Janet's illness we were looking forward to a period of freedom from the gnawing worry of another's misfortune. Harry was improving fast, Harris would soon be seen on the horizon. We were poised to feel young again and then there was Betty. Batty Dalby, we used to call her. For the two years we were at Ripon we were taught to be dedicated teachers in a Church of England College, but life there had been tremendous fun and the roots of that had been in Betty Dalby. She had nurtured in all of us the ability to laugh. We did so until our ribs hurt, until we had genuine pain over the simplest of things. The war was not long over. We had no television and no outside college entertainment. We were restricted with rationing and shortage of money. I don't think we ever listened to radio but we had fun. We were trained to teach children physical education by pretending to be children ourselves. During this well-remembered lecture in the hall we used as a gymnasium, we were given responsibility individually for small apparatus. The lecturer, demonstrating what we should do at the beginning of each lesson, said, 'Tell me your jobs.'

There was an answer from many of us calling out the apparatus which was our responsibility. Skipping ropes, hoops, mats, balls. When it became Betty's turn she said, 'I'm bats!' For the rest of our time in college she was Batty Dalby. She and her husband had come to Harry's seventieth birthday and had met Janet for the first time. Janet had not joined my Guide Company until 1951 when I had been a year out of college but, on being introduced to Betty in 1997 she said, 'Oh! Are you Batty Dalby?' I had forgotten and perhaps so had Betty but Janet, who'd never met her, remembered. Life is made up of little things and fun out of hardly anything at all. If, and I think we have, brought fun into the lives of many children and holiday-makers, we have brought it in the most un-material way.

Margaret was approaching her sixtieth birthday. Her ticket to a state pension would come while we were on holiday and it encouraged her to make a somewhat comical decision. We had had many stressful years of late departures when going on holiday. Aunty Mary was getting up later every day and leaving before midday had become impossible. When long-distance walking, or driving, or attacking a heavy workload, it is advisable to start early and begin refreshed.

'If we could just leave now,' Margaret usually said when everything was done before bed on the night before leaving. Instead all the unavoidable morning disorder of breakfast for guests and rousing our dependants, dressing and shaving and getting breakfast and filling flasks, making sandwiches and beds and re-checking cattle, wearied us unforgivably before a long journey. If Dorothy and George could just have come late evening and we could have crept out while order reigned it would have been lovely.

'We will!' Margaret said. 'We'll slip out and spend my first pension on a blissfully free night at Skipton Travel Lodge. Next morning we will have no Currer chores.' So we booked an overnight stay, just ten miles away and those we told thought it the funniest thing they'd heard for ages.

There was an exceptional flush of grass. Our cattle are let out to graze all winter, if the weather permits. There is, of course, very little for them to eat but the transfer from dried food, handed out by us, morning and night, to self-service salad is never as sudden at The Currer as it is on farms where animals are penned indoors all the winter months and only given their freedom in the spring. Ours had been getting used to the richer diet gradually but the exceptional growth took us all by surprise. Usually grass won't grow quickly enough for us with last year's harvest dwindling in the barn, a holiday approaching and one hundred and seventy mouths to feed. Margaret was worried. It is normal for manure to be quite thin in springtime. It may be because the grass is rich or it may mean the cattle need worming. The calves we always treat before we go north but the big bullocks are not supposed to need it. Repeated dosage in their youth should have made them immune. Margaret commented on the fact that their manure was like mint sauce, mint sauce with a liberal amount of vinegar. If they had worm we must do something about it and not wait until our return.

Margaret rang the vet who said many of his customers were reporting this condition and that he was sure a flush of grass was the cause. Nevertheless Margaret took a sample down to the surgery for analysis. A positive result would have meant worming the whole herd and not just the calves, but it came back negative and I, for one, breathed a sigh of relief. We had enough to do!

The idea that the first lap of our journey north would be a mere ten miles, in evening daylight, was the most comforting thought we had had for ages. To rise next morning free of the disrupting activity of The Currer promised to be bliss. There would be no telephone call to delay us as it often did. Guests would not hold us up with well wishing and goodbyes. Margaret's idea was great and if people wanted to laugh they were welcome to do so.

Everything was going to plan. The very last room to tackle is always the kitchen. We start at the extremities of our domain working inward until both of us end up in the kitchen. Margaret is outside, beginning at the boundary, which must be secure, and I deal with the indoor jobs working first in the B&B and cottages, then the upstairs of our farmhouse while the kitchen takes the flak. Animals and guests always come first but glancing at the clock assured me that we were on time. What was done no one would undo before our escape.

By 2 p.m. the guest rooms were spanking clean and our sitting room door closed on tidiness. There was a smell of polish, the family beds had been remade for Dorothy to occupy and I was vacuuming the carpeted passage and preparing to do the staircase when Margaret returned from outside to help sort out the untidy kitchen. In our farmhouse, as in most, entry from outside is via the kitchen. The sitting room is tucked away somewhere beyond which means the first thing visiting friends see is the kitchen. Mostly this does not matter at all for we find guests think our warm kitchen with its huge pine table and welsh dressers is a little bit of Heaven. It might be, but not a few hours before we leave for holiday. Then, I assure you, it resembles a rummage sale! There are cases to fall over, washing is hanging to dry above the Aga and the 8ft by 4ft table is littered with the conglomeration of small articles which must accompany us. They are swept into a holdall at the last minute and when the table is clear then we go.

Above the noise of the vacuum I heard Margaret's plaintive cry, 'Oh, Jean, you'll never guess!' I switched off and came downstairs. Two men were getting out of their car and coming towards the house. My heart sank to my boots. It was Jack Clay who had lived on our neighbour's farm when we were children and we lived in the village. His aunt's farm was adjacent to ours and he had been sent from Preston to spend the war years with her and had stayed permanently. He had shared that era with us and sadly this was the only memory his mind could retain. He remembered helping Father and me bring hay from Heather Lodge in the deep snow of 1947. Recent events were forgotten almost immediately, but how we had lived and how he started in business were as clear in his mind as yesterday should have been. He could talk with us as if his illness did not exist but he did not know that the man with him was his son. In our cluttered kitchen, at our piled-up table, eating scones Dorothy had made for us to take with us, we reminisced with him easily for two hours.

His has been a life which should be remembered, for from nothing he amassed an empire. From a stall selling wood and do-it-yourself tools he rose to building hundreds of houses, an exclusive fish and chip restaurant, a successful clothing venture and arguably farmed the best pedigree herd of cattle in the area. He could talk farming with Margaret as if nothing was wrong. He was as at home in our disordered kitchen as in his own lovely house with its Olympic-size swimming pool and, had we meant to leave in the hour, there was no way we could have sent him away. When the two men eventually went we had not just lost two hours, we had lost momentum, rhythm and direction. It was almost impossible to pick up the threads and accelerate.

In darkness, at well after 11 p.m., we arrived at Skipton Travel Lodge well and truly exhausted. We had meant the ten miles to be in daylight. How we hate driving in the dark. Both Margaret and I dearly wished we were spending the night at home. But, pulling into the car park, a feeling of peace began to envelop us and the holiday mood took over. We'd done the right thing, after all.

The receptionist indicated where I put our address and car registration number. I passed the form back to her.

'Keighley?' she queried.

'Go on, laugh if you want to. It will do us all good!' I said and we relaxed. Scotland here we come!

A holiday in the Western Isles never fails to rejuvenate us. We couldn't believe we were now all old age pensioners. Setting off on one of our favourite jaunts to the Hebrides, we felt as young as we had done backpacking many years ago. Age might be in bones but it is not in the head. Not in our heads anyway. Harris was beautiful, sunny as always by day and starlit at night. Guests from the city think that our star-studded Heaven at The Currer is incomparable but they are wrong. Lights from the town two miles away and the city not too distant pollute the sky with a vague redness non-existent in the Hebrides. There you can feel to be in space. On islands free of artificial lights the Heavens make us spellbound. Leaving John and Mamie's house, one moonlit night, I thought we would never get into the car, so hypnotic was the universe.

We totted up many more island miles on foot that year, pushing Harry in the wheelchair. He was an outdoor man. We should have taken him camping. He would have stayed outside perpetually if the British weather had let him. He did not need company either, he did not mind being alone. He loved the fresh air wherever and whenever it could be found. Most of all he loved moving in it and his wheelchair was preferable to the Range Rover. Wherever it stopped he wanted to get out which is why we bought a light-weight chair. Lifting it in and out perpetually must never become too difficult.

Harry was well again so we relaxed and found amusement in little things that would otherwise have frustrated us. We found that the powers-that-be had put toilet facilities at Horgabost. There is the most beautiful beach there from which the MacKay family sail out to Taransay, that lovely island they own and on which they keep a flock of sheep. There is an elevated plateau above this beach on which, in high season, campers pitch their tents to ensure, for themselves, sunsets out of this world. Until recently there has only been one toilet on Harris and that was at Tarbert where the boat comes in. We have long believed the islanders to be a more intelligent species so we presume that these new toilets have been built by the same idiots that have put loos for the disabled throughout the British Isles. Wheelchair user Joe Walters told me he didn't want a disabled toilet, he wanted one that worked. Most work all right if you can get in!

There are actually four toilets at Horgabost. One each for able male and female and one each for disabled ladies and gents, so more marks for Horgabost than for most places where there is only one which is in the ladies. There are thirty-degree gradient slopes to these beach toilets, which is not too steep, and a yard square, horizontal platform on which to pause to open the door. This, unfortunately, opens outwards so you have to reverse down-hill and if you self-propel your wheelchair you can't cope at all. If you are being pushed you need two carers. One to open the door and one to push you the last yard up the ramp! We had hysterics.

When coping with a disability, or with that of a dependant, it is necessary to have a somewhat earthy sense of humour so forgive me if I continue on this subject just a little longer. Those on the pier servicing the Iona ferry at Fionnphort, Mull, were impossible. The builders had kindly made facilities for both men and women. The gentleman's one was at the far end of the urinal and the ladies' one at the far end of the row of firmly closed cubicles. No woman pushing a man dare venture into a urinal and a man pushing his wife through a ladies would embarrass and be embarrassed. Almost all wheelchairs have passengers of the opposite sex to the pusher. We preferred to embarrass Harry and push him protesting into the ladies. One of us would stand apologetically outside warning newcomers that there was a man inside. In Mallaig the only disabled loo we could find was in the gents so Margaret stood, this time aggressively, outside until Harry and I reappeared. In Blackpool the unisex toilet was raised on a platform. The builder must have been told toilets for the disabled had to be higher than normal. Users had to step up and teeter dangerously and Harry had to be steadied. At Bolton Abbey the disabled facilities are through a short passage which also serves as a baby changing area. The outside door opens in and the toilet door opens out and there is not space enough between the two for the chair and the pusher. We complain to the staff every time but there is no change. Parking for the disabled, too, is often impossible. It is conveniently near the entrance to the Clog Factory in Calderdale but on a slope so steep no wheelchair user could cope.

We were ready to laugh at anything on Harris. We were not dependent on there being public conveniences, which is lucky for those in Tarbert close on Sundays. We know friends all over the island we can visit for pleasure and for purpose whenever we need to. Because there are two of us, we admit to being grateful for the ones at Horgabost. They could well be the most infrequently used ones in the country, for the holiday season is short and when all accommodation is full there are not enough holiday-makers to warrant four toilets on one almost empty beach!

There are no toilets at Northton but that does not matter for there live Jessie at No. 12 and Maggie at No. 8. It would not matter how many times we called. Sadly we rarely have time to call more than once at Jessie's and twice at Maggie's. We love her warm fire and the respite care we get as both her daughters take over Aunty Mary and Harry and relieve us of our duties. It is wonderful.

We knew we were going home to a thousand and one problems but on Harris we had hardly any and were totally relaxed. On the evening before we left, as usual, we chose to be in Luskentyre. In one way we are glad that we do not rent a cottage there because each house and each occupant is such a magnet that we may just be with them all the time and have no holiday. To talk to John MacDonald at No. 19 would please us all day. He was our crofter-host throughout all those happy camping-with-children years and his wisdom and wit are surpassed by none. His dogs are visitor-friendly to the extreme and would be all over us, all the time, if he didn't occasionally bellow at them in Gaelic. They obediently dive under the dresser only to reappear when they think he has forgotten.

At No. 8, only Farquhar of the original family of fourteen resides in the township. The old cottage where they were raised is empty now and he has built a new one for his wife and family, but the welcome she extends to us is equal to the one Lexey, his mother, and Dolly, his father, offered us for all of thirty years before they died.

Donald John is still weaving beautiful tweed at No. 6. He has extended the bungalow he inherited from his Aunty Annie whom we loved so much. Donald John's tweed is famous worldwide and though his wife is not island born her hospitality is.

Ben Angie is still at No. 4 and her son Donny has built a house within the croft. Morag is at No. 1 and she still has the most beautiful, shy dog who dives behind the chair whenever we go. Morag's is the first house on entering Luskentyre and she somehow sees us every time we pass. If we actually stayed in Luskentyre we would just hobnob with the crofters all the time and neglect the rest of the island completely.

We would frequently be down at No. 10 chatting so much to Katie and Angus that they would get fed up of us and be glad when it was time for us to go. We are so much at home with them and with their daughter Kathleen and husband Bobbie we hate to leave. We mourn the fact that Granny's cottage was pulled down when she died. We used to love her as if she were our own relation. Her sayings were so funny and she never wanted us to leave however late it was. She declared she only went to bed to give her teeth a rest.

But the last person we visit, and stay longest with, is always Rachel. She was our safety net during all those years so far away from home with other people's children. Frequently we marvel that we dared to bring so many to such a remote beach with only canvas to protect and then we remember that, when a solid shelter was needed, there was always Rachel's house, her welcome, her phone, her van and her comforting advice. She was a pillar of strength when we needed it and perhaps, had she not been there, we might never have dared.

It was with Rachel that we spent the bigger half of the evening before we sailed for Skye, and home, next morning. The atmosphere was as it always had been and Margaret remarked that she could almost believe that another camp was just behind us, that fifty children were all packed and tearful. In reality, those days were twenty years back in our personal history, yet the in-depth feeling was the same. It always is. On leaving the island there is always the comfortable awareness of success – in spite of which we nearly made an absolute failure of leaving Skye!

Throughout the holiday we had become more and more relaxed. We had a following wind and sunshine for the sail to Uig. Reaching Broadford we realised our field's-way speed had not made it possible for us to catch the 4 p.m. Armadale to Mallaig ferry but, as the islanders say, 'When God made time He made plenty of it!' We had more than enough to catch the 5.30pm. Enough time for us to pause and have something to eat. We discovered that in Broadford there is a fish and chip shop. In spite of 'mists on Ben nan Callaich' and 'rugged Cuillin soaring high' Skye always feels like the mainland, especially when you find a fish and chip shop open at 4 p.m.

We were very hungry so we pulled onto a parking area, looking beyond the Sound to the mountains on the mainland, and sent Margaret to buy us our evening meal. She found that it was an island shop after all. The fish had to be lifted out of the freezer and the chips took so long to cook she had time to sit on a chair and talk half an hour with the fish-fryer. She is always happy to chat with islanders and, having buttered bread and laid out the picnic things, I was content to absorb the wonderful view I expected to see again in two years' time but not before. Years are passing very quickly these days.

If I looked to my left I could see the Broadford Hotel where Margaret and I had stayed on our very first visit to Skye, when Margaret was just a child with a ball always in her hand. It occurred to me that Skye is an island on which we have only pitched a tent once. I almost said never but we camped one night at Uig, with Ann, prior to sailing to Harris in the early 1960s. Maybe it is because Skye has only been a place where we've had hotel accommodation which makes it feel like a return to civilisation.

It was 4.30pm when Margaret returned with our excellent evening meal. It doesn't take Aunty Mary long to eat her share. She was served first and usually got to the second course before we had finished dishing up Harry's. By that time ours was cold. It has been our lot for so many years that we have ceased to grumble. It took Harry a while to eat and he would never be hurried. After what seemed an age he asked, 'What is there to finish off with?' and I reached for the cake tin. In doing so I noticed the time and shouted, 'Nothing! Look at the time! We're going to miss the ferry!'

There was a sudden scramble. I reversed out of the car park while Margaret rescued the picnic things. We had sixteen miles to go down a single-track road. We'd not nearly enough time. The road was being widened. In parts it was finished and we could make up the time we lost where work was still in progress and traffic lights were causing delays. There are never any queues on Harris. Eventually the road works ended and the single track began. All too soon oncoming traffic told us that the ferry must be in and cars were being off-loaded.

'Make them use the passing places!' Margaret growled at me. 'You just keep going. We're going to miss it.'

It was the last ferry. We'd have to retrace our steps to Broadford and go east to Kyleakin for the bridge and the much longer route from Kyle to Fort William. Demon Darkness would harass us again. I put my foot on the accelerator. Gone was our fields-way speed. We could see the pier and the boat but we could also see the clock and knew we were going to lose. Boats belonging to Caledonian MacBraynes leave port on time. We have always known that. Only when there is a deterrent gale does the boat leave late. In May she is almost empty anyway.

It was as we'd expected. As we pulled onto the pier the open mouth of the car deck was closing and ropes were being taken from their moorings. The boat was moving. We had lost the race! I put my hand on the horn and my foot on the brake and lifted my hands in a desperate plea. For a moment the open jaws continued to close and there was an awful silence in the Range Rover. Then a miracle happened. The mouth began to open again and the ropes to tighten. The lower jaw rattled on the end of the pier and a member of the crew was beckoning that I should drive on. He motioned me straight to the foot of the invalid lift while the opened jaws began to close. We were suddenly all vocal. We said extremely nice things to that man. He helped us to get Aunty Mary and Harry out of car as if he were our best friend and he guided us up the ramp to the lift. We could feel the movement of the boat under our feet. We heard the recording that accompanies every departure. We heard the first bit. I don't think we heard the last. As we squeezed with the sailor into the lift, we heard the opening sentence, 'Welcome to The Lord of the Isles!'

We heard no more. Margaret and I echoed, 'It's The Lord of the Isles!' No wonder we were known and had received preferential treatment. This boat had served the Inner Hebrides for many years. Our Range Rover, with its distinctive roof rack and disabled occupants made us once seen never forgotten and we had been seen regularly for many years. Ever since it had been launched we had sailed on *The Lord of the Isles* and Harry had named Lusky after it.

The crewman beamed his pleasure. 'You're doing this route now,' I said.

'As from yesterday,' he answered. This is an autobiography about ordinary people getting the maximum of fun out of ordinary things. If it has any value on the bookshelf it is to say to other ordinary people that life isn't ordinary at all. It's a miracle from first to last and if you don't know how to find it so you have missed the most important truth of all (from *We'll See the Cuckoo*).

Chapter Eight

It is the business of anybody who can
to set right what anybody has set wrong.

Anglia Anthology.

S oon after our return home the Yorkshire and Humberside Tourist Board
told us they would no longer advertise properties which were not graded.
They had approved our plans in 1980 and inspected our premises and we had
paid membership for eighteen years. We had annually advertised in 'Where
to Stay' even though, being well established, we hardly needed to advertise
any more. When grading had begun we had felt no need for this extra qualifi-
cation. We had more customers than we could cope with. This quite new
ruling meant that we could still pay the £100 membership but we couldn't
advertise so we sent for the necessary forms to comply. We had recently
installed the en suite facilities. There would only be minor adjustments to
make. We would have to pay for a yearly inspection and have the bother of
an unannounced visit to add to fire alarm inspections, extinguisher updates,
alarm system tests and local firemen's visits. We have electric plug inspections and hygiene ones. A man comes from Animal Health, one from MAFF
to check ear-tags, and another from the Countryside Stewardship Scheme to
make sure the walls are being built correctly. Such is modern life. So many
of them do not know what they are talking about. The hygiene lady told me
to de-frost a twenty-pound turkey in the fridge, causing it to deep-freeze
everything in the refrigerator. She admitted no catering experience of her
own. The Fire Service made us put very strong springs on cottage and
bedroom doors which were used by self-catering disabled guests, seemingly
oblivious to the fact that they would not be able to open them, and the
Stewardship advisor really thinks bedding manure can be 'magicked' away.

The form, when it came from the Tourist Board, told us that the only
problem to becoming graded was that new regulations would forbid us to use
the room entered from the dining room. This was the most popular room
with the disabled or the elderly who did not like to climb stairs. It was also

a favourite with families of young children because parents could put them to bed only steps away from the sitting room instead of upstairs miles away. This too, was the room onto which we had had National Trust permission to build a lean-to ensuite suitably adapted for wheelchair users. This cannot be true, I thought, so I phoned the Tourist Board, told them they had approved this special room eighteen years ago and that we had just spent quite a large sum of money on improvements. We told them, too, that we were just about the only accommodation for the disabled within a very large area, other than one hotel and a Travel Lodge, both in a much higher price range than ours. Rules were rules, I was told, and could not be changed. We decided we could manage without them but, shortly afterwards, the Haworth Tourist Information Centre was forbidden to advertise ungraded property. Guests resident here at the time had enquired where they could find accommodation for an aunt in a wheelchair and had been given only two possible places, The Currer and the big hotel. There was obviously a very definite need for disabled accommodation. A severely paralysed man, a vet from South Africa who had been badly injured playing rugby, was using that rejected room when the Tourist Board called us all to Haworth to explain the new procedures. The injured vet exploded and made me promise that I never would close that room. He found it ideal. He had come specially to see Herriot Country and ours was the nearest suitable accommodation he could find. He could not move arms or legs but he could talk. I went to the meeting, pleaded my case but lost it. Who cares. We decided it was more important to provide holidays for the handicapped guests who frequently want to come to the Yorkshire Dales.

Not everyone thinks that what we provide is as wonderful as that South African vet did. A man booked a cottage for one week. He and his wife arrived on the Saturday saying their three children, all at university, would be joining them on the Sunday. When he saw the cottage he said it wasn't as luxurious as his own home and that he could not bring his educated family here. He asked for a full return of the £150 the cottage cost in high season. I gave it to him without argument. It is the easiest thing to do. I told him he shouldn't expect a low-cost cottage to be The Ritz. I didn't tell him Blind Date had booked or that Sir Anthony Quayle had been very happy in it.

We find that the gap is widening between farmers and the rest of the human species. There used to be a belief that country people were the salt of the earth. Almost everyone had a relative in the rural community and understood not just our lifestyle but our character, born of generations of people who have spent most of their time with animals.

As the millennium approached it was becoming more and more obvious that we were not only being misunderstood but there was a growing aggression towards us. From being respected as carers of the countryside and the animals grazing it, we had somehow become exploiters of domestic cattle and sheep and polluters of the environment. We were landowners and therefore rich, but our properties were dirty and our fields full of bacteria and potential disease. The media has aggravated this outrageously. Most of what is said is totally untrue. The welfare of our stock takes precedence over our own. Because our income has, for many years, been insufficient, farmers have been urged to diversify. We were certainly not going to get rich with the Blind Date booking which was our diversification.

Seven rooms were reserved for the one night only. We have never charged more than single rate if a room was booked for one instead of two and we stick to this rule. We decided that this was to be an interesting experience and abandoned the idea of it being a profitable one. We guessed, rightly, that the young couple would be really disappointed when the chosen envelope said they were, 'Going to the dogs'. The news would not be improved by the information that they were going by train to spend one night on a farm when they had every right to expect several in a high-class hotel.

The onus was put on us to make their date a memorable one, and we pulled out all the stops. It turned out to be quite an extraordinary and enjoyable experience for all sorts of unexpected reasons. We had thought the event would be planned with military precision but it was the most casual affair.

No one came to look or tell us what to do. Schools make more preparations. The production team made none. The menu was left to us and we were responsible for collecting the young couple and a member of the production team from the railway station. The meal did not cause us a problem. British beef cannot fail if served with Yorkshire puddings and what can be more appropriate, on the edge of the moor, than to serve bilberry pies with cream.

Collecting them at the station was a rather shabby affair for our old Range Rover was almost ready for the scrap yard. Like all our oldies it was just being allowed to die with dignity. We had been so overworked, preparing to offer the very best of which we were capable, that we had little time left to enhance the old lady or disguise the eaten seats for which Jess was responsible.

The camera team was coming from Blackpool and meeting up with the train party at the local station. We did not receive notice of expected time of arrival until two days before the event. Everything was unbelievably casual. It was obvious that the responsibility was ours to make this low-key date one to remember with pleasure and not with disappointment. I don't think we failed but we had to really make an effort to gain the approval of the two youngsters who had never been on a farm, would not have chosen to come and who were more than a little jealous of the other couple flying to the Seychelles. Can you blame them?

We had invited Betty to view the mini-drama from our sitting room window. The motor neurone disease was really getting control and she could barely move but, being a friend who loved fun, she had a great time. The Blind Date girl, Abby, was lovely with her, and with Harry, so she immediately endeared herself to us. She made a cup of tea on the Aga and declared she had never had a brew like it. In spite of it being summer with all the windows open, we had log fires everywhere and the place did look nice. There is nothing more welcoming than a log fire in an inglenook fireplace.

We were glad we had asked Barbara Sykes, the shepherdess, and her daughter and father to share their evening meal. That was a success in spite of the fact that they were continually on camera. Without them, there could well have been silence. As it was the laughter was as relaxed as it normally is in the dining room. Afterwards the camera team were ready to put up their feet in the snug and happy to poke the glowing embers. They were quite uninterested in going out. The young couple wandered out to the village pub where no one knew who they were. They came home in the darkness and joined the cameramen by the fire. We heard a hum of pleasant conversation when we went to bed

The next day dawned in summer splendour. The entrance to the dining room is the original entry to the barn, but the old oak doors have been replaced with glass and, facing east, the morning sun literally pours in,

Inglenook fireplace and beehive oven.

flooding the breakfast table with light and reflecting on the cutlery. Guests congregate outside if the temperature permits, for the view is spectacular. On mornings like the one of the Blind Date, a summer mist lies in the valley deceiving our guests into thinking they are in the Lake District. The camera men were just on a job and were appreciative that they were on home ground and not some exotic resort. I think they thought of their stay at a farm as a holiday, a brief respite, free of long distance travelling.

The young couple, Abby and Scott, came to breakfast with smiling faces. Abby had decided to enjoy herself. Scott came late and was gently teased for laziness. They were to go to Golcar Farm, for their sheepdog experience, at 11 a.m. Abby admitted that she was afraid of dogs. Neither she nor Scott had had any animal pet and both were apprehensive. We had been told to fill the gap between breakfast and coffee-time with a farm walk. This cannot be without an introduction to animals, but our goats and donkeys are friendly enough and cattle one views in the field, not the farmyard.

We had arranged that Tim would be building walls on the boundary because we thought a drystone waller would make good material for the hundreds of feet of film passing through the TV cameras. We loaned the two youngsters wellingtons and drove the cameramen down to the boundary with their heavy apparatus. Abby and Scott entered the spirit of the game and the atmosphere was one of fun. Whatever they did, both could say, 'Well I've never done that before!' Abby said, 'If we'd gone to the Seychelles I'd have spent my life never having been on a farm!'

Returning to the farmyard we suggested they feed Diana and her four black babies. We offered them the quad bike as transport but they had not been insured for such a 'dangerous activity'. Instead, as time was short, we took them up the hill in the Range Rover and they were introduced to our beautiful cow and her lovely calves. Scott was encouraged to go close enough, with the bucket of corn, for a film to be taken from an angle which would include the background view of Airedale in sunshine and Ilkley Moor catching the moving shadows of passing cloud. Just the job, we thought. The watching public will see the glory of the Yorkshire Dales at their best. We were very conscious of the fact that our land and animals and house were being filmed every time the cameras turned on the young couple. Driving back, down the road a cameraman was even filming our descent against no background at all!

So we gave them carrots and they overcame their fear of the donkeys, Jasper and Joe, who can be guaranteed to behave beautifully for everyone except the blacksmith. Donkeys are surely viewer-friendly. There would be smiles on couch potatoes when that was screened! Then came the fun of climbing the haymow and sampling the weight of the bales and Scott being applauded for strong-man stuff. The clock hands neared 11 a.m. and we all

Joe, a guest, and Jasper.

had a coffee while I phoned for a taxi to take them to Barbara's. We had grown really fond of those two youngsters. They maybe hadn't fallen in love but they certainly didn't hate each other. They possibly still thought they had drawn the short straw but they had enjoyed their stay enough to hug us tightly and wave an enthusiastic farewell. We know, too, that they had fun at Barbara's. Everybody does!

We had been afraid of the visit of a popular television production team only to find that it consisted of four nice cameramen, a research member and the two on a blind date. All were ordinary people, five were just doing a job and the competitors were good sports with a life ahead of them which, these days, would surely include many trips abroad. Abby, of course, believed that she was to blame. She had been the one to choose. From the three boys she had chosen Scott who had allowed her to pick the envelope that had brought them no distance at all, to a place more unfamiliar than any European resort would have been. To it they had travelled incognito by train to an old farm-house run by old ladies. Abby had initially been embarrassed but, just as we felt responsible for their enjoyment of the date, she felt she must make a positive response. Scott was a nice boy and both had excellent manners, which cannot be said of all young people who go on the Blind Date programme.

They coped with the individuality of our farm and they really had fun up at Barbara's. They won't forget. The memory will bring laughter, I'm sure, but it will be kindly amusement, which is how we received the screening of the programme in January the following year.

We had heard nothing at all from the production team. It had moved on. The series was incomplete. Our part was over and no acknowledgement of our effort was thought necessary. The researcher had thanked us on leaving, had paid and told us the programme would be shown sometime after Christmas, six months away. As far as they were concerned the operation had gone successfully and it was a case of here today and gone tomorrow. For us it was different. For us it was a one-off twenty-four hours well worth telling to all our summer guests. Guess who we entertained? We hosted Blind Date. Not the Cilla Black Blind Date? Exactly! I don't believe it! Well we did and make sure you watch it in January! We will. We promise. You won't see us but you should see Tim, down on the boundary, below the wood and you'll see Diana and Jasper and Joe. Surely you'll get a glimpse of the goats and they filmed all the meal and the fire in the inglenook!

We told everyone. We were amused and so were they. They told their families and friends at home saying, 'You know the farm we stay at, if you watch Blind Date you'll see it.' When I sent out Christmas cards I inserted a reminder and on the two nights it was screened we completed our evening chores at great speed. Everywhere our friends were poised to switch on their videos to record.

The first week, of course, we saw Abby choose Scott. We felt to be watching old friends. We saw the disappointment when she opened the envelope offering them both an unacceptable date in this country at the same time as the other couple anticipated a jaunt to the other side of the world. We felt deeply sorry for her and applauded the wonderful way they had come to The Currer and shaken off the feeling that they had been unfairly treated.

We had watched a few programmes preceding ours and knew that the replay was short. We acknowledged the fact that the Sheepdog Experience was the Blind Date so we told everyone there couldn't be much more than a few quick glimpses of the place they'd waited to see, on screen, for so long.

There was a deathly hush as the four of us sat before our television knowing that hundreds of our guests, nationwide, were waiting in silence too.

The moment of truth arrived. We saw an old white Range Rover coming down a road with no background possible and absolutely nothing more! Nothing! Our friends who videoed it said that one of the miniatures, of four on the screen at once, was of a boy eating but we never saw that. Shots of Scott floundering in a green field trying to control Barbara's sheepdogs brought appreciative laughter from the audience. Abby was laughing at him, quite relaxed at Golcar and only we knew how afraid she was of dogs. As an advertisement for the Yorkshire Dales it was a non-starter. The young couple were questioned as to the romantic success of a date on which they had barely had two minutes to themselves without the camera!

What d'ye know! We'd had a brief date with another world. We wouldn't have missed the fun it had brought for anything, though. Our disillusionment bubbled with laughter as we slipped thankfully into our backwater routine. Life is never humdrum at The Currer but the spotlight, presumably, is not for us. No one sent us a tape. They know, of course that we haven't a video but some anticipate that, one day, the Browns will invest in one. I doubt it. Olga did not send hers to the Barbaults in Lyon. What was the point? But we don't need any tape to remind us of a happy encounter with young people who knew how to behave and with men whose job it was to film and not to edit it.

This little excitement was not followed by an equally interesting summer. Emilie came again which is always a joy, but fewer guests came than usual. The strong pound made holidays abroad much less expensive than holidays at home. Driving the narrow lanes of our north country is not easy. I suspect that many people now have had an overdose of holidays and quite enjoy just staying at home instead of tearing all over the place. We had had close on two decades of being over-full and sleeping on the sitting room floor ourselves. We did not have to do that once in the summer of 1999. In our childhood days, when one holiday a year was the norm, we could not wait for the season to return. Our generation increased one holiday to two and even more. Passing retirement age, my contemporaries now have a car and means to holiday when and where they like. They must have totted up hundreds of holiday hours, maybe hundreds of holidays. Perhaps they were beginning to tire. Whatever the reason those who came reported vacancies in hotels and B&Bs wherever they motored in the Dales.

Families with children were fewer. We blamed bad propaganda in the wake of the BSE scare. The public had also been told that, on farms, children might get salmonella or E. coli. Children who came were more likely to want to watch early morning television than to want to help us on the farm. Instead of playing energetic games in the fields they sat playing with pocket computers. Not so Emilie. Before coming she had spent some time camping in Southern Ireland, with a group trekking with a horse and caravan. She was a tonic not to be surpassed by any bottled kind and Denis came for her last week and only he had to sleep on the floor.

While they were here we had another visit from Betty and her husband. We could not believe the deterioration. She had lost the use of her hands and was confined to a wheelchair. The one the NHS had provided was too heavy for Billy to handle and Aunty Mary offered her lightweight one until such a time as one could be ordered for Betty. Looking after his wife single-handed was becoming almost impossible even for a man with Billy's dedication. We began to recognise motor neurone as the most awful disease of all. There are others that paralyse, that make even eating and speech impossible, but motor neurone does not attack the brain. That remains normal and this creates the worst suffering of all. Ours was one of the few houses Betty could visit. Not many are as wheelchair-friendly as ours.

Betty was losing her battle but Harry had certainly put a brake on his. He passed his seventy-second birthday getting daily considerably better, thanks to the unexplainable merits of homeopathy. He was very fond of Betty for she had been one of the few people who talked to him on a one-to-one basis. He was very upset by her tragic illness. He knew more than any of us what it was like having difficulty talking and making others understand what he was trying to say.

We were suddenly on the doorstep of the annual selling of our cattle, which is enough to take our minds off almost anything. Whatever is urgent, either to do or to think about, must wait until we have sold. In September we begin to get short of grass for the herd that always approaches one hundred and seventy. Here on the hills, farmers cannot really finish cattle which means that hundreds of store cattle go through the bi-weekly cattle sales. They are bought by farmers on the plains who have harvested their grain and have sheds and food and specialise. By the end of September, were we to keep them, they would begin hankering after coming indoors and craving for corn. Our sheds are big and we have room for all when we let them out in spring, but they are twice as big by autumn and have outgrown anything we have to offer, so they are quite happy to go to more spacious indoor accommodation. They are sold with their friends and are sure of being well fed and housed for they not only have to be fat they have to be clean or be unacceptable to their final buyer.

Even though they go to luxury, we mourn them when they leave us and are very stressed by the process. If the prices reflect a good trade we are pleased. We are always proud of how well they look in the market for, selling only in September, we sell pen after pen of heavy animals which I think is impressive. A man sitting next to me, watching Margaret stay in the ring while more and more of our bullocks queued to go in, said to me, 'Are all those yours?' I nodded. 'Did you buy them all as week-old calves?'

'Yes,' I said. 'All in one week. Some at Skipton, some here and some at Gisburn.'

'I think I'll buy five hundred!' he gasped. ''Ave ye seen the price of calves?'

The Calf Processing Scheme had been stopped completely. The compensation for sending baby bulls to the abattoir had been gradually decreasing but now it had stopped and calves were worthless. They were being dumped, in protest, outside officials' houses and in telephone boxes. Farmers had had enough of slaughter at birth in order to produce milk. They were still taking them to market but there were so many of them they were sold for a song. That we would buy ours for something and nothing gave no pleasure. There is no joy in a system which is wrong!

Billy was desperately in need of some relief. He had applied for respite care for both of them, in some nursing home which specialised in providing such, but there was a waiting list. He rang and begged to come to us for a few days. He desperately needed to get some sleep and Betty had reached the stage when she could no longer lie down. At home she was sleeping in a recliner and we had one in the sitting room so we agreed and Billy got a few nights' sleep while I used the bed behind the curtain. Betty laughed as easily as she cried, sunshine and showers. My admiration grew for her daily. She was in a mess and she knew she was. She knew the diagnosis and that there was no cure but though her movement was becoming nil her personality was not changing at all. I had seen her laugh and cry in college fifty years before and the intervening years changed none of that. As for me, I had several comfortable nights in the bed behind the curtain. Upstairs I normally shared the job of settling Harry back into bed every time he got up to the toilet. For that performance he must have held a record. Poor Margaret was the one that really suffered with no halving of the chore with me while Betty stayed.

After a few days Billy was rested and our two struggling friends went home and we concentrated on selling the second half of our stock of twenty-three month old bullocks, after which we would have to employ ourselves getting ready for holiday. Knowing that we were soon to be away for two weeks and that we would come home to buy the year's intake of calves, Billy asked if he and Betty could come again for a few days prior to our leaving and we could not answer nay!

Somehow the house had to be left clean and orderly for Dorothy to take over and the remaining cattle had to be checked and boundaries secured. Accounts had to be brought up to date and still we had guests and breakfasts to prepare and evening meals to serve. We let everything take second place to Betty. We took out the heavy NHS wheelchair Harry had been provided with, years ago, to take with us to Aberporth. It was unforgivable that the NHS never succeeded in getting a suitable lightweight one for Betty. She and Billy left on the Tuesday evening and we had two days to prepare.

On the Wednesday it was necessary to pack our cases, but as usual Aunty Mary refused. She thinks it is tempting fate if she packs a day early. She made no attempt to come downstairs but sat in her bedroom armchair nodding all the time. By mid-afternoon I insisted she got into bed and slept properly, which she did. So properly I half wondered if she would wake again. At her age it could have been possible. I continued my packing, thinking that it was lucky we were still at home. She was asleep when Margaret left to encircle the land and do what was necessary and still asleep when she returned.

'Could she be unconscious?' we wondered. I finished packing and sat on the cases and pressed the clasps. We seemed to be in limbo. Things were happening over which we had no control. We have always been in authority. At school, in Guiding, on the farm and in the preparation of any activity. Suddenly everything seemed out of our hands but we were at home, not halfway to Wales in a Travel Inn.

We desperately needed to get away to revitalise. We needed respite too. Others in our position sometimes left their dependants in care and snatched a brief moment of calm. Harry is remembered for once saying, 'Would you be better leaving me behind?' He said it with confidence that we never would!

'Of course not,' we had said, just as he had expected we would. 'Well, wouldn't it be boring without me?' he had laughed. Too true!

Darkness falls soon at the end of September and Aunty Mary still slept and we continued the ritual of preparing to go. In mid-evening she woke and got up as if daylight was to be expected. 'Are you all right?' we asked.

'Yes,' she said. 'Why?'

'Well, we've been getting ready to go on holiday all day while you've just slept!'

'Well I don't pack until tomorrow anyway,' she said. Presumably she was all right after all.

We breathed again and on Friday we drove down to the Wrexham Travel Inn and having settled Aunty Mary in her room in front of the television, we took Harry out into the car park to breathe the fresh air he loved and to enjoy the lights and the incoming guests. Margaret went to let out the dogs and put them on a lead.

She rejoined us and said, 'I've just been thinking. Wherever do we go from here?' and I understood exactly what she meant. She didn't mean Wales. She meant, what next is round the corner and will we be able to cope.

Chapter Nine

'If you listen to me' said the old oak tree,
'I'll teach you the way to grow,
One inch in the year is the way, my dear,
In case you didn't know.'
'No listen to us,' said the firs with some fuss.
'That pace will not suit us at all,
You must double that rate – it's getting so late
And press up if you mean to grow tall.'

Enid Gush

I t was the last holiday we had at The Cedars for it was to be pulled down and rebuilt. The wooden bungalow opposite had already been removed and taken behind the family home of Jan and Tony to become a workshop. The foundations of a more permanent one, to be specially designed for the handicapped, were being dug during our stay. A bumper crop of apples showered the lawn each day and we were allowed to take them and most of those from the two trees Tony felled, which were too near the new site. The new building project meant that, when we left, The Cedars would immediately suffer the same fate. A bigger, four-bedroomed house was to be built and we, when we returned the following year, would occupy the specially designed one on the other side of the drive. We looked forward to the minor change believing, quite wrongly, that good things go on for ever.

Margaret had questioned, 'Where do we go from here?' The future seemed full of pitfalls. We appreciated that our road ahead, like those twisting and twining in the Dales of our home county, had never been straight. We had not wanted it to be so. Just as every bend of the tarmacked one can be expected to provide a different, beautiful view, another summit to climb and another experience to encounter, so we had expected and proved our future to be. There had always been a certain distance in our outlook, a freedom in our captivity. Suddenly we began to feel well and truly fettered, unable to make our own decisions, no longer driving along the road but rather being swept downhill, unable to control the brakes.

The first thing to do was to enjoy our holiday and the next step was the calf-buying. That far was straightforward. I must say we were rather jealous of Jan and Tony, all excited with their new project. We envied them their building plans and the excitement of decorating, and furnishing the two new holiday homes which would replace the old. Ahead of it was creative fun. We desperately needed something other than winter to look forward to. Margaret and I did hardly any talking during our Aberporth fortnight. Of the future, that is. Whatever would be must be. Whatever the heavy load we must carry it. There is no room for us to be pessimistic when we have a project. We stole joy from Jan and Tony's Aberporth one and that was all we talked about. While waiting for our increasingly old aunt to rise, we watched the workmen laying foundations with nearly as much interest as if they had been doing it for us. We examined the plans our friends spread out on the table and told them how much we envied them. There was so much creativity left in us in spite of our pensioner status. While retirement was freeing our contemporaries from the chains of responsibility, these were tightening on us. Our oldies were getting older. We laughingly remembered again Mother saying, when Bess our twenty-year-old dog recovered from a heart attack, 'You won't get rid of your old folks easily, either'. I assure you we did not want to then, nor do we now, but that does not mean that we do not feel the increasing weight!

Our holiday left us refreshed. It was reassuring to know that, if the opportunity presented itself with something new, both Margaret and I would be raring to go. Our enthusiasm is far more than a flicker. We returned to The Currer ready to face whatever life might decide to throw at us.

The first was a remarkable handout. We were not taken by surprise for we already knew that calves would be cheap, but not so cheap. They were almost given! One was. A farmer had brought in a calf and missed the sale so he just gave it to me. Margaret bought one for £1.50 and many cost only £2. We bought them all on the one day and never went to Gisburn. No one wanted calves. The man who'd wondered whether to buy five hundred had changed his mind but Margaret just bashes on. She might change her method of feeding, and frequently does a U-turn if something isn't working but, come hell or high water, she buys the same number of calves!

Betty and Billy were successful in obtaining a week's holiday at the previous home of Princess Diana's family in Norfolk. It was so lovely, and the care so exceptional, I think they could have stayed forever and then, almost immediately, Betty had to go into palliative care. Billy was allowed to stay with her all day and return to his own home at night. Again I had reason to realise my incompetence in the city. The nursing home was on the other side of Bradford and to drive there would have meant half an hour's journey through the city centre. Me? I knew I would want to visit her fairly frequently, alone, for two could not leave The Currer in winter. 'It's easy!' Billy said, but no way was I going to attempt it. I bought a street map but only to find the exact location of the nursing home. I solved the problem by driving each time to our Land Rover specialist's garage where I left my Range Rover while I caught a bus into the city and another one out to the nursing home. Instead of it taking half an hour it took three times as long but there was no way I would add the stress of learning to drive through traffic to the stress of visiting someone as ill as Betty, so I stood firm and went by bus. I'm just not a town person. Multi-storey buildings and high street shops don't turn me on. I'm not afraid provided my feet are on the pavement. I'm not afraid of people but have no wish to be one of a crowd. I don't want museums or cinemas, restaurants or markets. On wheels I come from another planet. Visiting Betty I found was much more difficult than having them stay.

The Range Rover parked outside Simmonite's show room was looking very old. We do misuse our vehicles, with on-field work, dogs, fencing posts, bales of straw and wheelchairs. We picnic in them with those who, in their infirmity, drop crumbs on the floor and spill coffee on the carpet. We climb into the driving seat with mud-caked wellingtons and we store bundles of binder twine for the hundred and one emergencies which can be coped with by using string. On top of all this we periodically take rubbish to the household tip which you wouldn't want to do in a new vehicle. Old corn and rusted barbed wire and ragwort. There was also the uselessness of our garage. Even if we bothered to put the Range Rover in, the roof was so badly in need of repair it offered no protection from rain or snow. We decided we must do something about the roof but neglected to do so, thank goodness, for it would have been wasted effort.

The annual MOT test coincided with the death of our goat Jimmy. It seemed no time at all since we exchanged the baby billy goat for a cockerel we had reared in the house. It had been hatched at Christmas and been abandoned by its mother. It had given us such joy as a baby but its domesticated upbringing had made it quite arrogant and even aggressive and I was quite glad to see it exchanged for a dear little billy goat. Jimmy had grown old more quickly than his foster mum, Rosy, for billy goats don't live nearly as long as nannies. We've proved that several times but, so the superstition goes, they bring good luck. Whatever other people think about our lifestyle we firmly believe luck is on our side so before it deserted us we'd have to replace Jimmy. However, the first replacement we had to make was on wheels, not legs.

We took Jimmy to Jerusalem Farm in the Ifor Williams trailer we had bought to transport live animals. Having deposited him at his last resting place we drove down to the Simmonite garage for a car check prior to an MOT test due at the end of the month. Harry, Margaret and I sat in the showroom while the test was being conducted. We had warned the mechanic that our over-employed and somewhat ancient vehicle must not cost us too much in repairs. If it was going to cost a lot we would have nearly a month to think about what we should do.

We do not take Aunty Mary to the knacker's yard so there were just three of us huddled over the radiator in the showroom, mourning Jimmy who had been born in Heptonstall but who had lived free to come and go, from field to barn, at The Currer, adored by holiday-makers and generating our good fortune for the last seven years. He had died in the company of cattle, a species he seemed to consort with in preference to his own kind. Perhaps it was that Charlie had pushed him into the wings when he was young. Whatever the reason Jimmy had chosen to sleep in the manger of the cattle shed with the bullocks and not with Rosy and the white nanny Snowy. She had run wild among the deer for eighteen months, before children, here on holiday, coaxed her from the hill into our farmyard and christened her. Perhaps Jimmy thought he was a bullock. We once had a pig that thought he was a dog!

Jimmy had no doubt known he was about to meet his maker and had settled down on the straw in the top shed where Margaret had brought a Belgium Blue stirk needing an antibiotic. The two had snuggled down together and had enjoyed each other's company for a few days until Jimmy died. Animals show an amazing amount of condolence.

All vehicles in the showroom were Range or Land Rovers, of course. Margaret and I gravitated towards a Land Rover station wagon identical to the ones we had driven before Father died. It was fourteen years old but in excellent condition. We admired it and looked inside but passed on to look at the Range Rovers also on display. We were not looking to buy but had decided that our next vehicle must have four doors. The Range Rovers we had owned had only ever had two. Whoever was on the front seat had to get out to let anyone other than Margaret or me get in. We could squeeze our way through but no one else could. The four-door Range Rovers were really only four-seaters. They were luxurious but inadequate for we often had Hilda. However we were not buying, so we went back to the station wagon and climbed into it and took a trip down memory lane.

There had originally been seven of us but Father and Mother and Aunty Janie were all gone. What fun we had had when there were seven driving northwards to the Highlands and Islands of Scotland. What fun we had had filling its twelve seats with Guides and their camping gear. What wonderful opportunities it had provided as a school bus during my teaching years. A station wagon had brought half a dozen calves back from market on innumerable occasions. We had a joint history with long-wheelbase Land Rovers. The first we had brought from an ex-army dealer in Bawtry but David

Simmonite had serviced it. The vehicle had cost £750 and David had been little more than a boy, working in a barn down Squirrel Lane. Our last one had transported all the materials, the tools and the equipment of our barn conversion in 1980 and had died after its completion. Mother had fancied a Range Rover. She had been amazing following Father's death and had survived the building site conditions and the extraordinary activity of that extremely busy year with the same enthusiasm she had brought to our removal to a ruin in 1958.

Then she had asked for an Aga for there was no electricity or gas here in those days. Solid fuel it had to be, so she had asked for an Aga. She was a competent cook, of course, even making scones in it on the day the removal lorry brought our meagre possessions down the field, for there was no road. After the barn conversion, more than twenty years later, she wanted a Range Rover so we bought a second-hand one costing nearly £4000.

The Aga cost only £200 in 1958, which had seemed costly. It was new and one nowadays would cost possibly twice as much as we normally pay for replacement vehicles that last about seven years. The Aga we bought forty-three years ago is still nearly as good as new. Certainly guests return year after year just for the quality of the meals it continues to cook. That an Aga improves the talent of even the best of cooks is not debatable. We would sacrifice electricity rather than do without our valuable friend. However poor we became financially we would forfeit all in order to replace it, for its services are not just as Queen of Stoves. It can do so many other things besides that and to be without it just one day, for some minor service, causes life to fall apart and us to go to pieces.

It is our early morning source of kitchen warmth. All day and night it generates the heat which we call home. It provides the hot water for an ever-increasing variety of uses indoors and out, and dries overnight as many sheets and pillowcases and personal garments as the bread rack and half a dozen clothes lines across the ceiling can accommodate. There is no need for us to pray for outside drying weather for our outsize wash, nor for us to spend hours at the ironing board, for folded bed linen and modern, easy care garments can be ironed merely by placing a pile on the chrome insulating lids. Harry repeatedly said there were three things he could not do without: car, wheelchair and sisters. There are only two I cannot function without: Aga and sister!

Mother needed the Aga to complement her skill and her personality and she loved the old Range Rover just as much. We preferred the station wagon for its benefits exceeded those of its posher relation. We gravitated toward the one currently in the showroom, even as we head for the cattle market if we are in Cardigan or Camarthan.

The mechanic returned with his assessment of repairs needed before we could get an MOT to see us through the next year. He was shaking his head. 'It's not even safe for you to drive home,' he said.

'But we've got to!' we gasped.

'We'll give you a lift,' he suggested.

We had Harry, two dogs and a trailer which had just conveyed a dead goat to Jerusalem Farm.

'We'd better send for Tim,' Margaret said. He would be walling and have his mobile in his pocket. He could come with a Land Rover in which we could put dogs and on which we could hook a trailer. By the time he came we had bought the station wagon. Twelve seats, we bragged, just the job for a Guide Campers' Reunion on the inviting Island of Tiree. We'd arranged for the garage hands to transfer our roof rack from the old to the new for, on consideration, there is one other thing we cannot do without and that is the roof rack and the fitted PVC cover we bought in Bowness on Lake Windermere.

Before Tim came we had also transferred what proved to be a shockingly large amount of clobber from the Range Rover into the trailer. There were cushions and rugs and tools and crowbars, odd bits of cutlery from forgotten picnics and plastic bags. We found articles that had been lost for ages. A hairbrush we had not seen since winter and a pair of sandshoes left there since spring. We were glad we had no spectators for we were ashamed. We applaud those couples who come with such tidy cars. Our problem is that, the moment we return home, we have those with us who need helping out of the car and into the house in urgent need of the low-loo. There is a necessity to slam on the kettle. Thank God for the always-hot Aga. A match must be put to the fire or a heater turned on and, very quickly, the food we have bought at the supermarket must be brought indoors and the frozen things put in the freezer before the irritable phone goes again. So the car is never completely cleared of the final bits and pieces and a conglomeration accumulates about which we are highly embarrassed.

Tim came and we took him into the showroom to show him what we had just bought and we told David to be as quick as possible in changing the road tax and getting our new transport to The Currer. We felt that Jimmy, who had brought us luck for several years, had not deserted us in death and we, who are not superstitious at all, quaked a little at not having a billy goat with winter and all its hazards approaching. A few days later we told our visiting blacksmith we had lost our resident luck. He looked up from his task of clipping the donkey's feet and said, 'My nanny's in kid. You can have the billy.' We have always believed that conception is the beginning of life and that abortion at any time is a form of murder. We took courage in knowing that our 'luck' was already restarted and, though for one reason or another, the billy when born in the spring was not to come to The Currer until the following spring, it made no difference to his non-resident capability. He was ours and his influence was felt even though we had to wait for his presence.

We had only to wait a few days for the delivery of our new-looking fourteen-year-old Land Rover, but when, with the roof rack sanded and re-sprayed, we attempted to drive into the garage we saw, at once, that the vehicle was too tall. This was a major problem. We knew the garage had to be re-roofed and we could have done that. The incentive generated by a lovely 'new' vehicle would have excited us to do the repair at once. Highering the roof was a totally different job, one we'd done once before, hurriedly and in bad weather, just before Margaret went into hospital for a major operation. To higher a building once is possible but to lift the cross beams a second time means re-building as well as re-roofing and we were fifteen years older, and involved in the annual calf-rearing, and it was December.

It would have to be John, we agreed. The garage was at the eastern end of a shed complex we had built during the sixties. The total area of garage, corn store, yearling shed and donkey hole was 90ft by 36ft. The land sloped to the east, we had lifted the garage roof once before. It was already higher than the rest of the roof which wasn't all that good either as corrugated tin goes. We had repaired it several times and, just before Christmas, while John and all his family were plucking turkeys by the hundreds, a vicious wind took off some of the sheets. Torn pieces of tin littered the yard and gaps were left through which rain and snow would fall. Margaret went onto the roof and did a poor but adequate temporary repair and we phoned John and told him to increase the work order from one garage roof to 360 square yards, as soon as possible. The yearling shed was hardly usable and the next wind might deposit the whole roof in the vicinity of the Bradford and Bingley Building Society's huge, ugly offices on the valley floor.

He came to look and the inevitable happened. If we were to re-roof, he said, we should think about highering it all. Not just the garage. It had been built before the age of big tractors. We had taken muck out, then, with a hand-fork. John always had a problem taking it out now, with modern equip-ment. We had to agree that a full lifting of the roof was sensible and while we were about it the northern face of the whole length of the several sheds would have to be highered. It was tin and it looked onto the farmyard, the entrance, the house and the cottages and it could do with a facelift, which meant a total rebuild and we ought to do it in stone, to match the house and, you guessed it, our bank account was going to suffer monstrously!

Betty was allowed home for three difficult days at Christmas and we visited her, there, on the same afternoon that we called at our builder Brian's Open Day to celebrate the fortieth anniversary of his marriage to Margaret.

Life is mainly just a series of extremes that are quite difficult to cope with. I had seen Betty a few times since October but Margaret and Harry had not and were shocked by the enormity of her illness. From there we had to change gear completely and celebrate with those whose life expectancy was toasted. Here's to a Golden Wedding, here's to health and happiness, here's to the millennium. We'd, moments earlier, been with friends whose fate was sealed, who had no future that wasn't painful. It was a difficult transition to make for all of us.

The December which saw the end of one millennium and the birth of another will always be remembered and so will be the struggle of the first three months of the new era and the difficulty of coping on a building site of massive proportions. The workmen's dedication to detail and perfection drove us to screaming point. The unexpected firework display that had held us enthralled was soon just history as we struggled to perform the winter feeding, exposed to all the seasonal elements. Roofing the garage, in our amateur way, had looked too difficult to contemplate. John and his men, making a professional job, caused us far more hard work for months longer than a dodgy re-roofing, by a couple of women, would have done! We were nearly at the band end, as Mother would have said.

When work began on the new shed, the demolition of the old one was instant and made working conditions for us almost impossible. We had not anticipated the complete exposure. John's tractor and trailer took away everything. All the old roofing tins and rotting beams and DIY hayracks and doors and partitions disappeared immediately. Everything unusable and usable alike, vanished before we had time to rescue anything. The men were like vultures ripping apart the amateur work of decades. We gasped but were unable to halt the demolition which left corn bins exposed to winter wetness and the electricity panel in danger of electrocuting us all. And they disturbed what mice we had or rather their Jack Russell did. He had a field day chasing the poor little unsuspecting creatures. Two found their way into the Loft Cottage where an American professor was living at the time. He was called Art Bruneau and he caught both of them. He did not complain or move house as many would have done.

The job of feeding cattle in the Top Bullock Shed was horrendous. It was not so much the exposure as the irregularity of the ground. It became riddled with foundation trenches over which we had to put bridges and Margaret's job of carrying heavy bales became a nightmare. Then, when the foundations were laid, the floor space became littered with beams and girders which had to be stepped over. Corn had to be taken from the bins and barrowed to elsewhere and we thought that maybe the completed beauty might not be worth it. What antagonised us most was the perfection of the builders. They might have been putting an extension on Buckingham Palace so perfect was their attention to detail. They were not prompted to speed by the difficulties we were suffering. Men! We wouldn't have one given!

The first two months of the new millennium were so difficult we would prefer to forget them but if I only remember the good things this account will ring false and in every detail recorded it is accurate. January and February caused us to have doubts about the year 2000 and for those to be justified.

A problem which had been building up for some time came to a head soon after the New Year, simultaneously with the purposeful arrival of the workmen. As I was the one in the house when Harry wakened it was generally I who brought him downstairs. For most of his life Harry could go up and down alone. At some forgotten point, probably before Father died, I'd considered the stair rail not enough and put in two bars, one on either side of the door from the kitchen. This is two steps from the floor and we must have considered extra precautions were necessary. At what point we arranged to be behind him when he went up and in front when he came down is forgotten. It must have been after Mother died in 1990. It was not a problem. I brought him down in a morning, as Margaret was always out, and she brought him up at night for I, who rise very early out of choice, went to bed before they did.

Neither of us shared our increasing worry. I was finding the descent a bit of a nightmare and Margaret found Harry was out of breath when reaching the top at night. Aunty Mary was equally out of puff when she climbed the stairs but as each only needed to do so once a day, following the installation of the downstairs loo years and years ago, we accepted that all these problems were normal, old-age difficulties we must just accept.

Then, one day early in January, I brought Harry down to the top of the two steps into the kitchen and he wobbled. He descended them and lost his balance once again. I lowered him to the floor but he banged his head on a pane in the door to the entrance porch and glass shattered everywhere. There was not a lot of blood but the pane had been splintered into hundreds of pieces. While he continued to sit on the floor I swept up those around him and went for Margaret. She admitted she was having problems at night and we decided this was yet another job we must never do again alone.

The next fortnight was horrific. I called her from her feeding chores every morning and she wakened me from deep slumber around midnight and we looked forward to many years of this routine unless we did something positive. Mornings were not too difficult but bedtimes were bad. Harry was so out of breath and I was dazed. Margaret and I were heard to say to each other complaints we'd never uttered before, such as, 'Other people have no idea what looking after the handicapped is really like!' and, 'Other people can

just go to bed and sleep till morning!' So, lest we should get too sorry for
ourselves we really addressed our problem and we got out the Yellow Pages
and looked for a firm who dealt in chair lifts. Friends recommended a stair
lift but we never followed that up. We had fire doors bottom and top of our
stairs and were not prepared to forfeit them. The bottom two steps protruded
into the kitchen at a point where the porch door was. And wasn't it highly
possible that Harry may have to be taken upstairs in his wheelchair very soon?
We decided to anticipate this and phoned a firm which specialised in wheelchair lifts.

Two men came at once and dismissed Margaret's bright idea that the lift
could be housed downstairs, in the cubicle below the landing, because it had
no continuous wall to the ceiling. They insisted one could be installed,
however, and told us it would cost £8,500, more than twice what we'd just
paid for a 'new' Land Rover. Outside men were building for cattle and
donkeys what was going to cost the earth. We asked if a second-hand lift was
available. Handicapped and elderly sometimes die, surely. The men admitted
they did, often, but they didn't have one at the moment.

Again we got out the Yellow Pages and this time we enquired for a second-
hand one and we found a firm that could provide one in good condition at
half the price. They came to see where it must go and did all their measure-
ments from upstairs. They told me to take up the floorboards and if necessary
arrange for an electrician to move wires and to get him to put in a suitable
plug. They said I must get a joiner to take out a square hole in the floor and
they would bring the lift almost at once. They had measured everything
without noticing the exposed beams in the kitchen, through which the lift
must rise. Without moving a beam the installation could not be. Brian said
he could do that but the idea of doing so did not appeal one bit.

We were disappointed but not yet beaten. Harry's bed had been brought
into our room some time ago, when his blood deficiency started, but there
was still space enough. Admittedly it was a 'Brown space', one into which an
object fits exactly. In this new location the lift could rise between the two
beams and miss the one in the bedroom which went the opposite way. So far
so good and work could begin but the wall it was to be fastened to was not
an outside one and the upper half was stoothing and plasterboard.

We were told to move everything out of the kitchen and vacate the
bedroom. 'Here we go again,' we said, carrying furniture into the sitting room
and duvets from the bedroom.

'We won't take long. Three days,' the men said, before they found that the
hefty inside wall was only randomly built and would not hold the necessary
bolts. So girders were bought and the lift bolts changed so that they would
go right through the wall to be attached to iron on the other side. We were

three weeks sleeping on the floor. All the while we stepped over workmen's tools in the kitchen and up the staircase and suffered increasing problems outside as the building work progressed. The weather deteriorated bringing snow and rain and everything had to be battened down against wind. The year 2000 was a stinker ninety-five per cent of the time.

The Land Rover had to stay outside in appalling weather. One Sunday I got into it to drive its nose into the shelter the house provided against the prevailing wind. Jess had the awful habit of chasing cars taught to her by Lusky, whose addiction had not only endangered his life but had punctured many car tyres. We had not thought this possible and had disagreed with those who accused him, until we actually saw him. Then we meekly paid for the repair and took him to the vet to have his teeth clipped. He wouldn't stop chasing cars and neither would Jess. As I got into the Land Rover, just to move the vehicle a few feet, she came belting towards me. I had hardly reversed inches but she fell over and I thought I had injured her. I was very distressed and called for Margaret who came running. She said she thought the dog had only collided with the wheel. She was almost certain I hadn't run over her but we phoned the vet who said we should take her down to the closed surgery and he would come from his home and check Jess over. I was still trembling and the feeling of guilt persisted until we were told she had had a heart attack and that news was so frightening I think we would have accepted an accident, with little injury, rather than hear she had a heart liable to attack. This first one had probably been caused by her eagerness to reach the car when she heard me press the ignition.

We were acutely aware of how much we loved that dog, not least because of her relationship with Harry. We called her his dog because she protected him whenever he needed moral support. All dogs are wary of those with cerebral palsy, where movements are less controlled and who find it difficult to stroke and fondle. No animal had ever shown aggression towards him but none had ever leapt upon his knee as Jess did, licked his face or snuggled up to him in the Land Rover as Jess had done for the last twelve years. We called her Harry's dog. Often we called her 'our little girl'. Apart from Diana all our cattle are bullocks. Our dogs had been male for some time so, on the death of Shep, we had brought this little bitch pup from Hubbersty in the Lake District. It had been so nice to have a baby girl. A bitch is quite different from a dog and Jess was no exception and, right from the start, she loved Harry.

She was given an X-ray and prescribed multiple pills and we entered an era of making sure she was indoors when a car was expected to come or go and we deprived her of the job of herding cattle. It became an increasingly difficult responsibility for she didn't feel any different except when it happened, which it did several times during the next month. She would one minute be walking naturally and the next rolling in the grass, or on the concrete yard breathing with difficulty and her lips and tongue would be blue.

Eventually the roof beams of the sheds were lifted onto the iron girders and feeding time no longer meant climbing over them. As winter progresses the wildlife gets weaker and so do we. The bathroom scales tell all and trousers, which were tight in summer, begin to fall down of their own accord. Hands become sore with frost and binder twine. Pipes froze and corn bins emptied. Two of these had to be moved and were deposited by the tractor into a much handier position for next year's feeding. We were getting there, slowly, but surely things could never be as hard as this again.

The lift was working. It had taken three weeks. The men had worked weekends but still it had taken twenty-one days instead of three. We re-laid the carpet in our bedroom and were able to re-make the beds and have a change of clothing. We scrubbed the kitchen floor and brought back the furniture from the sitting room and gave it a good spring clean.

When I rise my first job is to check the cattle sheds. I go alone for the dogs generally wait for Margaret. One morning, at the end of February, both Jess and Danny went out with Margaret when she went to feed first the calves and then the bigger cattle. She invariably leaves the outside door open. I stand the cool in-rush of air so long and then I leave whatever I am doing to go and close it. Jess had been down the Five-Acre and had returned. Because the door had been left open she had re-entered the porch and had lain down. Weary of the cold air filling the kitchen, I went in to close it and our little girl lay dead at my feet.

The realisation stunned me. I went down to the bullock shed to tell Margaret. She was unbelieving. She had watched Jess wander down the field not ten minutes ago. She had walked strongly. The Five-Acre was her most favoured field. In it at dark, she barked at her echo almost every night. If she has a ghost it will haunt the Five-Acre. It was too soon after losing Lusky for us to say goodbye to another dog. He had been an invalid for a long time and his death had not been unexpected. Our dogs live to a great age and Jess was only twelve and, more importantly, she was Harry's dog. He was going to miss her like nobody's business.

We have mourned the death of many, many animals in our long years of farming but Jess's fatal heart attack was the hardest to take. Harry did not always share our grief for he had never reared or nursed an animal. Death outside was something with which Father, Margaret and I had to handle. Harry had to cope with the death of Jess and it was harder because Aunty Mary had always found his dog's presence an intrusion. Her wagging tail, her paw attracting attention irritated our Aunty, hence the cardboard box I'd made to prevent Jess sitting on her feet. She did not share our emotion and it was a long time before Harry stopped talking about his loss. Danny, too, had a problem. He had run out of the front porch with Jess and Margaret. He and his friend had run down the field and returned together, yet the next time he came into the porch Margaret and I were standing over Jess and she was dead. He couldn't, surely, have thought that we had done this to his friend? He was worried. We left Jess in the porch all day so that he could absorb the reality but he was a very unhappy dog. We did not let him see where she was eventually laid to rest. Grave digging is always a difficult job with pick and spade, but the men were here shed-building and had tractor and shovel and we asked that they dig a hole in the paddock. They did so very deeply and there was no way we felt we could bury our Jess so far under the sod. So we half filled it again before we gently lowered her in and covered her over. Dealing with death is inexplicable. We can't say why we were unprepared to bury her so far from the surface. She had been a very close friend for many years and to put her so far away didn't seem right.

I cannot understand those who refuse to have a replacement dog because such is not possible, even though they are right in one sense. We will never get another dog quite like any we have had before but to never again know canine friendship is self-deprivation. It is loneliness self-inflicted. Where we could find another bitch was a problem we were eager to solve.

On leaving Harris we had told Angus that two years on we might need to bring home a little collie bitch, for Jess would then be fourteen and we do like Harris dogs. We thought we must first ring Luskentyre. Who knows, our island friend might have a suitable replacement and some member of his family might be visiting from Glasgow and would bring it halfway. It was unlikely and, when we phoned, Angus had neither collie bitch nor visiting relative.

We could only remember that Jess had come from Hubbersty. We did not know the name of the farmer or the address. What we did have was the telephone number of the orchard where we used to buy damsons, until ten years ago. I phoned and they remembered us. Why are we always recalled? Once seen we fail to be forgotten. Yes, they knew the farmer at Hubbersty and yes they could give me their number. These people also remembered we had taken a bitch pup from their litter twelve years ago but unfortunately they did not have any pups. Their son worked on a farm at Crook and they had a litter born a few days ago. Their dog had sired them. They could give me that number because they might have a spare bitch. They had. There were just two in the litter. The rest were dog pups but they only had one customer who wanted a bitch and, yes, we could certainly have the other. Few people will risk buying a pup without seeing it. We are never given choice and it never fails. We asked that the lady on the phone should call it Meg and teach it to bark. We need a dog which is an alarm. Jess always was. She knew if there was someone on the moor and alerted us. Danny is a silent dog except when he wants to come in.

We had another death in the animal family. For over a year we had had a goose that couldn't walk. Each morning she had to be caught, a noisy, flapping, potentially dangerous bird and taken out to join the only other goose we had at that time. He adored her and stayed dutifully in the paddock, keeping her company all day. There seemed no reason to deprive him, as Margaret was brave enough to grab the lame goose every morning. Whether I could have done so is debatable but I was never put to the test.

This performance lasted for more than a year. Passing strangers called to say one of the geese was hurt. Neighbours from the village knew and understood but early in April the lame goose flapped its way into the stream and died. Its mate was inconsolable. Margaret phoned anyone she thought might have a spare goose in order to pacify the bereaved gander. She found no one, but our electrician happened to be doing a job for us and he said he knew someone with every kind of bird imaginable. He said he'd get one at once and he did. The gander was delighted. The new goose accepted the arranged marriage immediately and thought she was in Heaven. It wasn't long before I was baking with goose eggs again and in May she was sitting and presently our flock doubled when two goslings hatched. When the twins were fully grown, however, Margaret noticed something hanging out of one of the beaks and realised that it was a dog lead clip. She caught the bird and pulled the clip and a yard of red lead came from its gullet. She showed it to the holiday guests and it was good for a laugh until, shortly afterwards, the young goose was found dead. We could find no other explanation for this other than an internal injury caused by eating a red 'worm' three-feet long.

At the annual Guide Get-together, on the first Saturday in March, nothing was discussed other than the coming May Reunion on the Island of Tiree. Most of those planning to sail out together were the pioneers of our island camping. Now almost all in their fifties, they had just been teenagers in 1957. Some who had never attended annual meetings would join them and reunite after forty-three years of separation. Excitement was even greater than it had been all those long, wonderful years ago.

The re-building of the sheds took over two months and the finished work was beautiful. It was a pity that cow muck would have to dirty the cleanliness of the new floor. Of course it had no doors. Why is it that John and his men are always needed elsewhere before they have completely finished? They have, over the years, built all our well-planned complex of sheds and barn but they have never put on the doors until long after completion. These on the

yard-facing buildings were not hung until just before Christmas, eight months
later. When they were, they were perfect.

The installation of the lift was a major operation. It was far more disruptive
than the floor tiling of the previous year. When it was completed we noticed
that the kitchen wallpaper was damaged and everywhere needed painting.
This also applied to the bedroom and to the staircase but we had no time to
decorate. We even neglected to whiten the rooms used by guests. We had
given them an annual coat of emulsion every previous year. Three weeks after
the lift was installed it broke down and we were back on the front room floor.
While the skilled men struggled to find what was wrong with it, we struggled with a growing intolerance for workmen in general. We longed for a
time when there were no alterations in progress and no enormous bills to
pay. Surely it was time to pause and have a rest.

We had two long-term guests. Art Bruneau, a professor working at the Turf
Research station in St Ives, lived in The Loft, and Jan Murphy was having bed
and breakfast. She was a singer performing in The Phantom of the Opera, in
Bradford. It is always a pleasure to have someone for a long time. Someone
nice, that is. We enjoyed having both. Each was a professional in a different
way. Frequently Jan's beautiful voice could be heard practising when she was
alone. Sometimes I would pause behind her door, just to listen secretly.

Easter came and went. As often as possible I made the ridiculous journey
by bus to visit Betty in the nursing home. Incredibly she lived on, unable to
eat or talk. She could not go to bed or move any part of her, but the person
remained unchanged. The tears she could not wipe were followed by a
laughter she could not express. I cannot imagine a disease more awful than
motor neurone or a friend braver than her.

Ken and Marjorie Ward came with relatives immediately after Easter. Ken
was the artist who had painted the lovely picture of The Currer hanging on
the wall. He was first to notice a drip from the dining room ceiling. We had
been aware of a dampness for maybe a year. We had blamed many things for
the vaguely discoloured patch on the ceiling. We thought it might have been
caused by people wetting the bathroom floor when having a shower. It was
so small a patch and almost unnoticeable so we had thought best to ignore
it and not make a major problem out of a minor one.

Suddenly, in the middle of April, a bowl was needed to catch a steady drip
and we had no alternative but to send for the plumber, who was Brian-the-
builder's brother. They pulled down the plaster and exposed a length of pipe
which was green and pitted. They told us that the piping used for the
conversion must have been inferior. It had lasted twenty years but probably
the whole of the holiday accommodation would have to have piping renewed.
Not on your life, we insisted. Do this bad bit and then let's wait and see.

There was no way we could do a major repair at the beginning of a holiday season and what wasn't leaking did not need mending. Indeed not! If the men wanted a job then they could put us a loo in our bedroom, before we set about redecorating it after the lift installation. They turned their attention from work which did not need doing to such that did and put toilet and wash basin in a room which seemed to grow bigger every time we wanted to put something else into it. First had come Harry's bed, then the lift. No one could believe there was room for anything else.

We were really chuffed about the very last bit of plumbing we are prepared to do. In the house in which we had all been born, the builder had put a closet over the bottom of the staircase. It had been entered from the bedroom and had housed our holiday cases and some clothes and been a useful store. We realised that such a cubicle could be built above the steps at The Currer. It could be entered from our bedroom and could house a loo. The last of twelve toilets will be just that. There will be no more. We have had great fun puzzling where and how to accommodate them but that is now over. Indeed we were ticking off finished improvements like wildfire. Was it just possible that we could look forward to a period when paying workmen and buying materials became history?

The en suites were finished. There would be no more extensions. The shed city was complete, or would be when doors were hung. Tim and Graham had built up the yard wall. There were no more roofs to tin, no floors to concrete. We had a more than adequate supply of water troughs. We had self-service feeding machines and the previous year we'd replaced our thistle mower. We were coping. We were coping fine. We had been at The Currer for forty-two years and we had never stopped making improvements. I remember a sarcastic remark of Uncle Joe's when we first decided to come to the ruin. It followed his wife's critical, 'No man would take me there!' Uncle Joe had said with warning, 'It will take you five years to sort that place out!' His estimate had intended to shock us into reversing our decision. He had been dead now for over thirty years. Only now, forty-odd years and not five later, we were seeing an end to major activities and massive demands on our purse.

If I were superstitious I'd get a hang-up about April. Mother had died during that month in 1990. Joan had died during April 1996 and Janet in 1999. Now in the year 2000 it looked very much as if Betty might do the same but I refuse to get hang-ups about anything, as long as we have a billy goat, that is. Our new one was not resident. Twins had been born on the blacksmith's holding but were being suckled by mum and played with as pets by his children. Not to worry, he was there and with him our confidence was assured and our much-looked-forward-to holiday on Tiree was fast approaching, and the excitement was growing for our planned reunion.

Another reunion came first. It was fifty years since we left college to begin our teaching careers and we were having our mini-get-together in college at Ripon instead of here. For all of that time I had been Year Correspondent keeping everyone in touch. Normally when reunion was in college we drove over to Ripon and Margaret entertained the family in Studley Royal while I dined and communed with past students. Those occasions were always in July. We could not possibly do that in April so I elected to go by bus as I had always done in the days before we possessed wheels. In my youth the four-bus journey had been no problem and I could not see why it should be fifty years later. Margaret was too busy. I didn't want to drive alone. I checked the bus times and quite looked forward to just sitting on public transport for a few hours.

Margaret was to reduce the buses by one by taking me down into town. Buses to Shipley were every ten minutes and the one I chose to take would give me nine minutes' changeover time. However, just as we were leaving so were two of our guests, Brian from Portsmouth and his brother. Margaret called out to them, 'Do you want a lift into town?' and the small delay, caused by them getting into the car, made me miss my bus in Keighley and all subsequent buses one after the other. I spent an hour in the bus station at Shipley, thoroughly cheesed off and unreasonably glad that the college at Ripon was due to close and that there would be no more journeys there. It was naughty of me because everyone was angry and sad that our much-loved teacher training college was to be sold and students and courses removed to the York campus. Others were retired and free, even to stay overnight. They never arrived late like I did every time. On that fiftieth occasion I was one hour late. Once, on Harris, we were laughingly called The Late Browns. It was true. We have so many pre-meeting commitments. I looked at my contemporaries eating at table. We were all fifty years older and my journey through life had been different from theirs. They had been teachers, too, but they had married and had children and were now showing photographs of their grandchildren. Life for most of them had been of the expected pattern, the one we had maybe all thought lay ahead when we had parted company, at the gate of the Ripon College campus, fifty years ago. It hadn't happened that way for me but I had no regrets and I certainly was not ready for retirement, which was fortunate as it was not possible on the agenda.

It was naughty of me but, yes, I was glad that, like The Currer improvements, it was coming to an end. I was tired of always arriving late, of the stress of getting there. If they wanted to close the college there was nothing any of us could do about it. Reunions wouldn't be over because we could meet here whenever we wanted, but the rush, the stress, the late arrival, the out of breath beginning of a meal the others had already begun, was over and

I was glad. The occasion was quite sad. The end of an era always is and a lot of the conversation centred around Betty's illness and that was depressing when the atmosphere should have been one of a golden anniversary. Audrey Ames, who lives at Austwick, brought me home in her car. I have seldom been more grateful to anyone.

There was another journey we had to make before holiday. We had to go to Crook, near Kendal, to pick up our pup, Meg. We could have collected her on the way north to Scotland a week later but we wanted to cope with her for a few days, before our holiday. To take a puppy such a long distance was not ideal and seven weeks old was rather too young to bring her away from her mother but we had really no choice in the matter. The jigsaw pieces fitted together perfectly, just a little too tightly for comfort. Order in the universe holds me spellbound. Surely it is governed. When man takes a hand it loses perfection. The timetable concerning Meg was an example of perfect planning by good fortune, by chance, by miracle worker, whatever you care to call the Supreme Organiser. She had been born just three days before Jess died. If there is reincarnation for dogs, I say with confidence that the soul doesn't enter the blind and semi-naked pup until it is three days old. Jess, I am sure, had a soul. She was not just flesh and bones, she was Jess and that other part of her transferred itself to Meg. Not a day passes but we see in our *new* canine friend, an image of our old one. In the things that matter, Jess is still with us.

Amazingly there was just time enough to slot into April a journey to Crook and just enough days left before holiday, to get to know our new 'Little Girl'. Every collie is a funny little so-and-so and we had no thought but that she would be gorgeous as we drove towards the Lake District with a full Land Rover. We had collected Hilda, who loved a day out whenever we had a job further afield. The farm at Crook was in beautiful, Cumbrian countryside. The north of England from east to west is pastoral and, because it is farmed by grazing animals and riddled with country roads, no part of it is less lovely than the rest. Only where horses pasture is the land anything other than a lawn. Where diversification is into horses and equestrian pursuits, the land deteriorates rapidly, but in Cumbria and the Dales, cattle and sheep are perfect landscape gardeners. Long may that be so and Cumbria in springtime is pretty unbeatable.

We had brought a puppy carrycot with us. We do not usually buy relatively expensive things for our farm animals. They are our friends and not our pets. We had paid £30 for this cage only because Meg was coming on holiday with us to Tiree, and we must be able to contain her. She had been ours for seven weeks, though not with us, and we already loved her. She had been taken from the barn, a farm dog's natural habitat, into the farmhouse to await our collection and when the door was opened she was having none of that restraint and headed off for the barn again. She looked very little to be taken away from her mother, but in little more than a week the mother who had suckled her would tire of her offspring anyway. Puppy play can exhaust an older dog and poor Danny was soon to find that out!

The bundle of joy took one look at us and disappeared under the barn door. It was cruel to pursue and to take her away from her birthplace but a fortnight on Tiree's beautiful beaches awaited her, followed by all the freedom of The Currer and the companionship of Danny. People seem to think animals who understand human language are intelligent and that we are the superior race because we have speech. Personally we think the boot may be on the other foot. We think animals do have a language and we are of lesser intelligence because we cannot understand theirs. That animals communicate becomes more evident every day. Cattle certainly tell each other things and just because we cannot comprehend what they are saying only puts them in the same category as foreigners whose mutterings cannot even be separated into words. We are confident that Danny talked to Meg on the journey back to The Currer, in the same way Lusky had told him not to worry on the long, two-day journey away from his island home at Luskentyre.

Jess had travelled very badly and had been sick all the way from Hubbersty but Meg found the movement of the car no problem which relieved us of one anxiety. It is a long way to Tiree! She became head-over-heels in love with Danny and seemed to have no homesickness at all. She just followed him everywhere and we really need never have feared that she would stray, but we still netted the fence enclosing the entrance to the front door so that she was safe from incoming cars, and she slept in the carrycot under the table at night, where she could see Danny. During the day she slept in Danny's bed. We thought he might object because she wanted everything he had but tolerance is his middle name.

We entered the last week before leaving for holiday. There were two things we had to do. We had to visit Betty and we had to go to the cash and carry to buy food for the eighteen who were gathering on Tiree in expectation of re-kindling that flame, in them, which has been burning in us, it seems, for ever. As Margaret and Harry wanted to see Betty we drove to Wibsey and we left the Land Rover and the two dogs outside their house and Billy took us to the nursing home. I cannot, in words, describe how sad, yet how lovely that occasion was. Margaret initially found the visit almost impossible. She was unprepared to see how fast the disease had progressed. She hardly knew what to say but Harry stepped into the fore. He knew exactly what to do and what to say. Composed and compassionate he greeted her.

'Hello, Betty. How are you? We've come to see you.' He continued to say all the right things. We watched spellbound. Margaret followed his example, grateful for his leadership. Our brother was as amazing as Betty. The way in which she tolerated that awful disease will remain with us for always. We tried not to make our parting sound like 'Goodbye' but we knew that it was.

So now there were just days to holiday but each one required that we make an evening meal. Among our guests there was Tom, who had been in a wheelchair for fifty years. He had come on holiday for years with his wife, Judy. They had met in Australia, married and come back to England where they had lived in County Durham. Judy was disabled too and after the recent amputation of her legs she had wanted to return to Australia and the comfort and care of her family. Tom had gone too, but the climate had not suited him and he had returned. They both suffered from the hurtful separation and phoned each other constantly. Tom was having his second holiday without her at The Currer during the week before our holiday and that was a mistake for those pre-holiday weeks are always ill fated.

He had a very poor start to his holiday health-wise but recovered and picked himself up, determined to enjoy his stay to the full. After a few days he felt well enough to buy himself a fishing licence and head for the canal. He had a pint at the pub alongside and was so welcomed by the landlord that he forgot to pay, which meant he must return next day to settle his debt. He was in great spirits and did some shopping. His van is fully converted so that he can get in and out with ease. He enjoys the shopping centre in town and paid a visit to Boots chemist which has a ramp at one of the entrances. He chose the wrong exit and catapulted down two steps and was thrown out of the wheelchair into the precinct. Two men picked him up and put him back into the wheelchair. He came home but did not tell us. He refused his evening meal and next morning did not rise before noon and was extremely stressed. He was to go home the following morning and his agitation increased towards evening and we insisted he tell us what was the matter. He did. He told us about his accident and his fear that he was hurt and could not drive home. As we were poised for holiday we feared that, too, and sent for the doctor to come and check him over and give him assurance that he was only bruised and could safely go home.

We went somewhat tardily to the cash and carry warehouse and bought £400 worth of food, some to leave behind for Dorothy but most of it to pack onto the roof rack for transfer to Tiree in a couple of days. It was like old times buying stores for camp. Aunty Mary, Harry and the dogs were all in the Land Rover. Margaret climbed onto the rack and we put everything on the roof and set off home. On the outskirts of Wilsden the Land Rover hesitated and then stopped altogether.

'I can't be short of petrol, can I?' Margaret said. 'The gauge said I was low but not empty!' Our Range Rover had gone for miles after registering empty.

We decided something else must be wrong, then started to panic because it was 5 p.m. and our specialist garage would close and we'd be stranded with all that food, two dogs, two human dependants and everyone waiting for an evening meal at home! I opted to find a phone and ran to the nearest house. The owner was washing dishes and all her worldly goods were neatly packed and stacked on the living room floor. It was the eve of her removal to another house. Her children were playing quietly and the atmosphere was one of extreme competence and order and I compared it with the chaos which would reign in my house if we had transport problems.

She let me phone and while I waited to be re-called I dried her dishes, conscious of the neat piles, the filled cardboard boxes. This lady was organised, and we would have to be in a few hours' time. The Simmonite mechanic said he would come with a breakdown wagon to pick up the Land Rover and as we waited we wondered how to get our passengers into the cab, then decided it was impossible and we must order a taxi if necessary. The enormous recovery vehicle arrived and Margaret admitted the problem might just be an empty fuel tank. 'We'll try that first,' said the patient man who should have been having his tea by now. He went the two miles to the nearest filling station and came back with five gallons of petrol in a huge container. When the engine burst into life we did not know whether to be extremely embarrassed or very relieved.

'I'm so sorry,' Margaret apologised. Then, 'We really are under stress at the moment. We go on holiday the day after tomorrow. We very nearly panicked!' The good man laughed. He has known us a long time. We drove home wiser owners of a Land Rover that exhausts its supply of fuel before it actually registers so.

We had a lady staying from Gourock who bought crystals. She gave us a pink corner stone for the mantelpiece to ensure for us peace and the ability to see beauty. We had the latter already. Peace as the alternative to war has always been our hope. Peace in everyday activity, we could do with plenty more of that!

The next day was our last and we must pack, or rather I must do so and Margaret must check the boundary. She came back saying there was a very dangerous branch of hawthorn above the mini-cliff in the Eight-Acre. She feared an animal might trip over it on the narrow path above the ledge and plunge to its death. 'We must saw it off,' she said. She was not going on any holiday until we did, so we went up in the Land Rover, with brother in the front seat and tools in the back, and we made a mullock of the job. Having sawn halfway through the branch, which was a mere six inches from the ground, it dropped slightly and trapped the bow saw permanently – well, for that evening anyway! So now we not only had a dangerous branch but one with a wedged tool that, try as we might, would not budge. As it was almost dark we drove home defeated, planning to return next morning but minus an idea as to what we could do. Much later, but long before we had any hope of bed, Margaret went out on some forgotten errand and found that the herd of seven month old calves, that had been sleeping out for several days, had broken through the paddock fence behind the house and were camping illegally. We were incredibly tired so all she did was to shut the yard gates to prevent them entering and doing damage to the visitors' parked cars. I don't think The Currer ever wants us to go on holiday. Wearily Margaret came in and announced we must get up early, perhaps not even go to bed, we had so much work to do before we could leave.

Serving B&B breakfasts next morning a well-wisher asked if we were on course for departure. 'Guess what!' I said. 'Calves broke through the paddock fence last night. That's to mend before we go and we've a bow-saw stuck in a hawthorn branch, above the cliff in the Eight-Acre.'

The listener happened to be an agricultural merchant so I described how we'd tried to take off a low branch we thought could trip up an animal, if several took to the path at once. 'Take your car jack up,' he advised. We could see it would solve our problem immediately but I don't think we'd have thought of it ourselves. It's true: it's not always what you know but who you know, at the right moment in time. Carrying the jack from Land Rover to tree was the hardest bit. Lifting the branch so that the sawn half gaped wide enough for the saw to be released and the operation to continue was mere child's play. What a nice man that agricultural merchant was.

So now we had only to wash the dishes, make the beds and sort out the fifty metres of flattened fence and isn't that the most disliked job we ever do? Margaret hunted up new posts and brought out the sledgehammer and a bale to stand on, for we were once described as 'the diminutive ladies'.

As we needed only one stop on our journey to Oban for the Tiree boat, we had booked a Travel Lodge at Penrith so it was not imperative that we leave home too early. An early start was preferable but not essential, so we made as good a job of repairing the fence as we could and went indoors. We'd put the luggage on the rack and encased it in the Bowness cover before breakfast, so we were ready to go. And then the phone rang. Unbelievably it was the son of the same friend whose visit had so delayed us the previous May. 'My father is in hospital,' he said. 'Do you think you could call in and see him? He can talk to you.' It was true. Jack could talk about the past for hours.

'We're just leaving for holiday,' I heard her say. 'We're passing the hospital. We'll call in.'

'We'll do what?!' I gasped as she put down the phone.

'I said we'd go to see Jack on our way out,' she admitted.

At 4 p.m. we pulled out of the yard. We spent nearly an hour pretending we had all the time in the world, talking about the snow of 1947 and the Ayrshire herd we had at the time, to a man who had once lived as a neighbour, who remembered us and what we did then, but hadn't a clue what he had done yesterday. Finally, long after tea-time we left the hospital and headed for Penrith. Phew!!

Chapter Ten

> *To whom do I owe the magic of*
> *This Incredible Reunion,*
> *This God-given week when we were one?*
> *One family sharing memories*
> *Of halcyon days when we were young.*
> *To whom can I attribute*
> *This affinity, this ease, this joy,*
> *This unplanned serenity,*
> *This Pentecostal radiance?*

We were away at last, turning right on reaching the exit from the hospital grounds and heading towards Skipton and the A6, the faster route to Penrith. It was late and the A629 was very busy for it was rush hour and everyone was hurrying home from work. We were driving along the Skipton by-pass when Harry said, 'Go to Grassington.' He repeated it several times and when we reached the roundabout we obeyed and followed the A65 as far as the Grassington turn off. We were on holiday and needed to leave tension behind. So the Fields Way it was and the relief, when we turned off the highway and took the narrower road with no vehicle in front and none behind, was palpable. Anxieties, tension, weariness, stress all dissolved within the comfort of the Dales. The upper fells of Wharfedale belong to the National Trust and the route through Buckden and over to Hawes, in Wensleydale, is well known to us.

April had barely gone and, as always in sheep country, there is a temptation to sing, albeit untunefully, 'All in an April evening, I thought of the Lamb of God.' The sheep and their little lambs passed us by on our road but no other traffic did. We were at peace among the woollen landscape gardeners of the Dales. I do not think enough people appreciate their debt to the native herds. They too often believe the exquisite beauty of the countryside is a permanent thing that can be preserved without grazing animals. It cannot. It is totally dependent on the continuation of farming practices pursued over hundreds of years. To our left, as we drove northwards, we could see the

Lakeland Hills etched on the skyline. Without sheep the character of them would change completely.

Beyond Kirkby Stephen a B-road shortens the journey and misses Brough. We drove along it with blinding sunshine striking our port bow and we dare not turn west onto the Penrith road until it, in glorious splendour, sank below the horizon. We pulled into a lay-by and waited and watched the dazzling ball disappear, painting the sky as it did so, an impressive shade of scarlet and gold.

I did not know that, even while we sat there watching the Heavens ablaze, Betty had slipped into unconsciousness or that news of her death would reach Tiree before we did. Even had I done so it would have been inappropriate to grieve. To mourn is necessary but death is welcome after so much suffering and Heaven couldn't have looked more beautiful than on that May Thursday evening, waiting for the sun to go down and it to be safe for us to enter the A66 and head for Penrith.

We arrived at the Travel Lodge at the same time as the curtain of the night enveloped us. Our little pup had been angelic. She had been quiet in her carrycot and sensible on a lead. She seemed to be far too small to be going on such an adventure. Forgive me if I repeat it too many times, but I really would like to know what thoughts pass through doggy minds as they follow their human families wherever and whenever.

There was yet again a hitch at a Travel Lodge. Two rooms had been reserved but they were both upstairs! I couldn't believe what I was hearing. I always, always, always explained we had a brother in a wheelchair and needed ground floor rooms.

Since the installation of the lift Harry had never walked stairs again. The receptionist tried to insist that I must have neglected to tell the booking clerk but I couldn't have. When we first accommodated the handicapped on our own converted premises I was quickly made aware that those who have a disability, or who are caring for a wheelchair user, ask innumerable questions about height and width, about ramps and toilets and parking spaces. Until a few years ago we never had to say Harry was disabled because he could, with help, negotiate almost anything. Margaret had even taken him to the top of the sand dunes at Luskentyre. Recently we had to join the army of those asking questions about wheelchair friendliness and I was willing to swear, under oath, that I had booked ground floor rooms.

Our only complaint about Travel Inns and Lodges is that bookings are unconfirmed by letter. A reference number is meaningless to the customer and nothing on which to build a case. Fortunately the receptionist could re-arrange two other bookings and give us ground floor keys. It wasn't her mistake but I am equally sure it wasn't mine. Seeing Harry enthroned on wheels she did some quick thinking and solved her problem.

Sadly, for twenty years it had been unknown for either Margaret or me to bathe before leaving. Travel Lodge baths are not so comfortable as the one at The Currer, but ablutions can be taken at leisure which does compensate. As ever we crawled, clean and scented, into bed.

Morning sunshine streamed through the bedroom windows as we leisurely went through the somewhat lengthy operation of rousing our dependants, feeding and dressing them, all in holiday mood. Margaret took the dogs for their morning stroll and I filled the thermos flasks. Then she and I entertained departing guests by repacking the roof rack. Margaret, the nimbler of the two, goes up and I, the taller, throw up the overnight things. Everyone is smiling while saying a cheerful, 'Good morning'. Everyone seems amused by our necessary antics but the car park is empty when we finally push the wheelchair past the busy chambermaids blocking the passage. They too, are cheerful. We can relate to them for we are chambermaids also.

Couples, unhampered by dogs and relatives, have all departed in a freedom we do not know or want. It is our fault that we have had so little personal space. We did not have to take other people's children. There are kennels in which to leave dogs and respite care homes in which to leave the elderly and infirm. To take dependants with us has been our choice. It has been fun. All those years with children were joy. Given a replay we would do the same again, without hesitation, but when personal freedom comes, if ever, we'll know what to do with that also. In the meantime, as Harry once said, life would indeed be boring without him.

It would be boring, too, without Aunty Mary. We arrived at Longtown at lunchtime and we admitted to being very hungry. Margaret sent me to buy fish and chips so that we could picnic in a convenient spot we have used many times, close to the river and not far from the toilets.

'I'll be taking them to the loo,' she said.

Returning with my steaming purchases, I found confusion. The toilets were closed for repairs. A lady passing by had told Margaret to take them to the nearby pub, The Tavern, which was almost adjacent to the public conveniences. No way, Margaret told me, was she going to take them into the pub to ask for help.

'I'll go,' I said. I was a headmistress used to commanding help when surrounded by a multitude of children. I remembered being in Inverness, waiting for a train connection, late at night. We had been in camp on Harris for a fortnight and had travelled down from Ullapool and every child needed the toilet. I remember marching into the posh Station Hotel and asking if fifty children could please use the toilets and was welcomed with a smile. I'll never forget ushering them all across the foyer to the elegant Ladies. They entered smelling of sand and salt water and tiptoed out, shining and fragrant.

Their camp tablet of Lux may still have borne its name but the rose-scented hotel liquid had been depleted!

To me a brother in a wheelchair and an ancient aunt were child's play. My confidence weakened, on entering the pub, when I saw a huge notice saying that the toilets were for customers only. At almost three score years and ten neither I, nor my companions, had ever been customers of public houses. However, though less sure of being welcomed, I ignored the notice, entered the dark saloon, full of working class men, and went to the bar.

'We are on our way from Yorkshire to Oban,' I told the barman. 'I've got a seventy-two-year old brother in a wheelchair and a ninety-three-year old aunt [How many times have I used this and it been a successful excuse?] and the toilets are closed. Would you mind?'

'Come right in,' the good man said. 'You're welcome!'

There was no way we were going into the Gents with Harry. We dragged him, protesting, into the Ladies and made our invasion as brief as possible. The premises were absolutely empty for it was lunchtime and only men were drinking in the semi-darkness of the saloon. We wobbled out, dragging Harry between us, said a grateful thank you and returned Harry to the wheelchair we'd left on the pavement.

It takes Aunty Mary much longer. We had left her safely behind the closed door of a cubicle so Margaret went back into the pub to collect her and guide her safely out.

She was not there!

Margaret reappeared saying so.

I had pushed Harry to the station wagon just a few yards away. 'She must be,' I said.

'Well, she isn't! You go and look. She's not there!'

The toilets were just inside the pub entrance. Coming out of them the open door onto the street could be seen. I insisted she must be still in there or we would have seen her walking behind us. Had she done so she would not only have seen us, she couldn't possibly have missed the Land Rover with its PVC Bowness cover!

Thinking Margaret must be stupid, I went inside and into the Ladies to the open door of the cubicle our aunt had used. 'Aunty Mary,' I called. 'Where are you?' There was no answer. Margaret followed me and we opened every one of the seemingly many doors but she was not there. It was ridiculous to be searching emptiness so diligently. Even when we knew there was no one there we still kept on searching. Aunty Mary is large but we searched those premises as if we were searching for a contact lens. We asked the barman. We asked the dour men in the darkened room. Nobody had seen Aunty Mary. ' She must have gone out,' the barman said without interest.

'A small lady went out,' one man said.

'That was me,' Margaret answered. There was a rising panic in both of us but it was unintelligent to think Aunty Mary could have really disappeared. Nevertheless we were getting desperate.

'She'll have gone out and turned the wrong way,' the barman said after he, too, had searched, called, 'Mary!' several times and been unable to find her.

So we went out and Margaret said she'd go up to the High Street and turn left and that I must follow and turn right with Harry. We were beginning to lose our composure. We didn't see how she could possibly have come out and not seen us parked so close. She had no dementia that we were aware of. We had lost her a few times in Carmarthan Market but that was because she was bargain hunting. We had not indicated we would go into the town centre. She knew I had just bought fish and chips and that they would be going cold. Her memory is not so bad as all that!

Margaret hurried off and I struggled to get the wheelchair turned and back onto the pavement, then I began to follow. I could see Margaret at the T-junction looking east, then west and shaking her head. Our aunt couldn't walk fast and she invariably needed an arm to help her. Surely she could have got no distance. A child might have run. A child might have been abducted but no one would run off with a ninety three year old! I don't believe in magic or aliens whisking people into outer space, but disappeared she had!

I hurried along the pavement regardless of the fact that the wheelchair was rattling and Harry almost bouncing out. I was watching the uneven pave-stones ahead. I don't know why I glanced sideways. Had I not done so we would have searched the High Street and then we would have gone to the police for we would not have found her. Adjacent to the end of The Tavern wall, there was a huge wooden gate. I do not think I am exaggerating if I say it was seven feet high and more than that wide. It was made of six-inch slats, each separated by a space and the two halves of it were secured with a huge padlock bigger than my fist. Nettles and grass escaped from behind it onto the street, suggesting the gate had not been opened for some time though, between the gaps, a normal, overgrown, pub-yard could be seen. No doubt the jumble would have been identified as beer barrels, dustbins, boxes, Calor gas cylinders, bottles and crates had I not been held spellbound at the sight of an old lady, handbag in hand, standing among the nettles, bewildered by her unexpected location.

I left Harry outside the gate. He could see her, though the gaps between the gate slats were small, and I ran to the main street and yelled for Margaret to stop looking. The lost lady had been found. May we be forgiven. We stood in front of the locked gate and we creased with laughter as we might at a monkey, behind bars in a zoo. We do not know how she got there nor the route the barman went to rescue her and reunite us but we couldn't wipe the smile from our faces nor suppress the laughter. We realised, of course, that had I not glanced sideways as I hurried up the street, it might have been a long time before anyone, barman or policeman, had found her. Oh, yes, without Aunty Mary, too, life might be boring!

We spend more time than other people do visiting public conveniences and it takes us half an hour whereas it only takes other people minutes. Having attended to family, we then have to find a field or woodland for our dogs to use. Our first and last experience of Meg being unable to wait any longer was somewhere in the Loch Awe area. We were approaching Oban via Inveraray and had not broken our journey there because Aunty Mary was asleep and time was running out. Only by the skin of our teeth had we caught the Gourock/Dunoon ferry. Harry was comfortable and we were used to dogs who could almost wait for ever. Danny had waited two days on the journey home from Harris, on the year Angus had insisted we bring him home. We had released him from the British Airways box he was travelling in, several times, but he was too stressed to take advantage. We had never travelled with a pup before and when we were approaching some botanical gardens, Meg became as talkative as a monkey. We have never heard her speak that language again. It was full of words and sentences and she was not quite nine weeks old. We started to laugh and look for a lay-by but the road was narrow and the only convenient place seemed these botanical gardens. Cars were parked just within the gates and it was evident that there was an open evening of some sort, for an attendant was organising the parking. We had to admit we were only looking for a place where an agitated and chattering puppy could spend a penny. It would have been embarrassing if the man had not been a dog lover. As it was he adored our baby collie nearly as much as we did and didn't mind at all. He helped Margaret lift out the talking pup and the river she made would have watered several flowerbeds. Never again have we heard such a dramatic display of linguistic ability. It was baby-talk of the rarest, most endearing kind. What a joy Meg was all holiday.

Unlike Janet, I only give reincarnation a brief, negative thought, every now and then, but there is an awful lot of Jess in Meg. Each dog is different but Meg is too much like her Lakeland predecessor for it to go unnoticed.

In Oban we spent the night in an hotel near the pier. It was only the second night we had spent in one, since we began using self-catering cottages in 1973. It used to be possible to sleep in berths on the Inner Isles steamer but not any more. We find this a nuisance. Anchored in the harbour, safely in our cabins, we did not need to rise early. The boat could leave harbour and sail up the sound as far as Tobermory before we need emerge. Now this is no longer possible, we had to rise at 5 a.m. in the Kelvin Hotel. Fortunately it was situated conveniently near the pier and the public car park opposite could be used for the overnight parking of the Land Rover.

Meg had her first breath of sea air walking on the harbour and she caused so many eyes to turn adoringly in her direction, Margaret was almost afraid to leave her in the car all night, lest someone stole her. For a fortnight she was to become a beach puppy with an immense amount of freedom to chase sea birds and find stinking remains of dead lambs. She dug far too many holes in the steading cottage garden for sand is easy material. She learned that we were suitable people to follow and that Danny was a playmate to tease and wrestle all day, if she could keep awake long enough.

It had been arranged that we would spend the first week of our holiday alone, principally to have a much-needed holiday, a battery charge, before being joined by the pioneers of camping, the 1957 Guides. Hughie's second cottage in the steading was bigger than the first and we chose to use that. It was as beautiful as the first but had two bedrooms and more bathroom space. The Guides would use the smaller cottage and two others nearby. Between the two steading cottages the barn had been emptied, carpeted and furnished with chairs and a dining table to accommodate us all. Perfect!

The weather, during the first week, was simply glorious. We spent long hours on the beautiful beaches scalloping the island. We visited friends and made reunion plans galore, desperately hoping that the good weather would last. We need not have worried.

It was forty-three years since we had begun our twenty-five years of island camping with hundreds of children. Nearly all of those waiting to join us had been on the first camp and I had been only twenty-seven at the time. While we were reunited, I was to reach my seventieth birthday. I had catered for many, year after year, on wood and peat fires and I say and will say it again and again, that if I should be remembered at all, it should be for the fun I have given children in beautiful places.

Margaret was just as excited as I was. She was more anxious than I that it should be a perfect performance, this attempt to replay without rehearsal. Father had grown too old, in the early 1970s, to leave with all the responsibility of family and farm. Margaret had sacrificed the annual camps and stayed at home, almost a decade before I was forced to call a halt. I risk being told I lie when I say that each of the twenty-five summer camps in the Hebrides was equally good, equally enjoyed whatever the weather and whoever the children, but I speak only the truth. To pick out the best, or the worst, would not be possible. There is magic, for us, in islands and I was relying heavily on this and predicting that this experience of return would not be disappointing. I had confidence in my returning children, irrespective of their being in their fifties, and I knew instinctively that the island and the islanders would not let us down.

Campers' reunion, Tiree, 2000.

Every morning Danny, Meg and I went down to the nearby beach to stretch our legs and welcome the new day. The pup gave continuous joy. She caused no trouble other than holes in the garden which we filled in every night. She slept in her carrycot, in the car and only argued with us when we wished to drag her away from a dead lamb or a stinking sheep half buried by drifting sand. Father had said that if a dog was allowed to eat a dead animal it would never worry a live one. He had many old-fashioned prophecies, most of which were reliable. Babies in the animal kingdom mature far too quickly. If we had been more abreast of the times we would have had a camcorder to film Meg and preserve the moving pup, but we would also have needed a video and we do not have one of those either, so it was terribly important to enjoy every minute we could. That first week on Tiree was the moment to do so, for when Saturday came she had to take a back seat while we became Skipper and Flim again.

The good weather continued. May, in the Hebrides, seldom disappoints. We went down to the pier, in the tiny township of Scarinish, to wait for the steamer from Oban. While it was some distance away we could see the line of our grown children, leaning on the deck rails and waving and the lump in my throat grew until I thought I would choke. The years roll back so easily, I find. The pages in a still-open book are easily turned back. I cannot imagine senility in my confidence that to forget is impossible, but I found I was not quite sure that I could cope with the experience of watching the boat dock and waiting for the invasion. Always, before, I had been on the deck with them, and any emotion had been aroused by the approaching island. It had been well controlled by the activity of ensuring that everyone was assembled to disembark, with kit collected and rucksacks shouldered. There had been scarcely any time for private joy as the boat slid too quickly against the pier and the gangway was too speedily lowered. Standing waiting on the pier was different. The steamer sailed too slowly over the bar and into Gott Bay. It approached the pier at a snail's pace. My campers were all waving and I was getting more and more tense.

The docking seemed to take ages. Twenty years ago it had all happened so quickly I hardly had opportunity to take the fifty and more sailing tickets from the depths of my rucksack pocket, before they were needed to lead my party down the gangway. In May 2000 I stood on the pier first on one foot and then on another, silently screaming at the crew to go through their motions more quickly, while I could still greet everyone tearlessly.

It was an emotional reunion. I felt tears against my cheek that were not mine. I had been their teacher and their leader, to be obeyed and respected but not embraced. On 13 May 2000 their arms encircled Margaret and me and their still-white cheeks brushed our already sunburnt ones and that precious moment, before all the talking began, I will treasure all my life and take with me into eternity. It was an emotional start to a wonderful week, an almost accurate replay of forty-three years ago. Barefoot and in shorts, these grown children even looked the same and as the sun daily coloured their legs and their bare toes, and as they grouped frequently in a different kaleidoscopic pattern and talked the same language, it seemed that yesterday had not given way to today.

So how do I begin to tell you about it, you who did not experience the first camp or any of the twenty-five years of island camping that followed, you who have maybe never been on Tiree in the springtime, with children in the sunshine? May is the month of calves and lambs and the sea birds have finished nesting and behave protectively towards their young and, though you may waken early the sun has beaten you and is streaming on your pillow, for your curtains are not drawn. To know is to have been there and though I am always writing for my children this chapter is unnecessary for those who shared our millennium experience and will never forget.

So I must write it for those who were not there and hope that, in part, they will comprehend.

Reunion is such a lot of talking but ours had to be accompanied with activity. Kit had to be loaded into Donald Brown's Land Rover, which he had driven to the end of the pier. Shy, competent, island Donald has been

our mainstay for many years. At our 1957 camp he was only a child. As the
number of camping years grew he, too, added age and understanding, became
teenager and then man. He can always be found, can always provide, can
always repair, transport and support. He is there on arrival and departure and
Tiree without him is unthinkable. Sylvia, too, was on the pier. She had been
my pupil, then a Guide who had gained a Queen's Guide Award, an island
camper and a Ranger. She had spent almost twenty years taking holidays on
Tiree and had recently gone to live there permanently. Her car and our Land
Rover were parked on terra firma and she was to loan hers so that wherever
we went there was room for all.

To see the pile of their kit, first on the pier and then outside the white-
washed steading, among the daisies, was to bring the past into the present.
The memory of the heap of tents and skips and personal gear, being unloaded
from Johnny Kennedy's lorry onto the machair carpet of the small valley near
the shore at Salum, was brought suddenly into focus. All week I was to
remember the words I had written at the end of *A Song to Sing and a Tale to
Tell*:

> I do not believe that the grand boys and girls who have wandered with us
> are unusual. They are ordinary children whose good fortune it has been
> to see great beauty and know fine people.
>
> I am sure that there are thousands of children everywhere who would
> be just as happy, tolerant and sensitive; just as considerate and aware as
> ours; just as inventive and resourceful if they were given the same
> opportunity and the same simplicity.
>
> If I am wrong and by some unfair twist of fortune, we have indeed had
> the best of Britain's children, for over twenty years, then Hazel, Margaret
> and I have been singularly blessed.

During the six days of that reunion I believed we had, indeed, had the best
of Britain's children and been singularly blessed! The sun thought so too and
shone on us everyday. Many people think that, over the years, people change.
I think they are wrong. Character and personality may develop and mature
but, I have found, that to know a child is to know the adult that child will be.
To think there has been change, I believe, is not to have known well enough
in the first place. We saw no change in our grown children. What they were
they still are. If they thought they saw change in one another it was only
because, as teenagers, they missed what they were seeing now. We who had
been older than they then, small though the age gap was, saw the same char-
acteristics which had made them individual children over forty years ago.

Only Barbara, and Sylvia who lived there, had ever been back to the island
often. Kathleen had been back only once. The others – Ann, another

Margaret, Toots, Joan, Valerie, Brenda, Christine, Jenny, Enid, Helen and Pauline – were returning with only childhood memories of an island paradise. They had feared disappointment if they returned alone but reunion had been irresistible.

On the beach at Caolis, on the machair where we'd camped so many times, at Brock among the once-thatched cottages, stretching sunburned legs along the wide, white, empty beaches of Gott and Baugh and Balephetrish, it proved to be much more beautiful than they remembered. Their memories had been of childish fun, of freedom, frolic and food. They had remembered life in a community but only adults really remember a landscape and, though they, like Barbara, had been spellbound being driven along Gott Bay, all those many years ago, it was as adults that they appreciated the sheer beauty of the island and they were wide-eyed. Most of them had travelled abroad. They had all seen more places than I had, but Valerie spoke for them all when she said, 'I think I have died and this is Heaven!'

They could not believe how easy it was to communicate with each other. Some had not met again in all those in-between years, yet not one found it difficult to talk to another. They were amazed how much they had in common, how much they agreed, how similar were their morals, their philosophy, their accepted code of behaviour, their parenting and grandparenting and their Christian values. They each nearly fitted the same mould, understood the same language and had the same delightful sense of humour. What amazed Margaret and me was that they treated us as they had then. When they were children it was always them and us. Between us was always the distance of leader to led. If we had thought about it, Margaret and I would have prophesied that the gap would have disappeared. It hadn't. Their respect for us was just that little bit more than for each other, their relationship with us was different enough for me to remark, to Margaret, with a smile, 'Guess what! It's still them and us!' and that was both amusing and acceptable. If that had changed perhaps the experience that followed would have done so also.

On that first day we went to Salum, to the hollow in the machair which had been our summer haunt for many years. It was as if we stood on hallowed ground. How small it always seems without the tents, and how empty without the children. The drop onto the beach is steeper than it was for there has been some erosion which would now make it quite difficult to carry full buckets of water from Calum's for cooking and drinking or from the sea for everything else. Hughie has increased his herd and now makes silage so perhaps if we were to camp in July now, we would first have to pick up the dry cow dung and pile it to use as fuel alongside the pine strippings shipped from Tobermory.

After singing grace, as we always do when together, we ate the meal

Margaret and I had prepared. We sat round the extended table in the carpeted barn and we talked and we talked. Eventually we were all exhausted, they the more so with two days of travelling on top of the excitement of unstoppable tongues. There is nothing so invigorating as conversation, nothing more tiring. Arm in arm they went to their three cottages and we went to bed even without talking to each other.

The following day we began to feel the real magic of the island. I drove Harry and Aunty Mary to the other end of Gott Bay while the others walked, a happy, healthy, wide-eyed group who had not aged in more than four decades. Only Jenny came in the Land Rover. She had had a too-recent broken pelvis to attempt too much walking. Some, with recurring pain, would have cancelled coming to the reunion altogether but not Jenny. I pushed Harry's wheelchair along the flat extent of the Traigh Mhòr to meet the walkers. They took the handles and pushed him back. This became a ritual followed for most of the week. It was a respite care experience. My one-time Guides pushed the wheelchair, took Aunty Mary's arm, made the picnic, filled the flasks, made the meals, set the tables and did the washing-up. Helen even drove the Land Rover. Margaret and I knew a freedom we'd not experienced for a very long time.

Mary Davis and her daughter Monica opened up the closed-until-high-season Centre, at Hynish. They had baked pancakes and scones and afterwards took us over the machair to Happy Valley. Margaret and I had never been there for the simple reason that it meant leaving Harry and Aunty Mary, and Mother when she lived, for quite some time. To do so, in the May of 2000, was easy for we left Jenny behind to care for them during the hour of our absence and I am glad that we first experienced the beauty of that tip of Tiree with friends. The sun was high and hot and we were all in shorts and shirts. and though most of us were greying none had lost the agility to climb over the rocks, or the desire to wade through the breakers, or just sit on a promontory, silently watching the changing colours of the Atlantic.

Because Tiree is relatively flat, apart from the three small hills of Hynish, Hough and Cean a Bhara, and has no rivers bigger than a small stream, a valley has to be small. Because Tiree is tree-less it has to be empty of everything but pasturing sheep and wheeling seabirds. Because Tiree is so small, everywhere has to be beside the sea, which is turquoise, having a bed of white sand. Sunday, in the Hebrides, is a silent time. The pink crystal corner-stone donated by our visiting guest may ensure peace in our habitat but the pink rocks of Tiree, the washed pebbles in their thousands on the shore, the Iona marble found at Balephuil taught us, half a century ago, how to appreciate splendour. We had been born with eyes that could see beauty and so had this adult group of children, reunited, slim, healthy, barefoot, sun-worshipping grandparents in shorts. They scattered themselves singly or in couples, bright dots of red and yellow against the green carpet of the valley or silhouetted against the blue of the restless ocean breaking on the shore.

Then, in the evening, after sundown, they gathered cross-legged in front of the sitting room fire, in the bigger cottage we occupied, and we sang until midnight. That first campfire was amazing. How could we possibly know so many songs and ditties and campfire circle games? How did we so easily remember all the words? I had painstakingly typed out many from my song book but the effort (all typing with two fingers is an effort!) had been quite unnecessary.

To lead the campfire was still my responsibility. I have no singing ability. I change key at random and, recently, at the first crescendo I become mute. Even though I cannot finish a song I can still begin them all so that there is never any silence. If I pitch the wrong note, years of practice have taught them how to adjust and one song grows out of another in our 'Song to Sing' community and at that first campfire the spirit of the week was born. We felt the surge of returning memories. This is what we had come for! This is what we had waited so long for!

That Evensong, rich in the folklore of Guiding and in the music of the Hebrides, was a spiritual experience. We laughed at the witty ditties of child-hood and cried when singing 'The Creed' and sentimental tunes like 'In my Father's House' and 'Kumbya'. There was little doubt but that we had all been smitten, again, with the magic of islands which 'lie dreaming in the west'.

I remembered that last campfire of the first camp, forty-three years ago. We had been in Calum's kitchen singing to his very old mother, and her contri-bution, 'The Eriskay Love lilt', had reduced children to tears. Those children were with us now. They had been the ones to open the door for the hundreds who had followed, in the twenty-five years we had been able to continue, and my gratitude to them for re-opening the door in the millennium was immeasurable.

Harry's most frequent query was always, 'Have I done all right?' Margaret and I went to bed that night feeling we had done so, too. We had done all right, beginning with these our first campers and continuing to do so for enough years, for our Hebridean invasions to become a legend.

Did anyone else have a seventieth birthday amid such beauty among such good friends? One of our group had not yet arrived. Toots, whom most had not seen for over forty years, was to arrive by the small plane which lands on Tiree almost every day. While most walked via Salum and Vaul, climbed to Dun Mor, the brock we had seen excavated many years ago, and made a pilgrimage to the Ringing Stone, I drove a Land Rover party to the airport to meet the plane. Immediately, Toots was one of The Clan and we all gathered on the machair, enclosing the magnificent Balevulin Bay, for a pre-packed picnic, immensely glad to be together. Conversation was unbelievably easy. There was no small talk. All subjects were profound as each shared an affinity one could never have accurately predicted.

It would be stupid to say I felt young again for the truth is I have not yet ever felt old, but I did feel the youngest person ever to reach three-score-years-and-ten!

Ann, Enid, Helen and Pauline shared the cottage at Miodar, on the tip of the Caolis peninsula. It provided unexpected luxury with spacious kitchen and enormous lounge. It was ideal for seating many at an extended table and having a birthday celebration such as I had never known before. We are not birthday people. Harry's seventieth had been created by our guests and mine was totally in the hands of my ex-campers. Funnily enough the only other time that I can remember, when I was so prominently the centre of attraction, was at my retirement from active Guiding when Hazel and those organising the evening on Tiree, planned the first annual reunion on home territory. Scores of ex-campers had attended that occasion. It had been secretly planned and cancelled because of deep snow. The secret had been let out by Jenny who had written from Stokesley, Middlesbrough, to say how sorry she had been not to be able to attend. Not knowing it had been planned or cancelled, her news had let every cat out of the bag for me.

The more recent occasion will be as remembered as the first, not least because every time we raise our eyes in the sitting room at The Currer, we will see an original watercolour on the wall. A Keighley artist painted it from a colour photograph of the shore below the minute township of Brock with its traditional once-thatched, black houses. Though the thatch has been replaced with tar, so that the roofs look like up-turned boats, and their walls are whitened, as are almost all the houses on Tiree, they represent the island we first explored fifty years ago. They are reflected in the shallow pools left by the outgoing tide and the colours of the land, sea and sky are so Hebridean; it is the work of a fine artist.

The birthday cake was unbroken in spite of its long journey and amazingly it had a frill on which was an original camp form for 1957 advising parents of the date, venue and cost of the very first camp on Tiree.

One of the highlights of every camp was to hire Johnny Kennedy's bus for a trip round the island. It always ended with a picnic and a swim at Balephuil on the southwest tip of the island. The two-mile stretch of twice-daily washed sand is very beautiful, the Atlantic continually roars and, even in calm weather, great white rollers break on the shore. On a clear day a glimpse of the Skerryvore lighthouse, miles out to sea, is a reward for children fed on Arthur Ransome.

We spent the day after the birthday on Balephuil's glistening beach, watching the might of the ocean crashing on the pink rocks below the village. Margaret said she'd painted a picture, at school, on returning from Tiree in 1952 and the teacher had disputed that the rocks were pink, but those at Balephuil certainly are.

The number one highlight of every camp was, of course, the dance. On Tiree this had usually been in Calum's barn, and all the day had been spent clearing it and building benches with oil cans and pine strippings. Calum, our piper, was long since gone, his big house divided into two and his barn no longer available for revelry.

Charlie, too, had died. He had been our accordionist not only on Tiree. He had worked for a time at Hipperholme and had been the musician for our Christmas barn dances. Nevertheless, the sons of Tiree continue to play traditional instruments and Lachie Campbell, whom we had seen grow from a child, was currently pipe major. Sylvia's friend, Billy, plays the accordion and a teacher from the school the fiddle, so we were not short of instrumentalists when we planned a dance during our reunion.

While we were scattered on the beach at Balephuil, Ellen and Hughie were busy hosing out the barn nearest to the converted steading. Situated only yards from our cottage it was ideal. Donald could take a cable from the house to provide temporary lighting. He also brought some chairs, and plastic garden seats appeared from everywhere. We knew that the food we had prepared would be supplemented with scones and pancakes and sandwiches by the islanders.

All our children loved to beautify themselves for the dance. In camp they'd had time but we had not. They'd washed their hair and some of the 'LUX' had disappeared from new bars of soap. They'd ironed their uniforms with metal mugs full of boiling water. They'd polished their belts and badges and looked a treat. For staff it was different. Tents must be secured, refreshments taken to the barn, morning's wood brought under cover lest there was rain overnight. There was never any opportunity for us to turn our tent into a salon. A thoughtful Guide had polished our badges and we'd been more skilled than they in keeping best clothes protected but we'd had no time for feminine pursuits.

Nothing had changed. Margaret and I were left to cope with administration while they disappeared to bathe and shower and make themselves into ladies. Unbeknown to us they called at the barn to decorate it with the bunting they had used for the birthday, so they were very late dashing to their separate cottages to take turns in the bathroom.

Islanders began to arrive. The piper stationed himself at the door of the barn and began to play and still their hostesses did not appear; I confess to becoming agitated and cross. How dare they invite islanders and employ musicians and not be there to greet them. They shouldn't have decorated the barn if it was going to make things late. I became nervous. Could I cope? Would they dance? Could they? I never could. As children they were game for anything and they could cavort. They didn't have to dance properly then. What would I do if these middle-aged grandmamas just sat on the fringe, tapping their feet and not daring to dance?

We had pushed the two wheelchairs, with Harry and Auntie Mary, into the barn and we had chatted up all our friends and apologised profusely for the absence of the English and still no one came. Islanders are not used to starting on time. We learned that long ago but they were usually the later ones. Though far from early we had always been the ones tapping our feet and waiting for the music and the dancing to begin. I realised I had not changed either, I was exhibiting all signs of a frustrated Guider, cross because her Guides were taking too long. This was their dance! They should not be late. My agitation was getting the better of me. I was forgetting that people do not change. I had never been afraid that my children, uninhibited after two weeks under canvas, would not dance. I was scared that these ladies, who had been my children, were no longer to be trusted. They were married women who had lived more than half a century. Would they be shy? Would they refuse to sing? Would they find seats round the perimeter and just watch? And if they did what was I going to do about it? I was the world's worst singer and, twenty-five years ago, on the morning after the dance, John Lachie had asked, 'Were you at the dance, last night?' We had both been waiting our turn in the travelling shop and when I had answered yes, he had warned, 'Och, well, and it's dangerous to do when you are old what you didn't do when you were young!' Now I was much older than then and I knew I could not lead in this evening activity. Everything depended on these ladies presently titivating themselves, wanting to look their best for an island event of a lifetime.

They came and I loved them to bits for they could dance and sing until morning. The married island men swung the married Yorkshire-born ladies on to the well-brushed and hosed barn floor; the piper and the other musicians increased their tempo and enough heat was generated in the cattle shed to keep Aunty Mary and Harry warm in their wheelchairs. What a night it was!

Had Margaret and I been responsible for the learned healthy lifestyle these ladies must have followed to be able to walk and climb and dance even as they had when they were children? How sad it was that we were no longer taking children to camp in out-of-the-way places on the edge of the Atlantic. To do so for so many years, obviously, had been rewarding if others left at

home were anything like those who had come with us. I feel confident that
they are. I 'know' them. They honeymoon on Harris, they are Guiding in
Canada. They travel the world, they are teachers and nurses, doctors and
physiotherapists. They take their children camping and they are healthy
and fun-loving still.

I should have known and not had cold feet waiting for them to come. I
should have known that Ann would sing, alone, even as Janet MacIntosh from
Urvaig did, and the fiddler's small daughter. I should have known they would
still know the reels and the Highland dances, but to have expected it
would surely have been a form of arrogance.

The twenty-five years of dances, in island barns or village halls or just on
the machair of the campsite, have become just one with time. None stands
out more colourful than the rest. Over the years all the children behaved the
same, barefoot, browned with the sun, red-cheeked with exertion. But this
millennium dance will remain highlighted for many reasons and not least for
the contribution of the accordionists, the fiddler and the piper, Lachlan
Campbell. He did us proud that night. Everyone wanted to dance with him.

The wonder of reunion continued. After activity there was always the joy
of restful strolling or lingering on beaches, sharing thought-provoking hours
with understanding friends. For me there was the long-remembered thrill of
just watching. Then it had been children. Adults were no less interesting. Ann
was still singing alone at the water's edge, Barbara was entertaining, Kathleen
was doing her Florence Nightingale act. Some were searching for shells, some
looking among the tidal debris, some cross-legged in a group, one with a
camera in hand. Nothing had changed. The convivial atmosphere was there.
Everything was all right!

There was the delightful afternoon when we entertained the Brownies from
the island and I saw my group as parents, knowing how to entertain and play
with children. It had once been my role. Now it was theirs. Their parenting
years had taught them all the tricks. And every day the sun shone on our
activities. Impossible, you may say, and complain that my spectacles are rose-
tinted. The impossible happens many times. Miracles are happening every
day. Unfortunately the millennium shocked us more than it pleased us, hurt
us more than it delighted us, but I can say truthfully and sincerely that the
days we spent on Tiree were, to quote Pop Larkin in a Gaelic manner,
perfick, chust!

Donald had been accumulating driftwood and old and rotted fencing for
the sole purpose of lighting a campfire on the shore. This had been the way
we had spent the last evening, every year for a quarter of a century. The
Guides had collected the fuel in those days and they had collected more than
plenty, but Donald collected enough for a beacon. He took it by tractor and

left it where rocks jutting out across the beach have been covered with centuries of sand. Coated with sea pinks and marram grass they have become a spit of land dividing Salum Bay into two. As children they had referred to the half as the whole when the activity was to swim the bay and even so it was no mean feat to swim from Calum's to the halfway spit. Christine, who was with us, had gasped with amazement when she first saw the wideness of the bay, at the beginning of the week.

'Now I know why you tried to stop me from swimming so far!' she said.

Christine had been born with a physical handicap, which she had almost overcome but we had tried to deter her from swimming such a distance, in such cold water. What others did so did she and would not listen to us. Seeing the distance with adult eyes she understood why we had tried to detain her.

Had we been available to see how much wood Donald had transported to the beach we would have said he'd brought far too much. His hard work embarrassed us, especially when the first soft rain of the fortnight began to fall as we foregathered for campfire. Had he not spent so much time preparing the bonfire I think we would have abandoned the idea and assembled in the cosy sitting room as on previous evenings. To do so was not even discussed. Dressed in hooded cagoules they looked even more like they had done forty years earlier. We were as tough as ever and the cloud above recognised this and stopped crying. The tremendous heat of the leaping flames dried our waterproofs immediately and the fire was so intense it was all flames and no smoke and we sang on the rocks for all of four hours. How could we? Where had our voices got such energy? We oiled them halfway with thermos coffee and cocoa and we talked and we put on more wood and some went towards the incoming tide and the darkness was without rain. The smell and the feel and the noise of waves lapping on Salum shore was as familiar as ever. It was like coming home after a short absence. Only the Land Rover parked on the beach and Harry's wheelchair in front of the embers was an addition.

At midnight we sang Taps and bundled Harry into the Land Rover. A few of us drove back to Caolis. Many stayed behind. Some would have stayed to watch the sun rise in the morning but eventually we were all round the fire in the steading cottage. To them it was an unforgettable experience but to Margaret and me, who had enjoyed more years of camping than they, it was just another encore in the long history of encores which have been our privilege to enjoy. We were no longer deluded into thinking revisits and reunions were one-off experiences.

Because they had to catch a Saturday train our 1957 campers had to leave the island on Friday. They had arrived in tears. They left with smiles from ear to ear. They left on what I think was the most beautiful day we had had all fortnight. It was absolutely calm and the sea was turquoise. Sitting in it, as from the beginning of time, was the Dutchman's Cap and beyond that Staffa and the mountains of Mull. Peace and fulfillment there were in plenty. Utterly exhausted we sat with Marie Campbell on the lawn outside Corrairigh, at Cornaig Beg. Toots had not left by boat so we'd taken her to the plane. Ann was staying to sail with us next day but she wanted time alone, which was so like Ann who had spent so many island holidays with us. We wanted time to be with our island friends.

In the evening we spent the first half at Sackhill with Margaret and Duncan MacInnes, at whose wedding we had been, nearing fifty years ago. There we had another unexpected reunion with a 1957 camper. Hugh from the mainland had been staying on holiday with his grandmother at Salum. Then he had been a boy and he had come daily to the camp to join in the fun. Year after year he had joined us, certainly often enough for the Yorkshire invasion to be imprinted indelibly on his memory. He was married and bringing up a family in Australia. He had come back to the island on the morning boat and had not known his childhood playmates were just leaving. How he would have enjoyed the previous night's campfire.

The second half of the evening we spent with Hughie, Ellen and Effie. It was a traditional way to end a holiday, round the fire in the house standing where once there had been a crofter's traditionally thatched house. Quietly and serenely we had supper with our dearest friends, they who had made not only 1957 possible but also the millennium Reunion. We could sit comfortably and say that the seeds we had sown together, they our island hosts and we the teachers of a generation of children, had resulted in an abundant harvest.

Chapter Eleven

Every road through hill and valley leads to Heaven by and by
And the winds that sweep the valley point a finger to the sky.
Campfire song 'I go my merry way'

W e travelled home safely and the euphoria of our holiday remained with us as we journeyed south. All was visibly well at home. Harry and Meg had shared our unique experiences with enthusiasm but Meg was wildly glad to be home. As the days went by Margaret and I were less inclined to believe that homecoming was bliss!

If we had expected millennium May to herald a period of contentment and joy, of calm water after the white rapids of the 80s and 90s, we would have been sorely disappointed. There was an element of nastiness hovering over mankind's step over the threshold into the unchartered regions of 2000, reminding us that the devil is still around, the devil in people and in the elements. Were we those who only see the negative and unable to reverse the lesser forms of it into almost positive, then the final pages of this book would make sorry reading.

The news in print or on the screen seems to prefer to be bad. People, according to their choice of viewing, favour murder and crime and sin in all its human forms and I flatly refuse to join the journalistic trail and record just the downside of the new era. We have a reputation for looking on the bright side, seeing miracles though they be small and for turning what seems like failure into a lesser disaster, even a minor success.

However, truth cannot altogether be avoided and I have a responsibility to tell it so I must admit that the turn of the century was far from trouble free, for our profession, our family, our friends, our country; the world was certainly taking a battering. Fortunately our ability to say and feel that things could be worse, that clouds have a habit of breaking and allowing sunshine to filter through is what keeps us going. We trace the rainbow through the rain continually.

Storm may rage on a mountain top and peace dwell in the valley but ecstasy lives on peaks and plains are full of hollows, trouble and strife. I remember when with Guides we climbed Ben Luskentyre, each year, and at the pinnacle we were exuberant but descending we were exhausted and, back in camp, we noticed all the imperfections of normality.

Our return from our extraordinary holiday was similar. We had to lower ourselves from cloud nine and almost immediately we were aware that the year 2000 had variable fortunes. When good, as it had been on Tiree, it was wonderful, when not it could be pretty horrid and occasionally downright cruel. Indeed the twenty-first century seemed determined to offer the planet far more downs than ups but, with a philosophy developed over many years, we met Triumph and Disaster and treated those two imposters just the same.

Meg had not been let into the Tiree cottage. Allowed into The Currer, on our return, she explored every nook and cranny, even before Dorothy and George left things once again in our over-full hands. We should not have allowed her to cavort all over the place in case Dorothy, a Border Collie expert, thought we had a badly behaved puppy but Meg was so, so happy we were even more inclined to think the soul within her belonged to Jess. Happiness in man or beast is a precious gift and Meg was happy. So what? We could not turn her out. She was only ten weeks old. In a world increasingly short of joy, she was a tonic for all depression.

Indeed it seemed all summer that every time Margaret went outside she found an animal needing treatment! A donkey was lame, a bullock had a temperature, a calf had Foul, the one we called Puffy, because of his damaged lungs, was worse!

Inside we had a leaking pipe, a tap washer problem and water to mop up from the floor, one toilet was badly blocked and in another en suite, a toilet seat unexpectedly fell off.

Incredibly we had no tourists for the spring bank holiday. The mid-week periods of late May and June were fully booked with school parties but, since opening in 1981, we had always been brimming with guests for every bank holiday. We wondered why things had changed but then realised that the pound favoured holidays abroad, British weather is inconsistent and modern man nervous of wind and chill. Fear of bank holiday traffic sends holiday-makers to the congestion of airports and cheap flights to Spain. Also, we feared we were still suffering the backlash of BSE. There was increasing belief that farms harboured disease. CJD, e.coli, salmonella and dear knows what lurked on our premises and no one can understand why farmers' children are the healthiest in the land!

We washed the linen after the school party went home. We remade the beds and became farmers-only for one weekend. It was the year the Countryside Stewardship earmarked for the rebuilding of the lookout, locally called Fairfax Coppy because it had been built and used by Thomas Fairfax during the Civil War. Tim and Graham made an excellent job of sorting out the curved stones which, when correctly assembled, made a mini-tower. A little bit of local history was once again preserved for posterity.

A few days later and we were full again. An alternative medicine convention coincided with a visit from relatives from Canada and, inevitably, we were sleeping on the floor once more.

Puffy continued to be brought in at night, due to his wheezing lungs, and in June he was joined by a friend whose breathing was also noisy. It was a good calf so Margaret sent for the vet, despite the cost. He came and agreed that an unnatural noise was being made but could not identify it. However, the calf appeared to recover with the antibiotic Margaret had already begun to use and, though both calves were let out during the day, both were brought in at night.

It was on the cards that, one day, Puffy, brave though he was, would die. Damaged lungs do not easily repair. His companion, however, seemed to have recovered. Puffy was thoroughly enjoying having a friend so the other calf remained in the shed at night and was restricted to the roadside pasture by day.

I am always the one who makes the early morning visit to any animal having overnight accommodation. I went down, one morning a couple of weeks later, and found the better of the two calves lying dead in a lake of blood. Blast! I kicked the concrete of the manger. Blast! Blast! When it was Puffy who died, quietly and with dignity, at the end of summer, it was more acceptable for he had struggled for a long time. When an animal seems to have recovered and then is found having haemorrhaged so much blood, the reaction is to swear and kick the concrete!

A few days later a calf appeared which wasn't ours. It was a Limousin bullock and George, our neighbour, said it belonged to David Bailey. Several efforts were made to return it but it was wild so Margaret bought it. David handed over the passport and the calf joined the herd. The fiasco of trying to catch and return it to its owner had resulted in a lameness which never properly recovered. While grazing he sometime knelt on his front legs and when walking he was somewhat stiff legged but he had achieved what he wanted and that was to stay at The Currer.

Almost immediately we had another problem. 'There's something wrong with that bullock!' Margaret announced, with binoculars focused on one left behind at the top of the road. She went to investigate and brought the un-resisting animal home. She was pretty sure she knew what was wrong but she phoned the vet and he agreed that all the symptoms pointed to photo-sensitisation, an allergy to sunlight, for which he had no cure. Several cases had been identified in the area recently. Eating St John's Wort causes it but it can be that a harmless plant has suddenly become dangerous to certain animals more susceptible than the rest of the herd. Treatment, said the vet, was to keep the animal indoors all summer. The allergy causes extensive damage to white skin. The affected areas are very painful to touch and form a dry, leathery crust which eventually drops off leaving red, raw tissue exposed underneath. Healing takes a long time and results in poor growth for the liver may have been damaged. Years ago we had had a case but it had been at the end of summer and the heifer had remained indoors. To have to keep this bullock indoors throughout midsummer was unthinkable but the vet was adamant. So Margaret turned to homeopathy, which sometimes succeeds against all odds, and the animal recovered completely and was sold sound at the end of September.

I went to the last full College Reunion in July. Emilie was already with us for the summer. Ripon College was to be sold and the amalgamation with York St John made complete. Future reunions would be in York for all those wishing to participate.

Increasingly I did not. I had missed only one such get-together in fifty years. For thirty of those years, returning to Ripon had been a joy but the last twenty more like a nightmare. With no free weekends we had to be very organised even to get there late, which was unavoidable. I remember that on this last occasion Harry had one of his fairly infrequent early morning seizures and slept late. We could not wake him and had to wait until he roused. Very belatedly we all clambered into the Land Rover and collected Hilda. Arriving at College I crept into the dining room halfway through the meal and Margaret and Emilie took the others to Studley Royal to push Harry round the grounds of Fountains Abbey

The speeches after the meal were long and drawn out and I had no opportunity to converse with my friends. I couldn't get away quickly enough. I'd read the last chapter and I closed the book firmly and went to wait outside the entrance gate for my already full taxi. I remember thinking, 'That's that. It was good while it lasted but, OK, it's good that it's over!' Margaret thought so too. It hadn't been easy coping with people and dogs.

Sixteen-year-old Emilie was preparing to spend the next twelve months in Germany, with a host family, in order to become fluent in yet another language. She was slightly apprehensive and spent a lot of quiet hours collecting bilberries and sitting on the Altar Rock trying to solve the problems of the universe.

All the Barbaults are philosophers with whom we've shared a similar relationship, for though they are French and we are English, though they live in a city and we in the Dales, we have shared something in common which transcends age and race, language and environment. Emilie is well aware that there is a great deal in this world to try to understand. She formed a unique relationship with Meg who, on entering the sitting room, invariably made a beeline for our French friend and showered her with licks and kisses, completely ignoring us. Emilie called her Madame Meg and adored her in return.

She desperately wanted to be here for the birth of Diana's third calf but had to leave on the morning of the day before Diana calved. This was something we were apprehensive about for the previous two deliveries had been none too easy. At a crucial moment we yelled for a couple resident in the Loft Cottage. The man added his strength to ours and another member of our herd was born. I cannot remember the man's name, only that it was a moment in his life he will never forget. He admitted to never having seen anything quite like that before and he and his wife sat wide-eyed while the newborn creature, perfect in every way, was thoroughly licked, struggled to its feet and began to suckle.

And the summer slid into autumn and hauliers and farmers stopped petrol tankers from leaving depots and supplies in filling stations dried up! Guests arriving with only enough petrol to get them home, abandoned four wheels for the duration of their stay, preserving, sensibly, what they had left. They were all good-humoured about this. The estate, St Ives, was visited far more than usual.

We kept what was in our tank in order to drive to Otley for the second of our cattle sales. Everything depended on Milford having enough diesel to transport the last thirty-six. Harry had a hospital appointment. Barbara Sherriff had enough petrol for her less important needs and insisted on driving us there to preserve ours for the Otley sale, without which we could not leave The Currer and go to Wales.

I found myself wishing some outside deterrent would stop us going. It was unusual for me to have no appetite for holiday. I began to view the long journey down to Aberporth with, not exactly dread, but certainly with fatigue. I did not accept for one moment that this was due to the three score years and ten or the fact that we had just rounded up seventy-two big two-year-old cattle to show at Otley.

I have felt before, as I did then, that perhaps a change was due. Margaret too was viewing the coming holiday rather warily for a few big animals had not been taken to market with the others and must be left with Dorothy and George. Two had been so obstreperous they had jumped the five-barred gate of the loading pen and escaped removal to market. Two had been fractionally too young and must await our return before sale, and one had a very large abscess the vet was unwilling to lance until the season of flies was over.

But the petrol crisis passed and the holiday date came and for the life of me, writing this, I cannot remember any pre-holiday hitch, which was unusual and should have warned us. If it had and we had bowed to gut feeling that we maybe should not go we would have made a wrong choice for we had a lovely first week. The long journey I had dreaded was easy. After eight years, we at last knew the way without the help of the map.

A new cottage awaited us at Aberporth. The Cedars at Pennfyionn had been demolished and a new house, far too big for us, had been built on the site. We were to occupy the bungalow built on the opposite side of the road where, last year, we had watched the workmen dig foundations. The newly built substitute was called Dolphin Cottage and was specially designed for the disabled. It was lovely. The view, of course, was the same. It did not really matter that Aunty Mary slept till late. We realised that we could no longer have walked Harry up the steps into The Cedars and noticed that we had to wheel him from the car to the inside of the cottage. Almost imperceptibly he was getting gradually more disabled. Each morning we pushed him in a zigzag way down the dangerously steep road from our home to the promenade. It is minute. There is a car park for a dozen cars, no more. Each morning we pushed him back, I behind the handlebars and Margaret pulling a rope in front. Always, previously, we had unloaded him for the steepest bit and, both taking an arm, walked him to the top. A year on and those days had gone.

It rained more than it usually did, but that was unimportant for it did so when we were inside and was sunny when we were out, walking the sands at Newport or St David's, Poppit or Aberaeron or Llangranog. When it rained it did so with a vengeance and the lawns of Pennfyionn were like wet sponges.

Meg behaved beautifully. Though she does not stay close she shows no inclination to wander and responds instantly to her name. Most of our language she does not comprehend. Because she behaves well she does not need reprimand and does not understand the contrary. She hasn't any idea what we are talking about when we praise. We are even very busy on holiday and a good dog gets ignored. We appreciate that most people dedicate many hours to training their dogs but we have had to leave Meg to Danny. He has no bad habits unless clinging too closely is counted. Meg could never be called Super Glue as Danny is.

We phoned home more frequently. Dorothy said a yearling was ill. She'd called in the vet. A younger member of the practice had come, diagnosed a virus and given an injection, but Dorothy's excellent, detailed description of the symptoms told Margaret we had another case of photo sensitisation, in which case the vet's treatment would not work. She told Dorothy what to do. Dorothy said the vet would come again on Friday, the day before our return, as the abscess needed lancing.

Putting the phone down Margaret said, 'I think we should go home, leave here on Tuesday and get home on Wednesday.' We phoned Crewe Travel Inn for an earlier booking but they were full on that date. We managed to get one at Middlewich instead and pressed on with enjoying our holiday. I am sure Dorothy was relieved. Margaret was!

On Sunday there was torrential morning rain but sunshine in the afternoon. We were cruising along a by-way in the Llangranog area when we saw masses of floating apples in the ditch and hundreds all over the road. I was driving and stopped the Land Rover for I could not pass by a harvest going to waste. We grabbed plastic bags and began to rescue the bumper crop. The trees over the wall were still heavily laden and apples lay two deep on the orchard floor. A passing man stopped, obviously amused, and we asked him who owned the orchard so that we might report and ask permission to steal. 'Oh, just go on picking while I go and phone the police!' he said but he took out plastic bags from his pocket and picked for us. I'm sure he had no idea how valuable apples are to those who make evening meals for paying guests!

He told us who the owner was and Margaret found the farmhouse hidden by the trees and informed the lady of the house what we were doing. 'Don't take from the road,' said the farmer's wife. 'Take them from the orchard!'

'We'll buy some,' Margaret said. 'We'll call on our way home on Tuesday, if we may, and buy a lot!' And when we talk about a lot we talk in sacks, not bags. We insisted on paying and we hauled the treasure-trove onto the roof rack, wondering if there would be sufficient room in our autumn empty freezers.

We had thought it might be our last visit to Wales while we were wheel-chair pushing and while we had an old lady who seldom rose early but, when the time came, we felt we could not say goodbye. We had made friends and everything, except the steepness and the distance from home with fewer daylight hours, was so perfect that we booked one week for October 2001 and left a deposit.

Arriving home on Wednesday we got things under control. A more experienced vet came to lance the abscess and took away a bucketful of pus. He assured us the wound would completely heal and it did. He also confirmed Margaret's diagnosis of the yearling's complaint, although it had definitely begun to respond to the homeopathic treatment. Unfortunately we were unable to show him the two year old with a identical condition for we had sold it healthy in September.

There was an abundance of cheap calves at the Skipton and Otley Marts on the Monday, and at Gisburn, on Thursday, we completed our annual buy and found we had over eighty. Are we crazy? One of the last bunch of calves was a strong Simmental, a bargain for £20. However, instead of having to be

coaxed and pushed out of the haulier's wagon, this baby leapt into space and
careered dangerously and clumsily into the shed.

'That calf's blind!' Milford said. 'I'll take it back. It'll cause you no end of
trouble!'

'I bought it. It's mine,' Margaret said. 'We'll cope.' For some obscure
reason we called it Jack. It was the only named calf in the baby herd.

Rearing calves is a full-time job for Margaret. Add to it two steers with
complications, a left-behind group still to sell, an influx of self-catering guests
and hundreds of apples to peel and freeze, and our work load could scarcely
have been heavier.

For something like twenty years we had been responsible for much of the
social life of Aunty Mary's friend, Hilda. They went to Chapel most Sundays
and Hilda dined at The Currer. Every other Tuesday they attended the
Welcome Hour, before which Hilda had lunch with us, and she came for
Christmas, often for Easter and we took her almost everywhere we went. She
came with us to Cumbria for Meg, to Colne for sheets and pillowcases, to
Foulridge for sheeting and curtains and Bank Newton for homeopathic items.
If we just went for a run in The Dales, we took her. Her presence was never
a problem.

Realising that she was growing frail, the Christmas before her ninety-
eighth birthday, we had insisted she was fitted with an alarm system, a press
button round her neck which, when activated, would bring help. One Sunday
in late October I took her home before dark and an hour later she fell and
couldn't get up. She pressed her alarm, help came and she spent the next six
weeks in hospital. She returned home shortly before Christmas having been
instructed that she must not climb into a Land Rover again. It was tragic for
we had been her lifeline. However, she was given ample care from the NHS.
Carers came four times a day, and she became a very well looked after
prisoner in her own home.

We hardly noticed we had a job less for we had only taken her where we
were going already and, simultaneously, the weather turned vicious.
Torrential rain, nationwide, brought the worst floods in living memory and
Keighley suffered seriously. The River Aire burst its banks at Stockbridge
and acres of the valley were flooded. Harry said that the last time that had
happened was in 1946. I cannot detail for posterity the horror of the
millennium floods because, sitting perched on the hillside, we did not share
the fear and the loss felt by those on the valley floor.

From our near-summit lookout we could see the lake below us and television told us that Keighley was only one place in hundreds all over the
country to be suddenly submerged. Colin Jones drove into the yard to say
his family had been evacuated from their home early that morning and had

we, by any chance, a cottage free. He and his wife, Liz, and their three little girls had been annual holiday-makers from the south for several years. They had grown to love the area and Colin had secured a job in Leeds and they had bought a house at Stockbridge. They had been occupants barely a month before the flood. The Mistal was empty so we were able to offer refuge. Fortunately their home escaped the worst. Many had to wait months to return to their devastated properties.

Returning from a hospital visit to see Hilda, we found the old A629 was flooded, not by rising water from the river but from torrents plunging down the hillside. In some places between Steeton and Utley the road was submerged under eighteen inches of water. Suddenly we saw a resident from a nearby nursing home, running down the centre of the road in her night-gown. Traffic was slowing down but no one was stopping. Margaret turned abruptly off the road to alert the matron of the home and suddenly doors opened everywhere and carers erupted to give chase and rescue their patient. Life certainly is a comedy!

Every street in Keighley is a hill and down every one water was gushing. The drains were full and water leapt out of them. The Aire had burst its banks at Low Bridge and our route home was impossible. Slushing through less flooded roads and back streets we eventually climbed the hillside home, vowing to stay there for as long as it took.

The advent of so much rain, so suddenly, swamped even our sloping pastures so that the cattle could find no dry place to lie down. As they stood lakes formed round their hooves. They crowded round the gates leading into their winter housing and pleaded with us to be let in. It was still October; two months earlier than usual but Margaret opened the doors and let them in onto clean straw. Next morning they were fed hay and turned out but they were back at nightfall and every evening thereafter, they were back for bed and breakfast, almost doubling our workload and drastically depleting our winter store of food. It was going to be a long, long winter!

Milford took the last of the season's bullocks to the next cattle sale. The one with the abscess stayed behind and was housed with Diana and her three-quarter adopted family of four. They occupied the first shed we had built on coming to The Currer some forty years ago but which had been re-roofed and re-fronted nine months earlier, but was still doorless. All summer we had kept animals out with old gates tied on with binder twine, five-barred iron gates which would not keep out the rain, or wind, or snow. All summer the garage had had no door. Men! In December John sent his workman, who came, measured the three gaping doorways, and then made excellently fitting doors. Our gratitude was heavily coated with sarcasm!

I think it was the leanest Christmas we had ever had but it no longer seemed to matter. We've been there, done it all. Family parties in childhood, Christmases in a village school, carol singing with Guides and house parties with paying guests. We've made Christmas dinners for thirty plenty of times, cooking two 20lb turkeys, rising at 4 a.m. to put the first into the Aga. We've had over a decade of Christmas runs up the whitened Dales. Now there was not even Hilda to swell our foursome and we are not a family who will light candles and bring out china unless we have guests. Dirty routine work has to be done all through festive seasons.

I decorated the sitting room with a quarter of the three hundred cards we received. I brought up holly and hung baubles and tinsel on both trees and put most of the fairy lights in rooms belonging to the self-catering holiday-makers, whose presence proved to be so unobtrusive we hardly knew they were there.

Janet Bullock, in the Mistal Cottage, thought to take pity on us and suggested we leave Harry and Aunty Mary with them so that the two of us, Margaret and me, could go for our Christmas outing free of care.

'Thank you,' we said. It was a kind thought but we only ever went on jaunts like that for Harry. We would never have dreamed of going anywhere without him. Were he not there Margaret and I might become hermits.

But he was there and eager to go so we went up Street Lane out of Morton and over by Robin Hood's stone to Brunthwaite and Swartha, over Addingham Moorside and down into Bolton Abbey. There was little snow, just a scattering of icing on a rather soggy cake. We wrapped Harry up warmly and pushed the wheelchair until his cheeks began to go blue and then we went home the same way because it was just as beautiful scenery in reverse.

Because there was nothing else on the agenda, on Boxing Day afternoon we put family and dogs in the car thinking we would go over Slippery Ford to Cowling, but Harry fell asleep so we turned round and drove back home. In retrospect we wonder if this was a pre-New-Year glimpse of what was to come in 2001.

We felt very much alone and apart from the traditional festivities. Little did we know that we were to spend the best part of 2001 almost as castaways, in a world of our own which, in different circumstances, would have been pleasurable, a welcome idyllic return to the once-was.

There was enough snow on New Year's Eve to please Janet Bullock and to frighten Paulette Schrader. Like Colin Jones, she and her friend Lillian had been coming on holiday and had fallen in love with the locality. Paulette had secured a job in Leeds and had brought her three horses up to pasture on the outskirts of the city. Lillian wished to join her so that they could search for a smallholding together, so they booked The Loft for as long as either it was empty or for as long as it took to find and buy a property. Paulette brought her three horses to the livery stables owned by our friends Dolores and Raymond Shaw-Smith and she came to attend to them on New Year's Eve and dare not drive back for snow was deepening. She phoned for accommodation. We were full of self-catering Hogmanay guests and could only offer her Harry's old bedroom which was used as a store. I tidied it, removing things from the bed, but I could not empty it of the clutter. She left her car on the top road ready to drive into Leeds next day, leisurely and in daylight. She went to bed early and we did not bother to celebrate the arrival of 2001. It was a far cry from the way the millennium had been born. The outside world was under a blanket of snow and we had no premonition of the length of the winter ahead or the horror and hardship of the summer. It is fortunate that very little of the future can be predicted. A few days later Paulette and Lillian, two dogs and three cats took occupancy of the loft. We were disturbed to learn that they also had ferrets and guinea pigs, whose hutches they put behind the fencing of the loading pen, safe from our dogs. Neither Danny nor Meg could leap the gate which had been so easy for the two bullocks not wishing to go to market, but though they could not reach the hutches they could smell those animals and harrassed them with barking and howling almost continually along the fence.

Had we known the two women had ferrets we would, I feel sure, never have offered them The Loft, in which case we would have deprived ourselves of excellent friends, a distraction to ease the monotony, a panacea for the hurt and hatred which were hallmarks of the year ahead. Fearing that the small animals would be traumatised by the constant barking of our dogs, Paulette removed them to the Shaw-Smiths' farm and Danny and Meg had to look elsewhere for their entertainment.

Bookings came in so fast we envisaged a bumper season. In and among the serviced accommodation, we began to get group self-catering enquiries and reservations. This was a road we increasingly wanted to go down. A week here and there when we did not have to cater was just the life we wanted. We had to admit that the years of constantly making evening meals, of forever making beds and washing sheets were taking their toll. And Harry and Aunty Mary consumed more of our time. Some weeks away from constantly attending guests, suited us fine.

Two ladies from Dublin booked The Mistal for all of March in order to attend a dog grooming course, and ramblers from Wales made a block booking to self-cater towards the end of the month. They would use The Loft also and at this point Paulette and Lil would have to go.

The cattle were fit. So, presumably, was our nanny goat, Rosie; either that or in her dotage. She decided she wanted company and while the ground was still snow-covered and January frost defied the weak winter sun, she climbed the wall on the eastern boundary and disappeared. We searched in vain. However, a resident from the hamlet of Marley, on the valley floor, rang to say a goat had joined Harry Raw's flock of in-lamb ewes.

The weather was far too extreme, we thought, for an ageing goat and we tried to encourage her back but the terrain over the wall is not suitable for such an activity and it was not until our white nanny, Snowy, came to bleat in the gateway that we eventually succeeded. Even then she was loath to return to the barn. When she did we imprisoned her overnight but the next day she was off again.

We began to have great respect for her response to the call of the wild in mid-January. She must be tough, indeed. Should her stupidity end in her death, we decided, that was her problem, not ours. She knew where home comforts were. She could leap the wall whenever she felt inclined. She had always been a law unto herself. We quite envied her the opportunity to disappear and camp out. We would like to do that, in the summer of course. Fortunately Harry Raw eventually took his ewes into the barn for lambing. He put Rosie into his Land Rover and brought her home. Without her foreign friends she stayed.

We desperately needed some distraction for her and again reminded the blacksmith that he'd promised us his spring-born billy. Margaret said he could bring the nanny, too, if he wished but it was the luck billies are supposed to bring which we really wanted. We claim to not be superstitious but we like to have a billy goat around and we don't care who knows.

Things were seemingly OK in our domain but luck was not with our friends. One disaster after another seemed to haunt them. Messages of death and accident dominated phone calls so that we became nervous of picking up the receiver. We were horrified to hear that Dorothy had broken both her ankles. She and George, who so admirably looked after our house, were standing in for the Davisons at Transfield, next to The Altar farm, a mile from civilisation. She had neglected to put on the light in the middle of the night and accidentally turned at the top of the stairs instead of into the bathroom. It was a mistake that cost her six weeks in hospital and months on crutches. For her and George 2001 was a nightmare. But, for us, January was relatively gentle, unusually so, which is not the best of omens.

At the beginning of February Diana's second family became twenty-two months old. Their passports had been retained for two months by MAFF, and subsequently returned to us, so we were now allowed to sell. It is the Government's way of making farmers keep their bullocks eight weeks after claiming premium for which animals have to be a certain age. It is all very complicated but rules have to be obeyed. The four passports, allowing sale, were now in our possession but we were in no hurry to go to a cold store cattle market. We could wait until March. There was, we believed, plenty of time. The big animal, fully recovered from his abscess, need not be sold for another two months, either. We were working round the clock feeding a hundred and seventy animals and any sale could wait.

But when Milford, our haulier, came with his annual bill, he suggested we sell immediately. The market was healthy at the moment, he said. Good store bullocks were selling well. He thought the older bullock would also find a buyer. He thought we ought to send all five to the fortnightly sale on Friday 16th.

Margaret hesitated. She never likes selling, especially when there is no immediate rush to do so. We were all right as we were, she dallied. We were too busy. It was too cold. We were sitting at the kitchen table, having a cup of tea and I was writing out a cheque in payment and Milford was persisting that he thought Margaret should sell now, while the going was good. There was no frost on our road. It was still only February. We could be snowed in for six weeks yet. So she gave in, told him to come on Friday and me that it would have to be my job. Harry was all smiles. It meant a day out for him.

I planned not to take Aunty Mary. She was too old. It was too early in the year and she habitually rose too late, but trips out are few and far between in the winter and she was up in time and determined to go. The cold spell had passed and the sun was strong for the time of the year and bore down benevolently on the market car park, keeping my two companions warm for as long as it took to sell.

The place was teeming with animals. Back-end calves, fifteen months ago, had been unbelievably cheap. Farmers had kept more than usual. That must be it. Winter fodder was beginning to dwindle so young stock, in their hundreds, were being sold, for the most part at rock bottom prices. Older, strong stores were selling well and when my turn came, three hours after the commencement of selling, Milford was proved right. Harry was never bored, sitting in a Land Rover in a busy car park, and Aunty Mary could sleep. The sunshine was brilliant. Everything seemed to be going well for us and when the blacksmith rang to say he was coming on Monday, that pleased us, too. We were putting one hurdle after another behind us and every day was one nearer spring.

Margaret insisted that the blacksmith brought the promised goats but when he came he was without them. Our luck had been resident long enough in Otley. 'Can we come to your place and collect them ourselves?' Margaret asked.

'Yes. You can,' said the man. It was going to be the only way.

'We'll come over on Thursday with the Ifor Williams trailer.'

'They're only little,' said the blacksmith, 'Two sacks will do in the back of the Land Rover.' We doubted that but never like pulling a trailer so we were prepared to take a risk. We paid him in advance. Everything was going smoothly. I helped feed the cattle then went indoors to make the evening meal. I paused to watch the six o'clock news.

Foot and Mouth disease had been confirmed in pigs at a farm in Northumberland and that was the beginning of a farming nightmare. We, and probably every farmer in the country, stopped breathing properly. It was many miles away, but wherever it was it excited fear. Foot and Mouth disease is a plague of enormous proportions.

On Thursday we drove over to Otley. We had always had goats which were sheep-size. As yearlings, these twins were minute, no bigger than month-old lambs. We couldn't do anything but laugh at them. Danny, too, thought their presence in the Land Rover was fun. Meg gave them a wide berth. We'd asked what breed they were and the blacksmith had said, 'Anglo Nubian/Golden Guernsey,' but that had given us no clue as to what their size would be. Nor should it. Even their owner didn't know why they were so little.

So Mopsey and Cottontail became members of our family and brought a ray of sunshine into an environment which had suddenly clouded over. We put them into the Poorly Pen, which was empty for all calves were well and thriving. They slept so closely together that they looked to have only one body and two heads. We felt like Dr Doolittle, and we laughed every time we passed them. They didn't sleep much, however, for they appeared to be constantly eating and when they chewed their cud they did so in unison.

That same day MAFF imposed a ban on the movement of all cloven footed animals and on cattle markets until further notice. By a hair's breadth we had sold our cattle. No more sales from The Currer were necessary until the very end of August. By one day we had brought home our goats, one a billy which should bring us luck. We began to breathe normally.

Chapter Twelve

With all its shams, drudgery and broken dreams, it is still a beautiful world
Found in a Baltimore church

At this point I feel I should define what we call luck. It is not maybe how others see it. Having good luck doesn't mean freedom from problems in our daily lives, it just means that these problems, small or gigantic, have the decency to space themselves out so that, somehow, we can cope, even when coping seems barely possible. Just when every avenue seems blocked, the load too heavy, a problem insolvable, for us there suddenly appears a way out. That is Good Luck. Is it because there is a God in Heaven? I think that, if so, it is because he has delegated the job of rescuing us in time to a very competent guardian angel. There are people and conditions far more needy of His individual attention than we. We don't really believe that it is a billy goat, but who knows. Or it could be that hard work solves most of our problems. Something does. So far, any way!

And, by the skin of her teeth, Meg survived an argument with the postman. She has an interesting personality, this flying dog of ours. She is incredibly beautiful and she loves everyone except our very nice postman. It is his fault. He drives too quickly. He is frightened and electric waves communicate this to Meg. He approaches us but does not stay and his hasty retreat would excite a chase if we did not prevent it. If he could come at the same time each day, as did all our other postmen, on the stroke of 7 a.m., then we would have no problem but we do not know until he has entered the yard. Both dogs are obedient and come into the fenced and gated area in front of the door, but then they bark like mad and Meg looks formidable. She, not Danny, can jump the gate so they must not be given freedom until the post-van is well up the road. During the first week of Foot and Mouth, Meg and Danny chased the van into the yard and Meg must have leapt against it and was thrown into the side mud. The postie was very upset. Meg had a nasty cut on the fleshless part of her leg which needed stitching and somehow to be kept clean. We brought her back from the vet with a plastic stocking, which hadn't a hope of staying on, and a plastic collar as big as a bowl. We had enough trouble!

Were we more exhausted than usual after a longer than normal winter, more muscularly weary and strained than on previous years? I doubt it. All others in our profession would be feeling the same as winter drew to its annual close. As always we prayed for spring, aching with every movement but also – which was new – fearing with every moment.

A car drew into the yard and a man I did not recognise came to the door and said, 'How are you for testing?'

I stopped breathing. Foot and Mouth has that effect. We were extremely nervous.

'What!' I gasped

'Is it a good time for a test?' the man repeated.

'Test what?' I asked though I was sure I knew the answer. The virus must be on our doorstep.

'Your electric plugs. I do it every year. Remember?'

I was too stunned to recover immediately. 'Oh not now,' I stammered. 'Later when Foot and Mouth is over.'

Rather unkindly I repeated what he'd said to Margaret and made her tremble likewise. It's the little bit of Grandfather Smith in me. It was good for a nervous laugh whenever anyone phoned. There was so little to laugh about where Foot and Mouth was concerned.

We did a little stocktaking. We had enough hay, straw and corn to last until the middle of March but we were desperate to have the muck taken out before movement of plant was stopped. Margaret phoned the contractor and immediately snow began to fall and the entrance gate, at the top of the road, was blocked by a drift. With the inclement weather came severe frost and frozen pipes to the cattle sheds.

Foot and Mouth disease was spreading rapidly all over Devon and Cumbria, while we were being tormented with hose pipes and water carrying, too much bedding muck in the sheds and too much carrying of heavy bales over slippery surfaces. We saw nothing on television except the killing of healthy animals. We did not need to be told what infected animals look like, though, belatedly, weeks into the outbreak, the Ministry sent us details of what to look for. Farmers already knew. They spot an ailing animal immediately it stops eating. They see instantly if it is lame. It is more difficult to spot Foot and Mouth in sheep but no cattle farmer would miss it. It is not one animal which is ill. Almost immediately it is many. Sores on feet and tongues and mouths are noticed at once and even we, who tend sick animals as if they were humans and never put down an animal unless it is absolutely necessary, who bury our dead and would not dream of cremating our loved ones, could see no alternative, at that moment, other than slaughter of infected herds and the traditional burning of carcasses on railway sleeper pyres. But we did not see film of sick animals being killed, just of hundreds and thousands of healthy, beautiful creatures, massacred on suspicion, before confirmation, because they were contiguous to suspect cases or merely at risk because some vehicle passed by, some relative had called.

Our annual Guide reunion falls on the first Saturday in March. We first realised we must cancel it when Ann rang from Aviemore. The enormity of Foot and Mouth hits one immediately but not the implications. The small hindrances are hidden. Acceptance of a total shut-down does not bring instant understanding and my reaction to Ann's phone call was hesitation. Did a ban on animal movement, on buying and selling, also mean no guests? Joanna rang from Manchester and that settled the fate of the 2001 reunion and prompted me to ring MAFF and enquire about our early season bookings.

Their advice was not entirely negative. We were told to keep alert. The disease was not in Yorkshire. We must use our own judgement. We were to find that advice from the Ministry, if it came at all, was always weeks late. Booked guests were much more positive. The two ladies from Ireland, due to attend a dog grooming course for the duration of March, were told by the Irish Government that their visit must be cancelled until after the epidemic.

We were suddenly in the grip of quite a severe freeze-up. It was a relief, as it always is in these circumstances, to have no guests with cars that cannot get up the hill and no one in The Mistal cottage when we need to attach a hose to the kitchen tap. We struggled with buckets and troughs and air-locks until we thought we would go mad. The cattle couldn't be let out for the first continuous period that winter. They ate an increasing number of bales and the bedding manure deepened. Margaret rang the contractor again and we opened a bale of straw at the entrance gate, soaked it with disinfectant and put a footbath there. We bought a tyre spray and prayed the muck-spreader would come before such activities were condemned. We did, however, assume responsibility for stopping the daily visit of the post van and the weekly refuse collection. Each was a farm-to-farm service and the risk too great.

The Council rang to say footpath closure notices must be collected from Haworth Tourist Office. They were flimsy bits of paper so we bought stiff plastic covers and nailed them at a dozen places where footpaths entered our land.

Two weeks into the outbreak we drove down to the vet's to have Meg's stitches removed and collect our letters from the village post office. There was one from Sheila Johns, in Cornwall, with a photostat copy of the Crossgates News Letter. Ours lay in an unopened envelope I had presumed was just an invoice. The letter advised us that the homeopathy service had something to offer which might be a deterrent to the virus. It had proved valuable in the outbreak of the sixties.

The next day saw us driving to Bank Newton to pick up a pre-arranged bottle of Borax merc corr syphilinum psorinum, an imposing name for 500ml of what looked like water, left in a dustbin at the end of the lane. It was to be squirted twenty-four times, every two days, into our five hundred gallon storage tank. Homeopathy always sounds and looks to be utter nonsense, but it was keeping Harry alive, had cured laminitis, lumpy jaw and photo-sensitisation. We were willing to try anything rather than witness all our animals being shot.

A guest who keeps horses once told me that she uses homeopathic products, not because she believes in them but because they work. That said everything.

It was a truly beautiful day of frost and snow on the hills and winter sunshine everywhere. We took the Lothersdale road to Elslack. 'Lo there's a dale!' Cromwell is reported to have marvelled, and when Elslack, they say, Heaven is busy. We appreciated the sun but hoped it would not weaken the frost before our muck had been taken out. Tractors make a sorry mess of soggy pastures.

There was no Foot and Mouth anywhere in Yorkshire but every farm had its carpet of disinfected straw and every one of the county's many footpaths was closed. We wondered if this would affect the walkers who, from Wales, had booked a self-catering holiday in March. Their booking had meant we would have to say a brief farewell to Paulette and Lil. We had pre-booked a cottage for them, owned by one of our Guides in Haworth, just for one week, after which they could return for the rest of April. However, even before we knew what was happening, the Welsh party cancelled. Without open footpaths their holiday was not possible. Paulette and Lil need not leave after all. I must admit their presence was comforting.

The newly cleansed and spotlessly clean muck-spreading equipment came and the painstaking task began of emptying one shed at a time of its inhabitants, removing the deep accumulation and re-spreading straw before returning the animals. The job takes two days and is strenuous. Fortunately the frost held. A few days later the fields were like sponges and mutilation would have been inevitable. Yough Leigh handed back the field gate keys and I went, belatedly, into the house, dirty, tired but content. I had missed the six o'clock news.

Aunty Mary said, 'There's Foot and Mouth at Queensbury!' A case, the first in Yorkshire, had been confirmed the day before, at a farm in Hawes. Our county is big and Hawes many miles away but Queensbury is on our doorstep. Aunty Mary is so often wrong, for she will not wear her hearing aid, that I was not unduly worried. Harry was not in the front room. He would not have heard incorrectly. I did not tell Margaret. She, too, was tired and had still a lot of work to do.

Pauline Raw rang. She delivers our milk every Monday. 'I think I'd better not come down,' she said.

'Fine,' I reassured her. 'I'll meet you at the top. Just give me a ring on your mobile.' Pauline was a pupil, a Guide, she came to Tiree for the millennium reunion and her husband's sheep pasture over the boundary wall.

'There's Foot and Mouth at Queensbury!' she said. So Auntie Mary was not wrong after all. The dreaded virus was only about six miles away as the crow flies.

Paulette called in with some bright red laminated footpath closure notices which made the Council ones look feeble. Since nailing them to the gateposts we had only had to shout at two joggers who deliberately ignored us but did not come again. One family only passed through our paddock. 'Can't you read?' we asked.

'I didn't come on the footpath,' said the father. 'We just came across Rawson-Chad's.'

'And our neighbour's. Both have got cattle. Now you're coming through our herd and up our road!'

'I'm sorry but my wife and baby are sitting on your seat at the top of the road,' the man apologised. 'I didn't see a notice.'

'But you don't need to see a notice. Everybody with a television knows there are no open footpaths. Get real!'

After that we did not see any more walkers for many, many months. A friend in Buckden accosted a lady ignoring the closure notice. 'Oh, it's all right,' said the trespasser. 'It's all right. I'm a vegetarian!' Who teaches these people, for goodness sake? What hope was there for farmers in distress?

Not much, but local people did keep off our land and we were eternally grateful. The footpaths began to grass over. We began to stop worrying in case someone left a gate open. I phoned Julia in Buckden, whose life mirrors our own for they are farmers and have diversified into tourism. I was interested to hear her comment on her feeling of serenity. We are perpetually harrassed by inspecting officials from MAFF and Environmental Health and Fire Safety. Even the absence of tourists was lovely. There were no visiting children to leave shed doors open, trespass on hay or tinker with equipment. There was no one to leave electric plugs on or taps running. We were quite at peace in our isolation. No one would come and no one would need attention. For over twenty years we had not known this environmental bliss. We had no indoor improvements to necessitate the daily arrival of a plumber, a builder or an electrician. There was no outside building to do. Even the shed doors had been hung.

Julia said, 'Just keep buggering on, Skipper! You don't need to worry if your kitchen floor crunches!'

It was a funny kind of serenity. It was false security but the sudden stalemate in the tourist trade was a panacea. It is not easy to play a waiting game. One farmer, speaking on television, said it was like watching a juggernaut hurtling towards one, not knowing whether it would veer to the right or left or hit you full on. The dreaded virus, it seemed, could only be fought with the most draconian of Ministry methods and everyone waited on tenterhooks. Every pre-booked guest cancelled for March and bookings for the summer came to a halt. We had been urged, along with thousands of others, to diversify. I could not think of one diversification which would sustain us all in this crisis. All sporting activities stopped. Golf, fishing, equestrian pursuits, farm shops, you name it, died alongside the disease. The tourist trade came to an abrupt halt, caravan sites were empty, B&Bs and hotels, holiday cottages abandoned. No tourists visited stately homes, tea shops, museums, abbeys or safari parks and village shopkeepers faced bankruptcy. People were losing money, not by the day but by the hour.

All our drystone walling had to stop. Tim is a farmer as well as a waller and farm to farm movements ceased. While he and Graham had been working on the meadow walls, gates had been closed against cattle. Before we dared open them we had to make sure that the dewpond was safe. The two men had cleared it of stones and grass, ready to take out the cobbles and do whatever was necessary to make it a working feature once more on the landscape. Cleaning it out had exposed an alarmingly deep hole. Re-filled with water it would serve four fields. Left empty it was dangerous. Margaret was sure an animal would fall in for two feet of water had gathered in the centre and the sloping sides were steep. The cobbled cone was five feet deep but no work could be done on it so we decided to put a fence round it so that our fear of an accident would go.

We drove into town to pick up a roll of sheep netting and a drum of barbed wire at the agricultural merchant's. On the road approach to his shop and warehouse there was a huge disinfected carpet, Foot and Mouth notices and a footbath. A visit to him was, for many months, a source of up-to-date news. This began to be saturated with rumour. Early on in the outbreak gossip had it that the F and M notices had been printed ahead of the disease. The press said that a phial of the virus had gone missing from Porton Down Laboratory in November, and that the Forestry Commission had been asked about sleepers, now being used to burn carcasses, long before the need came. The virus was spreading so quickly that rumour had it that it was being helped.

With wire and binder twine and our two decrepit relatives in the Land Rover, we headed across the moor towards the meadows. There was standing water everywhere and our vehicle was sliding all over the place. We realised that it had been insanity to come with our dependants but Aunty Mary had recently frightened us. Left alone she had realised her spectacles were upstairs so she had tried to bring down the lift. It had stopped in mid-air for there was an obstacle underneath, so, for the first time in twelve months she had climbed the stairs, collected her glasses and walked down. I had been concerned. 'Just fall and break a leg and it's hospital! With Foot and Mouth in the area, how could we come and see you?' We decided she was safest in the Land Rover but were quickly changing our minds as the wheels skidded dangerously. Harry we could never leave behind but, in an emergency I am sure, between us, we could have carried him. There is no way we could lift our far-too-heavy aunt!

But we made it to the meadows and the going was safer. We had not bargained for the fact that the four stone gateposts, round which we had planned to wrap the netting, tapered towards the top. No matter how tight the bottom of the fencing wire was, the top was limp and frilled.

'We'll have to have four wooden posts,' Margaret said. She believed we had these spare, on a redundant fence on the boundary and she tried to drive there but the land was far too waterlogged. We abandoned the Land Rover on a square of firm ground and walked to the disused fence only to find that the posts were rotted. We re-traced our steps, struggled once more across the sodden earth, to the firmness of the track along which runs the MacDonald ditch, so called because it was paid for by workers at the beef-burger restaurant, when they stayed with us one year. It was currently heaving with water. We returned to the agricultural merchant's, arriving as he was closing, bought some posts and called the activity off until the next day.

Tomorrow was Saturday and we coaxed Lil into coming with us, for we planned to leave the Land Rover on firm ground and walk nearly half a mile carrying the posts.

We made sure Aunty Mary had her glasses and left her at home but Harry we took with us. When we reached the end of the track the way beyond looked less wet and the carrying distance frighteningly long, so Margaret said, 'I'm going forward. Hang on everybody!'

We slid a bit but it wasn't so scary and she drove right to the dewpond where we began the job we dislike most, knocking in posts and stretching wire, particularly the barbed variety. Meg went crazy in the two feet of water in the cone. She should have been a dolphin. The Heavens opened long before we had completed the job and we were wet through almost immediately. We persisted, unconscious of the discomfort but fully aware that an

already waterlogged track home would be becoming impassable. Margaret
wished she had not given in to temptation, that she had left the Land Rover
where we had planned. The rain was torrential, each drop twice the size it
should have been. Water ran down our wet trousers into our wellingtons but
we were determined to finish. All the way home our vehicle skidded and slid
and the steering wheel was useless for the wheels went every which way. We
thought it impossible that we would reach terra firma but we did. Lil went
to her cottage and we to the farmhouse to take off every article of clothing
and leave it in a heap in front of the washing machine. We stoked up the log
fire and Lil returned. We ate something hot and acknowledged the fact that
for two whole days we had forgotten the Foot and Mouth crisis. The way
forward must surely be to work. There is always plenty of that commodity
at The Currer.

We were aware that we would have to have more fodder. The ground was
too wet to open the meadow gates and, to be honest, there would be no
growth of grass until the earth dried and the sun shone more warmly. We
did not know whether transportation of food was allowed or even whether
there was any available after the disastrous last summer but, one day in town,
we saw a load being taken somewhere so Margaret phoned our Green
Hammerton supplier, for there was no Foot and Mouth out York way. He
could not get straw but could get a load of hay. When it came, Mark said,
'This is the heaviest load I have ever delivered!'

The good news was that there was a heck of a lot of hay. The bad news
was that is was the end of a long, hard winter and to manhandle such heavy
bales in our weakened state was cruel!

It is necessary, whatever life throws as you, to look for joy, to leave room
for laughter. Our greatest joy was Meg. All winter she had learned to play
alone. She knew how to fetch Danny should there be something really
interesting. Without dog walkers she had to focus more on the inhabitants
of the sheds. The big cattle she avoided, but the kids were just right. The
barn had enough bales to make play enormous fun for both dog and goat.
Watching them was far more uplifting than switching on television. We had
no inclination to watch Comic Relief. Red Nose Day seemed an insult even
though its intentions were good. We had an obsession with Ceefax. The rapid
spread of disease terrified us but we were hypnotised by it. We had to watch
the news, had to see the pyres and the smoke. We were continually searching
the atlas to identify the infected areas.

Watching Meg splashing in a water trough, even on the coldest of days,
was a sedative for our fears. Responding to her once-a-day cuddle was TLC
sorely needed. Wet and exhausted she hogged the warmest place on the
hearthrug in front of the fire. If our feet had got there first she sat on them.

Even without guests and cars and other people's dogs, The Currer is still an interesting place to live for any pup. There was a downside for us in that she made a mess, played havoc with a newspaper, a lump of wood, our chair legs or a cardboard box. She devoured biro pens by the dozen. Where she managed to find them I do not know, and she ruined my glasses. The frame was in pieces, the two lenses under the sideboard.

Harry found Meg a source of fun. Our other amusement was not available to any but Margaret and me until spring brought out the goats onto the yard stage. The twins were a laugh a minute. They called the Poorly Pen their home until spring but all afternoon they played in the barn, sparring with Meg, dancing and cavorting and eating almost continually. For my seventieth birthday Pat Roberts had brought me a wall plaque which said, 'Everything grows with love'. And food. They suddenly began to grow and within months were Rosie's size.

The Currer is an extremely interesting place to live for animals which are entirely free, as are goats and dogs. The donkeys are semi-free but must be kept out of places where they can pick up corn for they are not sensible eaters. Like dogs they are biddable and if asked to come out they obey immediately. Goats do no such thing. They do exactly as they want, all the time. It is impossible to chase them out if they do not want to go, so it is a waste of time to try. The donkeys know who will give them carrots and have memories of those guests who are a soft touch and recognise them immediately. Their four front feet are on the doorstep of The Mistal within minutes of the arrival of Janet and Bertie Bullock, who come every Christmas. Goats only eat when they want to. They only do anything when they want to and Mopsey and Cottontail were no exceptions. They did, however, want to eat more than most.

No directives came from MAFF. Well into the epidemic we got a letter instructing us on the welfare of animals, telling us, the professionals, how to do a job our ancestors had been doing for centuries. What farmers and shepherds most needed to do was to move their animals to new pasture. Just to take them across the road was forbidden. The fields in which sheep were trapped became just acres of mud. Farmers knew what to do, all right, but they were forbidden to do so by inexperienced civil servants, bulldozing their way through disaster, blindfold.

In mid-March we fenced the gaps in the Five-Acre wall in preparation for letting out the calves. On the first sunny day we opened the nursery door and allowed them to joyfully leap into a new environment of fresh air, a green carpet at foot, a blue sky above and space, glorious space! Spring was still to come. Technically it was winter and weeks would pass before we could stop supplementing diet but, on the first suitable day in March, we do not hesitate to give the calves their first taste of the joy which is to come. We are tempted to do it before we should, for the sight of their terrific enthusiasm and energy is an annual tonic. Off they galloped as if led by an invisible Pied Piper, leaving behind the maimed one just as in the story.

Jack, the partially sighted one, went no further than the apron of concrete at the mouth of the shed. We decided to leave him be. He alone could work out his problem. We did not know what he could see. Perhaps a mist or a distortion was more frightening than blackness. Samson, our totally blind calf, had bashed on with the herd at the first opportunity. He had frequently lost his mates and had to be brought home alone but when the door was opened he was off. Not so Jack. He stood there, at the edge of the firm ground, and he stayed there until the others returned. We decided not to urge him forward on that first occasion outside.

With so much coverage on television, we hoped the general public was revising its ideas on farmers. It was surely obvious that we all loved our animals. Big strong men were being shown weeping as the cremation pyres burned and thick smoke polluted the countryside for miles and miles. They were weeping for the loss of their animals. There is an isolation in farming so that our animals are not only our dependants, they are our neighbours and our friends. Our precious friends! Margaret could be heard singing, some-what shakily, 'You my precious friend, to the very end, I'll be there'. Farmers do not kill. They are professional carers, servants even. They nurture. They are only concerned with the living. They bring the sick back to health and grieve when they do not succeed. They have to send the older animals away because a new generation is constantly being born and the proceeds of such a sale is needed to buy food for those that are left. Every farmer has to buy food supplements and provide shelter. Ours is a modest business but £20,000 is needed for this purpose every winter.

There are rogue farmers who bring us disrepute but the majority farm like us, the welfare of animals coming before our own. I apologise if I repeat that, in this household, as in all farms, it is animals first, guests second and family last.

If people think there is no difference between sending an animal away for slaughter at a certain age and the killing of it prematurely on the farm, they had only to watch those grief-stricken farmers.

A farmer's wife was asked, 'Will you now give up farming?'

She answered, 'My husband's soul would die if we did!'

Every one of us trembled at the thought of what might lie ahead. Some were crying for lost companions. Soon they would cry for lost work. Those used to a sixteen-hour day take unkindly to inactivity. When bills kept coming in and there was no money to pay them, then they would weep for a different reason, but the greatest of all three would be for their animals. One man, writing in the *Farmers Weekly*, likened the killing fields to civil war. Another to genocide. Margaret said it was a crime against God because we knew, and every farmer knew, that the number of infected animals was minimal and millions of healthy ones were being sacrificed.

Suddenly the voice of the tourist industry and the cries of the subsidiary rural businesses became deafening. They were casualties in somebody else's war. Farmers were sincerely sorry about this. Those like us, who had diversified, ignored the death of our holiday trade and were glad to be left alone. For those wholly employed in tourism it was total disaster. The Government recognised this and, with a General Election on the agenda, the message was sent to the public that the countryside was not closed. Those who had unselfishly given up weekend walking and overnight staying must be allowed back into the villages. Their sacrifice was unnecessary. Middle England, with its wealth and leisure opportunities, its cars, its dependence on weekend golf, horse racing and multiple holidays must be placated. The countryside, the media said, was open. No one believed this and the public stayed away. It was still very early in the season. Things could get a great deal worse. Indeed they could and they did.

As every one of our potential guests cancelled, people thought we would panic. A few years ago we might have done but we feared what they might bring if they came and were content for them to stay away. They would come back to the Dales but could the herds and flocks? That would not be easy. Over the generations animals have learned to belong to the place in which they were born. They have passed on that knowledge to incomers. They have known an unfenced boundary. Many hefted flocks have developed over the centuries. Tourists would come back but could farming practices be restarted? It was doubtful.

We realised that we were in a better position than most, selling and buying only in the autumn. We had no dairy herd. Each animal in such knows the hour and the routine of a normal day. New ones introduced into the herd learn from the majority. All new at once and chaos would reign for ages. If we had to restart, the baby herd would have no yearling herd to imitate. Nevertheless, somehow pastures must be grazed, or grass cut, for land soon reverts to wilderness.

Two good sunny days allowed us once more to let out the calves and, on this occasion also, Jack still did not step from the concrete onto the soft earth and we feared there really was going to be a problem. Then came a spell of bitterly cold weather when the yearlings didn't want to go out either and when pressed to do so returned early, long before darkness, to huddle against the shed doors, desperate for us to open them.

On St Patrick's Day a second farm at Queensbury fell prey to the virus. As, we were told, infection was rapid, the delay of ten days between the two infections had deceived us into thinking there was not going to be a second. I think we had begun to feel nothing really local was going to happen and that, by Easter, things would be returning to normality and we would be going on holiday, as usual, to the Hebrides. The second Queensbury case killed all thought of that and prompted us to write to Mary Ann, at Scaristavore on Harris, to cancel our booked fortnight. This upset all of us for we are always in need of an island holiday. What to do with a cottage we had reserved two years ago was a problem. We preferred to send someone in our place. We told the MacSweens to re-book if possible while we phoned around. Our first call was to Joan and Steve McInnes whose joint history with us spanned decades. It had been Joan who'd introduced us to Sue Aspinall, at the Homeopathic Clinic in Skipton, without whom Harry's life would have posed far too many problems. She had been with us on the millennium Reunion on Tiree. Who better to ask first?

'You've won a holiday for two, on Harris,' I said. 'We can't go and it's going to be wasted!' She was so sorry for us but over the moon at the thought of an almost imminent holiday on the island where she had camped with us on so many occasions. I phoned Mary Ann and told her not to re-book, that Joan and Steve were coming instead.

To sacrifice a holiday on Harris was painful. We do not have weekends or free evenings and we had broken sleep with Harry every night. On holiday we were far from carefree for we took our canine and human dependants with us, but it was always a lifesaver to go to the islands in the spring. Denied our holiday, it made us nearly as happy to send Joan as it was to go ourselves.

We had many things to be thankful for, work-wise and money-wise. For the first time in the forty-three years we had been at The Currer, we had no project under way other than the drystone walling, which had had to stop. All our shed building had been completed and the ensuite facilities in the B&B were done. No lift was being installed, no floor being laid, no windows replaced. We'd sold the only animals ready. Diana would not calve until September. The markets surely would have re-opened by then and we would be able to sell the eighty two-year-olds and buy calves for Diana to adopt and, in October, buy our autumn intake of week-old babies. Providing we avoided Foot and Mouth, we could hold our course. Money-wise we had our four pensions and Harry's attendance allowance to pay the overheads which remained, though B&B business income was at a standstill. We would cope, providing the virus was kept at bay. We even had our billy goat luck, safely resident. Very tentatively we looked on the bright side and settled into our isolation. We could 'bugger on!' like Julia said.

The weather was insufferable. The bales in the barn dwindled to almost none. We were desperate for the grass to grow, impatient for Doctor Green, the cure-all magician of the spring. The weekend was cold but sunny and we let out the calves for their third experience of the Five-Acre. This time Jack went with the black tide, off the concrete, onto the grass. When they disappeared over the brow of the slope, he did so also. We did not know what to expect. We feared he might lose the galloping herd and that, if we had to fetch him home, he might not be easily driven. Fully exhausted the majority of the calves returned, late afternoon, to flop onto the newly laid straw and chew their cud at peace. Jack did not appear to be there but one third of the calves had not returned. When they did I checked them for the brown and white Simmental with the awkward gait, but he was not there. Nor was he down by the fence. Margaret was otherwise occupied but I called her.

'Isn't he by the fence?' she asked.

'I can't see any animal in the field at all,' I answered.

Cattle are very gregarious animals. Like pigs they are happy bedfellows. Given the freedom of a large shed, pigs will sleep on top of each other and be mistaken for a pile of dead. Cattle are nearly as neighbourly. We believe all animals should have space but people who think cattle are ill-treated if they are in a crowd should have seen our baby herd ruminating so close to each other no one could tell which head belonged to which body. Among the black and white carpet no brown could be seen but all heads were lifted, all mouths were moving and one of them belonged to Jack. It was resting comfortably on the back of a friend and he was chewing like mad, one of the lads, a fully-fledged member of The Gang!

We laughed in spontaneous relief and the black Foot and Mouth cloud lifted briefly. One problem was definitely solved.

The calves did not go out again for a week for enough snow fell to disrupt life in the North Country. It was cruel. Since the torrential rains of October we had had six long months of a winter which still showed no signs of departing. Margaret had carried thousands of back-breaking bales and it wasn't just my imagination, she was more bent than before. Tendons between knee and thigh were tightening under the strain.

On the twenty-third of March an outbreak was confirmed at Rawden, a similar distance as Queensbury but northwest instead of south. We were being encircled and on the same day the Chief Scientific Advisor warned categorically that Foot and Mouth was out of control. Something had to be done quickly and drastically or by June, he said, four thousand farms would be infected and eventually half the country's sheep and cattle would be lost.

So the army was called in to occupy the accommodation rumours told us had been booked in February. A massive trench was dug, on a disused air-field, in Cumbria. Half a million sheep, we were told, would be buried there, and cattle galore. So there began the transporting of carcasses, some infected, some just contacts but potentially dangerous, and the highways of the North Country were blocked with container wagons travelling through trouble-free areas, and frightened farmers writhed in anger, watching them pass by.

Waking early, roused by Harry who needed helping to get back into bed, I could not face sleeplessness in a cold bed. We were so angry. I made myself a cup of coffee and hugged the Aga trying to control my rage. How could Government officials, well-dressed and clean, expect any human being to daily round up healthy animals and kill, kill, kill? Kill the newborn, kill the heavily pregnant, kill the pedigree, the hefted, the beautiful?

How long, I wondered, before these employees, bribed by huge salaries, eventually cracked and could stomach their task no more, before they vomited in the hedgerow, before they were demanding compensation for stress and were joining the farmers on the brink of suicide?

We all felt powerless to do anything. When another case was announced at Rawden we rang the office of Ann Cryer, our local MP, and put it on record that we were pleading for the use of a vaccine. It was time, we said, to pocket pride, to stop worrying about exporting until we had something for sale. To continually buy meat from South America and Southern Africa, where vaccination was used, and deprive our farmers of the opportunity to protect their herds, was hypocrisy. Our request, the man said, would be faxed to London that morning.

Container lorries had begun taking live animals for slaughter on the airfield and Margaret rang the RSPCA to ask if they were monitoring this and ensuring that humane methods were used. We all knew, deep down, that there was chaos in which nothing could be done properly.

Almost immediately vaccination was discussed to pacify farmers but confusing information was louder than ever. It was broadcast that vaccinated animals, injected to form a firebreak, would then have to be killed. Rubbish! We were told that warehouses and supermarkets, openly buying and selling meat imported from countries where the disease was endemic and vaccination a routine, would not buy home bred if we did likewise.

Because they could not burn dead animals quickly enough, rotting carcasses were piled high in all the infected areas. They posed no risk, the Ministry said, while disinfecting individual premises to the cost of £100,000, sealing transport lorries, daily throwing away white coats and using so much disin-fectant that stocks ran out nationwide and all waterways must have been polluted. But, no, the Ministry said, the smelling, rotting carcasses and the toxic fumes from the pyres were no risk to other farmers, nor to the general public. No one believed this. How could they when they were told infected farms would not be allowed to re-stock for six months after disinfecting?

Why, if the virus disappeared on death, was the countryside open but not fields belonging to farmers? Everything was a contradiction.

We began to be inundated with letters and phone calls enquiring after our safety. Were we escaping the disease? Were we closed? Were we well? Everybody seemed to care about us. People in France, America, Canada, Australia and from all over the UK were concerned. We are praying for you. We think of you often. No one was bitter because holidays had to be cancelled. We were confident the summer bookings would be safe but our empty spaces were not being filled. Reservations came to a complete stand-still. Routine work was dwindling and the weather improving. The waiting game was beginning. We had a problem: what were we going to do with inactivity?

We had more time than usual to admire our pastures. I wish I was as competent a lawn mower as our animals. Where the cutting depends on me, the green square, in our tiny garden, is a shambles. Fortunately Lil handles our strimmer professionally and has come to my rescue, but the real masters of the craft are our one hundred and seventy animals. They keep the 180 acres evenly grazed to perfection. The only fertilizer we use is bedding manure, composted for at least a year and a spring scattering of Grasstrack minerals. That every square yard of our pastures is eatable bears witness to the sweetness of the forage. In the spring of 2001 we viewed our land with pride.

Chapter Thirteen

Shy of the gatepost we turned for the stars,
Leapfrogged transgressions over Saturn and Mars.
Trapped all our worries, laughed them asleep,
Poured false conversation down drains in the street.
Climb the sterile biscuit moon, inflate the carnival balloon.
Remember when we'd just begun? Remember when we rode the sun?

Quin

This on a card from Margaret, the wife of Brian our builder, reminded us that in the midst of trouble we must never forget the heights we had climbed. All our lives have been a succession of beginnings and, yes, each has brought an excitement comparable to the riding of the sun.

Without breakfasts to make for holiday-makers, I could spend the hour before the family wakened to remember with my pen. I could capture again the delights of the milestones in my life, each new step into the future had been fun to take and impossible to forget. Kitted out in khaki smock, at eight years old, I had started life as The Little Milk Girl. I radiantly rode the sun on that occasion, knowing my status as a member of the working family team was assured.

My first day at grammar school, my entry into the Guide Movement, my acceptance at teacher training college were all times when the sun shone brilliantly and I was astride it. Unforgettable was the time Margaret and I began taking children to camp in the Hebrides, and the year when, with a decrepit Austin Gypsy, we began the thirty years of taking family to islands sparkling in sunlight and washed by the Atlantic. Those were moments when my sister and I rode the sun together, as was the beginning of life here at The Currer. Boy, did we ride the sun in those early days and years bringing the house from ruin and re-claiming the land. Mother rode the sun every day, singing from her kitchen window, 'Oh what a beautiful morning, oh what a beautiful day'. Father grinned from ear to ear and Harry climbed the hill with agility to fetch groceries from the village shop.

Alone I rode the sun as I took up my headship at Kildwick School and held it for twenty-one years. Aunty Mary, in her dotage, repeatedly asks, 'Wouldn't you like to give all this up and go back to teaching?'

'I am old,' I tell her. 'They would have thrown me out twelve years ago!' I am satisfied that I was astride the Kildwick sun for twenty-one years and grateful that I am still close to many of my grown children.

What a beginning, too, was our conversion of the barn into holiday accommodation. Our feet never touched the ground. Inactivity has never been a way of life. The starting whistle has blown for every lap of our journey through life. At the closing of one, another door has opened and not until 2001 has the way ahead not been beckoning.

We are eternally grateful for that card from Brian's wife, reminding us and I think promising us that there would be a new beginning, hopefully, of the way of life we so love and that soon all this tragedy would be put behind us and we'd gallop again in sunshine! We had to wait many months for that to happen for Nick Brown, Minister of Agriculture, admitted that the disease was not under control and the army officer, in charge of disposal, said the job was bigger than expected and, believe it or not, the chief scientist was advising vaccination! This must be true for a record of it was scribbled in my notebook at the time. It is, however, difficult to believe for vaccination was never practised, millions of animals met their death and several farmers committed suicide.

The epidemic was creeping down Wensleydale but came no nearer to us on the run-up to Easter. Suspected cases were culled before confirmation and all the adjacent farms were taken, too. This happened in Doncaster. The results were negative but came too late. This was unforgivable.

Everyone cancelled for Easter. Who could blame them? There was nowhere to go and should the virus suddenly appear locally no one wanted to be a spectator. We did not know what to do about the May and June school bookings. They could not be cancelled at the last minute for parents often take a break while their children are away. Once it had been my profession and I knew that, when I was looking after their daughters, Mum and Dad often had a weekend in Paris or a holiday in Spain! With Skipper or Teacher safely baby-sitting, a taste of freedom was snatched.

I phoned MAFF and enquired what would happen if we had visitors here and disaster struck, only to learn that these would be grounded, unable to leave. But May was still distant and no new cases erupted in Queensbury or Rawden and we hesitated. The local education authorities did not. They forbade schools to visit farms and that settled that argument. Speculation was silenced re the date of the General Election with the announcement that it would be postponed until the outbreak of Foot and

Mouth was satisfactorily dealt with, and on 23 April, St George's Day, we received a letter from MAFF saying that vaccination was not to be feared. Many questions were answered positively and hopes rose. It was a perfectly safe procedure. Milk could be drunk and meat eaten. No one need worry! That was the last word from Government. No steps whatsoever were taken beyond that!

The Prime Minister went to Cumbria to view the carnage and the media reported that he had vomited in the hedgerow. Not everything the media said was true but this could well have been. There seemed no end to the awful news. Then, on the six o'clock bulletin, it was reported that a newborn calf, drip white, had survived the killing of an entire herd in Devon. Five days afterwards, with the carcasses lying unmoved from the killing field, this small calf had apparently appeared. It was headline news. It was christened Phoenix. A whole nation rose to protect it. Men, sent to finish their bungled job, were obstructed. The voice of the people was loud enough to worry authority and the Prime Minister told the nation that indiscriminate, blanket killing was no longer necessary. The calf would live. The worst was over and an election could be held at the beginning of June.

We expected that, following the MAFF letter and this premature announcement, at least selective vaccination would follow. It did not. Indeed everything remained as it was.

What to do with inactivity? We did not have to look far. Margaret started the room-to-room decorating she does every spring, but for once un-hampered by tourists. Paulette and Lil did the garden and cut the grass. The daffodils were beautiful and Red Admiral butterflies awakened and appeared everywhere. A few peewits, so long silent, called from the high ground. Mallard ducks made their brief spring visit to the pond. It had silted up over the winter and weed was quickly making it bog instead of clear water. The heron feasted on frogspawn every morning. Later in the season, every year, he disappears.

The goose became broody and the gander quite vicious. Doctor Green, the cure-all magician, was back.

It seemed as if we had a herd of goats for the two minute kids had grown to full size. The blacksmith could not believe what he saw. We continually marvelled at our luck in collecting them from Otley on the day before all cloven footed movement stopped. They were deliriously happy. They danced. To watch them was a joy. They followed Rosie and the white goat every-where and our January wanderer stayed at home. The deer trespassed as usual, which was illegal, but the sheep on the Marley Banks could not leap the highered wall or squeeze through the re-inforced gate. There was always the danger that the eighteen deer we could not keep out would bring disaster but it was a risk we had no power to avoid. They were so beautiful and elegant we could only fear for their safety and not dwell on our own.

The donkeys, Jasper and Joe, left the precincts of the farm and feasted on the hill but, after grazing all day, the cattle still preferred to come home. The field depressions continued to hold water but the bedding manure was drier. I was reminded of my teaching days and the February poem with the line, 'Every step the horses take, turns into a little lake'. The fill-dyke month had been left behind but still the earth would not drink enough. The last bales of straw disappeared and we sent for more but the coffers were bare, everywhere, and we had to be satisfied with a load of last season's very weathered hay and pray for a dry spell. Eventually it came and we closed the gate on the higher acres and the herd was happy.

I envied them. For longer than most people I'd had the opportunity to sleep out of doors. There is nothing more tempting to drink than the night air. The smell of it approaching the nostrils surpasses all other. It is best savoured from the grassy carpet beneath an old-fashioned tent, a tent with hessian sod cloth which can be lifted, while lying, so that the white tents of dependent children can be seen and the stars above and an early dawn just lightening the eastern horizon; an old fashioned tent with a sod cloth which can be brailed at noon to air it and ensure that the grass carpet lives. Not for me is a modern, unhealthy canvas home, with sewn-in groundsheet and zip-up doors for, should there be no rain, I want my doors open.

Deprived of this intoxication, I am grateful that, of necessity, my bed must be pushed against the window seat in our somewhat crowded bedroom. I can open my window wider without rising even as I used to lift the sod cloth to savour the breeze. We never draw the curtains so, on a clear night, when the moon is full, it floods the room with light and, at a certain time of the year, Orion can be seen perfectly framed in the second of the four mullions. In spring when the evening air is fully scented, I can smell the growing grass, even as I did the machair from a tent, and with that I must now be satisfied.

Another fragrance penetrated my little white tent those many nights I spent, each year, under canvas. It was the perfume of wood and peat smoke drifting from the embers of our dying fire. Next day it would be re-kindled but the best aroma comes from the embers and heralds a peaceful night. Nothing is more soporific. Aunty Mary sleeps badly and was advised to put a bag of lavender on her pillow. She would do better to open her window wide for the scent of wood smoke pervades The Currer, too. It curls up the chimney, from the dying embers in our sitting room, and floats through our open window ensuring we, at least, sleep well. We are not disturbed, either, by the continuous screeching of the little owl, only by the screaming of the vixen. That wakes us every time!

On 2 May there was glorious sunshine and I decided outdoor work must take precedence over all else. I was employing myself making a ramp for the low step leading into The Mistal kitchen. Handicapped people who self-propelled their wheelchairs normally entered via the dining room door. This was fine except when those in the B&B half of the conversion were also self-catering. The kitchen step was only three inches high and the job essential but not difficult.

I was thus happily employed when I heard the cuckoo!

That we had not recently heard him calling, actually on our land, had been more than just disappointment. Since we had first lived at The Currer in 1958, the arrival of the cuckoo had been a sign that we had survived the winter. His wife is, of course, dependent on there being small, unsuspecting birds to hatch and rear her young. We wondered if his absence was due to there being fewer each year of these foster parents. The bird population was diminishing. Everyone was agreed upon that. Bird lovers consistently blamed modern farming methods. We could not believe that we had altered our seasonal programme at all. We no longer let the meadows grow to make hay but those few fields were but a fraction of the whole. Our moorland had become pasture but all around us there was a landscape untouched through centuries. There was heather and bracken, bilberry and gorse. There were acres of woodland. We did not use fertilizers or pesticides but the bird population's demise frightened us. The swallows went from the barn before we converted it. More recently the wrens had left the walls and the sparrows had completely disappeared. The hilltop used to be noisy with peewit and lark. It was alarming and we had no explanation. The winters being less severe, one would have expected more survivors, not fewer. A dry summer can take its toll but we had plenty of wetlands. It was a mystery.

The return of the cuckoo was exciting. His failure to return to Jimmy's Wood for two years had been not just a natural tragedy, but was a spiritual one. Our souls needed his promise, equal to that of the rainbow reassuring us that 'The morn would tearless be'.

Making a ramp for The Mistal door I heard the cuckoo and went bananas. I went flying to find Margaret. On no account must she miss this unmistakable sign that, come what may, we would survive. Harry had been watching me make the ramp and he heard it too. We weren't going on holiday but we lived in a beautiful place which the three of us loved to bits.

With time to ponder we noticed again what a man of the open air Harry was. He was seldom indoors all summer. He loved fresh air as much as we did and none of us was deprived of it in 2001, with no washing up to do and no beds to make. Cups of coffeee could be enjoyed outside and in doing so we became aware of other birds returning. We commented in whispers, lest we speak to soon, but other people began to notice it and comments were appearing in magazines. We heard a curlew and a lark and a few pairs of peewit swooped ahead of us. I saw partridge in the Five-Acre and a green woodpecker was stealing from the peanut holder put out for the tits and finches. Starlings were nesting under the eves and wrens once more were running up the walls. We were invaded with wagtails and sparrow droppings appeared on the concrete below the laithe porch roof. We held our breath!

The most exciting return was that of the swallows, Father's birds. He waited for their arrival as we did the cuckoo. The Swallows far more rewarding for they become neighbours who air-dance, who teach their young on the washing line and who come to say goodbye before flying thousands of miles over the sea to Africa.

Joan and Steve left for Harris, where the sun shines brightly every May. The growth on our Pennine pastures was only slowly quickening but summer had come to the Outer Isles. We laughed every time we switched on a weather forecast for a whopping great sun persisted in sitting plumb on our island. Harry followed every yard of their journey north and every minute of their fourteen-day sojourn in an earthly paradise. For us not to be having a holiday, when the weather was so extremely beautiful, was only bearable because Joan and Steve were enjoying it so.

News of Foot and Mouth left the headlines as the Members of Parliament canvassed for re-election. They made promises galore for education and health and transport, all of secondary importance to food, but all parties left farming off their agenda.

The crisis, the Government said, was controlled and the polling date would be 7 June. Not a farmer in the country was deceived. The urban population might not know it but we farmers did. The virus was still being spread, animals were still being slaughtered and contiguous killing continued. Footpaths remained closed and B&Bs empty.

It was suggested that the returning bird population might be due to the fact that no walkers or ramblers, or dog owners frequented the countryside. It was a wild guess, and flawed, but voiced by many. We wondered whether the manure, lying deep in our sheds because we hesitated to send for the spreader, was beneficial in that insects galore must be living in it. Farmers' more hygienic methods, of late, may have reduced the bird larder drastically. We stopped trying to answer the equation and merely took joy. Most of life's puzzles are unanswerable, anyway. The calves stayed out permanently but the muck stayed in.

We desperately needed a future. We found it in our valley of tranquillity where the pond was quickly silting up and grass and weed were competing to hide it. I love the pond and it was gradually disappearing.

The idea of rejuvenating it was born when a Wilsden man rang to ask whether we would like eighty 4ft by 8ft sheets of wire netting for 50p each. Paulette and Lil expected to need fencing. Their removal to a smallholding was imminent. We all went to Wilsden and we bought the netting and then we wondered what we could do with it. The goats provided the first opportunity to use six pieces, for Rosie again showed an interest in the forbidden territory so we put a hasty stop to that.

Increasingly I wanted ducks. We had not replaced the flock almost wiped out eleven years ago by a fox who entered their den because of our negligence. A broken garage door had allowed him access. It had been ignored because Mother was dying and this had occupied all our thoughts and time. Reynard had entered and run riot, killing all but a few. We had been extremely distressed and when, eventually, the few survivors died we had not bought more. Because of this the pond had lost its inhabitants and its identity.

We decided, in our almost-isolation, that we had time and opportunity to do something about this emptiness and, while in town, we visited the DIY store and saw garden huts were for sale, reduced by £50. It was sheer extravagance when we had no income other than pensions, but we bought one and it was delivered in pieces for us to erect.

A heatwave tempted us to steal a day at the east coast. This area of North Yorkshire was free of disease and we took a chance for Harry's sake. He had missed his holiday. This proved to be one of our all-time regrets that we had to forfeit this annual, island holiday through no fault of our own. A Government decision to vaccinate would have adequately halted the disease for relatively hardly any cost at all. Less than a pound per animal! Any farmer would have stood the cost himself.

Tragically we missed our holiday so we stole a day at Filey, just to see the sea. It was a Saturday, 12 May, so Paulette and Lil were around just to keep an eye on things. We roused our family as early as possible and found that the way we went was free of traffic. Others seeking sea and sun had gone ahead of us. Those going to Filey had taken all the parking places so we dined on the cliff top at Hunmanby Gap where there was the privacy we like and a lovely view of the sea. Later we found a place on the Filey promenade so I was able to push Harry's wheelchair on every inch of the sea front, which enabled us to pronounce the excursion a success.

The cold weather had slowed growth. The heatwave now dried everything. The muddy field gateways became treacherous pavements, crusted on top and waterlogged beneath. We spent Sunday's heat being mud-larkers, dragging sods and weeds out of the pond. Harry viewed the performance from his wheelchair. For seventy years and more he had been an onlooker of our major activity. His continual regret had often been expressed in his cries of,

'I wish I could help!' Margaret barrowed manure to tip beneath the fruit trees. Only the plum has a substantial harvest and, that year, the deer got into the orchard. Could it be they who stole most of the ripe fruit? We gathered all the gooseberries. It could be that they are too sour for any animal. Certainly they are too prickly!

We had been praying for rain and it came on the Monday and forced us indoors. Margaret took up her paintbrush and I papered The Mistal kitchen. Grass began to grow profusely almost as it does when rain falls in the desert. Cattle frequented the hilltop and were silhouetted against the skyline. The appalling weather had delayed the spring spreading of Grasstrack minerals. Suddenly John's man could do this and, as we had no guests, he cleaned out the septic tank, too. Margaret ordered some magnetic rock shavings recommended by the homeopathic veterinary group. We had to do something, but we sincerely wished we hadn't when the lorry delivering the load arrived with 'Penrith' printed on the cab door. There was Foot and Mouth rife in Cumbria. 'Whatever possessed me to do that?' she gasped. That was not the end of it. The man tipped his load and a few days later a spreader came from further up Airedale, to scatter the stuff on the chosen area.

'I've been busy, lately,' said the driver. 'I think I must have spread thousands of tons of fertilizer this spring!'

'Good show!' said Margaret. 'That's the way! We must all keep going! Forward always.'

Margaret swept up the remains of the heap and filled five sacks. These she decided we would scatter manually on the hillside which falls from our homestead down towards our nearest neighbours at Jack Field. This pasture is neglected, being unsuitable terrain for a tractor. Paulette and Lil elected to help, so we loaded the sacks onto the ATV trailer and took Harry in the Land Rover. Margaret excitedly told us again of a strange circle she had seen as long ago as last autumn, which still mystified her.

It was a beautiful day. The ground was a rich carpet of meadow flowers. From the slopes the view up Airedale, towards and beyond Skipton, is always breathtaking. On most days, Ingleborough, fifty miles away, is etched on the horizon. The twin mounds of Sharper and Blunter, just beyond Skipton, cannot compete with the easy-to-recognise table top of one of Yorkshire's famous three peaks. To the north is the Pennine rib of Ilkley Moor. On the floor of the valley, Keighley peeps out from its hideaway up the banks of the River Worth. Easy to pick out, a mile up the Aire Gap, is the grammar school I attended. Steeton Hall, where I spent so many Guiding hours, is not so easily identified but lifting its head proudly out of the trees, on the hillside above Steeton, Jubilee Tower can always be seen. There, under camouflaged canvas, we camped during the war years. It's a terrific view and it was a glorious Sunday morning.

'I want to show you that strange circle,' Margaret said again. She had been bemused by this phenomenon since last autumn. She had said, then, that there was a perfectly marked circle, about ten metres in diameter. She was interested in its origin. Could it have been made by some animal ritual? Had it been made by hares, or deer whose habits we did not know? She even suggested it had been scorched by the landing of some UFO. I had been sent to look at it in October and had been interested, too. We'd expected it to have disappeared by spring but Margaret said it was still pronounced and when we went to look we found that she and I went to different spots on the hillside.

'Not there!' Margaret corrected me but I was looking at an identical circle and on investigation we found there were five similar rings and we became more intrigued than ever. They were not touching but close enough to be all seen at once and we began to speculate as to what had caused them.

'Must have been a squadron of UFOs!' we laughed.

'Could it have been the site of a cluster of round houses?' Margaret's imagination was having a field day. Normally, with our day filled with B&B chores, we would not have had time to mess about trying to solve unnatural phenomena. The summer of 2001 released us from duty and it was lovely. Having fairly recently been to the Stone Age encampment of Castell Henlys, in Wales, the idea that we might have the foundations of something interesting ourselves compelled me to ring the archeologist at the Manor House in Ilkley and he arranged to come and see this unusual ground pattern the next day.

Early in the morning, I went down to the place of interest to make sure the circles were still there and not just a figment of our imagination. I dare not think what we would let ourselves in for if there should actually be a site of historical interest on our hillside.

I told the archeologist, 'I thought it might just be the fairies and all five might have vanished!'

He was interested but said immediately that the circles were not the foundations of Stone Age round houses. The walls of those would be twice as thick.

'I think you might be right about the fairies.' He was serious. He scratched the discoloured surface to reveal a fungus. This one he identified as St George. It would have begun as a minute cluster. Spores are only thrown outwards so that a circle grows radiating from the initial cluster. The circle grows but a few millimetres a year. The size of the present 'fairy circles' would indicate they had been growing for at least fifty years. It wasn't what we'd expected but we were suitably impressed. That there were fairies resident at The Currer, when we came to live here, accounts for our good fortune and our happiness. What's more, they are still here! And we have a billy goat! The archeologist was far more interested in our inglenook fireplace. Because of it he thought his journey had been worthwhile.

His journey would not have even been requested the next day because Foot and Mouth was identified on a cluster of farms at Stainforth and Malham and what became know as 'The Settle Triangle' emerged. It was horrific! The disease spread down Airedale as rapidly as it was doing in Cumbria. It was only days since the spreader from Settle had scattered the magnetic chippings on our Eight-Acre, after putting fertilizer on scores of farms within that triangle. We admitted this to no one and were apprehensive to say the least. No amount of decorating could distract our minds from the horror that was unfolding not many miles away.

Settle is no more than thirty-six miles away and almost immediately it became a hot spot of disease. Outbreaks occurred daily at Malham and Gisburn and Gargrave. The virus swept down the valley like a lava flow. There was no mention of this on national news. An election was imminent. There was plenty coverage on regional TV. The Harrogate Brownies cancelled their Spring Bank Pack Holiday and the Nicholsons cancelled the Mistal Cottage. A mass cull began involving hundreds of farms. The virus was at Coniston Cold and Kirby Malham. It seemed unstoppable.

Do things always look even more beautiful when you are sad? It is not a reason for wanting to be so, but it is a comfort. I remember that when Father died during the great snow of 1979, the white world was amazingly beautiful and that in the late April of 1990, when Mother died and we had already cancelled an Arran holiday due to her illness, the spring was touchingly lovely. Saltburn beach, on which we pushed Harry's wheelchair the day after the funeral, was nearly, if not quite, as beautiful as Arran where we should have been. I think that in moments of sadness one must be more sensitive, that emotion must magnify and glorify. Sight and smell seem more efficient and hearing more acute. Work, of which we have always had too much, dulls appreciation and there has always been an increase of that commodity prior to holiday and on return. Spring, in the Hebrides, has been breathtaking. Could it really be that we had missed it in our homeland? Had we been too busy being happy and too active? In 2001 when we were sad, and mostly alone, with no demanding routine jobs, we were aware of the sheer beauty of our hilltop perch and our well-loved acres.

Our floral pastures began to look like parkland, so evenly were they grazed. With no detaining chores we could walk them more frequently, praying beneath the cathedral dome of the sky, that our contented cattle would not be prematurely deprived of their exceedingly beautiful habitat.

'If ever you should leave us,' I sang to them, 'It cannot be in springtime!'

A late season develops far more quickly than an early one. Just when we feel we cannot bear another day of a too-long winter, whoops, buds are bursting, blossom weighs heavily on the trees, the hawthorn is buried under 'snow', bluebells reflect the sky and birds quieten as they nest. When the air-system is turned off in the calf shed the silence is heard. It was so much more noticeable in the year of the greatest farming disaster of all time. The washing machine stopped repeating its grumble in the kitchen. No cottage radio was heard. The telephone seldom rang. No cars accelerated up the slope to appear, too quickly for comfort, in front of the house. Grass grew in the concrete cracks in the yard and the notice on the shed wall, which said, 'Cars parked at owners' risk', was ludicrous! No neighbours from the village walked their dogs through the paddock, exciting ours to a loud display of welcome. We were back to the once-was, before we built the road, when we had youth on our side but, unlike then, we had no exciting future ahead.

As our decorating progressed, the interior of the house began to look pristine and, unexpectedly, we wondered if we would ever want to fill it again. The tourist trade was so minimal everywhere it was bankrupting businesses, but we seemed immune to our financial loss and obsessed only with the beauty of emptiness within and our animal-populated pastures without. In our farming status quo we were so much luckier than almost anyone else. To wait for our cattle sales cheque until September was normal. To be empty of guests was not but, for the first time in twenty years we were not dependent on a diversification income to pay for sheds being built or ensuites added to each bedroom. We had our pensions to pay for day-today living. We could survive. We just wanted our animals to do so, as did every farmer in the country. With no ongoing project, paint was our only expense. We had two freezers full of food. It was summer so we hardly used any electricity. It was not necessary to go into town, so the petrol bill almost disappeared. Even the tardily hung doors on the glamorous sheds had been paid for. I creosoted them with pride!

Everything was unusually tidy. The heat made the opposite slope of the valley recede and softened the scar of roadside development along the A650. Leafing trees hid the houses climbing higher up the hillside than we approved.

The twin goats continued to be a comedy act. The nanny, Mopsey, was a ballerina. She could stretch her neck higher than the billy, reaching tastier silver birch leaves than he. She balanced precariously but confidently on the yard wall, an acrobat of distinction. She also believed the grass to be greener on the other side of the fence. Her head easily squeezed through the netting one way but each time her ears prevented retraction. Hearing her bleating for attention we went in her direction, with the wire clippers necessary to free her.

Butterflies became numerous. One morning I walked across our land as far as the Druids' Altar. The ground was a carpet of flowers: daisies galore, bird's foot trefoil, cotton grass, yellow rattle, bugle, hawkweed and hordes of buttercups. I met no one except Margaret who had brought Harry to the green Altar Road and pushed him towards me to meet at our boundary. She returned to collect Aunty Mary and I took the wheelchair and my brother through the gateway into St. Ives. It was the first of our many visits to our neighbouring parkland, during the summer of the Foot and Mouth epidemic.

No animals are farmed in the estate. Horses are kept, but the dairy herd went when the Booth family retired to live in the village. Since then the home farm has remained empty and the land has the appearance of set-aside. There is little more ugly than neglected land. Docks and nettles and ragwort invade the meadows immediately. Where man interferes and then walks away, nature is no longer beautiful. Most of the estate is wooded and the lanes have hedgerows. There are uncultivated acres of heather and this untouched landscape is lovely, but the ungrazed pastures and the uncut meadows are an eyesore environmentalists should see before they encourage farmers to back off. The beauty of the countryside depends on continuity. Land, which has been farmed for centuries, must not be neglected.

St Ives was open to the public for only horses have homes in front of the Mansion House; that field used to be the nursery for the newly born members of the resident milking herd. It used to be green and lush. Horses ruin land and what was a pleasant pasture is now a mess of docks and nettles which contrasts unfavourably with the beautifully cut greens of the golf course. Nevertheless St Ives is a very pleasant place to be and Harry loved its wheelchair-friendly paths which we are all too often too busy to frequent.

I was acutely aware that the estate farmer had gone. What of the farms devastated by disease and cleared of animals? Should the plague reach us, and our hundred and sixty-seven lawnmowers be sacrificed, then those beautiful pastures of ours would become a wilderness. Perhaps the neglected landscape would be the incentive for farmers to re-stock. I had wondered if they would want to restart. Would they feel like we did about the B&B? Would they really want to go back to all that work? Would they want, again, to get up at 4 a.m. to milk every day? I think they would not be able to ignore the changing view and would yearn for pasturing animals once again, just as we could not bear to think our converted barn would be empty for ever. Only time would tell and that would soon be a commodity of which there was plenty.

Is beauty something you most appreciate when you are sad or am I just making excuses for being so aware of it when I should have been blinded by tragedy? Tiree was so beautiful the year eleven-year-old Lesley had to be taken home because her father had suffered a heart attack and died. The snow was never more beautiful than the year Father died, the daffodils never prettier than in the April Joan, my teaching colleague, finally lost her fight with cancer and the Isle of Man was so beautiful and so silent a place in which to mourn.

The army had been booked in at a big hotel this side of Skipton, twenty miles east of the first outbreaks in the Settle triangle. Rumour said the booking had been made long before the arrival of the virus. Soldiers infiltrated the dale, travelling west each day and returning each night, and the disease spread rapidly eastwards and outwards on either side of the railway. Malham, Airton, Gargrave, Rylstone. Blame was being thrown at farmers, who were not on the move, and seldom on the vets and soldiers and carcass hauliers who constantly were. MAFF officials demanded the right to go from farm to farm, dead animals lay rotting for days in the fields in which they had been killed before being transported miles to distant burial places. Some were buried where watercourses were polluted. Some had to be dug up and taken elsewhere to be buried. The job was a shambles!

The bank holiday came and went without tourists in the Dales. Our converted barn was empty. A relic. A museum. We spent the holiday putting up the elegant duck-hole, helped by Paulette and Lil. Though there was a stiff breeze, Harry watched the activity with his usual interest. The pieces of the garden shed went together like a dream and when it was finished, and creosoted, we highered the fencing with our 50p sheets to keep out the fox. We were well satisfied with our somewhat expensive buy, which we could ill-afford, and were ready to welcome ducks.

Pauline Raw told us of a farmer at Malham who had lost his flock and herd.

'What will our dog do, Daddy?' his child had asked.

'We'll get some ducks,' the father had said.

We are all made with the same farming genes. Animals are our way of life. We cannot live without them. Our electrician provided us with some ducks and the good old days returned. The pond had its resident swimmers and the cakes for the family were made with duck eggs!

We hadn't stopped spending money on the white flotilla. The summer heat, and the demise of the watercourse which habitually fed and aerated it, soon threatened to dry up the pond. Our source of constant water, from a natural and lively spring, was twenty yards away and lower than the pond. We decided to buy a pump and pipe and pay for our electrician to install it. We justified the expense by reassuring ourselves that, during the winter, the pipe could serve a water trough. The spring never freezes so, should the mains do so, we would still have a source to tap. We were confident we were not just wasting money but insuring ourselves sensibly against whatever a severe winter might throw at us. The spring had been our only source of water for seven weeks in 1963 and we had had to bucket it to house and shed. Should this happen again our problems would be comparably minimal.

What now to do with all this time we had because we had no tourists? Margaret said she'd had a struggle to drive a calf out of the bog which was a permanent feature of the Dyke Field. The wet lands had been extended and deepened by the floods of the previous autumn. Everywhere water levels were higher than usual. Margaret thought we ought to fence the area and that perhaps it was a job for John. But Foot and Mouth was confirmed at Thorpe, that tiny hidden village between Burnsall and Grassington, and another area was emptied of its livestock and another Dale had been infected. Wharfedale is an even bigger tourist venue than Airedale. It has Bolton Abbey and Ilkley, Kettlewell and Buckden. Upper Wharfedale is National Trust country and really dependent on a visiting public.

And still there was no mention of all this on the national news as the election drew close. The party candidates laboured away at inner-city problems, education, transport, health and crime. Nothing was said about the rural communities and industries rapidly hurtling towards financial disaster.

The outbreak reached Middleton on the other side of Ilkley Moor. The practice of contiguous culling meant that thousands of animals were being killed and rumours were loud that, after the election, there would be a mass cull. The Settle triangle was an embarrassment. 'After 7 June,' farmers said, 'a mass cull is certain'.

At all costs we must keep busy. Margaret said, 'Oh, come on, we'll do that fencing ourselves!' It was sensible for we were losing money by the hour and banging in posts releases trapped anger. To do so would be good for us. We were putting no money aside to pay the autumn bills. We must stop spending unnecessarily but we ordered fencing posts and wire from the agricultural merchant in town. Collecting them we talked to two farmers who told us the army had booked the Skipton hotel for eleven weeks. Eleven weeks! We were aghast! 'The vets are all booked in at The Craiglands in Ilkley!' one man said. 'Slaughter pens are being built at Addingham Moorside,' said the other.

It was time that we really prepared ourselves against the governmental weapon of mass destruction. Terrorism can be defined in many ways. We felt that we, and all our colleagues, were victims. We went to the cash and carry and stocked up our larder against seige. The display cabinets were still full of meat imported from South America and Southern Africa. In both continents, Foot and Mouth was endemic and vaccination practised. We angrily accused the butcher of disloyalty.

It was advisable to appoint a private valuer, should our herd be killed, so Margaret phoned Otley Cattle Mart to make sure of the support of the auctioneer. I chatted again with the former pupil and Guide, Julia Horner, in Buckden, who was an excellent source of information. She asked if we had received a 'Help Pack for Farmers'. We hadn't so she faxed one to our accountant and he made a special Saturday morning journey to deliver it by hand. It contained a mass of 'Farmers' Rights' and suggested ways of standing against MAFF to protect healthy stock. Margaret gave our name to a Bristol solicitor in case we needed help.

We were all so much in the dark. We were not used to phoning neighbours and most of our information came from friends. Bill and Dorothy had driven to Morecambe and had met thirty full containers of dead animals on the road between Skipton and Settle. Two more, Joe and Evelyn, had driven south past an empty Catterick Barracks and again north, not many days later, and found it a-buzz with personnel and tents and fortified with stacks and stacks of railway sleepers. Paulette used the internet and brought us information that way. A protest group emerged. Celebrities joined, including Noel Edmonds in Devon. The cry for vaccination echoed everywhere but there was an election, a result, and then a Tory Party leader resignation. The fact that 250,000 animals in this area were killed went unnoticed.

We were afraid vets from the Ministry would cross our cattle grid, a quarter of a mile away, and just appear in the farmyard. There were instances where they had wrongly interpreted a map reference and had come and wiped out the wrong herd. We knew that, further up the dale, there were farms also called Currer Laithe. We were taking no risks. If our animals remained healthy, no way were they going to be killed. Farmers who had lost their stock began ringing to say they would police the gate for us if necessary. Strangers were suddenly friends.

We lifted a barrier from the cattle grid by the pond and took it on the ATV to the farm entrance. We hung it on gudgeons, putting the top one upside down so that it could not be removed. We put padlocks on the gate and the barrier and barbed wire on the rambler's gate. We gave one key to Paulette and Lil and put the other on our car keyring. No one, now, could come unannounced.

Simultaneously we realised that, in our isolation, we were neglecting to lock the front door at night. We hadn't done this since the days of a field gate at the entrance and no easy access over a cattle grid. For twenty years we had had strangers in the house and their cars in the yard and we had not neglected to lift out the car keys or lock the front door. Suddenly we were forgetting both and speaking of our small estate as an island.

The fencing took nearly one whole week and provided entertainment for

Harry. We were conscious of the fact that we had a summer in front of us to devote more time to him than usual and we made as much use of it as possible. Daily we took him, and occasionally Aunty Mary, in the Land Rover to the edge of the bog to watch us bash in the sixty fencing posts round the perimeter, stretch on the three rolls of sheep netting and uncoil the drum of barbed wire. The task was not as unpleasant as usual for we need not hurry. The earth outside the bog did not resist too strongly and the poles penetrated it with each blow. Margaret did most of the hammering in with the mallet. She always does. The enclosed area was more like a water-garden than a bog. The spring yellow of the flora had given way to the blues of May and the scarlet of June/July was the prominent colour. The pastures were populated with red clover, the hedges and copses with red campion and foxgloves stood sentinel, in hundreds, along the wall sides, but the flower that blood-coloured the bog was the ragged robin. There was ground ivy and bugle and cotton grass among the rushes. We couldn't possibly ignore the joy of the life we led while weeping for the imposed agony from without.

We were conscious of something we had always known. We were pensioners who were not suited to retirement. Not for us were the weekly over-sixty meetings. We were not suitable material for Third Age societies, coach trips with the elderly, coffee in the shopping centre or any of the things our contemporaries seem to do. For us, to live is to work! We had always known this but the truth shouted at us daily, waking us each morning with the query, 'What can you do today?'

There is one main stream in the Dyke Field, into which the slope has been drained, unsuccessfully in the region of the wetlands. The gully is there but it is useless. Margaret found that the calves would not cross it. A feeble jump would be all that was needed but they would not attempt it and stranded themselves on the other side.

'We'll have to make a bridge!' she said. That was a fun game which occupied us for a while. Then I decided to use two sheep hurdles to enclose a donkey/goat-free zone outside The Mistal door. These are gates of metal tubes and when the job was done we noticed that the wind could enter and play a tune. It is pleasant, if somewhat ghostly, for the melody it plays is haunting. If cottage holiday-makers begin to leave early we will know why and will have to take away the fencing.

Still almost imperceptibly Harry was getting weaker. We began to walk him less and push the wheelchair more. We pushed it into the lift. For twelve months we had not done that and we shuffled furniture so that we had a clear run to wherever he needed to go. Instead of walking him to the Land Rover we took him by chair. When we had time to worry about it we knew his mobility was decreasing.

Eating was also becoming a problem. Harry liked his food. He liked his food a lot. He never put on weight which was lucky, but he firmly believed it was a godsend that his sisters could cook as well as his mother. He wanted everything homemade but enjoyed expensive cream cakes on holiday and appreciated it when Tim brought some from the village shop. It wasn't his appetite that was at fault; it was the eating process, keeping food in his mouth until it could be swallowed. It was a problem but not a big one. It did not worry us unduly. Our brother had been disabled for nearly seventy-four years but we had not been especially aware of his handicap because his intellect and his attitude had been nearly normal. His disability was an accepted part of our life and, though we made it our first object in life to keep him alive, we did not make it an obsession. We were normally too busy to anticipate and worry about what the future might hold for Harry, until the summer of Foot and Mouth when fear became an unusual neighbour. Fearing for our cattle, we gradually became aware that we were fearing for Harry.

St Ives was a haven of peace and we frequented it as often as we could. We pushed both wheelchairs on a double circuit of the lake whenever we had the opportunity. The Mansion House now accommodates handicapped young-sters and a wheelchair route has been made all round the perimeter but we never met any of them enjoying the quietness which hangs over the water. We found the solitude there to be a balm for the wounds summer was inflicting. After our promenade at the water's edge, we would wander towards the children's play area to see if the ice-cream man was there. His takings must have been sadly low. St Ives is not a tourist attraction, but normally, it attracts scores of local people. In 2001 it was almost empty.

The lake is a sanctuary for wildfowl but their numbers seemed unusually low. If there was one fisherman casting his fly and sitting patiently beside his rod that was all. The countryside was asleep.

One Saturday afternoon it was unseasonably cold and grey and outdoor work was only an attraction if Harry could sit in his wheelchair and watch. It would have been an opportunity to watch a film on television, to get out my scribbling pad or open up the sewing machine or just to fall asleep by the fire, but Harry said, 'What are we going to do this afternoon?' The weather was never a deterrent to him and the era of jigsaw making had gone. For years this interest had occupied the hours when there was nothing to do. Lately the joy of this activity had died. A pile of boxes stood in a corner of the spare bedroom but Harry did not ask for them.

'Where can we go?' he wanted to know, on that grey, end-of-the-week day. It was too cold and miserable to do anything really, but Margaret came up with a most unlikely suggestion.

She who, like me, avoids all unnecessary contact with the town, who hates shopping as much as I do, who never ever goes window-gazing, said, 'Would you like us to push you round the indoor Airedale Centre?'

The beaming smile on Harry's face clinched the bargain. 'If you want to,' he said. Well, that was debatable but we drove out the Land Rover and put both dependants in, one wheelchair and the two dogs and we went to find a parking space in the crowded town. To find one big enough for a station wagon, we had to go into the supermarket car park and there we left Aunty and dogs and we took Harry along streets and into shops he had never been in since childhood. We went several times around the covered-in market and we wandered repeatedly in the shopping precinct. We pushed the chair through Boots and Marks & Spencer and Woolworths, buying nothing. We went round W H Smiths and to see the foundations of the new bus station-to-be. We went through the Town Hall Square and followed Cavendish Street under its glass canopy and met at least two friends who certainly hadn't expected to find the country-loving Brown threesome walking round Keighley, among the crowds of a Saturday afternoon.

Two hours later we returned to Morrisons' car park and I indicated I was just going inside the supermarket to buy something, in order to get my parking ticket stamped. 'Take Harry back to the car,' I said.

'No. I'm coming in with you.' Harry was still game for anything so we pushed him all round the stacked shelves, buying little but entertaining a happy brother.

We have told many people of our Saturday jaunt. No one else has, as yet, thought it was a very, very funny story, one we will laugh at for many a year to come. It makes us wonder, in retrospect, where we will eventually, ever find such fun as we had with Harry!

He was struggling to overcome a blocked nasal passage and needed oodles of fresh air so we chose a breezy day to do an annual trampling of the bracken, willow herb, goose grass and nettles which grow behind the north wall of the pastures we still call the moor. Cattle do not really enjoy eating it and never sample enough to make themselves ill but, tempted to try it, they knock off the top stones of the wall. There was a time when Aunty Mary would have wanted to sit out in the sun, but that time had gone. She nodded in the passenger seat and Harry sat alone. We kept an eye open for the herd of eighty increasingly heavy and curious bullocks. We had little hope of selling them, for no movement of any sort was allowed. Cattle are always curious, but in the summer of 2001 they were more so than ever. Human beings crossing their domain were non-existent and their dogs belonged to a bygone age! Had they approached Harry, sitting like the Lord of the Dales, they wouldn't have left him be. This awareness, that our one hundred and sixty-eight-head herd roamed in isolation, worried us. Should normality be restored and all our numerous footpaths re-opened, the cattle could well be dangerous, so curious would they be of trespassers. There was, however, no sign of normality returning.

There had been a time when a circling helicopter caused near-stampede. During the Foot and Mouth crisis the Ministry helicopter hovered several times a day. Farmers believed it was bad news. The disease followed the helicopter, they said. The cattle became so used to this overhead noise they hardly noticed. Anger was growing in the Dales. Contiguous killing, it emerged, was illegal. A stand could be taken against authority but few dared resist. There were plenty letters and signatures. After the election the name of the Ministry was changed to DEFRA. Farmers locally called it Death Row and Margaret Beckett became responsible. Hilary Peters was organising protests and came to see us on 24 June, telling us that Margaret Beckett was coming to Skipton the next day. She hoped there would be an angry crowd to greet her. All those still escaping the disease dared not go but those who had lost the 250,000 animals already slaughtered jeered angrily when the visiting minister said, 'You expected a mass cull after the election and, you see, it didn't happen!' There is nothing so deaf as a brick wall!

We began to take liberties we would normally never presume to take. Julia wrote an excellent article for the newspaper. She sent a copy to Prince Charles and received an understanding letter in reply. I sent one to the Queen. You can't get higher that that. I dared because both Julia and I are Queens Guides! A sympathetic reply informed me the article would be sent to Margaret Beckett. That was useless. Whatever we did nothing changed. The killing machine bulldozed its way relentlessly.

We began to feel sorry for ordinary, urban people who were having to cancel holidays they had been looking forward to. It wasn't fair! It seemed that everyone had to suffer.

But there is no cloud without a silver lining for those who look upward. To do so in the otherwise blighted summer was, miraculously, to see swallows. I have recorded only one year since 1978 when a tiny few had nested. Nationwide the swallow population had been dwindling. That they survive their long flight to and from Africa is a miracle in itself! We could not but be aware that they were back in droves. They were swooping about their daily business, every which way, and we were ecstatic! How many of them, we could not determine. They were like bats, flitting everywhere, and we went dizzy watching them. There were so many of them we could not watch an individual flight. They concentrated by the sheds but we could not see them within or identify their nesting places. When they settled, momentarily, it was on the telephone wires. Maybe there was truth in the theory that dirty sheds provided bird food and Margaret said, 'I'm tempted to keep it in every summer if it means we have swallows again!'

A few days after Margaret Beckett's visit there was an outbreak at Silsden and Kildwick and several farms were culled no more than four miles away, westwards along the valley. The Government boasted that there were just a few hotspots of Foot and Mouth left in the country. We did not believe them for the mass cull, predicted in Powys, began. More farms were identified in Wharfedale and the epidemic leapt onto the North Yorkshire Moors. The fear was that it would spread to the huge pig population south of the moors and a programme of intensive bio-security led to all farmers being sent a video showing them how to properly disinfect. Many of us didn't even own a video!

We knew that Harry Raw's animals were being tested every two days but within our ring fence our cattle placidly grazed. We saw no white-coated officials, no transporter wagons. It was all happening to someone else, some place elsewhere. We had problems other than Foot and Mouth. We would have been blind not to see that Harry's health was deteriorating. Disabled he had always been, ill never. At least not until the Epilim fiasco and that had been sorted. We began to be afraid that momentum on a downward slope couldn't be stopped. We loved our brother dearly and we were scared. But Emilie was coming and Harry loved all members of the Barbault family. Emilie would be a diversion. There would be no beds for her to make and only cakes for the family. A happy month was ahead. We hoped her presence would immunise us against the disease and tried not to think how awful it would be if our turn should come while she was here! However, the billy goat and the guardian angel, the fairies and homeopathy were not letting us down, yet, so we awaited Emilie's arrival with optimism.

One amusing incident, just before she came, highlighted the tension within us. Rumours that infected pieces of sheep, tongues and tails, were being thrown over walls by Ministry employees were even reported in the press. Margaret found herself checking the chained entrance, at the pinnacle, daily. Cars could be driven to that out-of-sight gateway and rubbish was sometimes thrown over the wall. Increasingly, modern humans are litter louts. It was just the most suitable of places for any well-paid Government employee, wishing to prolong his lucrative job by keeping the disease going, to drop something over our wall. What sad depths had we reached that we could even think such a thing might happen? Then, one day, Dorothy phoned to say she had just been walking up Altar Lane, from the Bingley entrance, and an official looking vehicle had passed her with a number plate MAF. There were two men in it and it had not stayed long at our boundary before returning and passing her again. She was sure it was a MAFF vehicle and convinced they had been on some sinister mission. Margaret did not pause to hesitate. She grabbed a plastic dustbin bag and some tongs and ordered Harry and me into the Land Rover.

'Don't you think we ought to ring the Davisons at Transfield,' I said. 'See if the vehicle actually came as far as their house and Altar Farm.'

So we gave them a ring and learned that MAF were the initials of the owners of Altar Farm! It didn't stop us driving over the moor just to check and it illustrated just how nervous we really were. We laughed at our stressed condition and returned with an empty bag somewhat ashamed. There are, indeed, many forms of terrorism!

Chapter Fourteen

I saw in a vision the worm in the wheat
And in the shops nothing for people to eat,
Nothing for sale in Stupidity Street

Ralph Hodgson

We had warned Emilie that things would be very different here, that there would be few household tasks for there were no holiday-makers. She had had no experience of this isolation having always known The Currer as a hive of activity. For the most part she would be a prisoner, like us, visiting only disease-free places, and we told her that, while she was here, things might happen none of us would ever want to see.

She was determined to come and we needed her company – Harry in particular! We were losing Paulette and Lil who had finally taken possession of their cottage at Hainworth. Their presence had been a comfort and a distraction. They had helped us with some of the jobs which had needed more than just the two of us. They had brought news in from the outside world. Paulette had searched the Internet for more detailed accounts of the spread of the virus. It was our good fortune that, as they left, Emilie came.

We collected her from the National Express coach at its temporary street stand in use while the new bus station was being built. She had successfully completed her year in Germany, learned another language and another way of life. Denis had spent a teenage year out in Russia and come home unchanged. His sister came back from Germany the same person she had always been. It had been a learning experience but not changing one. It had been a new environment and she had matured but she re-entered our household as she had left it and for a month Harry had a great time.

If we had expected, too, that there would be a change one way or another in the farming status quo while our French friend was here, then we were wrong. The disease crept ever nearer but that was all.

On the day following her arrival we unlocked the entrance gate to allow Ana Chylak, from East Riddlesden Hall, to bring the new National Trust land agent to visit us. It was an eerie experience showing her round our emptiness. We entered the unused dining room. The newly decorated rooms had not been used since the outbreak. I had oiled the beams in the snug and washed the many curtains and cushion covers but Margaret was going to enlist the help of Emilie to whiten the walls. I hastily re-hung the curtains for Ana's visit and took them down immediately they left. Walking round the tidy rooms, with their un-slept-in beds and gleaming ensuite facilities, was really sad. All our work, all our earnings spent, our devotion and our pride were for nothing. All we had was a museum no one visited. We had been dedicated to the preservation, in perpetuity, of a five hundred-year-old property of a yeoman farmer. For what? For nothing at the moment. The soul of the place had gone.

Margaret and Emilie finished the decorating and we closed and locked the door. Twenty-one years ago, when all was painted and polished, we had closed the door in November 1980, fearful of opening it on the new life ahead. In July 2001 we closed it aware, I think, that change was inevitable. There was little or no excitement in the way ahead.

'What I will most remember about the Foot and Mouth,' Margaret was heard to say, 'is the locked gate!' It had been an open welcome for so many years but, locked, it gave us a security, holding terror at bay.

During the month Emilie was with us nothing changed on The Currer hillside. Our Precious Friends ruminated in blissful contentment. Within the family things were changing. Harry was definitely losing ground. We knew, and I think Emilie did too, that every day our normally independent brother was less so. He, who for over seventy years had drawn away from touch, began to lean his head affectionately on our shoulders. We noticed his legs swelling with water and were scared into taking a viral risk in order to take him out in the Land Rover. We looked for every available opportunity to push his wheelchair.

Above all we realised that even semi-retirement was not for us. We feared that, when Emilie went, we would be bored. Initially we had felt that to re-start the B&B was not attractive. Six months without it and we couldn't wait to get back to normal. Harry, in particular, missed people and needed a holiday. He needed Tim doing the walling, Pauline bringing the milk, guests driving into the yard and kitchen encounters with Ian and Angie. He needed interest. We took risks which were dangerous just to feed his enthusiasm.

The first fortnight of Emilie's stay was a heatwave. We risked a visit to Yeadon Tarn and she pushed the wheelchair round the lakeside. Harry Raw cut and made hay in the two Marley meadows and brought bales overland through our gate and stacked them in our barn. There seemed no hope of selling any of our one hundred and sixty-eight cattle. We could not go into winter with an empty barn. There was talk of mass blood-testing on the York plain so Mark beat the commencement by bringing us two loads of hay. Tim's summer programme was disrupted and he made hay instead of silage and brought the bales to us, but the barn was nowhere near full.

An infected farm at Silsden resulted in the mass cull of sheep on Baildon Moor. The villagers were angry, with reason, for the killing took place close to where the village fête was in progress. They had no disease but belonged to a farmer living within the 3km radius of the Silsden outbreak. Uninfected cattle were killed close to the back gardens of houses in Bradley. There was public uproar but to no avail.

Emilie and I brought up logs from the low pasture, where a rowan had fallen some years ago, in a feeble attempt to increase our fuel store. Margaret took out the ATV and flail mower and cut down the thistles.

Every time we looked at the eighty big cattle, the ones we would normally sell in September, we cringed. They were far too big for us to keep, and feed, and handle over winter. The problem was highlighted, as it always is in summer, when one was ill and needed attention. The fox had not been very vocal recently but instinct must have told him we had ducks. They paraded from their waterfront villa every morning and exhausted themselves swimming on the pond before taking a siesta among the rushes. Before dark, every night, Margaret drove the ducks into their manor house and securely latched the door. The goose had hatched two goslings and this larger and noisier lock was driven into the overnight safety of a shed. The fox could not get them but he came to try. We heard the commotion. The thundering of bovine hooves awakened us. We shot out of bed to the open window. The disturbance was in the vicinity of a fallen hawthorn tree by the wall separating the younger generation of cattle from their seniors.

Next morning Margaret found that five of the calves had jumped a potentially unjumpable wall and that one heavy bullock was maimed. Some unexplained damage to his left foreleg had doubled its size. He was limping too much to follow the herd and Margaret was able to open the gate and let him into the road. She brought him to the crush and gave him an antibiotic and a painkiller. There was no way she was going to send for a vet, disinfected or otherwise! There was nothing he could do more than she, except charge a call-out fee.

A few days later she put another bullock into the road showing unmistakable signs of Wooden Tongue. There was no way she was going to send for a vet for that either! The effects are not dissimilar to Foot and Mouth but from one they recover with a jab of Streptopen, almost immediately, and from the other they do not. Margaret was never going to risk a killing on suspicion.

Handling big animals is awesome. We asked the cattle market staff to remember we had eighty two-year-olds to sell, should permission to do so ever come.

'We've plenty of eager buyers waiting for the green light,' the office lady said. 'But there's not a hope in sight.'

One evening Margaret and Emilie went to check the yearlings in the rented field and Margaret stepped on a stone both she and I knew was wobbly but neither of us had done anything about it. This time she stepped on it she fell flat and next day she had a purple face and, weeks later, blamed the accident for a torn ligament in her leg. It was the beginning of a mobility problem she could ill-afford. She limped and the better leg of the two took the strain and years of carrying heavy loads suddenly took their toll. The easier lifestyle did not help, for sitting more and walking less tightened, rather than loosened, the tendons between knee and thigh and if we had not had so much else to worry about, I'm sure we would have been more alarmed. As it was we were sufficiently so to make anticipation of a winter with unsold animals quite frightening!

Emilie walked over to Haworth, via the road called Hog Holes Lane and the country pub at the summit, called The Guide Inn. We remember a time when it was called The Gormless. Close by this, the road forks. Travel left and you go to Haworth by road and right you go through Hainworth village and to Haworth by footpath. Emilie went via the track and called at the cottage where our ex-neighbours now lived, to see their horses, dogs, cats, ferrets and guinea pigs. They had acquired two pet lambs which could not be moved until after the restrictions were lifted. Emilie did not seem to mind mostly being confined to barracks and I think that, when we took her on one jaunt or another, it was not actually for her but for Harry whose summer seemed important. Having lost one holiday, and most likely a second, autumn, one, we had to salvage what we could and take what was offered.

The weather was unusually hot. Record temperatures were reached. The south had rain. We needed it but had to wait for several days during which the earth dried up in our pastures and we knew that, though a little rain in spring will work wonders, in summer, for it to do any good, it must be torrential.

At last the Heavens opened their floodgates over Yorkshire. Water catapulted down the MacDonald Ditch and a stream reappeared and flowed merrily into the duck pond. Were they happy! Ducks are so silly and we love them. The pump keeps their mini-lake full but a stream brings a harvest of aqua-food. Of course the deluge brought mud and it coated tractor tyres and the headache of cleansing was worse than ever.

We, too, are like ducks. We do not mind the rain. We dodged the drops to transfer Harry from his wheelchair into the Land Rover, and forced Aunty

Mary to go at a speed she never takes. We jumped in with the dogs and went to Wycoller. There was no Foot and Mouth in that area but there were no tourists either. Water poured down the hillside creating tributaries to the roadside gullie and they, in turn, overflowed and flooded hollows on the roads. Our Land Rover wheels sent fountains of spray sky high, thoroughly cleansing it and, as we neared Wycoller, and drove through the heavy foliage lining the single track, we could believe we were passing through a rain forest.

We do not normally disembark and go into a tea shop but, with Emilie to help, we fought the downpour and treated ourselves to tea and cakes. The cafe was absolutely empty. The proprietors were idly waiting for the hour to close. It was incredible that we, who were so diligently avoiding infection, should be the only visitors. Perhaps it was the rain that kept people away for the Government was adamant that virus-free villages, such as Wycoller, were open to business. The owner of the teashop said, rain or no, the summer was almost completely without tourists.

There was no disease in the Halifax area so, one day, we ventured to Shibden Hall which was equally deserted. We found an inglenook fireplace almost identical to our own but lacking the beehive oven. The curator told us that the Shibden inglenook had been put in the house in 1540 so now we can believe that when Arthur Currer bought the house in 1571, ours was already in it. That knowledge was worth a visit to the Hall! Margaret and Emilie walked the dogs in the grounds and found the boating pool deserted and no children in the play area. The summer of 2001 was certainly a universal disaster.

The spread of disease seemed to be abating and rumour had it that, if thirty days elapsed after the Silsden outbreak, selling within a restricted area might be allowed. This meant we might be free to apply for a licence on 22 August. On the 17th there was another outbreak in Addingham. The virus appeared again in Northumberland and that decided the issue.

Harry had a hospital appointment and the specialist said his white blood count was fairly low. He could have a transfusion now or wait a week or two. She decided on the latter but brought the next appointment forward. His legs were so swollen we frequented the village doctor's surgery quite often and each time I pushed Harry through the village. Once he had known who lived in every house but, living at The Currer for over forty years, we now knew hardly any. I pushed him into the village shop. He had not been in there since it was a Co-op, years and years ago. He had a great time!

Nothing really changed throughout Emilie's stay. She gathered lots of bilberries from the rough hillside. We talked endlessly round the dinner table. That Harry was finding difficulty in eating, she accepted. Emilie is never a problem. She can cope with our family as few others can. Denis rang to say he would come for a week in September and that brought a brilliant smile to Harry's face. The cattle continued to cause little trouble. The horrendous national tragedy was over the horizon, outside the limit of our sight.

All summer September had seemed a long way off. When Emilie went home all our problems seemed imminent. The first was the expected arrival of Diana's calf. Normally we would go to the market immediately, to buy three more calves to drink her enormous supply of milk. Obviously that could not happen. Could one calf take all or would we have to milk her? That was not a pleasant thought. Trading Standards warned us that if restrictions allowed us to bring in a calf we would then not be able to sell anything for twenty-one days, so buying was out of the question.

We had cancelled our holiday booking in Aberporth and pre-booked a holiday cottage in Grange instead. I rang the estate agent and asked if there was any chance of postponing it and was able to put back the date a fortnight.

The biggest problem would be the retention of eighty, two-year-old bullocks for whom we had neither grass, nor winter fodder nor big animal accommodation. The thought of this was a nightmare. It is annually necessary for us to reduce our herd by fifty per cent every back of August/ beginning of September. Our pastures will not support more than the year-lings in autumn. A full barn is needed for winter and it was only half filled with precious calf hay. Margaret ordered fifteen tons of corn and shopped around for more hay and straw. Farmers, who normally sold from the field, were hanging onto their stores until after Christmas, but we found a haulier whose normal customers had had their animals destroyed in the epidemic, one whose sales had been, predominantly, in the wiped-out Settle Triangle. We secured three small loads over three weeks.

We had another bullock with Wooden Tongue. It continues to amaze me how a sick animal comes home. It hangs back from the herd, in the vicinity of the steadings, always within sight of the house. Sick animals at The Currer do not object to being driven home and will go meekly into the shed. It is as if they acknowledge Margaret's remedial skill and say, as would a human, 'I think I need a doctor'.

We gossiped with a neighbouring farmer who said he had a heifer with what he thought was an abscess under its throat. Margaret said she'd had two with Wooden Tongue and the next time we saw him he said he'd called the vet and that had been his diagnosis, too. We can go years without that particular infection and then there is a mini-outbreak. Though our second case willingly came home, he was a maniac in the crush. Thankfully Margaret had spotted his problem early, before it had stopped him eating. Our lunatic, therefore, could be tamed with a bucket of corn, long enough for him to be jabbed!

The ducks were a constant joy. The pump fed their pond admirably so that they could frolic all day. They had to be chased into their hut every night and every morning I picked up three eggs. With no breakfast customers we had enough to give some away.

But the greatest joy of the summer was the antics of the twin goats. They had trebled their size and looked almost like deer. To watch them was to see ballet. The nanny was the most agile. She was first to arrive when the corn bin lid was raised. She was first to leap onto the wall near the silver birch and she reached higher than her twin. He ran with the herd but she ran in front. Her dominance was more apparent every day.

We had to learn, somehow, how to cope with a situation we could do nothing about. There was no point in continuing to be nervous about Foot and Mouth. Our attitude towards that changed from total fear to relative calm. I have no experience of war on my doorstep but know that those who have must get used to it or go mad. I suppose the truth is that you can get used to being afraid! From having almost nothing to do, we suddenly had problems to sort out and that is a healthy occupation. Our first was to separate the two-year-olds from the yearlings. We left the youngsters on the hill and brought their seniors home. We were happy organizing. We were tired of nagging Government to vaccinate, tired of cancelling bookings. October was a long way off and, we decided, even if it became possible to resume our tourist trade we would have no heart to bother re-opening before half-term at the earliest. We had lost interest. We talked about an autumn holiday. We are eternally optimistic!

We began to wish that Harry had had a blood transfusion after his hospital appointment. I worried that I had not insisted we take the safe option, when the specialist had hesitated. His new appointment, after one month instead of two, was for the end of August and his health was deteriorating too fast for comfort, so I phoned for an urgent appointment which resulted in an immediate transfusion. This emergency put Foot and Mouth well and truly into the background.

Normally we left Harry alone at the hospital when he was given blood, but because he was to be treated on a ward, instead of in the clinic, I elected to stay. It was the Saturday before August Bank Holiday Monday. His blood had to be matched, so the activity would take six hours. It was too long to leave him alone, so I stayed. There was nothing to do at home. Had things been normal, as on previous Bank Holiday weeks, the Gang would have been arriving for their annual get-together.

I took Harry home pink once more. It was already seven o'clock and we were ravenous. Margaret had made a mutton stew and the delicious aroma of it filled the kitchen. 'What's for pudding?' Harry asked.

I remembered seeing a frozen lump of rice pudding, preserved in the freezer, waiting for an emergency. Just the job, I thought, commending myself for being well organised and ever prepared.

'Pudding? No problem!' I grinned putting the white lump into a dish to be defrosted and re-heated in the Aga.

The mutton stew was a lifesaver equal to a blood transfusion. Our fears began to disappear. We had been getting very worried about Harry's health. I know I had become increasingly concerned about his eating problem. Margaret was ever more diligent about the homeopathy treatment which had kept him so well. We had become fearful of the weight of water in his legs and the paleness of his fingers. Well, he was nice and pink once more and tucking into a great bowl of stew and licking his lips for the pudding. I ladled it onto four plates and we each sprinkled the pudding with sugar and poured on milk and cream. I took the first spoonful!

'Hold on,' I gasped. 'It isn't rice. It's tripe and onions!' This may well be one of our favourite meals but not served as pudding, liberally sweetened. Tripe and onions is an easy meal for anyone with an eating difficulty and looks remarkably like milk pudding. Laughingly I hurried to the kitchen to put on a pan of milk and make a semolina. Hilarity saved the day and the episode was good for a laugh for ages. 'Do you know what Jean did?' was a phrase Harry used often before telling guests my imperfections.

We were laughing again! And on Bank Holiday Monday Harry had the best opportunity ever to say, 'Do you know what Margaret did?'

The weather was perfect. We could spend the whole day out. But Aunty Mary took some encouraging to get up earlier and it was approaching midday before we left the farmhouse. I had suggested we just go to St Ives. Harry preferred being outside and it was a simply glorious day. Margaret argued that it was Bank Holiday and a longer run was more appropriate.

'We've missed our holiday,' she said. 'We can't just go over the wall!'

'We'll need more petrol,' I said so we pulled into the filling station and I looked in the family purse. 'I've only enough money for ten pounds' worth!' I said.

Like Mother, I always have the purse. There is only one in our house. When filling up with petrol Margaret manipulates the pump and I go into the kiosk. The newspaper placard outside the little shop displayed some bad news. The body of a missing Ilkley boy had been found. It attracted our attention and momentarily clouded our holiday mood.

I climbed back into the driving seat for Margaret was having real trouble with the tendons in her legs. My suggestion had been rejected so I left her to decide our route.

'Go up Fell Lane,' she said. 'Let's go via Slippery Ford to Cowling, turn off the Colne road and go to Trawden and over the moor to Heptonstall and Hebden Bridge.'

So I drove out of the petrol station and almost immediately I felt a lack of power in the engine. I pressed the accelerator but did not get a normal response. 'The engine's cold,' suggested my usually intelligent sister.

'It's midday in a heatwave!' I said, dropping a gear. 'There's no pull in the engine.' I forced the choke right out and turned up Fell Lane on our way to the Outback.

'Do you really think we should be leaving civilisation?' I asked but I kept moving until we finally came to a halt outside The Three Horses Inn. The loyal vehicle stopped by the roadside, under a canopy of trees for which we were to be grateful for a long time.

'Well! What do we do now?' Margaret is more expert in these things so we got out. She lifted the bonnet and we tried to look professional. There was a Bank Holiday fête day at the pub and droves of happy people were assembling at the rear where there were stalls and competitions. Only one man looked our way. He came to peer into the engine but was no expert either.

We told him we had driven from home with no problem, had filled up with petrol for the tank had been low and, almost immediately, we'd had problems.

'Was it petrol you put in?' he laughed.

'Oh no, we put in Coke!' Ask a silly question and you deserve a silly answer.

'I think we must send for the AA.' Margaret pointed me in the direction of the pub. The mobile phone we never use was at home, but a pub we never use was across the road. In a bar we are aliens, albeit friendly ones, from another world. I pushed my way through a seething mass of Bank Holiday lunchtime revellers in the foreign environment. The barman lifted his head for my order.

'We've broken down on the other side of the road and need to call the AA. Can I use your phone?'

The man was obliging but busy. He indicated I could. I squeezed myself past the predominantly male, drinking public and passed my message over the phone. I could scarcely hear the reply, the din of happy chatter was so deafening. I gathered help would arrive in about an hour.

Back in the Land Rover we decided to have coffee. There was plenty of outside entertainment. We would just have to have patience. When help came the problem was not solved immediately. For half an hour the AA man checked and re-checked everything under the bonnet and under the car.

Eventually he said, 'When you fill up with petrol, do you get a receipt?'

'Always,' I told him.

'Can I see it?' I took it out of my almost empty purse.

He looked at it and said, 'You put diesel in!' He wasn't critical. 'It's something drivers are doing all the time!' but he had a smile on his face all the same. 'A garage will cost you the earth,' he continued. 'I know a man who will empty your tank and get you to a filling station for about £70. That's if he's free to come.' He phoned and the answer was that the man would be with us in approximately an hour and a half. He was a nice AA man who told us he remembered helping us some years ago. Why do people always remember having come into contact with us? The experience must have been memorable but pleasant for he treated us with the utmost kindness, but he left us without any name or contact with the man designated to empty our tank. We had to have some money. I had not even enough to pay for a taxi and even if I had gone home there was no money there. During the epidemic our only income was pensions and you cannot collect them on a Bank Holiday. We raided Aunty Mary's purse. Miraculously she had £80. She never spends any money so she had an accumulation. Just enough to pay for the emptying of the tank and a modest re-fill with petrol.

After two hours we began to panic. There was no sign of this nameless man. We had no number to phone him. We dare not send for a garage mechanic and risk having to pay twice. It was 4 p.m. We had been nearly four hours outside the pub. We ate our picnic and drank every drop of tea from our flasks. We felt totally helpless.

At 5 p.m. we felt something must be done. I went to a Fell Lane address. The lady had been a neighbour of Aunty Mary thirteen years ago. She was still there and I phoned for Tim who was out, and for Barbara and Arnold and they were out. I phoned for Dorothy only to hear that George was ill. She said she would come but she hadn't driven the car since breaking her ankles, seven months ago. She insisted on coming but before she left I was able to phone her back to say the barman had received a call to say that help was on its way. The good man had brought out ice-cold drinks for our stranded family.

When the rescue car came we laughed at the sign on the roof which said, 'Wrong fuel in tank? No problem. We can empty it.'

The man had come all the way from Fleetwood. Amazingly we were still laughing. Perhaps it hadn't been diesel, after all. Perhaps it had been laughing gas. We chuckled while the emptying was in progress but not one smile crossed our lips while being towed downhill, on a solid tow bar, to the nearest petrol station. That was a nightmare!

So we arrived home at 7 p.m. having left at midday and travelled no farther than The Three Horses. It had cost us an arm and a leg and we would not have needed to fill up with petrol if we had just gone into St Ives and enjoyed the lakeside walk. We would not, however, have had the fun of telling a good story to our friends and when next we went to fill up, and on every occasion thereafter, Harry would not have been able to say to his sister, 'Petrol, Margaret!'

Next year, we told him, on Bank Holiday Monday, he would say, 'Can you remember what we were doing a year ago? We were going mad outside The Three Horses!'

Sitting for seven hours in a cramped back seat position, even though relaxed and happy, could not possibly have helped the increased swelling of his legs. The transfusion did not have the desired affect. Harry was his usual cheerful self, but we knew something was terribly wrong. One day, when we were struggling to cope with him being so immobile, he remarked with a smile, 'I'm a sorry mess!' We tried to laugh it off, but it was true. To the dread of Foot and Mouth was added the greater fear that we were going to have an impossible task bringing him back to normal.

During the week, on 29 August, we celebrated his seventy-fourth birthday. He was so proud of his age. He laughed, remembering again the grim prognosis he had been given at birth. He desperately wanted to do so. Denis would soon be here and we believed that would be a turning point and were relaxed enough to leap out of our armchairs when I read in the Friday edition of the *Farmers Weekly* that the cattle movement ban would possibly be lifted on 17 September. We couldn't take it in and I read it again to make sure. There was, of course, the stipulation that movements would still be impossible in areas where there had been an outbreak within the last thirty days. All being well the last case close to us, which had been in Addingham on 17 August, would leave us free on 17 September. We would have to sell within a certain area of high risk but we would, hopefully, be able to do so.

We were working all this out, sitting somewhat dazed in the sitting room, when the phone rang. The family always expects me to answer it. A Mr Nigel Donaldson, from North Stainley, near Ripon, was calling. Was it true, he enquired, that we had some big cattle for sale?

'We have eighty, two-year-olds,' I said. Mr Donaldson had bought our animals fairly frequently at September sales. The ban on movement was going to be lifted, he told me.

'We've just read it in the *Farmers Weekly*!' I said.

'I'll come on Monday. I'd like to buy them all!' he said. 'Would that be all right?' Would that be all right? It would indeed! Happily I handed over the phone to Margaret. She is the farmer. Three days later we were walking the pastures with this eager buyer and agreeing to a price. It was fractionally below that we had received, selling at market a year ago, but these were strange times. To sell them all at once, to one buyer was almost certainly a miracle. There is nothing Margaret wants more than that her animals go to a new place with friends. She always sells in groups so that none is ever alone and nothing pleased me, the secretary, more than that I could hand over the identity passports en masse, without sorting them out individually. There would be no trying to see numbers on dirty ear-tags. No decision to make as to which animals to send, on which sale day. Oh boy! Would it be easy? It was a miracle. There would be no time wasted at the ring-side while our turn came to show cattle. No long wait for our brother and Aunty, sitting in the Land Rover.

The next day Denis came from Lyon. We expected that this would re-vitalise Harry but we had to call out the doctor on several occasions. I remember warning Denis that it might be the last time he saw him, but our French friend would listen to no such pessimism. Harry was a survivor, he was sure. Our doctor ordered another blood test and prescribed pills which caused unpleasant side-effects. We hoped Harry's body would learn to tolerate them. They made him very tired and we were glad of the sitting room bed-behind-the-curtain. Our brother never complained. When he was wallowing in a risky depth of bath water, asked if he was all right, he would always answer, 'I'm fine!' It was ever his catchword. Even if the wind was chill, asked if he wanted to go in, he would say, 'I'm fine!' In bed he could not move. Where we rolled him, there he stayed. 'I'm fine. Just shake my pillow!' he'd say. We always had to try several times before the pillow was just right. Many times a day he would say, 'I'm lucky!' We loved him to bits!

Having separated the herd into those eighty to sell and yearlings and Diana to keep, Margaret decided she really must begin supplementing the diet of the sold animals with some of our inadequate store of hay. She needed to do this for two reasons. On no account must the fat animals be allowed to lose weight. That was one. The second was that these animals could well eat all the grass needed for the yearlings, until bringing-in time in November. Denis began taking out hay on the ATV and trailer and distributing it down in the Dyke field, a thing we hadn't done for many a year. Margaret didn't really want to bring them in for feeding until she had no other option. Having never had the bedding muck taken out, it lay dry but deep and the sold animals were big.

We had a great ten days with Denis and began to be quite optimistic. We expected Diana to calve while he was here but she went overdue by more than a week and that was not good news. We anticipated an enormous calf and she was a bad calver at the best of times.

Margaret was still suffering from her fall. The purple had gone but she was walking badly and we could do without that! She suspected that the fall had aggravated a problem which had resulted from carrying too many heavy bales for too many years. We had been buying hay from the east coast Ings and the bales were monstrous.

The day before Denis travelled back to France will be remembered history for as long as the human race is interested in its past and records are kept. The event affected not one nation only. The whole world felt the repercussion. On 11 September hi-jacked planes flew into the twin towers of the World Trade Centre in New York and America embarked on a war against terrorism. We were shocked, but it was thousands of miles away and our lesser problems had to be addressed. There was nothing we could do about America except pray that the whole thing would not escalate into all-out war.

On the home front we were digesting a letter in the morning's post from Lord Whitty at DEFRA, saying that changes had been made and that, although some autumn movements would be possible, they would have to be within newly imposed boundaries. These would be no longer dictated by the spread of disease. The Ministry had decided, quite illogically, that county boundaries should determine areas. Furthermore Metropolitan Districts should be separated from within counties. It was a decision born of ignorance. The hot-spot called the Settle Triangle included farms in North Yorkshire, Lancashire, Cumbria, West Yorkshire and the Metropolitan Districts of Bradford, Leeds and York. The whole was designated High Risk and had previously been a single area. On 11 September we learned the awful news that a ruling from Government now prevented us from selling to Mr Donaldson! Prevented us from selling to anyone at all, for who, in the urban district of Bradford, ever bought eighty, two-year-old stores? Our land was right on the boundary. Others like us reared and sold to finishers. There was not one buyer in the imposed boundary to whom we would be able to sell. It was a complete nonsense. I phoned Trading Standards and a representative of the NFU was there. He agreed with me, said he was in the same situation with cattle to sell but trapped in the Metropolitan ring fence. He said the Ministry had been alerted to the problem and had promised to look into it at a later date. But everything was put on hold because of the terrorist attack on New York. Every farmer will tell you that Foot and Mouth died on 11 September when a new tragedy gripped the world.

We were, however, told that we might be able to appeal after 24 September.

'I'm going to have to bring the big ones in at night!' Margaret said. 'It's the only way we can cope!'

But first we must get Harry back on course and Diana's calf brought into the world. Fortunately the latter happened on a Friday when Tim and Graham were walling and could be called to assist. They came in haste and when Diana saw them the look of relief on her face was a picture. All four goats stood on the bales in the maternity ward and watched every detail of the labour. The head of the calf was enormous and the aperture seemed far too small. It took the strength of all four of us, and Diana, to birth that beautiful black baby. How anything, human or otherwise, can stand such a stressful entry into the world beggars belief. The last seconds were sudden and I fell backwards onto the hard concrete and that was me with bruised ribs for a fortnight. The calf looked big enough to consume all Diana's milk. His sire was a Canadian Aberdeen Angus called, appropriately, Lord Harry and we wheeled its namesake to the shed to view the new arrival in the herd.

Margaret with bad legs, me with bruised ribs and Harry a 'sorry mess' trying to get a tolerance for his new pills prescribed to reduce the water in his legs. It was a poor workforce to cope with animals for which we could not get a movement licence. Then came far more serious news. Dorothy's husband, George, was very ill in hospital. If we had had any hopes of an October holiday in Witherslack near Grange-over-Sands, still a month away, they quickly receded and his ill health took precedence on our worrying list.

In unrestricted times we would, by now, have sold and been going to market to buy more calves for Diana. We had no contingency plan. Even if we could get a licence to buy one from a next-door neighbour, we knew that would scupper our selling anything for another three weeks. Selling to Mr Donaldson was still out of the question. Our Government was far too occupied, with war elsewhere, to sort out farmers' problems in a countryside they didn't even understand. I believe they knew more about the situation in Afghanistan than on the boundary between Bradford Metropolitan District and North Yorkshire!

We anticipated trouble with Diana's expected overload of milk but had none. Her whopping offspring just drank it all. She was fed very little corn and her output never reached the maximum it had done in previous years.

With that problem solved Margaret turned her attention to introducing the big animals back into their overnight occupation of sheds. These had been big enough for them as yearlings but were far too small for them eight months on. Each afternoon we spread straw over the deepening old bedding and put hay, in readiness, in the mangers. Each evening we let them in. It was a risky business for they were twice as big and heavy as when let out in the spring. They were ravenous and hay and straw began to dwindle at the rate of one load lasting barely nine days. We needed to buy more but none seemed available.

We were only able to handle these big animals because they were ours and the routine of coming in every night was a known one, remembered from winter. In the morning they were given corn and hay and let out while we replenished the mangers and spread clean straw. Their heads were enormous and the effort to push past to feed corn was almost impossible. We dare not enter the sheds while they were in, for the depth of manure was dangerous.

We dare not send for the muck to be taken out for then we would have eighty cattle with unrestricted movement, slipping around and making a mad dash for corn. The deep manure had them relatively tamed. So we were coping. We stood well back when we let them in at dusk, a pushing, shoving sea of black and white, fearing we could not keep it up for long.

After a few days there came an evening when they did not come home. The night sky was clear. A multitude of stars decorated the Heavens. The September air was wonderful.

'They're staying out,' Margaret said.

At midnight I was already in bed when I heard the noise of their return. It frightened the life out of both of us. Cattle can be very spooky at night. An owl, a police car siren from the town, anything can startle. Margaret risked opening the two doors to let them in.

Our current situation was dangerous, we knew that, but there was nothing we could do but live a day at a time. We nearly had a blarney, as Mother would often say, every time the cattle came home. We'd left the yearlings on the hill and brought the mature gentlemen into fields surrounding the house and buildings and they objected. Every morning, eighty strong, they paced the boundary wall, searching for access to the higher ground they preferred. Not until noon did they stop wandering eastwards and westwards in anger! Too late they began to pasture, so that during the first week, before they accepted their restricted area, they came home hungrier than they should have been and more bales of dried food had to be opened.

What had happened in New York was as if it was on another planet as we tried to pull Harry out of his hole. It was proving to be a longer and bigger struggle than expected.

Aunty Mary was blind and deaf to his deteriorating health. 'Harry is really poorly,' we told her repeatedly but she never noticed. She was an old lady oblivious of anything and everything going on around her. Every day she enquired if we had 'got the disease' and when told we had not she believed everything was hunky-dory. Because Harry was not in bed, he was well.

The pills the doctor had prescribed took away some of the water in his arms and shoulders and we suddenly saw how thin he was. Unfortunately the medication failed to take away the heaviness in his legs. It seemed as if his problems multiplied every hour but all our efforts to solve them were positive.

We perfected his wheelchair route. I made a ramp to the front entrance. We cleared the upstairs passage of the bedding box so that we had perfect access to the bathroom. Harry loved deep baths. We cut a chest of drawers in two and recessed it in the kitchen so that the wheelchair could easily be taken into the sitting room. We pushed the wash kitchen table against the sink to allow access to the downstairs loo. For twenty years Harry had leaned against that table drying thousands and thousands of dishes. Now the few utensils the family used we carried wet, on a tray, for Harry to dry them seated at the kitchen table. The farmhouse adapted readily to all our needs. Nothing seemed impossible!

The back seat of the Land Rover provided too little space for heavily swollen legs so Tim moved the middle one back six inches. We felt capable of overcoming every problem. Harry's shoes would no longer fit his swollen feet so we ordered some from Cosyfeet and they fitted perfectly. There was no stopping us. A pair of jogging trousers, fleecy lined, were such a success we bought three pairs. We bought half a dozen new shirts. 'For your holiday,' we said. I sewed an eiderdown into a sack so that he could sit out in the wheelchair in comfort and warmth. There was no way we were giving in without a struggle.

We were increasingly worried about his difficulty in eating. Food had always been one of his greatest pleasures. He appreciated everything Mother had made and thought it was one of life's blessings that, when she had reluctantly handed over the task to her daughters, they could almost equal her. No evening passed but what he reminded me to take meat out of the freezer. Every morning he queried what we were having for dinner.

Our greatest fear was that the muscles in his neck were preventing him swallowing properly so we went immediately to buy a liquidizer for his main course. The result tasted quite nice but it would be monotonous for someone who liked meat and Yorkshire pudding to look like what they were. Though Aunty Mary was oblivious it did not escape us that Harry was very poorly.

We felt we must do something positive about moving our cattle to North Stainley. I rang ADAS and was told we would be able to apply for a Movement Licence on Appeal. Trading Standards sent me a form and I filled it in and posted it on 19 September. I remember this as being one of the most awful of days.

News of George was discouraging. Dorothy had slept exhausted after two nights of being called to the hospital. We had slept badly for Harry was wakeful. When sleeping he made no sound and his silence also kept us awake. We who are born optimists could see no solutions.

But this form came and I filled it in. Margaret was out feeding the eighty monsters. I phoned the buyer, the haulier and DEFRA and I wrote a letter. I went to the village shop and photostated copies of the eighty, thirteen-digit ear-tag numbers and a map of the route our haulier would take to Ripon. I posted the lot and crossed my fingers.

Margaret spent a good deal of the morning looking for our beautiful little nanny goat which seemed to be missing.

'Have you seen Mopsey?' she called as I returned from the post office. The other goats were there. We imagined they had worried looks but they were eating normally by the corn bin. Mopsey was always the first one to respond to the noise of the lid being raised. She was the one always underfoot, the pushing one, and she was nowhere to be found. She was also the one who poked her head through sheep netting and could not retract it. Normally she made such a bleating we knew exactly where she was impaled. She was a noise-making goat whose feet tap-danced on the corn bin lid and who rattled buckets when eating. She was the exhibitionist, leaping higher than her brother. She was a girl, a ballerina. She waggled her little bottom and charmed us all. She was addicted to leaves and her balance on the yard wall was perfect. Her absence spelled disaster.

The twins had come with collars, one red, one blue but they were unnecessary for, though they were almost identical when they came, they were now easily identified, not just because they were a slightly different shade of brown but because, like Diana and Meg and Emilie, Mopsey was all female. She was a girl.

It was inconceivable that she was missing. Every shed was searched and it became obvious that she was not at home. There are few places in our bovine city out of which an agile goat cannot escape. Cattle and donkeys, geese and ducks can all be penned safely but goats are nearly as gifted as cats at getting free.

She had last been seen, the day before, down the hillside above Jack Field. Margaret went to look over into our nearest neighbour's garden but she was not there.

'I must ring Harry Raw,' Margaret said. 'Perhaps she's done a Rosie!'

Because of Foot and Mouth, the low boundary had been really well secured. Nevertheless Mopsey was exceptional and getting over would be considerably easier than getting back. Margaret crossed the Low Pasture hoping to find her stranded on Marley Hall land but she was not there. She might, of course have joined the flock and it could be anywhere, or she might be with the deer. She looked like one.

In the Low Pasture there is a dry hollow with trees on either side, a small valley edged with oak and ash and a favourite haunt for my fire-lighting Guides. There was always a wealth of dead twigs and branches and several hawthorns excellent for burning. There we cooked sausages and dampers on sticks. There we boiled water in paper bags, and fried eggs on hot flat stones, or poached them in orange skins.

The valley is only a few metres wide and a rope bridge could be made to span it. An oak on the west matched an ash on the east and, should you wobble on the bridge, it was not far to fall.

It is not necessary to skirt the valley when going towards the boundary and had Margaret not made a detour to do so, on the way back, she would not have found Mopsey. The beautiful creature lay dead, on the ground, hanged by her own red collar. By an almost impossible stroke of bad luck, it had become impaled on a branch while she had stretched to nibble leaves. The branch had swung with her weight and twisted the collar, strangling her in an instant. It had stayed, telltale, in the collar, evidence of what had happened. Margaret was so upset she could do nothing but stem her tears and come home. The pretty collars had been only ornament. The first thing Margaret did was to take off Cottontail's and henceforth he became known as Billy. The fancy name of Cottontail was dropped.

We couldn't talk about the accident and we never told Harry or Aunty Mary. The one would have been upset and the other was preoccupied with the morbid possibility of Foot and Mouth and would have thought that Mopsey had died of that. It was some months before we even told the blacksmith.

The pain of that sudden death was incredible. Mopsey had been so young and beautiful. She had all her life in front of her, maybe twenty years in this paradise of freedom, fun and food galore. She had comfortable accommodation, choice and warmth and friends of her own kind and she was dead because we had not taken off a collar which was not necessary.

We do not immediately bury a dog or remove a dead calf. We wait for the body to go cold and the soul, if there is one, to depart. Mopsey was already cold but Margaret was not ready to bury her. Neither of us wanted to do the job immediately for other troubles confronted us and while we battled against an unyielding DEFRA, Mopsey lay for a week where she had fallen. When Margaret went down to inter her in the wood, only a skeleton remained. It occurred to us that, had she been human, no scavenger would have eaten her. Are we such a discredit to nature that even our meat is undesirable?

Were they all fools in authority, allowing movements but putting a cordon round the Metropolitan District that could not be surmounted? If we had been at Kildwick, where Foot and Mouth had been, we could have moved cattle to Ripon but because we were three miles over the Bradford boundary, our application on appeal was immediately rejected.

It was a young Australian who phoned us the refusal. I pleaded but he was adamant. No movements allowed! I pleaded admirably. I said ADAS had told me it was possible. I said that we were old and I don't admit that even to myself. I said we couldn't handle such big animals, which wasn't quite true but we hadn't the skill to fatten them. I told him we would run out of food and that there was a long, long waiting list for animals to be killed on welfare grounds and I said the sheds were too small.

'What do you suggest we do?' I asked him and he replied that he did not know.

'For goodness sake,' I exploded. 'Just give me a phone number of someone in higher authority!'

He did not know who to suggest. I was exasperated. 'Give me Margaret Beckett's!' I said with a flippancy the situation did not deserve.

'Who's she?' the young Australian enquired.

'You must be joking!' I didn't laugh and he really didn't know.

'No,' he said quite honestly. 'Who is she?'

'You've made my day!' I gasped. 'You've made my day!'

There seemed no point in arguing further. The bewildered young Australian said he'd report our predicament and ring me next day. He, too, must have had to work on a Sunday! He did but the answer was still no. I insisted this negative answer was put in writing.

I said, 'Tell whoever writes the letter that we have eighty enormous animals. They have been sold. Last week we could have moved them to Ripon. This week we can't because someone, at a ministerial office desk, has moved a boundary, illogically. We haven't enough food. We haven't the skill or labour to fatten. There is a long queue of animals waiting to be killed on welfare grounds. Our accommodation is for yearlings not two-year-olds! Have you any suggestion as to what we should do?'

'Could you build another shed?' was the young man's brainwave!

Was the world really full of fools?

'What a good idea!' Margaret said. 'We'll do that this afternoon!'

Fools who think terrorism can be fought with military might!

Fools who think it is unnecessary for an island to be able to feed its people! There are only three ways of importing food to an island and unless there is guaranteed peace, and no inequality which breeds terrorism, neither air, nor sea, nor tunnel is safe, and we have fifty million people to feed!

Fools who would not allow Hughie, on remote Tiree way out in the Atlantic, to bring a calving cow a few yards along the road but still allowed meat to be imported from South America and Southern Africa! On Tiree it would have been one out, all out, anyway!

There was, the letter said when it came, the alternative method of slaughter for welfare reasons. It did not inform us of the 17,500 backlog in the queue and we swept the suggestion under the table. We had kept our animals alive and, though Big Brother was holding a gun at our throat, we were not giving in.

Others can be excused for being undecided about whether our fate is cruel or kind, whether it is trying its hardest to wreck us or providing a guardian angel to hold us up, come what may, and guide us into safe harbour. The temptation must surely be for them to say the devil is out to get us, that life to us is unfair, that fate throws more than our share of obstacles in the way. Why is it that we always end up thinking we have been singularly blessed, that we have been guided round the pitfalls and helped over the obstacles? I, personally, do not believe God singles us out for special protection and neglects so many others. I believe He must, of necessity, delegate and we are just very lucky indeed to have the right angel for the job, sometimes above and sometimes on the ground!

Margaret remembered we had been given the name of a Bristol solicitor on the Helpline For Farmers fax the accountant had delivered personally. Burges Salmon was recommended for Foot and Mouth problems. Margaret phoned, stated that our problem was the sudden, unreasonable altering of a boundary which had left us stranded. The good man recognised there was no logic in this and agreed to represent us. As it was costing £100 a day to feed the cattle we did not think it an extravagance. There had to be a way of persuading authority simply to return our small, unworkable Metropolitan District back into the safety of North Yorkshire, where it had been throughout the outbreak.

I wrote three letters, one to this solicitor, one to the Country Landowners Association and one to Lord Whitty, currently leading the DEFRA deadlock. Burges Salmon and the CLA responded immediately but we did not hear from the Ministry until shortly before Christmas when a man rang to enquire if we had been able to move our animals!

'I am just sending you an acknowledgement of your letter.'

'Of three months ago!' I interrupted him.

'We've been very busy,' he apologised.

So had we!

Our immediate problem had been to get more hay and straw. The bedding manure, which was high and slowed the movement of cattle from dangerous to reasonably safe, made spreading straw very difficult for us. Especially for Margaret with her painful, unyielding tendons. We were swimming against the tide, coping in a determined sort of way but decreasingly optimistic.

I had a hospital appointment myself on 1 October and it coincided with a visit of cousins from Harrogate, who were taking Aunty Mary out for the afternoon. Our relatively new doctor had spotted a fifteen-year old thickening on my neck, no bigger than a shilling. I laughed and told him it was age but he said I must get it checked. I kept the appointment, slightly embarrassed.

The man with the scanning machine asked why I had thought it necessary to come so I told him it hadn't been my idea. He said he didn't think it was worth the effort but complied. 'As I thought,' he said. 'There's nothing there but a little area of extra fat!'

I collected Margaret and we went onto the wards to see George, who had been cruelly told the nature of his problem which seemed to reduce even Harry's to size. Mine was, as I'd expected, non-existent. I felt to be a fraud. The movement situation was out of our hands. For a little while we could only worry about George.

There were still two weeks to the holiday in Witherslack. There was still time to get a Movement Licence, move our cattle to Ripon and give Harry his holiday. Obviously Dorothy would not be able to stand in for us as she had done for sixteen years. We would have to approach someone else, if and when we saw the hoped-for opportunity. We still hadn't told Aunty Mary about our cottage booking but with her away, roaming the Dales with her nephew, we talked openly about Grange-over-sands and the lovely holidays we'd had and about this new cottage, at Witherslack, and the possibility that we just might be able to go after all.

We had a pleasant day out, just the three of us and on our return I washed the dishes and carried them on a tray for Harry to dry at the table. Margaret and I teetered on the uneven depth of manure to spread the straw together. It was relatively dry. With their weight the cattle hooves sank into it but bullocks' feet are suitably adapted for such contingencies. Ours are not and when we sank we left a wellington behind.

The human wanderers returned. Fiona was full of concern about our ninety-five year old Aunt.

'She can't see properly,' she said. 'She should have some new glasses!'

Of course, we agreed. Aunty Mary should do a lot of things she flatly refused to do. New spectacles had been top of our list for twelve months or more. She used to read avidly, even in the car when there was a splendid view. If we mentioned that she had given up this activity, which we frequently did, she refused so adamantly she'd lift a hand and threaten Margaret. I can remember Harry laughing as we gave Michael the job of booking a Harrogate optician. She would do anything Michael said.

All attention was on the old lady but it was Harry we were really worried about. I made the evening meal and liquidized the main course for him and it really was appetizing. I could have enjoyed it myself but for him to live on it for ever frightened me.

Always after relatives visited, Harry was stressed. He, who greeted so many, from every place nationwide and from almost every corner of the planet, was unable to cope properly with relatives. If he hadn't found Aunty Mary so funny – funny peculiar not funny ha-ha – he would have found her very stressful, too.

I must confess that Harry found Margaret and me funny ha ha. Listening to our conversation, one memorable day, he laughed outright.

'You sound just like The Likely Lads!' he said.

Chapter Fifteen

Quiet like, some still day, I'm jes' go'-in' home.
It's not far, jes' closeby, through an open door.

William Arms Fisher

A t first we thought that it was this age-old problem which was responsible
for Harry sleeping badly on that Monday night. So badly that, for a
moment or two, I lay precariously beside him, only half of me on the bed,
holding him still. He could not move his heavy legs but the bones of his thin
shoulders shook beneath my arm as I tried to calm him.

As children we had slept together. I have only one memory of doing so
and that was knowing we were both in the same double bed when Father
wakened us and Margaret was being born in our parents' room. Harry must
have been twelve for I was nine. When Margaret outgrew the cot she replaced
him and Harry was given the adult, masculine status of his own room. He
was a private person. That he accepted my touch was an indication that he
wasn't very well at all.

'I'm all right. Go back to bed,' he insisted, so I did and I believe I even
slept some. I don't think Margaret did.

Harry was hyperventilating and she was worried and wished we had some
oxygen. We'd already called a doctor out one night during the previous week
and were shy of repeating this unnecessarily. She kept saying, 'Breathe properly, Harry!' It was not a new problem. I remember Mother saying she had
sometimes, as a baby, slapped his leg to make him breathe in again.

Both must have fallen asleep eventually for when I wakened at six, as I
always do, both were sleeping and I tiptoed out, desperately in need of a cup
of coffee. I couldn't shake off my anxiety.

I went outside to release the ducks and collect the three eggs always in the
nest. What fun they had been all summer! I am sure they hear the front door
close behind me and know that I am coming. I cannot hear them until I have
rounded the corner of the house but they are already making a fine old racket!
I climbed the stile into their domain, hearing their excitement reach a

crescendo. I let down the ramp and they half leapt, half flew, one behind the other, in eagerness to enter the water. They splashed vigorously and arrogantly while I stole their contribution to our larder. Few callers visited us in 2001, but none left without a bagful of duck eggs. One Dolina laid all double-yolked eggs which was quite possibly why she died prematurely.

When I returned to the house Margaret was already up, an indication that she was agitated. We sat drinking coffee together wondering what the day would bring, listening for any sound upstairs. The installation of the wheelchair lift had left two gaps where the iron runners penetrated into the bedroom, so that every sound can be heard. We were tense. Feeding the eighty bullocks that the Government would not allow us to move did not help us to relax. Their enthusiasm impeded the giving of corn and it was almost impossible to open bales, for their two-year-old heads were too big for yearling mangers. Even Danny stopped running in ahead of us, as he does all winter. We agreed with a writer in the *Farmers Weekly* who said he couldn't see the tunnel let alone the light at the end of it. We were all on common ground. Usually there is a choice of roads and one must be taken. In 2001 there was no crossroads, no way to go.

Margaret frequently said, 'There must be many like us, coping with problems of illness and disablement, plus Foot and Mouth!' The epidemic could not be seen in isolation. It was an extra, a problem over and above all the others.

I left her to finish the early chores and spent the next hour running up and down stairs. Eventually I decided to stay in the bedroom. I didn't like the way things seemed to be going and when Harry wakened and began hyperventilating again, I ran to the sheds calling, 'I think we are going to lose Harry!'

'Send for the doctor,' she shouted back.

I did and he came immediately and said Harry must go to hospital. A few days previously, Harry had searched the telephone directory for Dr. Gopal's address in the village, and told me to ask the doctor, next time he came, where he lived but nothing was further from our thoughts. For a non-reading adult, Harry could find any address in the directory, quicker than I could.

We needed to leave Aunty Mary with someone while we went with Harry to the hospital. We phoned Joan who lives close to Airedale General and when I left with the ambulance, Margaret followed with the Land Rover and left Aunty Mary with her. Harry's breathing was so bad I feared we would not reach the hospital in time but it is amazing what oxygen can do. His breathing improved immediately en route. He'd almost died at birth because of lack of it and suffered seventy-four years from the initial shortage of it. The supply in the ambulance made a new man of him so that he even became talkative. The increasing paralysis of his throat muscles had made his habitually poor pronunciation worse than ever and I couldn't catch what he was saying. I thought he was trying to tell us of some discomfort. His jibberish reminded me of Meg wanting the toilet on our way to Oban, or the occasion when he had spelled out www.co.bbc and asked what it read. That had left us in hysterics. Suddenly I realised he was only commenting on the fact that he knew exactly where we were on the journey and could identify every landmark seen through the darkened rear window of the ambulance. It was like watching a sick calf begin to chew its cud again. Our brother was interested in the journey. It was normal for Harry. There was oodles and oodles of hope. High, apple pie in the sky, hope!

Nevertheless our lifestyle changed abruptly for we were unacquainted with hospitals. In seventy-four years Harry had only spent two days, twice, in Airedale General. On the first occasion he had phoned to alert us to the fact that he was being discharged by saying, 'Do you do bed and breakfast?'

He was wheeled into an assessment ward and was immediately very sleepy and almost at once he had a fit. We had lived with the possibility of an occasional seizure since the Epilim fiasco. We knew that he would now sleep for hours, so Margaret collected our aunt from Joan's house and went home to fill the mangers and lay the bedding alone for the evening return of the cattle. There seemed no point in her returning to the hospital. Harry did not wake until nine. He seemed his usual self. He was hungry and enjoyed a very milky Weetabix. He wanted an update on all the news. What was happening at home? Had I phoned? Was Aunty Mary all right? Why hadn't Margaret shaved him before bringing him to hospital? Tell her to bring the razor next morning! Had anyone called? Had we heard from the solicitor? As our friends on Harris would say, he was 'in his usual' and God was in His Heaven! Harry's questioning amused the other patients in the ward and it was a tonic to me.

I wanted to stay overnight but Harry would hear of no such thing. I warned the other men that he would call 'Jean!' several times in the night, but they said they would tolerate him. So I called a taxi and went home, through the dark, empty streets of town, through the village and over the cattle grid. The lock on the bar had been removed. If easier access for us meant letting in a wandering virus, so be it! We had other things on our mind.

It was difficult to determine how really ill Harry was. His cheerfulness, his interest in his new environment, his abundance of questions, and his sun-bronzed complexion threatened to confuse, but we sensed that he was quite ill and that the prognosis for the future was uncertain.

An early morning phone call to the ward assured us that the night had been passed without a problem. 'I'm fine!' he had probably said to the nurses.

Hearing this we did our morning chores before going to the hospital. A cousin collected Aunty Mary, so that was one problem solved. We found Harry in great form, loaded with news and questions. Someone had shaved him so Margaret could take the razor home. He found beards very amusing. Denis, with the same sense of humour, had seriously thought of growing one just before his September visit, just to see Harry's amazement and hear his laughter.

There was no need for two to stay, so I drove home to lay the bedding and fill the mangers. This was a job we'd expected would not begin again until December, when the yearlings would demand entry to covered accommodation! These two year olds had cost very little to buy. Now they were costing the earth. I phoned Burges Salmon and told the solicitor that he was on his own. He must do what must be done for Harry was critically ill in hospital and there was now no time for me to phone DEFRA, the regional vet, the CLA or the NFU. I said that it was more than ever essential that we moved our animals to the buyer, otherwise we would need more fodder. We hadn't time to order it, receive and unload it, or move calf hay from barn to feeding area. I repeated that the only thing needed was the return of the High Risk Metropolitan District into the High Risk area of North Yorkshire. Everyone agreed it was necessary and possible. Even the Ministry admitted it needed prompt investigation but chaos reigned in the House of Authority. Harry was coping better than it was!

I relieved Margaret at the hospital because only she could let in the herd, a somewhat dangerous job. She was suffering from pain in her front thighs and avoided driving whenever possible. At 10 p.m. Paulette and Lil came to the hospital and drove me home and we chatted until quite late. We were all concerned for Margaret. Our work was heavy and we knew no way out. At midday, on Thursday, I dropped Margaret at the hospital but did not hesitate long. Aunty Mary was in the Land Rover. So that Margaret didn't have to drive it home, I phoned Barbara Sherriff and she took us back at teatime, after I'd done the outdoor work. She pushed Aunty Mary into the ward to see Harry, who was in fine fettle. To unload the responsibility for our nearly ninety-five-year-old aunt helped us to relax. We always seem to have two problems. To be relieved of one enables us to attend to the other in a less stressful way. Cousin Freda and her daughter were with him and he was having a good time.

He was pretty exhausted when they left and shortly afterwards he was taken from the assessment ward to a permanent one and he was sleepy so I went to visit George. He was still in hospital but waiting to be discharged, within the next few days, having been told his cancer was terminal and there was no treatment which could do any good. Amazingly he was coping, even as Harry was.

What role models there are in our non-too-simple lives. As I had no transport, Dorothy and her daughter said they would collect me later, when they were leaving, and take me home. We were hoping for Harry's recovery and our friends had no hope left. We were so very, very sad. It deserves to be said that, throughout the months of his illness, George never gave up hope, never lost his sense of humour. Applause for his performance should be loud and long.

When we phoned next morning we heard Harry had had a bad night and had been moved into a side ward.

'Yes,' the nurse answered my query. 'You can come at once if you wish.' Margaret had cattle to feed, so I rang Freda's daughter, Kathleen, and she took me to the hospital. In the side ward we could talk without an audience. Harry's hearing aid was a problem at the best of times, being frequently lost in the most unlikely places. In hospital it remained in its box, a useless piece of equipment.

So, he had had a bad night but he was sunny, like the weather, when I arrived. October proved to be the warmest on record. Outside the mini-ward, a weeping willow moved continually, soothing anxiety, a panacea for our fears.

Had I brought a clock, Harry wanted to know? Would I put it where he could see it? Would I read his 'Get Well' cards and put them in view? Had we phoned Denis? He would want to know. Had we phoned Sue at the homeopathy clinic and was Aunty Mary all right? He seemed to think that if she were, we all would be!

If the reader finds I relate Harry's time in hospital in too much detail, please forgive me. We have no video recording of his unique performance and his example was one to follow. He had coped with disability for seventy-four years and he was still capable of behaving with cheerful dignity. He had only one complaint. A notice said 'NIL BY MOUTH' and he was hungry.

An army of doctors visited him. A previously undetected heart murmur was found. A saline drip prevented dehydration while a catheter measured output. The model patient was certain of his recovery. 'We haven't given up on going to Grange, have we?' he said.

'That's up to DEFRA,' I said. 'We can't go if we've still got the cattle.'

'What about Dorothy and George?'

'George is really ill, Harry. We'd have to get someone else.'

'Will I be home at the weekend? If I am I want apple dumpling. Like me Mam used to make. I'm hungry.' He might be in 'a sorry mess' but he wasn't dead yet.

I have the feeling that none of this describes an old man. Our handsome, handicapped brother hadn't aged at all, with the passing of so many years. He wasn't grey or wrinkled and was scarcely bald. He had no old man's habits. His outlook was that of youth coupled with the wisdom of long experience. His interest and curiosity made him alert and his memory never faltered. He kept us young, too. To be with him was fun!

The nursing staff found him amazing. Their competence was indisputable and given unreservedly to all but it was obvious that they were fascinated. We regretted every moment we had to be away, lest we miss something of his on-stage performance. Would we ever be able to compete? We laughed together when we were alone. He did so want to outlive the last generation and step out together, just the three of us 'young ones'. Aunty Mary at nearly ninety-five, held us back. He didn't. He had everything to live for, everything he wanted. His dentures were ivory white and his smile was that of a young man, even as he proudly boasted, 'I am seventy-four!'

Margaret had insisted that she could drive. She arrived earlier than previously for Harry's removal into the side ward had panicked her. She had brought Aunty Mary but had left her in the Land Rover. Harry listened while she and I talked farming. We were so seldom together. She was getting uptight about the dwindling supply of bales assembled near the mangers. Before the weekend was over, we must move more from the barn up into the Donkey Hole, and the garage, for easy access. This operation required two of us and there was never more than one at home. To employ help was probably virus-safe but we remained scared. We knew the fear of infection would not leave us until, by hook or by crook, we had moved our animals to Ripon. Another outbreak locally would be a disaster. The previous year's deluge had brought the yearlings home early. Should that happen again we would be in a real mess but the mild, dry, last quarter of 2001 proved to be a godsend for farmers.

Eventually I collected the Land Rover and its occupant and drove home for the fourth time to re-fill mangers and spread straw. I felt to have been doing it for a lifetime!

I had promised to stay overnight if necessary. The nurse seemed to welcome the idea and insisted I have a recliner chair brought into the room, so that I could get some sleep. It was a major operation to squeeze it in but she persisted. Harry had a problem with his catheter and, having sorted it, the nurses winched him in a sling above the bed to sort that out also. He said the hanging position was comfortable and asked to stay there a while, talking continually from his roost.

One of the doctors had decided Harry must have three more units of blood. They were doing every thing they could to make body fit mind. The night staff came but there were only three of them for a ward of over thirty patients. It proved to be not nearly enough, even for their superior competence. Many needed attention and one person died. The nurses never paused in their active vigilance. No one can be expected to be everywhere at the same time.

In the early hours Harry had a problem with acute pain and every few minutes he gripped my hand in agony. It was too frequent and I could not stand it. I seemed to be always calling for a nurse who was desperately needed by someone else. Try as they would they could not sort out the source of the pain. I had had more than I could take and I sobbed at his bedside. We do not cry in our family, but I did. I cried as I had never done before, embarrassed and ashamed. I desperately wanted to ring for Margaret but dare not for, if she came, Aunty Mary would be left alone and that could not be.

I begged the nurses to do something to ease the recurring pain. The staff-nurse put her arm round my shoulders and promised to ring for a doctor's permission to open the drug cupboard for a strong painkiller.

'Don't cry,' she comforted me.

'I can't bear him to be in so much pain!' I continued to sob. 'I know there are thirty more in the ward, but he is mine and I can't bear it, and George is terminally ill and the Government won't let us move our animals. Margaret can scarcely walk and one of us is going to be killed and ...' I just could not stop crying.

It was decided not to give the third unit of blood for the time being. Twenty minutes later permission was sent to inject a painkiller. The waiting time went so slowly and the medication didn't work.

'If the pain doesn't go,' the staff nurse said, 'I'll put a better one into his drip.' This she did and the pain disappeared but my weeping persisted.

'Don't cry!' Harry comforted me. He was coping so much better than I was. I must have looked a 'sorry mess'. As long as we live we will use the phrase Harry coined and it will bring a smile to distress.

He slept. The nurse brought me a second cup of tea but it did not induce sleep. I sat at the bedside and wetted his pillow with my tears for the river from my eyes would not stop. He was sleeping peacefully and I realised that my weeping had not distressed him. Perhaps he accepted it as an expression of how much his sisters loved him. Maybe his pain and mine were a necessary shared experience.

When dawn came he was still sleeping. I rang Margaret to say Harry was comfortable but the night had been wicked. She hurriedly fed cattle, let them out and dragged our old lady to the car. Just before she arrived at the hospital a doctor came and asked me if I thought the blood transfusion should be continued. 'Not just yet!' I pleaded.

'He's comfortable,' replied the doctor. 'I think we will leave it a while.'

A speech therapist came wanting to discuss the future feeding of Harry. She had been told he had difficulty eating. 'On Monday,' she said, 'we'll have a family meeting and decide what to do. Maybe a tube into the stomach would be best.'

I told Margaret and we were both horrified. The speech therapist had talked as if Harry were a machine in which we could pour fuel. She had not been told anything about him as person with cerebral palsy and a healthy appetite, who was looking forward to going home to apple dumplings. All she knew was that eating problems could be solved by tube insertion in the stomach. God help Harry! And us! We felt almost angry.

Because she had come earlier than usual Margaret and I had a longer time to sit together at his bedside. We talked, then he wakened and was normal and without pain. That is if ever one could describe our brother as 'normal'. We sat answering his questions. It was so easy to get uptight about Harry and then have all fears erased instantly by normality.

'Is Aunty Mary all right?' he said.

'She's in the Land Rover. What about you?' Margaret said. 'Are you all right this morning?'

'I'm fine!' he replied. I felt a fraud. What had all that been about in the night, hey? He was fine and I was a wreck! The painkiller had chased away the trauma. He was almost well again. The drug had relaxed his throat muscles and his speech had improved. 'I'm hungry,' he complained. We were calm. As they say on the islands, Harry was in his usual!

I was very tired from lack of sleep and from the exhaustion that follows tears.

'Be careful driving home,' Margaret warned.

Reaching The Currer there seemed to be cattle everywhere. They lined up at the kitchen windows, looking in with bovine curiosity. From the house the view, from each of the many windows, was of cattle. They were impossible to count. In the field they were too big and inquisitive to meander through safely and in the sheds they were too congested to count accurately. We had to presume they were all there. A man had phoned from the council, Margaret had told me, to say she had left one footpath unopened. He'd walked along the fields we rented and a closure notice was still there. She'd apologised but said she'd thought it best to leave it so until all these big animals were moved.

'Have you dangerous animals on a footpath?' he'd been quick to chastise.

'Maybe not dangerous, as such,' she'd replied, 'but big and curious and quite unused to walkers and until I get permission to move them there is nothing that either you or I can do about it!'

I manhandled the bales into position before surrendering to fatigue. That was the hard bit, then I crawled upstairs to bed. The sun was pouring in through the windows and drawn curtains did not take away the heat. Only Harry's bed was in the shade. I crawled in that and leapt out immediately with painful cramp in my toes. I had pins-and-needles in my fingers. I stamped about the room until they relaxed, then climbed back under the counterpane and slept for half an hour.

I was instantly refreshed and spread the bales with vigour and speed, sweating profusely. I couldn't possibly go back to the hospital without showering, after which I felt enormously better and we went back, early, to Airedale General. I'd thought to call in first to see George but, having left Aunty Mary in the sunny car park, I changed my mind and went straight to Harry's side-ward.

He was sleeping. 'He's just had a bed bath,' Margaret said. 'He's only just dropped off. Jean's come back, Harry.'

I leaned over and kissed him. He was all warm, sweet smelling and rosy. I took off my sweater for it was warm in the room. Margaret couldn't wait to recount the last few hours.

During my absence she had been having a great time with Harry at his very best. Joan, with all her nursing skills, had come to see him. His pain had remained at bay without further sedation.

He'd said to Joan, 'Do you know what Margaret did? She put diesel in the Land Rover instead of petrol!'

So Margaret told the whole story and finished by saying that every time we stopped to fill the tank, Harry prompted, 'The green one, Margaret!'

He'd been having a Fête Day, laughing at everything. Joan had made him comfortable and taken the liberty of giving him a little sip of water. We had decided to arrange something for Aunty Mary so that Margaret could be free to stay with me overnight, if necessary, but it did not look as if it would be so. Joan had said she would come back to the ward in the evening to keep me company. One Guide or another supports us every time.

There were many things Harry just could not do. One of them was to sing. None of us can sing in tune, but Harry never could sing at all. Yet Margaret had heard him humming. She'd been flabbergasted. 'Hey! Do you know what you are singing?' He'd smiled brilliantly. 'You are singing Tobermory Bay! I'm yearning for my Hebridean Island, the mountains there are heather sweet today! That's amazing, Harry! I've never heard you do that before!' Together they'd tried to remember more of the words: 'If I could fly I'd lift my wings and wander. My dream of Mull grows stronger.'

'We've got the music at home,' Margaret had promised. 'I'll find it!'

A neighbour, whose husband is also called Harry, had come visiting him in Ward 7. She'd called to see our Harry on her way down the corridor and had handed him a get well card. He'd thanked her and said, 'Read it, Margaret'. Then, 'That's nice, Kathleen. Can you remember when Harry planted our garden with flowers while we were on holiday?'

Kathleen had gone to tell her husband that Harry Brown was doing fine.

There had followed the bed bath and an opportunity to curl up and nod off and I'd found him so on my arrival. All warm and pink.

I was sitting on the bed, for Margaret occupied the one chair, as she told me what had been happening and that Joan was coming back so that I would have company while she let in cattle and sorted something out for Aunty Mary, still abandoned in the Land Rover.

I was watching Harry while Margaret recounted the saga of her lovely afternoon and mine paled into insignificance. We were really relaxed. I was confident the car would be wreathed in sunshine and Aunty Mary comfortably warm. I had come earlier than usual. Margaret need not hurry home. Harry was sleeping peacefully with his cheek resting on his left hand, as always. We could talk awhile.

The four days of having no time to discuss things with each other had seemed an eternity. We needed to talk about his illness, about cattle movement and about ordering fodder. There was a lot of sorting out to do. Margaret was even contemplating asking for the help of the RSPCA. They had written offering their services to any farmer whose situation was becoming impossible.

But the opportunity to chat never came, for suddenly, quietly, peacefully, I sensed a change. I stood and said to Margaret, 'Is Harry all right?'

She turned and stood, seeing and knowing, too. 'I don't think he is,' she said.

We watched him breathing out but not in and we knew that he was dying, so peacefully, so beautifully we could only watch with awe.

No one can really be confident of a life other than this one we live on earth. To prove it one way or another one must die. There seems, however, to be much more to life than just a complicated engine, operating non-stop, sometimes, though disabled, for a very long time. We, who are farmers, and have seen animals be born, and die, do not dismiss the fact that what goes for us might well go for them. Mother, Father, Harry, Lusky, Jess ... who knows. For each, breathing is life and death is when it stops and, at that point, human or animal, it is difficult not to believe that life is more than a computer, that there is an intelligence we cannot begin to understand. I did not see 'something' leave, but I knew for certain that the 'something' which was Harry had gone. It had left his maimed body behind and found 'wings to wander'. I remember saying aloud, 'Now wasn't that easy, Harry?'

Entertaining guests is our profession. Until they leave we give, and give, and give again of our attention and our service but there is no point in staying, waving in the yard, when they have gone for there are chores to be done. The nurse said we could stay with Harry for as long as we liked. No one could have loved him more or stayed with him longer than the many decades we had all worked and lived together.

Now that he had died, we who had seldom left him and had, more recently, vowed never to do so, were content to go. We kissed him remembering that, until only days ago, he would not tolerate even a peck on the cheek. He had shied away from demonstrative affection. We gave silent thanks for all those treasured years and found no problem in leaving him, for he was no longer there and no one could have taken his curtain call more triumphantly.

Slowly we went through the ritual of gathering his belongings, talking to and thanking the nursing staff and then we dragged our weary feet back to the Land Rover to tell Auntie Mary, sadly, that Harry had just died.

Eighty enormous animals were waiting patiently. Now there were two of us to face the danger of letting them in. Nothing outside had changed. Inside the house it would never be the same again.

There was nothing about the week of work that followed to suggest that life would change and I can assure you that our diet of toil and wonder, and our appetite for perpetuity has not wavered. In a caring profession like farming, there is little time to ponder. Morning and night those animals had to be fed. We did little else except execute the necessary duties, following a death and prior to a funeral. Friends came to see us and the sideboard blossomed with flowers and the postman began delivering the 150 expressions of appreciation of Harry. Dr. Gopal came to see us and I asked him where he lived and learned that Harry had been right. When was he not?

We went to the Chapel of Rest to see him before the coffin lid was closed and he was beautiful. We could hardly take our eyes away and delayed leaving for as long as possible. There were no wrinkles and just the suggestion of a smile, a tiny parting of the lips exposing the teeth of which he had been so proud. I declared he looked like Margaret, a likeness I had not seen before.

The fear that we were never going to be able to move the cattle was lifted on the Thursday before the Friday funeral. A letter from Burges Salmon said the ridiculous boundary would be erased on Monday. The solicitor was pleased with the successful outcome of his negotiations. In the same post came a letter from the CLA giving the same message and enclosing a copy of a letter addressed to them, from DEFRA, saying the Ministry had hoped to lift the ban earlier but had had to give the Metropolitan Districts a week's grace to adjust their computers. I filled in the necessary form, photostated the eighty ear-tag numbers and sent in the application to move our senior herd. We experienced a relief that proved to be premature.

With no tourists there was seldom any need to go into their sitting room. We could have had squatters and never known. Forty years ago this sitting room we call the Snug had been our kitchen. We had not initially known there to be our magnificent inglenook fireplace hidden in the plastered wall. When we'd built a lean-to kitchen, on a more convenient level, we'd converted it to its former glory but never removed the immersion heater switch from the wall, or the many electric meters hidden behind one of the monstrous beams.

All summer we had not needed a boost to the hot water system, for the Aga had heated enough for family requirements. However, on the night before Harry's funeral, Margaret thought she should switch on the immersion heater. We would all need a bath that evening. So she went into the Snug, for the first time in goodness only knows how long, and found water had begun spouting out of the cold water pipe which feeds the conversion and the cattle sheds. It must have only just started, for though the carpet beneath was wet, it was not submerged. Water was coming out fast and furious, spraying curtains and furniture and more seriously, the electric meters. In a panic we turned off the mains supply of both water and electricity.

This was one more opportunity to demonstrate our quirky definition of good luck, our positive 'what if' attitude to incidents others would call disasters. What if Margaret had not gone in at that moment, had not thought it necessary to put on the booster heater? What if the pipe had burst at any time during those weeks of closed doors? What if it had burst while we were in church? What if ...?

Disaster has a habit of stalking us but it normally finds the right time to attack! We knew we would have eighty cattle emptying the five hundred gallon emergency tank. We knew we could not have baths. We knew we would have to bring a kettle of water from the spring and use a different loo every time, for no cistern would re-fill, but everything could wait till morning. Perhaps Tim, who was walling, could help us out. The guilty pipe was exposed, so the repair would be simple. We dried the meters and, later, we tentatively turned on the electricity.

Next morning, of course, we found the interruption of supplies had flipped the electric emergency fuse in the buildings and air-locked the water supply but daylight is the cure for most ills. Tim did an emergency, temporary repair with a jubilee clip, even as the phone was ringing madly in the kitchen.

I lifted it. The Council had received my application. I had answered the question, 'When do you wish to move cattle?' with 'As soon as possible'. I must give an exact date, the caller said.

'How soon can we?' I asked.

'Tuesday,' she answered.

'Put Tuesday,' I ordered. 'Don't dare send the form back. There isn't time. We are just going to my brother's funeral. You alter it for me. Please!'

We had quick baths. Margaret was still drying when the limousine came to pick us up, to join the waiting hearse at the top of the road. What's new? Amazingly we went to the funeral relatively composed.

The church was almost full and the organist was playing the haunting Gaelic strains of Tobermory Bay. We had spent a long time making sure that we had a beautiful funeral. There is beauty in sadness and I think it a mistake to think that it must be avoided. To mourn is necessary for a healing process to begin. A friend returning from a celebratory funeral had remarked, 'I hope someone cries at mine!'

There is no more poignant music than Gaelic played on the organ by a lady who in childhood was my Patrol Leader in the village Guide Company, as long ago as 1940.

From each service sheet, Harry's laughing photograph brought tears to the eyes of the congregation. That had not been our idea. Two of the hymns had not been in the hymnal, so it had been necessary to ask Tony Ainley to print enough for the expected many. His wife, Pauline, had asked for a photograph and we'd hesitated. Good ones of Harry were not plentiful. One taken at his seventieth birthday appeared as if by magic. Sometimes the hunt for something right takes a long time. It was as if this snap of Harry had placed itself first in the queue in readiness. It had taken longer to find the music for the two hymns not in Ancient and Modern. 'Loving Shepherd of Thy Sheep' seemed appropriate for one who had lived all his life on the land. We had no problem with that tune. For the lovely words of 'Beloved let us love,' a favourite from college days, we had to phone Dot, in Suffolk, and for 'Awake, awake to love and work,' sung mostly in the Service Horseshoe of half a hundred camps, a Methodist hymn book had to be used.

There were people from all walks of life. What used to be a big family is now reduced to a handful. There were friends galore, Guides, my school children, neighbours, farmers and even holiday guests from Newcastle and from the south of England. There were flowers from Tiree, from Raymond and Dolores, Paulette and Lil. There was Anna from the National Trust and Sue from Craven Homeopathy Clinic. All knew Harry yet there was not one, other than Margaret and I, who really knew him enough to pay him the tribute he deserved. That was our job and I knew we could entrust it to no other.

We asked Barbara Sherriff to read the poem Margaret had chosen to illustrate where Harry's faith and understanding had been nurtured. She did so beautifully. May we be forgiven for having taken a minor liberty with the words.

I've breathed the morning freshness, I've seen the day begun,
I've wandered in the forest, I've felt the early sun.
I've felt God all around me in the wonder scented dew.
I've climbed up to the hilltop and stood and gazed with awe.

I've seen the great waves rushing and sands silver in the sun.
I've loved the restless ocean with a strong and tender love
And known that all its beauty is reflection from above.
Oh, listen then, for having felt, I've understood.

We needed to remind the congregation of the pre-wheelchair days when Harry walked and stood straight. Though most of his friends were in tears, his sisters, in a carefully prepared tribute, honoured him as he deserved. We left the church to the strains of Dvorak's 'Goin' Home,' knowing where Harry had gone and then everyone was hugging us in the sunshine.

We have become increasingly aware that there is more cloud cover than there used to be. If the sun shines in the morning it is invariably shortlived, but on the day of Harry's funeral it shone brilliantly from dawn to dusk. I do believe it was the most beautiful day of the decade. It had the heat of summer and the mystique of autumn and an atmosphere reminiscent of Hebridean Sabbaths. When Father died, in 1979, sun shone from a blue sky onto deep, long lasting snow. We had only money to pay for a double grave. When Mother was buried, in the April sunshine of 1990, that grave was full but diversification into tourism gave us money to buy another plot, immediately, nearby. We hardly dared to hope that it would not be early dug. Harry had been quite groggy after Mother's death but had picked up well and had enjoyed eleven more, productive years.

On 12 October 2001, once again the day was so perfect no one hurried to leave the cemetery. We were not looking down. (In life you should resist doing that or you will fall!) We were looking up to the hillside which is ours, for Grandfather bought it in 1929. We were looking at the centuries-old house, etched on the skyline, where we had all lived so joyously, and proudly, for forty-three years. We could see the sycamore, standing sentinel below the eastern gable, and grazing cattle everywhere who, through no fault of their own, were posing us such a problem.

It occurred to me, standing above the grave with the coffin so far below, strewn with the thrown roses Fiona had insisted upon, that to leave Harry in such a beautiful place, with a view of home, was not a problem. And, moreover, I acknowledged that Harry had never been a problem to us. He had been one side of an equilateral triangle, the strongest of all geometrical shapes.

We have said frequently that almost everything we do needs two and it suddenly felt a precarious position to be in. One more loss and whoops-a-daisy! Three was an essential number of adults in every camp, three a requisite of every expedition. As only two we were going to feel far more vulnerable.

But we were surrounded by friends, most of whom grew out of Guiding. Unless we outlive them, neither of us will be absolutely alone. One of them, Barbara, came to my side and whispered, 'If Arnold and I come up later this afternoon, is there anything we can do for you?'

'No one can help with cattle,' I said, 'but you could help us mop up a sodden carpet in The Snug!'

'We'll come,' she promised.

So we went home to put on dirty clothes and wellingtons. We prepared the shed. We sorted out the airlock in the water system and the flipped electric and let in the bullocks. We welcomed our soulmates who had called at the supermarket and bought a hot, roasted chicken and some rolls and we ate them by the sitting room fire, in comfort. We finished the meal with cakes Joan had made for us. Because of her, my tins were full.

We mopped up the excess water in The Snug and put furniture in one half of the room. Then we lifted the wet carpet and draped it over the langsettle and chairs and plugged in the heaters.

Later the Ainleys came with flowers from the Chapel and told us Harry's had been a beautiful funeral.

So ended a period of our history. It is now recorded so that, as long as these pages remain, it will be remembered as a happy story with a precarious beginning, a long and successful lifetime with a happy ending, suggestive, surely, of an Eternity for those deserving of such.

We did not know, then, that at his home in Forncett St Mary, our competent artist was printing beautifully, a quotation from Dominican Bede Jarett.

> For Love is eternal and
> Life is immortal and
> Death is only an horizon
> And an horizon is
> Nothing save the limit
> Of our sight.

Chapter Sixteen

Fun is a delicate flower that doesn't stand up to changes
Neville Shute, *Round the Bend*

O ur daily activity had temporarily stopped being fun. We had always had more than just job satisfaction. Work had been an adventure, a game we played, winning, losing, laughing together as a team; five, then four, then three. Now we were only two, to be busy was not fun any longer. It could be so, once more, when we could get a grip on things. Sadly we wondered where we could find the happiness we had shared with Harry.

We should have been leaving for Witherslack near Grange-over-Sands on 13 October, the day which followed Harry's funeral. Had we had the opportunity we would not have had the heart.

'Rest if you must, but do not quit,' advised Paul and Bunty Bell. We desperately needed to rest but were in no mood to quit. We still had the eighty bullocks for whom a movement licence was imminent, in theory only, and their presence sealed our no-holiday fate. We handed over the keys of our Cumbrian cottage to Veronica, Tommy McGinty's widow, remembering all the work and kindnesses they had shown over many years.

We readjusted our compass and began a new era at The Currer. We had a lot of catching up to do. On the weekend after the funeral, Margaret and I painted the doors and wash boarding in the Loft Cottage. Pauline and Lil, after using it for six months of *annus horribilis*, had helped Margaret white emulsion the walls on leaving in July, but the gloss had never been done. We'd bought new carpets but had left them in store. Our first holiday-makers of autumn still expected to come on 20 October and in anticipation of moving our bullocks, we felt we must then honour the two half-term bookings. Both were self-catering and each cottage had been booked since spring.

We collected the new carpets and the two young women came, on Monday evening, to help manhandle them up the outside barn steps and to spread them on the lounge and one bedroom floors, ready for me to fit properly during the week. I had spent the afternoon hurriedly making new curtains and matching cushion covers. I had intended to re-paper the kitchen but abandoned that idea for time was running out.

We expected to get a Movement Licence on Tuesday morning, at 9 a.m. We had been told that the vet would ring with this announcement and come straight up to inspect our cattle. Milford Kemp would then begin taking the seven loads of animals to North Stainley, Ripon, and life, as we would have to know it, would begin.

The expected call did not come. We phoned and the veterinary receptionist said no Movement Licence had been granted. No fax had come from Bradford Metropolitan District. She didn't know why. We'd better phone Bradford.

'That's right,' said the lady in the Council office. 'We put the application in the computer but it is rejecting them all! Don't worry. I'll try again tomorrow!'

'That's too late,' I shouted. 'We have seven loads of cattle to move. Our haulier is waiting for our phone call. He can't be messed about with a postponement. He's harrassed enough! He's had no work all summer. Now there's a long backlog. Our seven loads represent three days' work!'

'Well!' she said. 'You can't move them without a licence and the computer won't give you one and there is nothing we can do until it does.'

We were furious. We knew that movement was legal. Everybody said so. The solicitor, the Chief Regional Vet, the CLA, even the Council said movement was legal. Everyone except the computer.

'Perhaps,' said the office girl, 'it will give the go-ahead, tomorrow!'

But it didn't. 'It must be that the computer isn't working properly,' the office girl said on Wednesday morning. Tough! The Metropolitan Districts had had an extra week to get their houses in order and had failed. I asked to speak to the man in charge of the Animal Heath Department of the Council.

'Don't shout at me!' he said. 'It's not my fault. It's the computer's!'

I sat by the phone all afternoon waiting for people who promised to ring back and I baked cake after cake in agitation. I dare not leave the kitchen. Margaret did the outdoor work but she was in when the phone rang about 4 p.m.

'You answer it,' I said.

It was the secretary from the Regional Chief Vet's office, with whom the Burges Salmon solicitor had negotiated.

'Have you got your Movement Licence?' she asked.

Margaret told her that the Bradford computer would not work and that we were exasperated, frantic even and definitely heading for a nervous breakdown!

'You'll have to have a licence,' the concerned lady said. 'If you don't move your animals this week, you won't be able to move them because Ripon is moving out of High Risk status on Monday.'

'On Saturday our first holiday-makers come into our cottages,' Margaret said. 'It's half term. We'll have children all over the place and eighty not-so-safe animals far too close!'

'I'll ring you back,' the lady said. We were considerably stressed. We'd wasted more time waiting for people to ring us back, during the Foot and Mouth shambles, than one could believe possible! Everyone's telephone bill was up by £50. Her call came at last, saying we had been granted a manually written licence. It had been faxed to Bradford. Almost immediately a call confirmed this from the Council and, sure enough, our vet received this specially written licence on Thursday morning. He came, said our animals were free of disease and warned us, the fragile ladies of The Currer, not on any account to enter sheds with so many such huge animals. 'Leave loading to the men!' he commanded.

We called Milford, our haulier, to say we had the go-ahead and he said he was on his way. We sent for Tim, who was again walling in the meadows, and we phoned cousin Freda's daughter, Kathleen, and begged her to come and clean The Loft bathroom and kitchen ready for weekend guests. We, who are habitually too proud to ask for help, were on our knees pleading for it.

For the first two loads of cattle transported north, Tim came down from the hill. Margaret and I were needed to hold gates open, and to close them at the right time, but we obeyed the vet and kept out of the shed. Milford intended transporting all night, so for the third load at 7 p.m. he brought a spare driver with him. The two returned for the fourth load at 1 a.m. In the small hours of Friday, they both looked alarmingly tired, eating and drinking huge mugs of tea at our kitchen table when all of us should have been in bed. We could go, but after leaving Ripon Milford had to take some fat animals to the abattoir, early, for another farmer before he came for two more loads. For these the vet had to precede him again to make sure that our animals were still disease-free. He told us that, if the final load did not go before 11 a.m. on Saturday, he would have to come yet again for licences lasted just twenty-four hours.

The stress of loading, the fear of someone, or some animal, being maimed and the worry in case a news bulletin announced another suspected case, did not leave us until the last load arrived safely at their new home. We did not have to wait until that comforting phone call came to hear the awful silence outside when the air system fans were turned off, or to witness the emptiness of the fields surrounding our homestead. We grieved again for those whose cattle had been culled, whose fields were emptied unlawfully. At great expense of time and money and sweat, we had completed our autumn sales. We were the lucky ones. It's funny but we didn't feel that way at all. We desperately wanted time to grieve for Harry.

We were aground, washed onto a sandbank. We need something other than work to float our boat. But work was all that there was. There were beds to make and curtains to hang in the cottages that would be occupied at 3 p.m. Barbara Sherriff came to assist. We were drained. Margaret's legs were too painful for her to attempt to check the eighty-nine remaining animals hiding, out of sight, in the meadows. Tim had reported no emergency so they could wait. Arnold came and re-laid the dried carpet in The Snug. I made some cheese toasties and we collapsed in the sitting room, totally spent. Then we talked about Harry. All week we had had no time to mourn.

Once again there was a semblance of the normality of the final twenty years of the twentieth century but there was no water under our keel, nor wind in our sails. Self-catering families arrived and cars were parked in the yard. People we'd known for many years occupied The Loft. Children played in the yard and peeped in the kitchen window asking for Danny and Meg to be let out for cuddles. Their semi-active, eleven-year-old brother was driving madly round the yard in his electric wheelchair, boasting that his speed limit of 4mph would rise to 6mph on his twelfth birthday.

We had to go forward. We must not stagnate. On Monday we went to Otley to thank the market staff for advertising our cattle in August. Their diligence had resulted in instant success. It wasn't their fault movement had taken seven weeks and cost us close on £3000. We collected Nigel Donaldson's cheque, paid the market commission and left our buyer luck-money. There was no way we would part with the billy goat.

We dare not pause. We must now buy calves. The age-old tradition of buying at market was no longer an opportunity. The market was a ghost town, empty of animals, so clean one could have eaten from the floor.

'How do we buy calves?' we asked. We were given a few addresses and phone numbers we could ring. We were told procedures re disinfecting and sealing vehicles and trailers and we drove to the man doing just this. He thoroughly cleaned and sealed the trailer with a minute piece of thin wire, before giving us the bill and paperwork, dated, as was necessary. This performance would have to be repeated every time we collected calves from outside a 10km area.

Apparently, we could buy from any farmer north and west of the B6161 from Pateley Bridge but not from Harrogate. We could not buy from south of the B6429 running east to west a mile south of us. We could have bought from most places in the Settle triangle had these not, almost all, been wiped out by the disease. Those remaining free were still under a D licence and, though in theory we could buy, they could not sell.

We had lunch with Olga Beardswood. She had represented Harris at the funeral and is our local link with the Outer Isles. We talked about Harry and Islands and Islanders and Harry. We could not stop talking about him. On the way home we collected the money from the plate which had been placed at the back of the church and, later that week, we left the muck-spreader taking out the tons of manure from all five sheds, and we went to White Windows Cheshire Home at Sowerby Bridge to leave with them the sizable sum of money.

When we first began our association with the home for disabled in the early sixties, the residents had slept in dormitories at night and spent daytime in common rooms. Now everyone has an individual bed-sit, beautifully furnished and decorated to suit its owner. This accommodates most of the residents fine. Each room has the occupant's own television, record player, radio, books, pictures and a mass of personal belongings and souvenirs, stuffed toys and even a live cat or two. We have no problem with this. It is wonderful, I'm sure. It's just that, occasionally, when we had wondered what Harry would do should he be the only survivor from a road accident or Margaret and I meet catastrophe in the cattle sheds, we had automatically thought he would be all right at White Windows. We realised then, in that almost luxurious atmosphere, he would have been extremely, desperately, inconsolably lonely. Amazingly he had no possessions at all other than a pile of jigsaws still to do and some finished ones under the bed, which we did not like to destroy and didn't interest him at all. He didn't watch television, listen to the radio or music. He didn't read, wasn't interested in photographs or pictures or magazines. He had accumulated nothing. He didn't want possessions. The only thing he ever showed anyone was his framed jigsaw photograph of himself and the Barbault family, at his seventieth birthday. All his life, his bedroom had been a place in which to sleep. He had everything he wanted. Therefore he was rich but he had nothing to take with him into a residential home. He just wanted the Land Rover and the numerous errands and opportunities to go out in it. He wanted his wheelchair, not to sit in but to take on holiday and go miles and miles on Hebridean beaches. He wanted people. Not ones to visit him. Few did that anyway. He wanted to be part of the business, at the kitchen table when Tim came, when Mark brought hay and Pauline brought the milk, when the corn traveller came and when holiday-makers came to tell us where they had been all day. Whenever the phone rang he came to listen to the conversation, he wanted to be there when post was opened and none of these essentials in his life could he take with him to furnish a bedroom. Never mind. It could now never be.

Before the half-term week was over the fated water pipe had spurted another leak. Water into both cottages had to be turned off and Brian sent for to replace the guilty length of copper. Margaret ladled water out of the five hundred gallon tank for our tourists. It was an unfamiliar experience for them. There were no animals in the sheds so there was no fear of an airlock.

The way forward, we knew, was to buy calves. I remembered the book agent advising me to leave this farming activity out of my manuscript, and concentrate on the abnormalities and idiosyncrasies of our bed and breakfast visitors. If my reader thinks likewise I apologise, but buying calves is our future, our hope of continuity. Without animals to graze our fields, The Currer will die.

We went into the newly mucked-out calf shed with annual determination, cleaned the passageway, scrubbed the table and fixed the feeding teats. Mr Lawson came from Cheshire to service the automatic feeding machines and Hargreaves Bannister delivered forty sacks of dried milk. Tim sat at the table with us and as he suggested neighbouring dairy farms where there might be calves to buy, I flicked the directory pages for phone numbers.

The hunt was on! There were plenty of older calves which we did not want. Farms were overstocked with them and, very reluctantly, farmers were having to destroy the newborn. A homoeopathic delivery contained a little note, 'We have currently one hundred and twenty animals more than usual!' One farmer, with a huge milking herd, was so overflowing with calves he had despaired. The knacker had been called to shoot a casualty and he had seen an opportunity, albeit an unpleasant one. He'd asked the knacker to shoot a few of his newly born surplus but the man had had no stomach for babies. He'd offered the farmer the use of the gun, but he couldn't do it either, so the herd, imprisoned by a D restriction, had grown and grown. Farmers who habitually send their calves to market had no calf accommodation and babies were being kept in garages and queer, unlit places, quite unsuitable but unavoidable, in the aftermath of Foot and Mouth.

Over-worked and over-stressed, accidents were happening. Here and there, a member of the workforce was breaking a leg, straining a muscle. There had been farmers in hospital, alongside Harry. The elderly became more infirm. There are deaths and funerals, always, but these seemed on the increase. Margaret's legs continued to be painful. We didn't know how to face winter if we bought calves but, like lemmings, we continued rushing into an unknown future. We began to buy, in ones and twos, not just on Monday but on Tuesday and Wednesday, Thursday, Friday, Saturday and Sunday. We phoned, we visited, we collected, we disinfected. We were unstoppable.

We collected the first two, Limousins, from a farm on Lees Moor at 9 a.m. and emptied them from our small trailer into the straw-strewn cathedral, a calf shed built to house eighty. We roused Aunty Mary and, after breakfast,

we attempted to approach a farm on the Slippery Ford road by going beyond
it on a parallel road and entering the road west of the farm, turning left and
so avoiding having to reverse the trailer. We are so poor at doing that. It
seemed simple. We were cocksure we were on the right, very minor road,
but missed the turning and went sailing down towards Sutton. On a steep
hillside we attempted to reverse along a track, couldn't, unhitched the trailer
and very nearly lost it on the down slope. Never will we do anything so stupid
again! How we controlled the two-wheeled trailer we consistently find so
difficult to discipline was a miracle, a fairly big one! It will be some time,
hopefully never, before we attempt anything quite so stupid on a hill. Tebbit,
the *Farmers Weekly* cartoonist, would have had a field day out of us.

We retraced our route somewhat shakily and took the right turning to
approach Lower Dene Laithe farm and collect four more calves. That was
on 6 November and it took us three weeks of buying and collecting, on a
daily basis, from umpteen farms. We went to Cowling and Guiseley, to
Pateley Bridge and Glasshouses, to Laycock and Newsholme, to Riddlesden
and Barden Towers, but the number of calves taking up residence in the shed
was minimal. After a fortnight we had only thirty and we began to think the
shed would be half empty all winter.

We'd ordered more hay from the man who had saved the day, in
September, by having a surplus caused by so many of his normal buyers being
wiped out with the recent catastrophe. He said he would deliver at 9 a.m. on
the morning of the only severe frost of a wet and windy winter. Before his
arrival we had to salt the whole of the quarter of a mile of road, cursing the
unfairness of the weather clerk. With hands smarting with the rock salt, we
then had to unload the heavy bales. We were not amused.

Although it was mid-November none of the trees had shed their summer
foliage. The sudden, very brief frost coloured the leaves gold and russet,
yellow and red, so that our wanderings in Airedale, Wharfedale and
Nidderdale became sheer delight. We were conscious of the fact that Harry
would have been in his element, being driven all over the Dales, meeting
innumerable farmers, looking at the view from their kitchen windows, as we
enjoyed their mugs of tea. We knew, too, that if this form of calf-buying had
not been necessary, we would never have got into the Land Rover, perhaps
until spring, for to do so without Harry was to do so without reason. I believe
that being forced to go on the calf-trail in our most beautiful home country
was a necessary part of our mourning, a coming to terms with our loss. That
brief night of frost, which coloured the hillsides with an autumn fantasia
without equal, made our 2001 experience a joy. Buying calves this way would
have been impossible without the automatic milk machines, baby-sitting for
us while we wandered God's acres. Yorkshire is so, so beautiful.

There were three farmers who could sell us calves if they could obtain licences. Jack Wilson at Green Hammerton had twelve Limousins and his brother had nine at Kelbrook but permission was not forthcoming. Robert Lofthouse had fourteen at Addingham but he was under a D restriction which prevented any movement, so we kept up the buying in small numbers and, very slowly, the shed began to fill. We collected one from Harden, two from the slopes of Ilkley Moor, and five week-old baby Friesians were delivered from Oldfield, to join our predominantly Belgian Blue and Limousin herd.

Our numbers were creeping up towards the mid-fifty mark. This was not really enough but it wasn't quite the disaster it had threatened to be. Then Jack Wilson got a Movement Licence and arrived with a dozen beauties. Henry unexpectedly got a licence, too. His vet came and declared the cattle disease-free and so he began loading his nine babies. A sudden message came to stop him. A mistake had been made. They could not be moved. He angrily unloaded, only to be told two days later that he could move them after all! Farmers were at their wits' end!

So we had well over seventy and enough. It was unbelievable. When another bull calf was born on farms where we had already bought, we had to reject it. We had plenty. Then the D restriction was lifted from Addingham and Robert Lofthouse applied for a licence, got it, called in the vet and phoned us. We had twenty-four hours in which to pick up the fourteen calves on which we had given up hope! Calves we didn't need any more. Wanting only seventy, we now had nearly ninety. We could have had many over a hundred, for farmers kept ringing, but we were adamant. No more! Definitely no more! No more buying another on Monday until next year, if we survived. In our exhausted state, even that seemed unpredictable.

But we did 'Buy another on Monday', long before then, though it wasn't a calf!

We arranged to call at Simmonites, as there was a minor job to do on our vehicle. It was so minor we were told we could wait while it was done. We arrived during the mechanic's dinner hour, so we drove on to the cash and carry to fill up with food. Our guests were mostly self-catering ones, but our stores were low and the opportunity to re-fill the larder was too good to miss.

Arriving back at the garage, the mechanic lifted the bonnet and said the engine was too hot to do the small job after all. He said he'd phone his boss and David would come and drive us home, empty the food and return with our vehicle. They would bring it back to The Currer next day. We were quite relaxed about it, for nothing was urgent. We were, I believe, his longest, maybe his oldest, customers. We had been shown too many kindnesses over the years to criticise.

We were parked on the garage forecourt and, while we waited for David to come back from dinner, we opened our coffee flask and, although it was long past midday, we had our Elevenses. There were several Land Rovers parked. One, just two spaces away, caught my eye.

I said to Margaret, 'I think that's a Land Rover Dormobile!'

She was sitting comfortably, her aching legs at rest. They were only painful when she walked. She wanted to be left alone but she said, 'Where?' and I answered, 'Just there!'

We had only ever seen a Land Rover Dormobile once before. Years ago one had been parked in the forecourt, belonging to a man just preparing to go on safari. This model has not been manufactured for many years.

'I'm going to look!' I said, opening the door.

Reluctantly Margaret followed but her interest grew as we approached the Classic Dormobile and saw that it was not privately owned, but was for sale. We tried the door. It opened and we clambered aboard.

'Hey,' we said. 'Just look at this!'

There was obvious comfort. There was a roof which raised. Two bunks, a cooker and a sink. It was carpeted and curtained. It was a tent we did not have to pitch. And it was cheap! We were wide-eyed. Almost speechless, but not quite.

'We could go the fields way, anywhere in this!' I whispered.

'Harry has sent it,' Margaret said. 'He knows we need a lifeline. This has been engineered. It's not an accident. It was meant to be. A one in a million chance!'

'We could just go,' I said. 'We could call it the Dorm'ouse. No need to book anywhere! Decide one day and go next morning, for the rest of our driving lives. It's an insurance. We could go anywhere and take as long as we liked getting there.'

We had been aground too long.

'It would float our boat,' Margaret said with confidence. 'It's just what we want, Jean. It will float our boat.'

We could not go to the Hebrides in May. We had already accepted that. We planned to take our frail, immobile aunty for a holiday, just a day's journey away. She was too old for two-day journeys and unpredictable crossings of a turbulent Minch. We could go to Saltburn, perhaps, and park our personal 'cafe' outside a cottage. She would love that. For her it would be a trip down Memory Lane for she had spent innumerable holidays there in the late 1940s. Then, later, perhaps we could leave her safely with other nephews and nieces and go island hopping alone. How Harry would have loved to go with us!

The wanderlust was gripping us. We heard the call of the wild. We could pick up where we had left off, many years ago, when we had sacrificed a two-man tent in order to take hundreds of other people's children in summer and the family in spring and autumn. While enjoying the one we had missed the other.

Again, forty years later, with a Dorm'ouse, we could experience the once-was. Together we could go to

> Far islands where the tide visits untrodden shores,
> Waiting for worshippers to come to Thee,
> In Thy great out-of-doors.
>
>   Van Dyke

WE'LL BUY ANOTHER ON MONDAY

Jean Brown
and
Margaret
Christmas 2004

Sunrise at The Currer.